ECSCW 2013: Proceedings of the 13th European Conference on Computer Supported Cooperative Work, 21–25 September 2013, Paphos, Cyprus

Olav W. Bertelsen · Luigina Ciolfi
Maria Antonietta Grasso
George Angelos Papadopoulos
Editors

ECSCW 2013: Proceedings of the 13th European Conference on Computer Supported Cooperative Work, 21–25 September 2013, Paphos, Cyprus

Springer

Editors
Olav W. Bertelsen
Department of Computer Science
Aarhus University
Aarhus
Denmark

Luigina Ciolfi
Sheffield Hallam University
Sheffield
UK

Maria Antonietta Grasso
Work Practice Technology
Xerox Research Europe
Grenoble
France

George Angelos Papadopoulos
Department of Computer Science
University of Cyprus
Nicosia
Cyprus

ISBN 978-1-4471-6148-6 ISBN 978-1-4471-5346-7 (eBook)
DOI 10.1007/978-1-4471-5346-7
Springer London Heidelberg New York Dordrecht

Printed on acid-free paper

Springer is part of Springer Science+Business Media (www.springer.com)

Preface

This volume represents the proceedings of ECSCW 2013, the 13th European Conference on Computer Supported Cooperative Work, held in Paphos, Cyprus, on September 21–25, 2013.

ECSCW 2013 received 82 competitive paper and note submissions. After extensive review, 15 were selected to form the core of the traditional single-track technical program for the conference. These are supplemented by exciting workshops and masterclasses that cover a broad range of topics and allow for wider and more active participation. These additional contributions will be published in the Volume 2 Proceedings, together with the expanded selection of demonstrations, videos, and work in progress.

Work in progress has been introduced as a new peer reviewed category for ECSCW 2013, and those papers will be included in the Volume 2 Proceedings that will be available online.

The technical program this year focuses on work and the enterprise as well as on the challenges of involving citizens, patients, and others into collaborative settings. The papers embrace new theories, and discuss known ones. They challenge the ways we think about and study work and contribute to the discussions of the blurring boundaries between home and work life. They introduce recent and emergent technologies, and study known social and collaborative technologies. Classical settings in computer supported cooperative work are looked upon anew. With contributions from all over the world, the papers in interesting ways help focus on the European perspective in our community.

Many people have worked hard to ensure the success of this conference, and we briefly acknowledge them here: all the authors who submitted high quality papers; all those who contributed through taking part in workshops, masterclasses, demonstrations, and the new category of work in progress; the 64 members of a global program committee, who dedicated time and energy to reviewing and discussing individual contributions and shaping the program; the people who helped to organize the program: the workshop and masterclass chairs, the chairs of demos and videos, work in progress, student volunteers, and various other practical arrangements. Finally, we acknowledge the student volunteers who provided support throughout the event; and we thank the sponsors and those who offered their support to the conference.

Olav W. Bertelsen
Luigina Ciolfi
Maria Antonietta Grasso
George Angelos Papadopoulos

ECSCW 2013 Conference Committee

General Chair
George Angelos Papadopoulos, University of Cyprus, Cyprus

Programme Chairs
Olav W. Bertelsen, Aarhus University, Denmark
Maria Antonietta Grasso, Xerox Research Centre Europe, France

Workshops and Masterclasses Co-chairs
Mattias Korn, Aarhus University, Denmark
Pär-Ola Zander, Aalborg University, Denmark

Work in Progress Co-chairs
Tommaso Colombino, Xerox Research Centre Europe, France
Myriam Lewkowicz, Troyes University of Technology, France

Demos and Videos Co-chairs
David Kirk, Newcastle University, UK
Abigail Durrant, Newcastle University, UK

Proceedings Chair
Luigina Ciolfi, Sheffield Hallam University, UK

Proceedings Volume 2 Chair
Mattias Korn, Aarhus University, Denmark

Doctoral Colloquium Co-chairs
Antonella De Angeli, University of Trento, Italy
Wayne Lutters, University of Maryland Baltimore County, USA

Local Organizers
Christos Mettouris, University of Cyprus, Webmaster
Petros Stratis, Easy Conferences Ltd., Finance Chair

ECSCW 2013 Program Committee

Mark Ackerman, University of Michigan, USA
Alessandra Agostini, Università di Milano-Bicocca, Italy
Antonella De Angeli, University of Trento, Italy
Gabriela Avram, University of Limerick, Ireland
Liam Bannon, University of Limerick, Ireland and Aarhus University, Denmark
Olav W. Bertelsen, Aarhus University, Denmark
Pernille Bjørn, Copenhagen, Denmark
Jeanette Blomberg, IBM Almaden Research Center, USA
Alexander Boden, University of Siegen, Germany
Claus Bossen, Aarhus University, Denmark
Nina Boulus-Rødje, IT University of Copenhagen, Denmark
Tone Bratteteig, University of Oslo, Norway
Susanne Bødker, Aarhus University, Denmark
Federico Cabitza, Università di Milano-Bicocca, Italy
Lars Rune Christensen, University of Aalborg, Denmark
Luigina Ciolfi, Sheffield Hallam University, UK
Gregorio Convertino, Xerox Research Centre Europe, France
Andy Crabtree, University of Nottingham, UK
Francoise Darses, Conservatoire National des Arts et Métiers, France
Prasun Dewan, University of North Carolina, USA
Monica Divitini, Norwegian University of Science and Technology, Norway
Benjamin Fonseca, UTAD/INESC TEC, Portugal
Sebastian Franken, University of Aachen, Germany
Víctor M. González, Instituto Tecnológico Autónomo de México (ITAM), México
Antonietta Grasso, Xerox Research Centre Europe, France
Marianne Graves Petersen, Aarhus University, Denmark
Tom Gross, University of Bamberg, Germany
Jörg M. Haake, Fern University Hagen, Germany
Richard Harper, Microsoft Research Centre Cambridge, UK
Kori Inkpen, Microsoft Research, USA
Giulio Jacucci, Helsinki Institute for Information Technology, Finland
Nils Jeners, University of Aachen, Germany
Nina Kahnwald, University of Dresden, Germany

Helena Karasti, University of Oulu, Finland
Wendy Kellogg, IBM T. J. Watson Research Center, USA
Michael Koch, BW-University, Munich, Germany
Timothy Koschmann, Southern Illinois University, USA
Charlotte Lee, University of Washington, USA
Myriam Lewkowicz, Université de Technologie de Troyes, France
David Martin, Xerox Research Centre Europe, France
David W. McDonald, University of Washington, USA
Giorgio De Michelis, Università di Milano-Bicocca, Italy
David Millen, IBM T. J. Watson Research Center, USA
Preben Holst Mogensen, Aarhus University, Denmark
Keiichi Nakata, University of Reading, UK
Iivari Netta, University of Oulu, Finland
Maria Normark, Södertörn University College, Sweden
Gary M. Olson, University of California, Irvine, USA
Volkmar Pipek, University of Siegen, Germany
Michael Prilla, University of Bochum, Germany
Wolfgang Prinz, Fraunhofer FIT/RWTh Aachen, Germany
Dave Randall, University of Siegen, Germany
Madhu Reddy, Penn State University, USA
Toni Robertson, University of Technology Sydney, Australia
Markus Rohde, University of Siegen, Germany
Mark Rouncefield, Lancaster University, UK
Pascal Salembier, Université de Technologie de Troyes, France
Kjeld Schmidt, Copenhagen Business School, Denmark
Carla Simone, Università di Milano-Bicocca, Italy
Cleidson da Souza, UFPA and ITV-DS, Brazil
Gunnar Stevens, University of Siegen, Germany
Hilda Tellioğlu, Vienna University of Technology, Austria
Ina Wagner, Vienna University of Technology, Austria and University of Olso, Norway
Volker Wulf, University of Siegen, Germany

Reviewers

Konstantin Aal
Steve Abrams
Jacob Bartel
Matthias Betz
António Correia
Juri Dachtera
Ilana Diamant
Ines Di Loreto
Roman Ganhoer
Friedrich Glock
Jan Hess
Timo Jakobi
Birgit Krogstie
Thomas Ludwig
Johanna Meurer
Drew Paine
Souneil Park
Christian Reuter
Torben Wiedenhoefer

Contents

“How Many Bloody Examples Do You Want?” Fieldwork and Generalisation

Andy Crabtree, Peter Tolmie and Mark Rouncefield

Abstract The title of this paper comes from comments made by an ‘angry’ ethnographer during a debriefing session. It reflects his frustration with a certain analytic mentality that would have him justify his observations in terms of the number of times he had witnessed certain occurrences in the field. Concomitant to this was a concern with the amount of time he had spent in the field and the implication that the duration of fieldwork somehow justified the things that he had seen; the implication being that the more time he spent immersed in the study setting the more valid his findings and, conversely, the less time, the less valid they were. For his interlocutors, these issues speak to the *grounds* upon which we might draw general insights and lessons from ethnographic research regarding the social or collaborative organisation of human activities. However, the strong implication of the angry ethnographer’s response is that they are of no importance. This paper seeks to unpack his position and explicate what generalisation turns upon from the ethnographer’s perspective. The idea that human activities *contain their own means of generalisation* that cannot be reduced to extraneous criteria (numbers of observations, duration of fieldwork, sample size, etc.) is key to the exposition.

A. Crabtree (✉) · P. Tolmie
School of Computer Science, University of Nottingham, Nottingham, UK
e-mail: andy.crabtree@nottingham.ac.uk

P. Tolmie
e-mail: peter.tolmie@nottingham.ac.uk

M. Rouncefield
Computing Department, University of Lancaster, Lancaster, UK
e-mail: m.rouncefield@lancaster.ac.uk

O. W. Bertelsen et al. (eds.), *ECSCW 2013: Proceedings of the 13th European Conference on Computer Supported Cooperative Work, 21–25 September 2013, Paphos, Cyprus*, DOI: 10.1007/978-1-4471-5346-7_1,

Introduction

> Anger can only ever be the object of the academic gaze, never the legitimate subject of academic style … Anger frightens because it violates the codes of rational detachment but even in this fright is contained a desire to communicate and include. (Keith 1992).

The angry ethnographer's position may at-first-glance seem untenable: fundamentally he is suggesting that general insights may be derived from very short periods of fieldwork and even single cases. At first glance this seems to be deeply wrong-headed. After all, ethnography as many people know is an anthropological and sociological approach that requires the immersion of a fieldworker in the everyday lives of the people he or she studies; surely that takes time if nothing else? However, the ethnographer goes on to remind us that ethnography is different in a systems design context. He emphasizes *in a systems design context*, telling us that context matters, that it shapes and constrains ethnography. He points us at a text and quotes from it to make his point, telling us about the "diminishing returns" that set in *for design* with long periods of fieldwork and the need to marry fieldwork to various stages in the design process if it is to be an effective resource *for design* (Hughes et al. 1994). He tells us that the demands of design curtail ethnography as it is practiced in anthropology and sociology, radically reducing something that traditionally takes years to months, weeks and even days, and that this was one of the very early understandings that came out of interdisciplinary efforts to incorporate ethnography into design.

He tells us too that immersion does not necessarily imply long periods of fieldwork. That the point and purpose of immersion is to apprehend a setting or some activities from the "native's point of view" (Malinowski 1922). He concedes that this may well take the anthropologist—who studies people in societies in which he or she is not a member—a long time to do; that he or she has to start from scratch, learn the language, and the ways in which people do things. *But*, he says, the same does not necessarily apply to the sociological ethnographer, who studies members of his or her own society. In this context, the ethnographer already shares a great deal in common with the people being studied. They share a common tongue for starters, which makes finding out what other people do much easier, and radically reduces the period of immersion. Furthermore, as a member of the same society the sociological ethnographer may even do the same activities as the people being studied—especially as design moves out from the workplace into everyday life—and this too reduces the time required to apprehend the native's point of view.

It depends on the context, of course, on what is being studied—the more unfamiliar the work, the more time it takes to apprehend. That's a practical problem the ethnographer has to contend with but it is not what the business of ethnography is all about. Immersion and apprehension of the native's point of view is not an end, rather they are means to an end. This is where the angry ethnographer becomes quite emphatic. There is a reason he is doing ethnography and from his point of view this is what underpins his claims to generality. The end, he tells us, contrary to current trends in anthropology and sociology, is not to represent the native and champion the user's cause—to become a proxy user in a design context as it were—but to uncover the *collaborative organisation* of a setting's work. He tells us that a single case may well be sufficient for that purpose because collaborative organisation is by definition social, tied not to individuals but to the activities that constitute the work of a setting, and that the ways in which activities are ordered provides for the generalisation of ethnographic findings even from short studies of single cases.

He cites, by way of example, studies of work in London Underground (Heath and Luff 1991) and how "surreptitious monitoring" is a generalisable property of the work insofar as it is manifestly not tied to particular individuals but to the *job* of controlling trains done by *whomever* is on shift or, similarly, how air traffic controllers "order the skies" through the collaborative orchestration of flight strips (Hughes et al. 1992), again regardless of which particular individuals are "working the skies" at any particular time. The angry ethnographer put the topic to bed with that but we suspect that the logic of generalisation inherent in his argument needs unpacking further if it is to be broadly appreciated. It is readily appreciable that fieldwork *in systems design* need *not* take a long time to do (a) because it needs to marry up with design and its inherently fast-paced processes, and (b) because the sociological ethnographer is already in possession of a good deal of the membership competence employed by the "natives", which is not to say that he or she doesn't need to work hard to further develop it as occasion demands or to convey "what anyone knows" to designers. Nonetheless, it is clearly the case that the duration of fieldwork can do nothing to assure us of the *validity* of the ethnographer's findings. That must turn upon other more exacting criteria, such as those that provide for and warrant general claims being made. It is to this matter in particular that we turn in the rest of the paper, explicating the sociological foundation that the angry ethnographer's claim stands upon and elaborating it through concrete examples. Why does it matter? If designers are to have confidence in ethnographic studies they need to be able to determine the veracity of the results provided by ethnographers. Understanding the basis on which generalisations can be made is a key ingredient not only of sound fieldwork, then, but also of interdisciplinary work *in systems design*.

The Sociological Foundations of Generalisation

The angry ethnographer's claim to be able to generalise findings from short periods of fieldwork and single cases turns upon the sociological reasoning of the late Harvey Sacks. Sacks is best known for establishing the field of Conversation Analysis (Sacks 1992a), which is today a staple feature of mainstream social science, taught and practiced around the world. Conversation Analysis emerged from Sacks' dissatisfaction with the ways in which sociology conducted its business in the 1960s and his critique of sociology played an influential role in the development of Ethnomethodology (Garfinkel 1967). Many in CSCW will be familiar with both Conversation Analysis and Ethnomethodology. The annals of CSCW are peppered with numerous examples of such work. Rather less visible is Sacks' critique of sociology and how this impacts generalisation in both sociology and systems design insofar as the latter makes use of ethnographers and ethnographic findings.

Sociological Description

In one of his earliest writings Sacks sought to "make sociology strange" in order to elaborate the problematic relationship between its "subject matter" and the "apparatus" used by sociologists (including ethnographers) to describe society and make generalisations about it. Sacks (1963) paints a picture of a machine to underscore the nature of the problem.

> At industrial and scientific exhibitions one encounters a machine which the layman might describe in the following terms. It has two parts; one is engaged in doing some job, and the other part synchronically narrates aloud what the first part does.

Sacks suggests that any attempt to make sense of the machine turns upon reconciling the parts of the object (i.e., the relationship between the doing and saying parts). Thus, the object might be understood by the layman as a "commentator machine". The sociologist might understand it as it such too, though he or she will offer a much more elaborate (and even alternate) description of the machine. Nonetheless it is with *description* that for Sacks the problem of generalisation starts. He takes it that sociology is in the business of developing some kind of "scientific" account of social life, which does not necessarily mean describing society in positivistic terms only that some kind of rigour is required. However, at the outset sociology proceeds to describe social life through the use of an unexamined resource—natural language—with the consequence that the "common-sense" that is built into and ordinarily expressed through natural language descriptions is imported without scrutiny. Sacks thinks this a deeply problematic move.

> The emergence of sociology will take a different course (when it emerges) from that of other sciences because sociology, to emerge, must free itself not from philosophy but from the common-sense perspective… The 'discovery' of the common-sense world is important as the discovery of a problem only, and not as the discovery of a sociological resource.

For Sacks, common-sense ought to be the subject matter of sociology. However, insofar as it is used as an unexplicated resource then it produces a very particular methodological problem, and one that has a profound impact on sociological generalisations.

> The sole difference between the writings of sociologists and the talk about society of anyone else turns on the concern of sociologists with a single methodological problem which sociologists have 'discovered'. I shall call this problem 'the etcetera problem'.

The etcetera problem recognises that general sociological descriptions—e.g., Marx's theory of capital, Durkheim's theory of anomie, or Weber's theory of rational action—are incomplete. More can always be said about the objects the theory describes, such descriptions can be extended indefinitely, and sociologists have of course been extending them for well over a century now. The upshot of the etcetera problem is that sociological descriptions are always *partial*. This means that the sociological object a theory describes cannot, as Sacks puts it,

> ...be recaptured by using the description as instructions for locating it... The reason these descriptions fail to be abstract in the sense typified by mathematics: general concepts of the latter sort retain the features of the particular cases—given the generalisation one can always recapture the particular object. Descriptions that neglect the features of particular objects prevent such recapture, and as the meaning of the etcetera problem is that even purported descriptions of particular objects neglect some *undetermined set* of their features, it is obvious that the mathematical sense of abstraction is not achievable given acceptance of the etcetera problem.

Take Marx's description of the division of labour in society, for example, and how it fails to elaborate how work in any particular setting is organised or accomplished. Marx's description is a treatise on the social character of work per se and says little about *particular* manifestations (Button and Harper 1996).

Of course Marx is not the only sociologist whose theory fails to describe its constituent social objects in locatable detail. We cannot recapture the commonplace categorisation of "suicide" from Durkheim's theory of society (Douglas 1967), or "bureaucracy" at work in Weber's description of rational action (Blau 1964), anymore than we can recapture the social objects described by contemporary sociological descriptions. Labouring under the auspices of the etcetera problem the founding father's of sociology created a methodological apparatus that, unlike their particular descriptions of social objects, is alive and well today. That apparatus trades on common-sense, exploiting it as a resource that enables the production of general sociological descriptions but they are general, as Sacks puts it, only in the "trivial sense" that they speak about and portray *society at large*. This is in large part due to the ways in which sociologists orient themselves to describing society in the first place. Sacks (1984) again invokes the image of a machine by way of elaboration.

> The important theories in the social sciences have tended to view society as a piece of machinery with relatively few orderly products... Such a view suggests that there are few places where, if we can find them, we will be able to tackle the problem of order... So we can have an image of a machine with a couple of holes in the front. It spews out some nice stuff from those holes, and at the back it spews out garbage.

Not surprisingly sociologists are generally interested in the "nice stuff" that the machine spews out. This is usually determined and controlled by the "big issues" of the day. The "mundane, occasional, local, and the like"—the garbage in other words—is of no interest or worth other than as a common-sense resource contingently drawn upon to embed sociological reasoning in visible features of daily life and to thereby warrant sociological description of the "big issues" that shape it (Bacchus 1986). However, treating society in this way results in the etcetera problem.

No surprise then that Sacks proposed an alternative treatment, which suspends the assumption that order is a rare beast to be found in only a few places and replaces it with a view that order is a mundane feature of everyday life and a constituent feature of the ordinary activities and common-sense reasoning that inhabits and animates it. We might therefore assume, as Sacks (1984) puts it,

> …wherever we happen to attack the phenomenon we are going to find…that there is order at all points.

Thus, in place of a view of society that is possessed of very few orderly products, with those products being produced through the operation of "big" social phenomenon—such as the operations of political and legal institutions, organisations and corporations—we have instead a view that suggests that just about anything and everything that occurs in everyday life, no matter how mundane, is possessed of its own orderly characteristics.

Take the following piece of text—as plain a piece of garbage as you are ever likely to come across—by way of example: *The baby cried. The mommy picked it up* (Sacks 1992c). What on earth could be sociologically significant about this fragment of ordinary language?

> When I hear 'The baby cried. The mommy picked it up,' one of the things I hear is that the mommy who picks the baby up is the mommy of the baby. Now it's not only the case that I hear it that way—and of course there's no genitive there to say 'its mommy picked it up,' 'his mommy,' 'her mommy'—when I hear it that way a kind of interesting thing is that I also feel pretty confident that all of you, at least the natives among you, hear that also. Is it some kind of magic? (ibid.)

How can something as seemingly trivial as a couple of throwaway sentences have such *enormous generalisability* built into them such that "all of you", or "at least the natives" (that is, competent speakers of English in this case), hear that it was the baby's mommy who picked it up when the words themselves *do not* specify that? The answer, for Sacks (1984), lies in the *"machinery of interaction"* that we natives (or members) use to order our everyday affairs. The interaction in this case lies in the reading-and-hearing of the text, though the machinery which orders this reading-and-hearing is also operative in the speaking-and-hearing of the words. It consists in the use of *membership categorisation devices* or MCD's (Sacks 1992c)—collections of natural language categories such as 'father', 'mother', 'baby', 'uncle', 'grandmother', etc., which members employ to characterise relationships between people—and *tying rules* Sacks (1992b), which provide for our hearing that the categories 'baby' and 'mommy' are first and second parts *of a pair*, that they belong together, and that the mommy is therefore the mommy of the baby even though nobody actually said so (Sacks 1992a).

The point in recounting the example, both for Sacks and us, is to provide a simple demonstration of the existence of an ordinarily seen but unnoticed or taken for granted "machinery of interaction". Furthermore, and perhaps most importantly for present purposes, the machinery is generalisable. You don't need 10 or 100 or 1000 occurrences or instances of *"The baby cried. The mommy picked it up."* to generalise MCD's and tying rules. You only need one, and you only need one because *in ordering interaction*, the machinery provides for its *own generalisation*, including its reproducibility and prediction. Thus, on each and every occasion of its occurrence "all of you" will hear the same thing again—that the baby's mommy picked it up—and you will hear it that way because that is what the machinery very specifically provides for. How can that be?

Sacks' response to the question is how could it *not* be, given that we are all individuals who only ever experience a random portion of our culture?

> ...any Member encountering from his infancy a very small portion of it, and a random portion in a way (the parents he happens to have, the experiences he happens to have, the vocabulary that happens to be thrown at him in whatever sentences he happens to get) comes out in many ways pretty much like everybody else, and able to deal with pretty much anyone else... Now if one figures that that's the way things are to some extent... you may well find that you got an enormous generalisability because things are so arranged that you *could* get them; given that for a Member encountering a very limited environment, he has to be able to do that, and things are so arranged as to permit him to. (Sacks 1992d)

In saying that members "come out pretty much like anyone else, and able to deal with pretty much anyone else" Sacks is not saying that we are all the same, but rather that our random encounters with our culture nevertheless provide us with a shared resource for 'arranging' the things that we find ourselves engaged in, even if we are familiar with those things or not.

> ...in a great deal of the stuff I've been considering, I've been regularly pointing to the fact that people do it with persons they've never met, extend things to occasions they've never dealt with, etc., and do it with assurance and some success. (ibid.)

The shared cultural resource is *order* and it is provided for not by the operations of overarching political and legal institutions, organisations, corporations, ***etcetera***, but through the operation of a machinery of interaction that may well have "enormous generalisability" built into it because members use it *to arrange* their everyday affairs.

Sacks' respecification of sociology brings an unsuspected phenomenon into view: the machinery of interaction whereby everyday affairs are ordered. The machinery not only consists of MCD's and tying rules. Sacks' work (1992a) revealed a great many other parts of the machinery ordering talk, not that he was interested in conversation per se, he "just happened to have it" available. His writings make it clear that he recognised there was much more to everyday life and that a great deal is left untouched and unexplicated by his work. In transforming sociology's subject matter Sacks didn't simply want sociologists and ethnographers to become Conversation Analysts, but rather he set up the broader problem of uncovering the machinery of interaction as sociology's goal. Thus, on any occasion of inquiry, no matter the social object,

> Our aim is to get into a position to transform…our view of 'what happened', from a matter of particular interaction done by particular people, to a matter of interactions as products of a machinery. We are trying to find the machinery. (Sacks 1984).

The machinery of interaction has been characterised by various labels, including members' methods, procedures, and most notably in the context of CSCW, work practices. Whatever the nomenclature, elaboration of the orderly ways in which people arrange their affairs in interaction reveals the "operational structure" of ordinary activities (Garfinkel 1967); in short, *how* they are *done* and reflexively *organised* as a *social* or collaborative enterprise in real time interaction. A single case of the machinery of interaction at work on any particular occasion is generalisable because it is a *shared cultural resource* for arranging the everyday affairs it elaborates. It is in this sense that activities may be said to contain their own means of generalisation. What we want to do next is move beyond an abstract elaboration of the foundations of sociological generalisation to examine a concrete example of it at work in design.

Shaping PlaceBooks

The approach advocated by Sacks and the angry ethnographer was adopted in the development of a system called PlaceBooks. It is not our aim here to provide a detailed description of the system but to *explicate the nature of ethnographic study and generalisation in its development*. Suffice to say that the development of PlaceBooks was occasioned by the recognition that multi-media solutions such as Google Maps provide inadequate support for people to map rural places. While it is possible to add a variety of user-generated content (trails, text, photos, video, etc.) the results lack sufficient granularity to be of much practical use in rural situations. The problem becomes more apparent when we contrast current solutions with the simple pen and ink sketches produced by the late Alfred Wainwright of the Lake District in the UK, which have sold in their millions since their initial publication in 1965. To this day there are no digital equivalents.[1]

Wainwright's sketches *contextualise place*, exploiting maps, text, diagrams of routes and landscape drawings to elaborate features of a location that are *salient* to human interaction with it: in this case features that are salient to 'walking the fells'. Researchers involved in the development of PlaceBooks sought to enable people to purpose digital resources to contextualise place and support a wide range of rural activities. Not only walking, but also cycling, climbing, surfing, sailing,

---

[1] Compare, for example, the various representations provided by Google Maps of Eskdale in the UK with Wainright's: http://2.bp.blogspot.com/-TuXyhpJX7tc/TmC9lZBtYbI/AAAAAAAAAsE/w2hfyfBaAms/s1600/WainwrightPage.jpg.

bird watching, and the rest. The initial problem that confronted the design team was how to get handle on what kind of system they should build? A range of approaches were adopted to help develop answers to the question, including envisioning new means of documenting people's experience of place using ubiquitous computing technology, new forms of map representation, and commissioning an ethnographic study to understand the cooperative work involved in the act of visiting place based on the premise that no matter what one is visiting a place for there may well be generic features of the *act* that frame engagement and raise requirements for systems design.

The Act of Visiting Place

The act of visiting place falls more generically under the umbrella of tourism and a large body of work has emerged over recent years that focuses on the invention of the rural as *a place of leisure* (Agyeman and Neal 2006). Labouring under the auspices of the etcetera problem, a range of different theoretical perspectives jostle together to elaborate that generic sociological character of visiting rural places. It is seen as response to the ways in which modern living conditions 'numb' us (Le Breton 2000), for example, and as a means of 'reconnecting' with ourselves at both a sensorial and spiritual level (Sharpley and Jepson 2011). Postmodern and critical treatments urge us to consider tourism as a performance enacted in place (Edensor 2001) and place itself as multi-layered and interconnected 'text' (Staiff 2010) whose intelligibility resides in the tourist 'gaze'. Whichever way you construe of it, the turn to the countryside as a major site of leisure is of demonstrable economic benefit to rural communities, and this in turn shapes a wide variety of theoretical views on the pros and cons of 'ecotourism' (Higham 2007).

Nonetheless, as we seek to treat the common-sense world as a topic for investigation—rather than as a resource for theorising tourism in rural contexts—we focus upon what visiting involves as a *practical sociological* matter (Crabtree et al. 2012), as something which requires collaborative work and organisation *by the parties involved* if they are to bring the act of visiting about. The specific visit we observed was that of a family of six to the 'Parc Naturel Regional de Chartreuse' in South-Eastern France, about an hour's drive away from where the family lived, in November 2010. The family itself was composed of Dave (50), Chloe (42), Paul (20), Jane (16), Marcus (14), and Sarah (8). The visit took place at a weekend and the nature reserve in question had recently experienced one of the first major snowfalls of the year (much of the reserve is above 1,000 metres). All of the data was gathered through natural, in situ observation and involved a mixture of video and audio recordings, photographs, and handwritten notes. All in all the study involved 20 h of fieldwork distributed across 16 days, with over half the fieldwork taking place on the actual day of the visit. It is not possible in the space available to provide an extremely detailed account of the collaborative work involved in making the visit happen (c.f. Tolmie and Crabtree 2013). Instead, and in sequential order of their occurrence, we elaborate the key organisational features of that work.

Occasioning the Possibility

The first step towards a visit occurring is the *occasioning of it as a possibility*. There a variety of ways in which such occasioning might take place. It might be that it arises apropos of nothing much in particular—'because we were bored', 'because the weather is nice', 'because we need to get out of the house for while', 'because the kids are driving us crazy', and so on—or it might be occasioned in a variety of others ways and for a variety of other reasons. Previous promises, for instance, or as a way of encouraging someone to do something else, such as a particularly onerous project for homework, or as a reward for doing something else. The time of year and recurrence of events might occasion the possibility. Recollections of places already visited, triggered by photographs or someone mentioning someone else is going to a place you've already been to and liked, often occasion visits too. But perhaps the most commonplace occasioning of all is the occurrence of some special event, such as Mum's birthday, or it being Easter Monday or some other one-day holiday, or an anniversary, and so on. In our case, what occasioned the visit was that we asked the family to 'go and have a day out in the country' so that we could study it. Whatever occasions the possibility, the occasioning itself brings with it a certain body of interactional work, which we shall explicate as we work our way through the sequence.

Making the Possibility Concrete

Having agreed on the possibility to visit a place the next organisational matter the cohort must address is to make it concrete by *deciding where to go*. This is wrapped up with such practical matters as deciding *when* to go and *what to do* when you get there. Family routines rarely allow for total spontaneity. Decisions about when to go on a visit have to accommodate the routine and the reasoning implicated in decision-making must here take the various commitments and obligations of family members into account (what about school, what about work, what else do we have to do, what time can we leave, when must we be home by, etc.). Decision-making here also turns upon matters such as what the weather is likely to be like on the day, whether the place might be heaving with people (for instance on a bank holiday), and whether there are things to be done the next day that might be impacted. Decisions of when to go are also quicker to make than decisions of where to go, but have to be made by a certain time, as the visit may occasion planning and preparation and space needs to be allowed for this, though they are more quickly resolved than decisions of where to go.

Deciding where to go depends upon the potential cohort. Not all days out will necessarily encompass everyone in a household, so not everyone has a say. Furthermore, some members of the household have limited discussion and decision-making rights, particularly young children. On the other hand, strong differential rights may be operative (e.g. if it's your birthday, you decide). For a whole family day out, when no one has particular rights of choice (such as the one we are looking at here), everyone is potentially involved in deciding where to go and this can make it hard for the group to ratify a decision. So it's not a case of saying "right, we're going hang-gliding", for example, but rather "shall we go hang-gliding?" which can then implicate either acceptance or rejection by the cohort. Once an initial proposition has been floored, subsequent suggestions may be considered iteratively. Consider, for instance, the following vignette.

Chloe Dad suggested visiting a glacier. A guided walk up into the mountains
Jane Yeah, that sounds good
Dave That's what I was thinking because the Alps are within striking distance and we could do that within a day trip
Paul (dubiously) Mmm
Chloe What else could we do up in the mountains?
Dave I don't know
Chloe Bobsleighing
Dave It depends whether there's snow'
Paul I'd like to do that'
Jane I'd be happy to go up into the Alps just to take photos
Paul Go skiing? Family skiing trip
Chloe Well I like skiing
Paul I haven't tried yet'
Chloe And if we go to a centre there's not just skiing. Ice skating! There could be ice skating
Jane I don't like ice skating any more
Chloe No?
Jane Well every time I do it I keep getting knocked down.

What can be seen here is that an initial proposal provides for the subsequent utterances to be ratifications or counter-proposals. Furthermore, two or more suggestions open the floodgates because apparent uncertainty provides the rights for proposal across a broader cohort. Add to this that there are numerous grounds upon which the appropriateness of a suggestion may be considered: time, cost, distance, weather, relative interest, majority and minority interest, novelty, risk, excitement, proximity, adherence to the original proposition, and so on, can all enter into the discussion. All proposals are potentially accountable to these considerations and rejections can be articulated on the same grounds.

Arriving at suggestions, let alone decisions, takes work then and not all of it discursive in the first instance. Dave had anticipated that making a decision on where to go could be problematic and had prepared a list of links in a text file prior to the discussion. This involved a substantial body of work on his part, with a range of Google searches, examination of specific websites, and copying over of links from the browser to the text file so that they could be quickly transported to the machine in the living room and thus made visible to everyone at the same time. In this way group discussion came to revolve around physical presentation and display of a range of different resources associated with the possibility of visiting *some* place, including websites, brochures, advertised events, maps, and so on. This meant that discussions of where to go bled into discussions of what to do and vice versa. Nonetheless, a decision was eventually arrived at and the Chartreuse Natural Park agreed upon.

Making Ready for the Visit

Decision in hand the next organisational matter to be addressed consists of *making ready for the visit*. In this case, making ready drew upon the use of a range of physical and digital resources, with some aspects being directly collaborative (e.g. deciding what to do about food), whilst other aspects may be undertaken by dedicated individuals (e.g. buying food to take on the trip). A number of considerations are potentially relevant here, including deciding what route to take, what things to take, what time to leave, financing, who to tell, contingencies to cover, and who should do what and when. Families do not just go out on day trips by walking out of the door. There is a whole range of mundane and taken for granted work implicated in *getting out of the door*. Things of relevance, things to be taken, have to be brought together and much of this cannot be done days ahead of departure. Often it is work that has to be done just before you go. So people have to be got up and organised in readiness for departure, and this itself may have to be discussed the day before. In this case Dave and Chloe decided an exact order of who would get up and wake who in turn in the morning. Things to be taken—especially food and drink—may take active preparation no sooner than the night before, perhaps even on the day itself. Houses may have to be prepared for a day of absence by locking doors, shutting windows, changing the heating, and so on. Things have to be loaded into cars. Verification may happen at a number of places that the right things are being brought together and prepared, as we can see in the following interaction between Dave and Chloe.

> Dave goes out to car with coat and boots—Opens the boot and puts them in—Goes back into house and gathers up all the other coats and brings them out to put in the boot as well—Goes back into house and brings out another pair of boots and a rucksack and plastic bag to pack—Goes back into house and gets stuff on table (batteries, cameras, wallet, phone, etc.) pulled together in one bag—Others getting coats and scarves on—Dave checking with Chloe whether there was anything else that needed to go in the car—Chloe comes over to look—Jane's stuff but she'll sort for herself—Other boots are going to stay there.

Then people also have to be loaded into cars, which can itself involve extensive negotiation as family members vie for what they consider to be preferred positions within the car. The work of making ready is distributed, collaborative work that may implicate and render accountable anyone in the household, yet only certain individuals may initiate certain activities (e.g., not just anyone decides it's time to load the car). Such matters fall within the larger organisation of relationships within the household and just who may appropriately ask what of someone else.

Making Your Way There

Making your way to a place can be an important feature of the visit, particularly if it takes a substantial amount of time to get there. Journeys occasion leisure activities—games and entertainment (whether it be watching a movie or remarking upon scenes of interest passing by)—and mundane work (fuel stops, toilet stops, food stops, etc.). It can also be the case that the exact proposition and details of the plan shaping the both the journey and the day out itself will get fine-tuned once the trip is under way, especially if delays, diversions or other unexpected contingencies arise along the way. In this particular case the priorities were established en route as the family decided that they'd go for a walk first of all, then eat, then do other things as they came across them. Although it's a vital part of how visiting is accomplished, the plan is neither complete nor rigid. Rather it provides a set of orientations and provisions that are negotiated into actual practice along the way as they are made to fit with the in situ and contingent events the family find themselves confronted by (Suchman 1987). This proved to be recurrently the case as the day out was seen to unfold and became especially apparent when the family arrived at their destination.

Arriving, especially when it's a visit to somewhere you've never been before, can itself involve a measure of work. Some of the attendant problems here include recognising you're there, deciding it is where you actually want to be, knowing where to stop, and ascertaining whether it's the right place to stop. Consider the following vignette by way of example.

Dave	Right, this is Saint Hillaire. Next question is where to stop. Just stop in the centre and hope we find it?
Sarah	I'd like to get out and stretch my legs((Carries on driving through village))
Chloe	Now we're coming out of town((Carries on driving))
Chloe	Commenting on coming into next village
Dave	saying looking for signposts
Chloe	Noticing signpost for station de ski
Dave	Yeah, I think stop somewhere around here and see
Chloe	What about going up to the ski station?
Dave	What I want to do is make sure we park where we're not too far from where we can eat—like near an auberge. I'm not going to be doing too much driving because I don't want to drive up into the high Chartreuse where we'd need snow tyres((slowing down))
Dave	How about there?
Chloe	There's a cafe restaurant
Dave	Shall I park up here somewhere?
Chloe	Yeah
Dave	Turns off road into parking area. Pulls into parking space next to other cars and stops.
Near	Tourist information office and just after cafe-restaurant Chloe pointed out.

There had been no prior decision made about an exact place to stop and it takes work in the course of driving just to figure out what an appropriate place might be. It starts with a vague effort to locate relevant signposts, but concretises around the spotting of a café restaurant by Chloe, which will facilitate part of the plan in view of providing somewhere to go and eat as well. However, parking near the restaurant had not been formulated as a part of the plan. Rather, it presented itself as an appropriate proposition in situ.

Once you have arrived there are still things to be done. The bringing together of things while making ready is essentially a provisional and contingent assembly of potentially required things. There is now the work of ascertaining just what should actually come along. Here, too, there are those who have the right to decide and do the actual apportioning, and others who are expected to do what is asked of them. A detail in this case is that it is snowy outside and everyone needs to don certain appropriate pieces of apparel. Once everybody is out of the car and ready there is still work involved in seeing what it will take to actually begin the visit. Just where do you go next? In this particular case the work involved is extensive. It involves decisions about whether to eat first or walk first, it entails researching what information is available in situ (the work of locating meaningful signs, of ascertaining what routes might be followed and what grounds would make them appropriate, such as duration), and preliminary to all of this, the work of uncovering just exactly where you are in relation to everything else that might be of interest.

Family walk across car park together to look at tourist information office
Get to map on board showing footpaths around the area
Chloe and Dave work out together which car park (marked P) they are at on the map

Chloe	OK, so there's a sentier [footpath] (pointing to map) just here
Dave	Just there, yes. Towards the parapente
Chloe	(tracing path around in a circle and back to P sign)
Chloe	Perhaps we can do that. (Looking up at tourist information office) It looks shut to me up there, but I'll go and look anyway
Dave	It is shut, yeah. There's no lights on or anything
Chloe	So, if we're here (pointing to map again) La Chappelle is there
Dave	We're at the tourist information anyway, aren't we. We're on the main road. I think we're here (pointing to map where there's an 'i' symbol)
Chloe	Which way are we facing then?
Dave	Errm, well we know that the er -

Making the Visit Happen

It is in the way of a great many kinds of rural visit that exactly what route is to be followed is something that is under constant potential revision, adaptation and elaboration. Almost straight away this becomes a feature of this family's visit as the prospect of visiting a waterfall presents itself to them:

Chloe brushing snow off of signs as Dave comes up

Chloe This is where it branches apparently
Dave Okay
Chloe So it's a one hour route that way (pointing to right)
Dave Okay
Chloe A 40 min route to the left
Dave Okay, we're probably taking the shorter one aren't we? In view of the fact they're fretting already
Chloe It says there's cascades as well
Dave Oooh!
Chloe I wonder if it's on the way? A frozen waterfall would be fantastic
Dave It would

Bundled up with the work of finding and taking a particular route is the work involved in actually finding one's way around. A particularly striking feature here is how much *wayfinding* is both collaborative across the whole of the family and informed by the traces left by other people.

Chloe There's a sign over by that tree (pointing to a tree in middle of large expanse of snow)
Paul We're not going to be able to read it from here are we?
Chloe (Pointing to a post with two arrows on it pointing different directions) I think we have to turn right. That's our most informative post there
Dave Right
Chloe We must be heading towards that signpost there
Dave We must be
Sarah Mum, there are footmarks leading that way
Chloe There are. We'll go that way

The preceding points are tightly bound up with how the family goes about managing the fashion in which it traverses the landscape. However, there are also a number of recurrently visible features that relate to what the family does as it is traversing the landscape. Something that particularly provides for the character of a specific visit is just what comes to be *taken note of* along the way. What all this amounts to is that there are things to be attended to and things that are passed by without remark, being oriented to as utterly mundane features of the environment in some way. It is also worth noting that it is not solely a case of people remarking for their own benefit. Much of what happens amongst groups is 'callings to attention' where some feature is explicitly pointed out to some or all of the other members in your party:

Paul suddenly runs ahead and stops, looking to the right: Everybody come here!
Everyone walks up to join him.

Dave Oh wow, yeah, I see. The mountains. (Spectacular view of the mountains with clouds banking up around them)
Paul A nice shot

As Paul's comment makes visible, something that can feature strongly in family visits to nature reserves is the *making of a record* of various aspects of the visit, usually by means of cameras. Much of this is once again premised around what is worthy of interest and capture, with the added element that family members themselves and their actions can count as part of this. Another part of the business of uncovering aspects of the environment worthy of attention or otherwise is the work that can happen with situated displays, i.e., noticeboards or information panels of various kinds inserted in the landscape. Consider the following:

Sarah	Chloe and Dave arrive at a viewing point looking across to mountains with two boards laid across the top of posts. Chloe walks up to one and starts to sweep the snow off of it. When snow is swept off it's just a blank board underneath.
Chloe	There's not actually anything on them right now
Chloe	Nothing either
Dave	tries to lift board and finds it is hinged so that you can raise it up
Sarah	Mum!
Dave	Because it opens up
PaulIt	is actually a workable display that knows that it gets snowy
Dave	Because it opens up
Chloe	Ah!
Dave	See

Clearly situated displays are positioned by those managing the site in an effort to explicate certain aspects of the locale in some way. A couple of things fall out of this, however. First of all something has to be recognised as a display to that purpose and, as the example makes clear, this is not always straightforward. Secondly, the explication turns upon the recognisability of the things being explicated in situ and this, too, can prove problematic. What the work of trying to disambiguate a situated display reveals is that there are ways in which it forms a part of a larger enterprise of trying to make the landscape one is passing through *situationally legible*. This not simply another aspect of wayfinding. It is, once again, as much about trying to locate within the environment what should and could be worthy of your interest as you go about the business of visiting place.

Calling it a Day and Heading Home

Days out like this do not typically come with a set end time, but of course, a stage is reached, especially where people are walking or otherwise exerting themselves in some way, where various members of the group start to voice a wish to 'call it a day'. Sometimes it is first voiced by children who are getting tired, sometimes it's voiced by teenagers who are getting bored, sometimes it's more immediately universal (for instance when the heavens open and everyone is getting cold or wet). However, it is important to note that bringing the visit to a close doesn't just happen by magic. This too involves work. Propositions or requests are made. Various people with various rights and responsibilities will ratify or otherwise, just as we have seen with regard to other matters along the way. This business of negotiation is an essential preliminary to the actual business of heading back. To ignore these interactional niceties and to just make a unilateral decision that you are heading back regardless would have powerful consequences, with others in the group immediately seeking out some kind of account. Here's how the visit was brought to a close in our principal example. Note in particular how the proposition of calling it a day is not just made on its own but also accounted for in various ways: initially it's about fatigue; then it also comes to be about the need to get back in time to eat:

Chloe I'm tired now, let's go back
Dave But we haven't seen the waterfalls yet
Chloe Let's go back. I want to be back in time for lunch

There comes a point where everyone in the group is back at the car (or other point of departure) and getting ready to go home. Departing retains some characteristics of both making ready and arriving. However, it is typically more constrained. The primary aspects here are: the relocation of the car; unburdening of individuals and replacement of things in the car; the redistribution of its occupants (which does not have to be exactly as it was before and can still be an object of negotiation); and the work involved in figuring out how to physically regain the route and head for home followed by the work of journeying and making your way home.

Getting Home

Something else our study revealed that should not be discounted is that a family doesn't just arrive home and that is it. Instead it takes work to get back into the house after a visit. Some of this work is obvious but nonetheless an important aspect of the overall sequence that cannot be set aside without ramifications of some kind. Thus there is work involved in physically getting out of the car and regaining entry to the home, with various people having various rights of precedence regarding entry. Then people will re-distribute themselves around the home in accountably appropriate ways. In this case Chloe started to get herself and Sarah out of their outdoor clothes whilst Paul took himself off upstairs and Marcus doodled on the guitar. Jane, meanwhile, was co-opted into assisting Dave with unloading the car. The actual unloading of the car can itself involve significant labour. On this occasion Dave systematically ferried everything into the living room first of all. Only after this did they begin to then re-locate various things to various locations, kitchen things (cups etc.) and rubbish to the kitchen, cameras etc. to the living room table, coats and boots by the door, and so on.

Beyond these moments of first entry the immediate post-visit phase can be seen to involve the rapid re-occupancy of the home and the re-constitution of the household routine. One of the first topics of discussion in this case, for instance, was what to do about supper. Arriving home can also involve the recognition and handling of the house's own contingencies (e.g. matters of heating and hot water, animals and their whereabouts, what would normally have been done during the day and hasn't been, who may have called, and so on). After a day out in the country has taken place the relevance of the visit to other matters becomes rapidly diffuse. Talk about the visit amongst the family mostly takes place in the car or immediately afterwards. Indeed, we should note that it would become accountably odd to continue to talk about it much beyond this. Instead one finds that talk about it amongst the family from here on in will address specific features as they are occasioned, for instance by other possibilities of trips, topics of interest, or looking through the photographs.

Informing Design

There is much that we have glossed over in our account of the family's visit, particularly the collaborative work involved in maintaining the family as a group that is collaboratively involved in having a pleasurable experience (c.f. Tolmie and Crabtree 2013 for further details). Nonetheless, we would suggest that even a single study of a single family having a single day out reveals a machinery of interaction that has broader purchase: which is, in short, generalisable. The design team, for example, recognised from their experience as ordinary members of society the operational structure of visiting place elaborated by the machinery of interaction. That is, they recognised that visiting place consists of a distinctive set of collaborative activities and cooperative work revolving around specific organisational matters. They recognised that the act of visiting place involves occasioning a visit, making the possibility concrete, making ready for the visit, making your way there, making the visit happen, calling it a day and heading home, and arriving home, and they recognised the work bound up with bringing these things about as a collaborative matter. The collaborative organisation or *social ordering* of the act of visiting—while inhabited by particular and contingent features (the particular cohort, the particular place visited, the particular mode of transport taken, etc.)—was not seen by the design team as being unique to the family but was recognised as something that their families enacted too. The *order* uncovered by the studies was seen to be *generalisable* by the design team then, and we suspect that those readers who have also enacted days out with their families and other small groups will recognise the generalisable character of that order too.

Our study had particular consequences for the design of PlaceBooks, elaborating the operational structure or embodied interactional order of the experience we could be designing for and enabling the design team to reason about the particular kinds of collaborative activity that ubiquitous computing technologies and novel map representations could be leveraged to support. The result was a suite of web-based, mobile and location-based tools that enable users to discover potential places to visit, to plan a visit, determine just what to do when they get there, to conduct the visit, and to create a record some time after that can be shared with others (see http://www.placebooks.org for further details). PlaceBooks has subsequently been adopted by the People's Collection Wales (PCW), a project funded by the Welsh Government to support the public in documenting the history and culture of the Welsh landscape.[2] PCW is currently exploring the use of PlaceBooks in a broader European context via its involvement in an INTERREG consortium.

Conclusion

The 'angry' ethnography is of course a rhetorical construct, which is not to say that the issues we make him speak about are not real or of consequence. What actually occasioned the writing of this paper was a review of a paper about the PlaceBooks system, in which several reviewers stated that it is not possible to generalise the findings of an ethnographic study of one family, especially given such a short period of fieldwork. This did indeed occasion an angry outburst from the ethnographers involved in the study, including many more choice expressions than the title of this paper can or should convey. The nature of the frustration is evident but it is not the first time we have run up against *assertions* like this, they are commonplace, and we don't expect it to be the last time we are confronted by them either. But assertions they are, rooted in positivistic and quantitative reasoning that insists upon a certain kind of generalisation procedure that has no cognisance let alone respect for the sociological grounds upon which generalisation works *within* everyday life and is 'built into' ordinary activities (Sharrock and Randall 2004). Not only *did* we find a generalisable social object in our ethnographic study of *one* family's day out, we found it through a very short period of fieldwork covering only 16 days. What we found—and what warrants generalisation—is a machinery of interaction whereby the members of a culture *order* a visit to a place for the purposes of having a family day out. That order does not belong to the particular family we studied. While locally enacted by them it is not theirs alone but belongs to the culture that they are members of. It is *a resource that the culture provides* for all families wanting to visit a place for a day out together, and other small groups too. As this kind of visit is extremely commonplace, then so too is the order that articulates it. The orderliness of other activities—controlling trains or planes, for example—may have much less scope or scale but is nonetheless generalisable across the cohort whose business it is to conduct such activities. Scale should not be confused with generalisation, however, and neither should the duration of fieldwork with validity.

Acknowledgments The research on which this article is based was funded by RCUK research grants EP/I001816/1, EP/I001778/1, EP/G065802/1, EP/J000604/1 and EP/J000604/2.

---

[2] http://placebooks.peoplescollectionwales.com

References

Agyeman, J., & Neal, S. (Eds.). (2006). *The new countryside?*. Bristol: Policy Press.

Baccus, M. D. (1986). Sociological indication and the visibility criterion of real world social theorising. In H. Garfinkel (Ed.), *Ethnomethodological studies of work* (pp. 1–19). London: Routledge and Kegan Paul.

Blau, P. M. (1964). *The dynamics of bureaucracy: A study of interpersonal relations in two government agencies*. Chicago: University of Chicago Press.

Button, G., & Harper, R. (1996). The relevance of 'work-practice' for design. *Computer Supported Cooperative Work: The Journal of Collaborative Computing, 4*(4), 263–280.

Crabtree, A., Rouncefield, M., & Tolmie, P. (2012). Doing design ethnography, Springer

Douglas, J. D. (1967). *The social meanings of suicide*. New Jersey: Princeton.

Edensor, T. (2001). Performing tourism, staging tourism. *Tourist Studies, 1*(1), 59–81.

Garfinkel, H. (1967). *Studies in ethnomethodology*. Englewood Cliffs: Prentice-Hall.

Heath, C., & Luff, P. (1991). Collaborative activity and technology design: Task coordination in London Underground control rooms. In *Proceedings of the 2nd European Conference on Computer Supported Cooperative Work* (pp. 65–80). Amsterdam, Kluwer.

Higham, J. (Ed.) (2007). *Critical issues in ecotourism*, Boston: Elsevier.

Hughes, J., Randall, D., & Shapiro, D. (1992). Faltering from ethnography to design. In *Proceedings of the 1992 ACM Conference on Computer Supported Cooperative Work* (pp. 115–122). Toronto: ACM.

Hughes, J., King, V., Rodden, T., & Andersen, H. (1994). Moving out of the control room: ethnography in systems design. In *Proceedings of the 1994 ACM Conference on Computer Supported Cooperative Work* (pp. 429–438). Chapel Hill: ACM.

Keith, M. (1992). Angry writing: (Re)presenting the unethical world of the ethnographer. *Society and Space, 10*, 551–568.

Le Breton, D. (2000). *Eloge de la Marche*. Paris: Métailié.

Malinowski, B. (1922). *Argonauts of the Western Pacific: An account of native enterprise and adventure in the archipelagoes of Melanesian New Guinea*. London: Routledge and Kegan Paul.

Sacks, H. (1963). Sociological description. *Berkeley Journal of Sociology, 8*, 1–16.

Sacks, H. (1984). Notes on methodology. In J. M Maxwell & J. Heritage (Eds.), *Structures of social action: Studies in conversation analysis* (pp. 21–27). Cambridge University Press.

Sacks, H. (1992a).In G. Jefferson (Ed.), *Lectures on Conversation Volumes I & II*. Oxford: Blackwell.

Sacks, H. (1992b). Tying rules. In G. Jefferson (Ed.), *Lectures on Conversation* (Vol. I, pp. 150–156). Oxford: Blackwell. Fall 1965, Lecture 4.

Sacks, H. (1992c). The baby cried. The mommy picked it up. In G. Jefferson (Ed.), *Lectures on Conversation* (Vol. I, pp. 236–242). Oxford: Blackwell. Lecture 1, Spring 1966.

Sacks, H. (1992d). On sampling and subjectivity. In G. Jefferson (Ed.), *Lectures on Conversation* (Vol. I, pp. 483–488). Oxford: Blackwell. Lecture 33, Spring 1966

Sharpley, R., & Jepson, D. (2011). Rural tourism: A spiritual experience? *Annals of Tourism Research, 38*(1), 52–71.

Sharrock, W., & Randall, D. (2004). Ethnography, ethnomethodology and the problem of generalisation in design. *European Journal of Information Systems, 13*, 186–194.

Staiff, R. (2010). History and tourism: Intertextual representations of Florence. *Tourism Analysis, 15*(5), 601–611.

Tolmie, P., & Crabtree, A. (2013). A day out in the country. In P. Tolmie, & M. Rouncefield (Ed.), *Ethnomethodology at Play*. Ashgate.

Understanding Mobile Notification Management in Collocated Groups

Joel E. Fischer, Stuart Reeves, Stuart Moran, Chris Greenhalgh, Steve Benford and Stefan Rennick-Egglestone

Abstract We present an observational study of how notifications are handled by collocated groups, in the context of a collaborative mobile photo-taking exercise. Interaction analysis of video recordings is used to uncover the methodical ways in which participants manage notifications, establishing and sustaining co-oriented interaction to coordinate action, such as sharing notification contents and deciding on courses of action. Findings highlight how embodied and technological resources are collectively drawn upon in situationally nuanced ways to achieve the management of notifications delivered to cohorts. The insights can be used to develop an understanding of how interruptions are dealt with in other settings, and to reflect on how to support notification management within collocated groups by design.

J. E. Fischer (✉) · S. Reeves · S. Moran · C. Greenhalgh · S. Benford · S. Rennick-Egglestone
The Mixed Reality Laboratory, University of Nottingham, Nottinghamshire, UK
e-mail: jef@cs.nott.ac.uk

S. Reeves
e-mail: str@cs.nott.ac.uk

S. Moran
e-mail: spm@cs.nott.ac.uk

C. Greenhalgh
e-mail: cmg@cs.nott.ac.uk

S. Benford
e-mail: sdb@cs.nott.ac.uk

S. Rennick-Egglestone
e-mail: sre@cs.nott.ac.uk

O. W. Bertelsen et al. (eds.), *ECSCW 2013: Proceedings of the 13th European Conference on Computer Supported Cooperative Work, 21–25 September 2013, Paphos, Cyprus*, DOI: 10.1007/978-1-4471-5346-7_2,

Introduction

Notifications play a key role in our communications and social media. They alert us that an email or text message has arrived, that a friend has tagged us on a photo or mentioned us in a post, or that a follower has retweeted us. Importantly, notifications may not just announce the arrival of a message—they may act as a *summons* (Schegloff 1968) that prompt the receiver to engage in a subsequent activity.

Particularly relevant to the CSCW community, notifications have been deployed to encourage user engagement in collaborative mobile systems for collocated groups; for example to support photo sharing and collective souvenir creation whilst in a theme park (Durrant et al. 2011), spectating at an on-going sports event (Jacucci et al. 2007; Salovaara et al. 2006), visiting a city (Patel et al. 2009), or to support the social fabric of a student group (van House et al. 2005). This paper addresses the question of how these notifications are dealt with in the context of such group-oriented activities through a field trial of a collaborative mobile photo system.

We accept notifications as a 'fact of life', this paper examines the social process that follows on the delivery of the notification. Accounts in the literature of how this is accomplished hint that *social* management of notifications is commonplace. For example, Tolmie et al. (2008) reveal complex ways in which mobile interruptions make the recipient accountable to other members of the shared setting. Harr and Kaptelinin (2007) have talked about the "rippling effect" an interruption may have on others nearby.

We present a study of the ways in which groups of people organise their interaction around notifications delivered through a system designed to support a collaborative mobile photo-taking exercise. Based on video recordings triangulated with usage logs we provide an in-depth analysis that unpacks the methodical ways in which groups employ *interactional resources* to deal with notifications. Explicating the interactional resources in face-to-face settings (e.g., talk, gaze, body orientation) is common in the literature that seeks to provide insights to support the design of collaborative technologies (e.g., Luff and Jirotka 1998).

Findings from the trial reveal the embodied and technological resources employed to manage notifications within the unfolding interaction. Drawing upon observations from our field trial, we contribute a detailed account of the social ways in which people accomplish *notification management within groups*, and implications for the design of notifications for collaborative systems. In particular, we identify a repertoire of interactional resources for notification management that can be used as a framework to inform the research and design of technology that employs notifications to support collocated group activities.

Notifications and Interruptions

We review literature that reflects the prevalent orientation towards interruptions in related work to motivate why notification management within groups is a common, yet understudied phenomenon. We then revisit previous uses of notifications in collaborative systems and highlight some group-specific issues.

Studies of workplaces have shown that interruptions are part of everyday life (e.g., Mark et al. 2005). The literature tends to emphasize the detrimental effects of the change in attention interruptions can instigate; for example that they cause frequent task switches (Czerwinski et al. 2004) that can lead to stress Su and Mark (2008), and failure to resume prior tasks (O'conaill and Frohlich 1995).

Adjacent research in interruption management often aims at minimising the cost of interruptions by deferring interruptions to more opportune moments (Adamczyk and Bailey 2004; Ho and Intille 2005; Iqbal and Bailey 2007), or by adapting the way the interruption is presented (Avrahami and Hudson 2004). This strand of work often proposes technical solutions that predict the cost of the interruption based on sensing salient characteristics of the interruption context, such as the environment (Avrahami et al. 2007), the activity (Iqbal and Bailey 2007; Avrahami et al. 2007; Adamczyk and Bailey 2004) and attention of the interrupted person alto06, as well as interruption content (Avrahami et al. 2007), and modality (Ho and Intille 2005).

However, Rogers (2006) notes that efforts of constructing such automated systems have failed to meet the expectations evoked by labels such as 'context awareness'. This is perhaps due to the unpredictable and dynamic nature of context (Greenberg 2001). Dourish (2004) argues that context is a "slippery notion" that is "continually renegotiated and defined in the course of action". In their ethnographic study of interruptions, Tolmie et al. emphasise the high local specificity with which interruptions are handled, that "pretty well precludes any principle judgment regarding its positive or negative character" (2008, p. 264); instead, they suggest that there are opportunities to support people's management of interruptions that arise from the identifiable and methodical characteristics of how people handle interruptions. The question this paper seeks address is, what exactly are these methodical characteristics employed locally to handle notifications?

Notifications in Collaborative Systems

The role of notifications in collaborative systems at large has been introduced as a feature to support awareness in distributed groupware (Dourish and Bellotti 1992), such as group editing (Shen and Sun 2002). Mark et al. (2005) highlighted their role in alerting users to the interdependencies within cooperative work, a feature we adopt for our own work presented here. Work on mobile photo sharing in collocated groups has shown how people use these systems as a site of self-expression within social groups (van House et al. 2005) and to support an on-going real-world experience (Jacucci et al. 2007). It has further emphasised the importance of a 'common space' to enable group access and use of resources to support collective creative practices (Salovaara et al. 2006), and social discourse around the shared artefacts (Patel et al. 2009). Our focus in this paper is to study how collocated groups handle and situate notifications within their ongoing interaction.

Rogers notes that notifications may contribute to people engaging in experiences: "A constant but 'nagging' mechanism may also be effective at persuading people to do something they might not otherwise done" (2006, p. 416). To that end, in our prior field study of a collaborative mobile photo-souvenir system, we revealed how notifications interfered with social group interaction, to the point that one participant described accepting them "all of the time would seem anti-social" (Durrant et al. 2011, p. 1772). Furthermore, the notifications of new shared photos in the photo pool often told the groups something that they could already physically see for themselves, being collocated. Redundancy and overload with notifications in mobile collaborative systems has also been reported by Streefkerk et al. (2008).

The literature indicates strategies employed within group management of notifications, such as ignoring (Durrant et al. 2011) and making interruptions accountable to various cohorts, is commonplace (Tolmie et al. 2008). However, it appears there is little discussion of how notifications are dealt with in situ and how this process might be supported by design, particularly for settings with collocated groups. The study we present in this paper aims at addressing this gap in the literature.

Application areas that may benefit from understanding and supporting notification management within groups include locally distributed work settings with high temporal demands, such as policing (Streefkerk et al. 2008), fire-fighting (Jiang et al. 2004), and disaster response. Moreover, technology support of leisure activities are relevant, such as cultural visiting (Brown et al. 2005; Bellotti et al. 2008), spectating at outdoor sports events (Jacucci et al. 2007; Salovaara et al. 2006) location-based games (Bell et al. 2006), and learning (Benford et al. 2005).

Exploring Notification Management Within Groups

The field trial was based on a collaborative photo-taking exercise to create orientation guides of a university campus for new students and staff. As part of the exercise, a group (four to six people) was split into two teams to collectively take photos around the campus to be used in the orientation guide. We designed the trial and system with a view to encourage the management of notifications by the groups. To realise this, we deployed audio-visual system notifications to support the interdependencies within the exercise.

Before we turn to the study, we briefly describe the photo-taking exercise, the application used in the study and its underlying notification mechanics.

Collaborative Photo-Taking in InstaCampus

To provide a realistic collaborative scenario, we devised a photo-taking exercise with interdependencies. Interdependencies were introduced by telling participants that a balanced amount of photos were to be taken of four different aspects of the campus: nature, building, wildlife, key services and information points. Notifications alerted group members to newly available photos, and also had the function of highlighting interdependencies between teams in the photo-taking exercise.

The notifications were implemented in a mobile app for Android called InstaCampus that participants used to take, access and browse photos. Newly taken photos are automatically shared across the group by being added to a shared photo pool integrated locally with the application's gallery.

Standard Android notifications were used (chime, vibrate, and icon + text in the 'notification drawer'). There are two types of notifications in InstaCampus.

- One teammate in the collocated team is notified when the remote team has 'shared' a photo (for the entire duration of the trial). When opening this type of notification, the app takes the viewer to the remote team's most recently shared image in the photo pool on the device. 'Shared photo' notifications are intended to provide a sense of awareness of the remote team's actions. To avoid notification overload, the rate at which shared photo notifications were delivered was limited by aggregating the notifications generated within 3 min after the delivery of a notification.
- Another teammate is notified when they 'found' a nearby photo (stock photos associated with a geofence; likewise for the entire duration). Opening a photo displays what was 'found' with the option to add it to their photo pool or to dismiss it. Notifications of 'photos found nearby' are designed to encourage team decision-making. Any notification overrides an unopened existing one.

Participants and Procedure

Four groups of four to six people were recruited for the trial, and consisted of colleagues and students in their twenties and early thirties who were familiar with the university campus. Upon gaining informed consent, each group was split into two teams of two to three people, with two phones assigned to each team to take photos through InstaCampus: one configured to receive location-based notifications, and the other configured to receive shared photo notifications. In groups with more than four people a phone was shared and the carrier was swapped when the teams met up for a halftime re-group after 15 min. We varied the group member-to-phone ratio to trial different naturalistic configurations.

The groups were briefed on their objective to take a balanced amount of photos of different aspects of the campus, focusing on nature, buildings, key services and information points. It was explained to each person that the pictures they take would be automatically shared amongst them. In addition, they would either receive notifications about the arrival of new, shared photos or notifications regarding images that were previously taken nearby, which they could choose to add to their collective photo pool. These instructions were also given to them on a print out.

During the trial, a researcher shadowed each team with a camcorder, and each individual's usage of the app was logged. The trial lasted for approximately 45 min (2 sessions of 15 min with a re-group discussion at halftime). The first group was used as a pilot study to refine the trial and was excluded from the analysis. Group 2 had 6 participants (3 female); Group 3 had 5 (all male), and Group 4 had 4 participants (1 female).

Method

This paper examines the ways notifications were dealt with whilst interactions within collocated groups unfolded. The findings are based on an analysis of video recordings of the trials, focusing on the way participants accountably organised their group interactions around the technology (cf. Crabtree et al. 2006). We draw on a framework to guide our analysis that "prioritises the situated and interactional accomplishment of practical action" (Heath et al. 2010, p. 1).

We catalogued the data corpus consisting of log files triangulated with the video recordings in a preliminary review that helped us to identify sequences of interest. The 74 location-based and 109 shared photo notifications generated for the three groups served to index the *fragments* in the data corpus (Heath et al. 2010), temporally framing (sometimes overlapping) distinct units of interaction. We then transcribed both the verbal and visual conduct in sequences of particular interest for an in-depth analysis of the accomplishment of interaction that makes the socially organised work of dealing with notifications observable and reportable.

Findings

We present relevant sequences from our data (fragments) that show key aspects of notification management. Occurrences of notifications mark the beginnings of the sequences we analyse (indicated in seconds by 0:00). We describe visual conduct and transcribe talk using a widely used orthographic notation (cf. Heath et al. 2010) as evidence for our analysis. All participant names are fictional.

Ignoring Notifications

Notifications were frequently ignored. For the purpose of this analysis, 'ignoring' a notification is defined by an observable absence of 'opening' a notification, i.e., the interaction required to 'open' a notification. 20 % of the 'images found nearby' notifications were not opened (16), and 62 % of the 'shared photo' notifications were equally not opened (68). The fact that the device was seen being carried in hand nearly all the time makes it less likely that notifications were unintentionally missed. Some/many of the notifications may have been overridden by the next notification despite the receiver possibly having the intention to open and examine it. However, for most of the unopened notifications our observations suggest that that they have been deliberately ignored. For example, in a fragment about 7 min into the trial (not pictured) Charlie and Dom are planning what kind of photos to take as they are walking towards a fountain. `C: I'll take it from this side. If you want to ((points the other way)) D: Yeah (0.2) ((turns the other way))`. As C is preparing to take a photo, he then receives his third 'shared photo' notification that he 'ignores'; i.e., C continues with his ongoing course of action without appearing to attend to the notification bodily or in his talk, and he does not subsequently attend to it in any way having taking his photo.

Ignoring frequently occurred when the handling of arising contingencies was prioritized over opening new notifications. Examples of actions that were prioritized over opening notifications were taking photos, negotiating physical environment, talking to teammates, being on time for the halftime or the endtime of the trial, or witnessing events such as a 'fish fight' in the lake on campus.

Notification Management Within Groups

When notifications were not managed through ignoring them, they were dealt with in a range of ways, one is through sharing its contents with one's teammates. Fragment 1 joins Simon, Pete and Oli (left to right) close to the end of the first half of the trial. Pete receives his sixth notification of an 'image found nearby' as the team of three is walking on a narrow pavement along a quiet campus road. Simon, to Pete's left, is not currently carrying a phone. Oli, who carries the other phone is walking slightly ahead of them.

Fragment 1 The content of a notification is shared with team members

(a) (0:04): Simon appears to have overheard the notification. He leans towards Pete and looks down at Pete's phone as he is opening the notification and they slow down. At this point, Oli carries on walking while Simon and Pete slow down to a standstill

(b) (0:07): Pete reviews the notification's content, while Simon leans in more, his gaze fixed on Pete's screen

(c) (0:09): Pete then slightly turns towards Simon, and lifts the phone up so it is easier to see, while simultaneously looking up at Simon. At the same time, Oli turns around towards the others

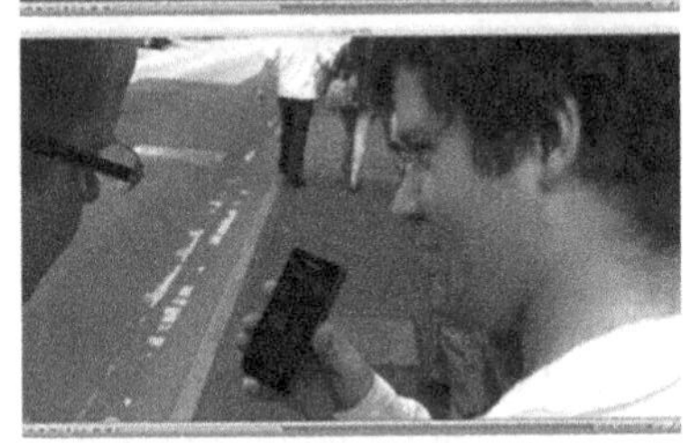

(d) (0:11): Oli is walking back towards them, as Pete briefly tilts the phone back to glance at it himself, with the screen showing the photo:

`P: ? think it's worthy (0.8)`

(e) (0:13): He then tilts it in a circular motion back past Simon to show the screen to Oli whilst saying:

`P: or not.`

Whilst Oli is looking at the screen, Simon replies:

`S: ? to keep (0.2) no!`

(continued)

Fragment 1 (continued)

(f) (0:15): Followed by Oli's agreement expressed by shaking his head. Pete turns the phone back to himself, and says:

`P: OK. (0.8)`

He then presses the "dismiss" button and, whilst lowering the phone he looks back at Simon and says:

`P: Somebody else took that one.`

Oli turns back the same way the others are facing and they continue walking in the direction they were heading before the interruption

The described sequence exemplifies the interaction through which the notification is socially shared within the group. On reception of the notification Simon signals interest in its contents through his bodily orientation towards his device and Pete. This indicates that this is a 'good moment' for the notification to be dealt with. Despite that there is no talk between the two as Pete shares the screen with Simon, Oli senses that they have stopped, turns around and approaches them, indicating his willingness to participate in handling the notification. P's question (`? think its worthy`) is heard as a request for S and O to share their opinion. S and O's agreement not to keep the photo is reciprocated by P's response both by dismissing the photo on screen as well as verbally by stating that somebody else took the photo.

The sequence illustrates how the decision on whether to add the photo 'found nearby' is made collectively within 15 s of receiving the notification. More generally we found that coordinate resources drawn upon within this process of notification management within groups usually included signalling readiness or receptiveness to the notification on side of the receiver, and at least a willingness and ability to share the notification on side of the sender. The above sequence presents an unproblematic instance of social notification. At the same time, it demonstrates the interactional resources drawn upon to achieve agreement and align their action: making visible that one has heard the notification sound, responding through slowing down and stopping (having paid attention to others stopping), turning one's body, turning the phone and making it visible and available for a recipient gaze etc.

Although groups in all trials employ interactional resources to manage notifications, it is important to note that this management is accomplished in nuanced, situationally, and individually distinct ways. For example in a different fragment (not pictured), Eva requests that Frank shares the contents of the 'new shared photos' notification he has just received, as he can be observed browsing photos.

E: What have you got there then? He replies, without sharing the screen with her, F: They are (2) ((browses pictures)) Colin Campbell building.

This fragment demonstrates that sharing the contents of a notification may be both requested explicitly, as well as performed verbally as opposed to visually as in fragment 1.

In the same team with Eva and Frank, Gerald receives the 'image found nearby' notifications on his phone. He frequently shares the contents, and he has a penchant to initiate sharing immediately after receiving a notification by stopping abruptly and announcing Oh I've got a notification!, or Oh I'm off again!, or, Oh hang on!—demonstrating that 'bringing to attention' and topicalising of a notification may be driven by a single individual rather than achieved in a more symmetrically co-oriented fashion observed in fragment 1. Overall, we have identified 51 fragments that feature visual or verbal sharing of notification contents among the collocated team.

However, reaching an agreement regarding how to deal with a notification is not always this swift. In the following, we provide an account of a second instance of how reaching agreement can be more complex.

Managing Concurrent Activities

The sequence depicted in fragment 2 shows how agreement to dismiss the content of the notification is reached whilst the teammates negotiate their ongoing photowork. This sequence begins about 4 min after the start of the trial.

Fragment 2 Negotiation of agreement is started in (d), pending during ongoing photowork in (e) and (f) and completed in (g)

(a) (−0:04): As we join the action, Ben is preparing to take a photo of the opposite ''Exchange'' building. He points while saying:

B: Yeah maybe from this side

(continued)

Fragment 2 (continued)

(b) (0:00): Angela receives her second 'image found nearby' notification on her device as Ben walks around the handrail in his way of getting a shot with more of the building on it, with his gaze still directed at the building

(c) (0:07): Angela follows him, positions herself to his side and then opens the notification as he prepares to take a photo by of the opposite "Exchange" building

(d) (0:10): Angela proceeds to lift and tilt the phone towards whilst pointing and saying:

`A: Got this one in a notification (1.0)`
`   same building`

Ben glances at the photo to be added or dismissed briefly (showing a photo of the same building he is attempting to capture), but then refocuses on his phone whilst saying:

`B: Yeah, you can't get a lot of it in.`

He lifts his phone higher and brings it closer to his face, framing the photo. She lowers the phone, points towards the building and says:

(continued)

Fragment 2 (continued)

A: ? Shall we try to capture exchange and the student shop.

(e) (0:13): He proceeds to take the photo, she glances back at her screen, still showing the photo to be added or dismissed. He then lowers the phone to a more comfortable viewing position for both, and then review the photo he has just taken

B: °It didn't (2.0) I don't know is it [()°

A: [Can't really see

what's that [just about (.) that it's Exchange (0.6)

B: [no

A: maybe like (.) ((tuts)) ah::m (1.0) what would be really

good to capture would be like (.) shop ((points)) and ah::m =

B: = yeah =

A: = and cafe.

B: Yeah

(f) (0:22): They start walking towards the Exchange building he just took a photo of, which has the mentioned shop and cafè in it. As they are walking she is carrying her phone upright near her face while he points towards the entrance

He looks at the paper with the instructions and reads out:

B: services (0.4) timetables n maps

They then stop in front of the entrance, she points towards the shop on their left:

A: the shop there

B: Ah OK.

They then take a few steps towards the shop until he abruptly stops:

B: Let's get the <u>shop</u> from the <u>ins</u>ide.

They turn back towards the buildings main entrance (shown in fragment 2(f)), as they enter the atrium he points at the shop:

B: You do the shop I'll do ((points the other way))

(g) (1:21): Angela then lifts the phone up hovering her finger over the dismiss button, saying:

A: °dismiss:°

To which Ben orients by leaning towards her device, glancing at her phone

B: °Yeah.°

(continued)

Fragment 2 (continued)

B: °Yeah.°

She then presses the dismiss button, after which she immediately turns her phone into landscape mode and proceeds to take photos of the shop, while Ben turns away from her to take photos on the other side of the atrium

The first feature of the interaction we wish to draw attention to is the focused way in which Ben accomplishes the photowork required to complete the overall task of the trial. Indicative of this are his remark at the beginning of the sequence (`maybe from this side`) that reveals his current objective to take a photo of the opposite building to his teammate. Further, his lack of engagement with Angela's attempted sharing of the notification that she has just 'found' a photo of the selfsame building shows his overriding concern with the framing of the photograph, causing 'trouble' for her concern to come to an agreement on her notification.

Most importantly, the sequence highlights the work Angela does to finally elicit her teammate's opinion on whether to add the photo to their shared pool, whilst also engaging in the concurrent and conflicting photowork Ben is focused on. Angela's more or less immediate opening up of the notification shows that she is receptive to the notification at this point. She shares the content of the notification (Fragment 2d), but perhaps due to a lack of Ben's expression of opinion she can be observed 'deferring' the decision whether to add or dismiss the photo. All the while keeping the device lifted close to her face or shoulder, glancing at it several times, perhaps to remind herself of the pending decision (Fragment 2e).

As they have entered the building and Ben suggests they split up to take photos separately, she seizes the moment to get his agreement on her suggestion to dismiss the photo. She immediately turns the device into landscape format in preparation to take the next photo. The immediacy and fluency with which she switches modes suggests that she probably planned this switch. In turn, this suggests she may have perceived the moment as the proverbial 'last chance' at which she can elicit his opinion without having to try switching back to the notifications view *later on*.

Contrasting this sequence of interaction with the one previously presented, features of the interaction emerge that make it remarkably different—most prominently the work to reach agreement and coordinate action (i.e., adding or dismissing a photo) in negotiation with a concurrently ongoing other activity.

Angela employs a range of interactional resources to support the 'pending' state, including holding the phone up and keeping it there even when walking (e.g., Fragment 2f), repeated 'bringing to attention' through talk and bodily conduct (e.g., Fragment 2g), finally seizing the moment to share just-in-time. The previous fragment contrasted with this one in that the 'good moment' emerged *in and through* participants observably demonstrating a (physical) orientation to the moment as an appropriate one for managing the notification. Through Angela's conduct she demonstrates a similar orientation, but also develops a strategy of momentarily deferring the decision to an appropriate moment whilst there exists the sense of the group's engagement in ongoing photowork (demonstrated through Ben's focus on his screen, limited attending to Angela's screen and relative silence in response to her requests).

We have identified several more fragments in which groups reach an agreement in negotiation with ongoing activity. For example, after Angela receives an 'image found nearby' during the halftime discussion with the other team, in preparation she opens but then defers sharing her phone screen with Ben while in conversation. In another group, Dom receives an 'image found nearby', a notification he opens as he is walking beside Charlie. Charlie himself then receives a 'shared images' notification a few seconds after. Dom 'defers' sharing his screen contents for a few seconds while Charlie is opening and reviewing his notification. In yet another group, Gerald has already shown his teammates the photo 'found nearby', as Eva receives a notification which leads to the team briefly discussing her photo before Gerald goes back to his phone, remarking, `I'm not gonna add that one.`

Overall, we have identified 8 fragments that feature a 'pending' decision and/or delayed content sharing as situational contingencies are dealt with between opening the notification and handling it in some way.

Distinctly different, the following sequence illustrates that participants exhibit alternative ways of dealing with notifications without sharing their contents with their collocated teammates.

Managing Notifications 'Individually'

The following fragment joins Charlie and Dom about 12 min into the second half of the trial.

Most notably, the decision to dismiss the photo is made by Dom without seeking the agreement of Charlie, or even bringing the notification contents to his attention. However, Dom demonstrates awareness of Charlie as he positions himself out of his way and turns towards him, and then turns with him as he is opening the notification (Fragment 3b, c). Yet Charlie does not even glance at Dom's activity while he is walking past him—perhaps he is already concerned with taking the photo. When Dom realises Charlie's action, his outburst suggests his approval and sudden co-orientation to his photo-taking. His temmate's activity appears to have 'overridden' any (potential) prior endeavour to share his

Fragment 3 The decision to dismiss is taken without seeking agreement with the teammate

(a) (0:00): Dom (wearing a black T-Shirt) receives his 12th notification of an 'image found nearby' (the notification chime is inaudible on the video). He crosses in front of Charlie and stops, looking down at his phone

(b) (0:05): Whilst shielding the screen from sunlight and opening the notification, Dom turns slightly towards Charlie who is approaching from behind. However, Charlie continues straight past him without stopping

(c) (0:10): As Dom reviews the notification contents (a photo of a student hall to their left) he continues to turn to face Charlie, who is walking towards and preparing to take a photo of a large information sign showing a Campus map

(continued)

Fragment 3 (continued)

(d) (0:13): With the decision whether to add or dismiss the recent photo on screen pending, Dom follows Charlie and just looks up from his screen as he is about to take the photo of the sign

(e) (0:14): Charlie is taking the picture, while Dom engages animatedly, pointing at the sign, saying:

D: Ah yes!

(f) (0:21): After the two briefly stand next to each other quietly, looking at the sign, Charlie turns away and walks off to take more pictures. Dom once again looks at his phone, and presses the 'dismiss' button

notification's contents. Another moment of 'standing still' together passes (without Dom seizing the opportunity), upon which Charlie turns and walks off.

The sequence shows the importance of (a) the exhibiting of receptiveness on the side of the (potential) receiver (Charlie), or lack thereof; and (b) the seizing of a moment to 'bring to attention' an outstanding decision (Dom), or lack thereof. Taken together, the absence of employing interactional resources to that effect results in a lack of co-ordinated agreement. This is not to say that the team has 'failed', simply that the decision is being made 'individually' as opposed to collectively.

We observed 21 instances where an individual dealt with a notifications without sharing its contents. In another team, for example, as Max and Linus are walking back to the meeting point for halftime, Max suggests where to go after the break. Linus does not engage in dialogue, and he never looks up from his phone on which he is browsing photos. This does not change when Max receives a notification a few seconds later, which he proceeds to deal with quietly as both continue. In a different group, Gerald and Frank are lamenting what kind of pictures to take next, as Eva receives, opens and reviews a 'shared photo' without comment. These examples show that more than willingness to share notification content is required; they emphasise that the sensitivity to interpret their teammates' actions as exhibiting (un-) availability plays a key role in deciding whether content is 'brought to attention'.

Limitations

The observed behaviours were occasioned by the nature of the task, which was the subject of the trial. Behaviours such as consulting team member(s) for decision making, commenting on the other team's location and reviewing their photos to inform what kinds of photos to take next are contingent to the nature of the photo-taking task the participants were instructed to carry out.

Further, the contents of the notification appears to have been critical in people's judgement of the value of the notification and whether it is worth a transforming the notification into a group concern, perhaps echoed in the frequency that participants opened notifications without sharing their contents. The content of location-based notifications presented a task that prompted a decision whether to add or dismiss a photo 'found nearby'. In contrast, the value of the shared photo notifications may 'only' be informational. Hence, the observations made in this study may not generalize to other settings. However, as the discussion will show, the findings support and echo the wider literature on interaction in face-to-face settings, which suggests that our study may have merit, particularly when considering the design of collaborative interactive notification systems.

Discussion

We now reflect on (a) the ways participants employ interactional resources to different effects and relate these to the literature on face-to-face interaction, and (b) the sequentiality of notification management within groups. Finally, we relate our findings to previous work on interruption management and ask design questions to support the collaborative management of notifications.

Interactional Resources for Notification Management in Groups

The introduced fragments have illustrated the nuanced, situationally and individually distinct ways in which notification management was achieved in practice within our field trial. Participants have displayed remarkably smoothly co-ordinated, shared agreement (Fragment 1), skilful management of a 'pending' decision in negotiation with ongoing work (Fragment 2), and the absence of content sharing and seeking agreement altogether (Fragment 3). However, in spite of these different effects, the interactional resources participants employed to manage notifications were drawn from the same repertoire. Table 1 summarises the embodied and technological resources and (some of) the effects to which they were deployed to manage notifications. A key insight is that in spite of a relatively limited repertoire of coordinate resources, participants employ them in ways and configurations to drastically different effects. For example, body orientation and movement can be equally employed to make visible availability and interest ('turning towards', 'leaning in') as well as to exhibit unavailability ('turning away', 'walking past').

Unpacking the interactional resources in face-to-face settings can be applied to provide insights into the support of collaborative technologies (e.g., Luff and Jirotka 1998). Our findings echo aspects of some of these accounts of interaction in the literature. For example, Hindmarsh and Heath (2000) describe how objects are brought to the attention of a colleague by another in the context of shared activities at work. Then the object is 'constituted', i.e., a mutual understanding or appreciation is achieved through talk, gestures and bodily co-orientation. Similarly, our study has shown that

- initiation (bringing to attention) is often accompanied by additional embodied resources such as gaze by the co-participant (e.g., Fragment 1a),
- co-orientation and understanding is displayed through body orientation (e.g., Fragment 1e).

The bodily co-orientation our participants exhibited speak to previous findings in nonverbal communication, e.g., Kendon's F-Formation (1990) is assembled as a 'transactional space' in which, for example, agreement is reached (Fragment 1);

Table 1 Interactional resources for notification management within groups

Interactional resource	Interactional achievement	
	Sender	Recipient
Body orientation	'turning towards' to signal willingness to engage (Fragment 3b, c)	'leaning in' (Fragment 1a), or 'turning towards' (Fragment 1c, 2g) to signal receptivity; 'turning away' signals unavailability (Fragment 3f)
Body motion	Walking together side-by-side, slowing down together facilitates glancing of screen, making visible screen interaction (Fragment 1a, b)	'walking past' signals unavailability (Fragment 3b)
Gestures	Making phone screen available for gaze to topicalise content (Fragment 1c, e, 2d, g); 'holding up' phone close to face to support 'pending' decision (Fragment 2e, f, g), 'hovering finger' to make action visible and accountable (Fragment 2 g)	
Gaze & Glance	Repeated glancing at phone to sustain 'pending' decision (Fragment 2e, f); monitor recipient availability (Fragment 3d) and reaction (Fragment 1c)	Gaze to view screen contents (Fragment 1c, e, 2d, g), to co-engage in screen activity (Fragment 1b)
Talk	Request teammate opinion (Fragment 1d); (repeated) bringing to attention 'pending' decision (Fragment 2d, g)	Express opinion (Fragment 1e); agreement (Fragment 2g) and co-engagement (Fragment 3e)
Audio	Chime affords co-orientation of participants to notification arrival (Fragment 1a)	
Visual	Performing visible touch screen interaction makes actions accountable to teammate (Fragment 2b)	Observing/glancing interaction gestures affords awareness of teammates actions; phone display is easily made available for glancing through simple 'sharing screen' gesture (Fragment 1, 2)

and Goffman's "body gloss" (1963) features, in that overall 'body gestures' may be applied to make facts 'gleanable'.

Sequentiality of Notification Management

We can now chart the sequential orderliness of the work accomplished by collocated participants. In the same way in which turn at talk is both *context shaped* and *context shaping* (Heritage 1984), the sequentiality of preceding and successive actions shape the social organisation of notification management. The sequentiality shapes when and whether a notification is opened or ignored, how it is brought to attention ('topicalised') and the matter resolved, and whether this happens immediately after arrival (Fragment 1), or in a delayed fashion (Fragment 2), or not at all (Fragment 3).

Our analysis focused on the actions through which the notification is dealt with once opened, within the course of ongoing interaction. The analysis of the 183 instances of notification management made apparent the sequential and interactional ways in which these were organised as a concerted activity between the co-participants in the setting.

On ignoring. In contrast to face-to-face interactions, the 'object at first is not brought to attention by the other, it announces itself through audible notification. Hence, there is no social obligation *per se* for the recipient to deal with a notification, 'ignoring' at this point is understood as a socially legitimate practice by the co-participants. In the same way that tending to a phone call displays to the collocated its relevance to the here and now (cf. Hindmarsh and Heath 2000), nonresponse ('ignoring') displays that the self-announcing 'object' is deemed irrelevant. In contrast, once the notification ('object') is brought to attention (e.g., through a question) by a co-participant in the face-to-face setting, there is a moral impediment to nonresponse (cf. Goffman 1963). We have pointed out interactional sequences in which the other held the recipient of the notification accountable and demanded to be informed of its contents. It is by virtue of the chime being and audible signal to those within earshot that co-orientation to its arrival can be established, which, together with the notification's relevance to the shared task at hand justifies this holding accountable of the other.

On content sharing. The notification content is topicalised for example when the recipient signals receptivity, and the sender is willing and able to share the contents. Once topicalised, the sender (the person who carries the phone) is accountable to perform an adequate presentation in a visual (e.g., by making the screen available for glancing) or verbal fashion (e.g., by commenting on the other team's shared photos). Of note here is that the small and light form factor of the mobile device affords the visual 'shareability' of the screen. Depending on the notification type the 'sharing' may support awareness of the remote team, or instigate team co-ordination on whether to add or dismiss the photo 'found nearby'. Body orientation and talk sustains the co-orientation and understanding until mutual agreement is achieved.

On filtering. In cases where notification contents was not shared with the group, the potential recipient of the notification can be observed producing actions that exhibit unavailability (e.g., being 'engrossed' in one's device) (cf. Sudnow 1972). As Sudnow argues, timing of glances, and more importantly, the other's "production of appearances under an orientation to their timing" (1972, p. 261) is a key issue to establish a co-orientation of participants in coordinating availability for social exchanges such as a greeting. The importance and sensitivity of this issue can be seen when contrasting fragment 2 and 3. In the former, B. finally signals availability, which allows for unanimous completion of the task. Contrastingly, in the latter, C. never signals availability, amounting in D's 'filtering' (never performing) of the (social) notification.

On negotiating concurrent activity. The case in fragment 2 illustrates that reaching an agreement on the notification sometimes requires careful negotiation with a concurrent activity. On part of the sender, assigning priority to ongoing activity was pivotal, alongside an ability to sustain the 'pending' state of the decision displayed through repeated glances and bringing to attention. Finally, detecting and seizing the opportune moment and adequate presentation (sharing screen and 'hovering finger') to come to an agreement is critical. In contrast, not seizing a potentially opportune moment resulted in 'filtering' of the (social) notification.

Supporting Human Interruption Management

By conducting the trial of a notification system designed for the collaborative task (photo-taking), we have examined how people readily exhibit social ways of managing notifications. Strategies that have featured prominently in the technical interruption management literature speak of attempts to mimic the human strategies we have observed. Technical strategies include "defer-to-breakpoint" (Iqbal and Bailey 2007; Adamczyk and Bailey 2004), "filtering" of relevant information (Sawhney and Schmandt 2000) and the adaptation of presentation (Altosaar et al. (2006). Our participants readily employed interactional resources to manage notifications in ways that amount to 'deferring', 'filtering' and 'adapting the presentation'.

However, the situationally sensitive and nuanced ways in which notification management is collaboratively achieved within groups raises the concern that automated systems that simply aim to replicate these strategies may not be appropriate. As previous work has suggested, this may be very difficult to do even for relatively controlled settings of desktop (Iqbal and Bailey 2007; Adamczyk and Bailey 2004) and office work (Avrahami et al. 2007). Our study highlighted how much more complex these difficulties could be when moving to mobile settings.

Instead, the account we offered echoes Tolmie's conclusion (2008) that people are already expert in how they handle interruptions. So instead of trying to replace human expertise with inadequate automated solutions, a challenge this insight poses for the CSCW community is how to support people's expert strategies in managing interruptions. Moreover, where is the design line between supporting expert strategies and attempting to automate or replace them? Our study attempts to chart the contours of that line. Concrete design proposals have to be left for future work. Rather, we ask designers to reflect on how might notifications be designed

- to ensure important content is not ignored;
- to maximise the interactional resources co-participants can employ to initiate and perform 'content sharing';
- to support the resources to 'keep alive' a 'pending' notification in negotiation with concurrent activity;
- to ensure important content is not lost when a participant 'filters' contents.

Conclusions

This paper has presented a detailed account of how notifications are dealt with during ongoing group interaction around a collaborative mobile photo-taking exercise. The account has broader relevance to the use of notifications in social and collaborative media in collocated settings, in that it unpacks how members manage notifications with sensitivity to the ongoing accomplishment of social order.

Our study has revealed the methodical ways in which participants organise the management of notifications with their collocated teammates. We had created a setting in which notifications are relevant because of task interdependence; and notification types are delivered to a different member of the collocated team to encourage social interaction. Our account pays particular attention to the interactional resources participants employ in situationally distinct ways to different effects, and to the sequential organisation of notification management. The study reveals that notification management within groups routinely features ignoring, content sharing, negotiating concurrent activity and filtering; we suggest that instead of attempting to replicate these sorts of strategies as part of an interactive system, technology design should aim to *provide support for these existing strategies themselves*. To that end, this paper has identified a repertoire of interactional resources that can be used as a framework to inform the research and design of technology that employs notifications to support collocated group activities.

Acknowledgments Thanks to the reviewers for providing constructive reviews. Thanks to Tom Rodden for valuable comments on an earlier draft of this paper, and to Mike Fraser, Peter Tolmie, James Norris, and Holger Schnädelbach for useful feedback on this work. The first author of this work is supported by EPSRC grant EP/I011587/1.

References

Adamczyk, P. D., & Bailey B. P. (2004). If not now, when? The effects of interruption at different moments within task execution. *Proceedings of the SIGCHI conference on Human factors in computing systems*. New York: ACM.

Altosaar, M., Vertegaal, R., Sohn, C., & Cheng, D. (2006). AuraOrb: Social notification appliance. *CHI '06 extended abstracts on Human factors in computing systems* (pp. 381—386). New York: ACM.

Avrahami, D., Gergle, D., Hudson, S. E., & Kiesler S. (2007). Improving the match between callers and receivers: A study on the effect of contextual information on cell phone interruptions. *Behaviour & Information Technology*, *26*(3), 247–259.

Avrahami, D., & Hudson, S. E. (2004). QnA: Augmenting an instant messaging client to balance user responsiveness and performance. *Proceedings of the ACM conference on Computer supported cooperative work* (pp. 515–518). New York: ACM.

Bell, M., Chalmers, M., Barkhuus, L., Hall, M., Sherwood, S., Tennent, P. et al. (2006). Interweaving mobile games with everyday life. *Proceedings of the SIGCHI conference on Human Factors in computing systems* (pp. 417–426). New York: ACM.

Bellotti, V., Begole, B., Chi, E. H., Ducheneaut, N., Fang, J., Isaacs, E. et al. (2008). Activity-based serendipitous recommendations with the Magitti mobile leisure guide. *Proceeding of the twenty-sixth annual SIGCHI conference on Human factors in computing systems* (pp. 1157–1166). New York: ACM.

Benford, S., Rowland, D., Flintham, M., Drozd, A., Hull, R., Reid, J. et al. (2005). Life on the edge: supporting collaboration in location-based experiences. *Proceedings of the SIGCHI Conference on Human Factors in Computing Systems* (pp. 721–730). New York: ACM.

Brown, B., Chalmers, M., Bell, M., Hall, M., MacColl, I., Rudman P. (2005). Sharing the square: collaborative leisure in the city streets. *Proceedings of the ninth conference on European Conference on Computer Supported Cooperative Work* (pp. 427–447). New York: Springer-Verlag New York, Inc.

Crabtree, A., Benford, S., Greenhalgh, C., Tennent, P., Chalmers, M., & Brown, B. (2006). Supporting ethnographic studies of ubiquitous computing in the wild. *Proceedings of the 6th conference on Designing Interactive systems* (pp. 60–69). New York: ACM.

Czerwinski, M., Horvitz, E., & Wilhite, S. (2004). A diary study of task switching and interruptions. *Proceedings of the SIGCHI conference on Human factors in computing systems*. New York: ACM.

Dourish, P. (2004). What we talk about when we talk about context. *Personal Ubiquitous Computing*, *8*, 19–30.

Dourish, P., & Bellotti, V. (1992). Awareness and coordination in shared workspaces, pp. 107–114. *Proceedings of the ACM conference on Computer-supported cooperative work*. New York: ACM.

Durrant, A., Rowland, D., Kirk, D. S., Benford, S., Fischer, J. E., & McAuley D. (2011). Automics: Souvenir generating photoware for theme parks. *Proceedings of the SIGCHI conference on Human factors in computing systems*. New York: ACM.

Goffman, E. (1963). *Behavior in public places*. New York: The Free Press.

Greenberg, S. (2001). Context as a dynamic construct. *Human Computer Interaction, 16*, 257–268.

Harr, R., & Kaptelinin, V. (2007). Unpacking the social dimension of external interruptions. *Proceedings of the international ACM conference on Supporting group work*. Sanibel Island: ACM.

Heath, C., Hindmarsh, J., & Luff, P. (2010). *Video in qualitative research*. London: Sage.

Heritage, J. (1984). *Garfinkel and Ethnomethodology*. Cambridge: Polity Press.

Hindmarsh, J., Heath, C. (2000). Sharing the tools of the trade: the interactional constitution of workplace objects. *Journal of Contemporary Ethnography*, *29*(5), 523–562.

Ho, J., Intille, S. S. (2005). Using context-aware computing to reduce the perceived burden of interruptions from mobile devices. *Proceedings of the SIGCHI conference on Human factors in computing systems*. New York: ACM.

Iqbal, S. T., & Bailey, B. P. (2007). Understanding and developing models for detecting and differentiating breakpoints during interactive tasks. *Proceedings of the SIGCHI conference on Human Factors in computing systems* (pp. 697–706). New York: ACM.

Jacucci, G., Oulasvirta, A., & Salovaara, A. (2007). Active construction of experience through mobile media: a field study with implications for recording and sharing. *Personal Ubiquitous Computing, 11*(4), 215–234.

Jiang, X., Chen, N. Y., Hong, J. I., Wang, K., Takayama, L., & Landay, J. A. (2004). Siren: context-aware computing for firefighting. *In Proceedings of the second International conference on pervasive computing (PERVASIVE '04)*, Vol. 3001 of *Lecture Notes in Computer Science*. pp. 87–105, Springer.

Kendon, A. (1990). *Conducting interaction: patterns of behavior in focused encounters*. Cambridge: Cambridge University Press.

Luff, P., & Jirotka, M. (1998). Interactional resources for the support of collaborative activities: common problems in the design of technologies to support groups and communities. *Community Computing and Support Systems, Social Interaction in Networked Communities* (pp. 249–266). London: Springer-Verlag.

Mark, G., Gonzalez, V. M., & Harris, J. (2005). No task left behind?: Examining the nature of fragmented work. *Proceedings of the SIGCHI conference on Human factors in computing systems*. New York: ACM.

O'Conaill, B., & Frohlich, D. (1995). Timespace in the workplace: Dealing with interruptions. *Conference companion on Human factors in computing systems* (pp. 262–263). Denver: ACM.

Patel, N., Clawson, J., Voida, A., & Lyons, K. (2009). Mobiphos: A study of user engagement with a mobile collocated–synchronous photo sharing application. *International Journal of Human-Computer Studies, 67*(12), 1048–1059.

Rogers, Y. (2006). Moving on from weiser's vision of calm computing: engaging ubicomp experiences. *Proceedings of the 8th international conference on Ubiquitous Computing* (pp. 404–421). Berlin, Heidelberg: Springer-Verlag.

Salovaara, A., Jacucci, G., Oulasvirta, A., Saari, T., Kanerva, P., Kurvinen, E. (2006). Collective creation and sense-making of mobile media. *Proceedings of the SIGCHI Conference on Human Factors in Computing Systems* (pp. 1211–1220). New York: ACM.

Sawhney, N., & Schmandt, C. (2000). Nomadic radio: Speech and audio interaction for contextual messaging in nomadic environments. *ACM Transactions* on Computer-Human *Interaction, 7*(3), pp. 353–383.

Schegloff, E. A. (1968). Sequencing in conversational openings. *American Anthropologist, 70*(6), 1075–1095.

Shen, H., & Sun, C. (2002). Flexible notification for collaborative systems. *Proceedings of the 2002 ACM conference on Computer supported cooperative work* (pp. 77–86). New York: ACM.

Streefkerk, J. W., van Esch-Bussemakers, M. P., Neerincx, M. A. (2008). Field evaluation of a mobile location-based notification system for police officers. *Proceedings of the 10th international conference on Human computer interaction with mobile devices and services* (pp. 101–108). New York, ACM.

Su, N. M., & Mark, G. (2008). Communication chains and multitasking. *Proceeding of the SIGCHI conference on Human factors in computing systems*. New York: ACM.

Sudnow, D. (1972). Temporal parameters of interpersonal observation. In D. Sudnow (Ed.), *Studies in social interaction*. New York: The Free Press.

Tolmie, P., Crabtree, A., Rodden, T., & Benford, S. (2008). Are you watching this film or what?: Interruption and the juggling of cohorts. *Proceedings of the ACM conference on Computer supported cooperative work*. New York: ACM.

Van House, N., Davis, M., Ames, M., Finn, M., & Viswanathan, V. (2005). The uses of personal networked digital imaging: an empirical study of cameraphone photos and sharing. *CHI '05 Extended Abstracts on Human Factors in Computing Systems* (pp. 1853–1856). New York: ACM.

Temporality in Planning: The Case of the Allocation of Parking Areas for Aircrafts

Ilaria Redaelli and Antonella Carassa

Abstract Several recent studies have focused on plans as coordination devices, demonstrating how organisational members use such plans to organise and make sense of their work. This research project aims to foster empirical research on plans showing how operators at the centre of coordination in handling activities at an Italian airport plan the allocation of parking areas for aircrafts. Based on the analysis of the operators' knowledge of the temporal features of planning, this research contributes to the understanding of how timely assistance for aircrafts on the ground depends on how spaces are allocated. This research highlights temporality in planning and promotes the understanding of the features of allocation and planning as situated and distributed activities.

Introduction

The Aim of the Research

Recent research has identified several features of plans and planning as well as plan failures in the organisation of the temporal order of work activities; however, investigations into how people's experience with the workplace setting's temporal structure might impact the use or setup of plans are lacking. This research project aims to address this issue by studying how the ramp control tower operators of an Italian airport plan the allocation of parking bays for planes. This setting offers the possibility to observe situations and behaviour that embody the topic under study

---

I. Redaelli (✉) · A. Carassa
Università della Svizzera italiana, Lugano, Switzerland
e-mail: ilaria.redaelli@usi.ch

A. Carassa
e-mail: antonella.carassa@usi.ch

O. W. Bertelsen et al. (eds.), *ECSCW 2013: Proceedings of the 13th European Conference on Computer Supported Cooperative Work, 21–25 September 2013, Paphos, Cyprus*, DOI: 10.1007/978-1-4471-5346-7_3,

in a perspicuous way (Garfinkel 2002; p. 182). It is our contention that understanding temporality in planning might foster our understanding of not only the procedures for establishing plans, but also plans as temporal coordination devices. Our study draws on the practice-based perspective of time to contribute to the understanding of the role of temporality in planning as a situated and socially constructed activity (Bardram 1997).

In order to develop our argument, we first present existing studies that have focused on planning and temporal coordination. We then introduce information about planning in the ramp control tower (RCT) and discuss the temporal features of such activity. Finally, we provide several suggestions for incorporating temporality into the design of software to ensure successful support in planning and coordinating work.

Debating Plans in the Computer-Supported Cooperative Work Community

The debate on plans in the CSCW community first emerged in the 1980s in response to Suchman's (1987) work criticising the possibility for plans to causally determine actions, as claimed by cognitivist theorists. Suchman demonstrated that actors' actions cannot be conceived as being determined by plans stored in memory in the form of formulated prepositions as actions are never planned in the causal sense, but rather always situated in the circumstances of the specific context. In addition, Suchman's characterisation of plans as weak resources for the control of actions affected subsequent study of the role of plans in work organisations. Schmidt (1999) argued that the development of the "situated action" concept increased scholars' interest in understanding situated actions, albeit to the detriment of the analysis of plans as "guidance for work". Suchman's work has also often been perceived as introducing a sort of opposition between plans and situated actions, presenting plans as poor resources that limit human actions; as a result, they cannot give an account of all the occurrences of situated actions.

Starting in the 1990s, several scholars began criticising some of Suchman's development (Ciborra 2002; Schmidt 2011; Vera and Simon 1993). For example, Schmidt (2011) disentangled some of the conceptual confusion about the "presumed weakness" and "incompleteness" of plans while Bardram (1997) demonstrated the situated nature of planning. Bardram's analysis of the daily clinical work showed that hospital patients' assistance is organised based on an on-going and socially constructed planning activity which is enhanced by and simultaneously shapes the work activities at the hospital. In fact, advanced planning, drawing on standard treatments for diseases, allows for anticipation of ways in which activities are executed while plan implementation allows for the adjustment of the plan to the conditions of the specific situation. Thus, the strength of plans is the anticipation of future ways of performing activities, detached from—but still taking into account—the conditions of the real-world settings.

Situated Use of Plans

According to Rönkkö et al. (2005), empirical research on plans has thus far focused on two main goals in that scholars have sought to understand not only the relationship between plans and actions, but also how organisational members orient themselves to plans to make sense of their work in contextually specific ways. Several empirical studies have explored how plans are used as artefacts for the coordination of work activities, analysing how plans' relevance is occasioned in the circumstances of their use (Bossen and Markussen 2010; Button and Sharrock 1998; Dant and Francis 1998; Koskinen 2000; Randall and Rouncefiel 2011; Rönkkö et al. 2005; Schmidt 1999).[1] Such research has demonstrated that plans can be used in various ways, such as for the reconstruction of courses of actions (Dant and Francis 1998) or as "perceptual background" against which to identify troublesome elements or situations (Koskinen 2000). These studies have also investigated what happens when plans do not work out (Bardram and Hansen 2010; Rönkkö et al. 2005) and the impact of the medium of schedule for the solution of problems of coordination (Whittaker and Schwarz 1999).

Temporal Coordination and Planning

Plans as "valuable mechanisms for giving order to work" (Bardram 1997; p. 18) are often employed in organisational settings for the temporal coordination of work activities. However, no systematic attempt has been made to link the study of temporality and planning. In the CSCW community, there is growing interest in the role of temporality in the coordination of work activities as more and more scholars have noticed a lack of research focused on temporal coordination compared with spatial coordination, thereby undermining the possibility for software to adequately support cooperative work.

Among the studies exploring temporality for work coordination, studies have examined long-term timeframe coordination (Karasti et al. 2010) as well as short-term timeframe coordination (hours or days), focusing more on temporal coordination within the organisation than within a single team at work (see: Egger and Wagner 1993; Bardram 2000; Reddy et al. 2006). Other research, even if not directly addressing the issue of temporal coordination, has shown both the failures of schedules in organising the temporal order of work activities and the modality by which plans can be used to achieve the temporal coordination of activities. These studies have shown that schedules might define deadlines inaccurately or in

[1] It is worth noting that this research defines plans as "we might intend this term in ordinary affairs" (Sharrock and Button 2003)—that is, artefacts that anticipate future ways of performing activities (Bardram 1997) and that might take the form of "formal organizational constructs" (Schmidt 1999) such as schedules, office procedures, classification schemes, and checklists.

a non-credible or consistent way (Whittaker and Schwarz 1999) and that particular efforts are necessary for people to meet deadlines. For example, Button and Sharrock (1996) found that the orderliness of work depends on the reflexive relationship between the schedule, which orients work activities, and the way in which such activities are carried out in order to meet the fixed deadlines. Meanwhile, other studies have examined the role of temporal patterns in providing means for the coordination of work (Reddy and Dourish 2002; Nilsson and Hertzum 2005). In the study of temporality for the coordination of work activities, an increasing interest is emerging in the practice-based perspective of time (Reddy et al. 2006; Karasti et al. 2010), which was first developed by Orlikowski and Yates (2002), who suggested considering people as "experiencing time through shared temporal structures [that] they enact recurrently in their everyday practices". Thus, people are oriented towards the means that organisations provide for the objective organisation of time (e.g., schedules) while such constraints simultaneously enable different actions so that "temporal structures both shape people's actions and are shaped by such actions" (pp. 686–689).

The Study

The empirical materials analysed here belong to a wider corpus of data collected in the course of an ethno-methodologically (EM) informed research (Crabtree et al. 2000; Garfinkel 1967; Randall et al. 2007) carried out in the coordination centre (Suchman 1997) handling activities in an Italian airport—namely, the apron tower.[2] The research lasted eight months.

Empirical materials were collected by means of direct observation of the field, interviews with RCT operators and tape recording of naturally occurring conversations. The researchers interviewed RCT operators, drawing on the ethnographic interview technique (Sherman Heyl 2001), during the plan setup and application phases so to gather information about their decisions regarding the observed activities. The interviews were not structured in advance and were triggered by the occurrence of particular events or situations. During the data-collection phase, the operators were observed for two to three days a week, according to the organisation and duration of their shifts, so as to observe all the activities carried out in the centre, which offers 24-hour service.

The objective of the data collection was the detection and study of the operators' practices in allocating resources during the planning phase. As such, particular attention was devoted to the identification of recurring patterns in the plan setup among the operators, following Llewellyn and Spence's (2009) suggestion for conceiving practices as members' phenomenon for the accomplishment of an

[2] In this paper, the terms "apron tower" and "ramp control tower (RCT)" will be used interchangeably.

EM-oriented study of practices. Therefore data collection was not oriented to the mere identification of patterns of activities, but to the study of the details of interactions so as to determine how activities are intersubjectively organised and recognised by operators as embodying (or not) a certain practice.

The EM-oriented study of members' practices is suited for the investigation of how local knowledge is deployed in the execution of everyday work activities as the detailed observation of members' active conduct allows for identifying the link between knowledge and action (Llewellyn 2008; p. 783). The term "local knowledge" (or local expertise), which refers to Normark and Randall's (2005; see also: Randall et al. 1996) conceptualisation, addresses a corpus of knowledge—mostly informal—that emerges from what people have experienced and whose relevance depends on local circumstances of work. Therefore, local expertise, which includes the knowledge of how to deal with procedures[3] and others' expertise, is necessary for the contingent enactment of organisational requirements and ultimately for the orderly accomplishment of work.

The RCT operators' practices analysed here represent patterns of activities not reported in protocols, but to which the operators are oriented in that they have demonstrated the knowledge that they are expected to follow these practices and justify any deviations with colleagues. In particular, our research focuses on how the local expertise on temporality in planning allows for the management of the contextual conditions of work. It is our contention that it is worth considering not only the temporal structure of practices—that is, "when people do what" for the accomplishment of their work—but also people's local knowledge of how others organise their own activities over time. When people do what they do as well as how much time such activity usually takes also matters.

Extracts reported here come from the ethnographic interviews collected in the course of the study.

The Setting of the Study

The observed airport has a simple structure (i.e., one runway and one terminal building) and small dimensions, but it is the third most active Italian airport for cargo air transport movements and the fourth largest in terms of the number of annual passengers, which has progressively increased from about 3 million in 2003–6.5 million in 2008, which corresponds with the growth of low-cost airlines. The airport

[3] The indexicality of rules and instructions has been widely investigated in ethno-methodological studies that have shown that (1) being competent in following instructions means being able to grasp the connection between an outcome and courses of actions based on information given in the instructions (Zimmerman 1971) and (2) rules and instructions often work as "prospective accounts". Indeed, rules can serve as accounts for what was done, "although in any actual performance a great deal more is necessarily done that can be comprised in the instructions" (Amerine and Bilmes 1988; pp. 329–331).

is home to a mix of low-cost, charter, and cargo airlines, although low-cost companies represent the majority of the airline companies operating in the airport.

The airport's RCT operators carry out two main activities: the coordination of the execution of handling activities and the setup of the plan for the use of aircrafts' parking areas (i.e., the stands) and gates. RCT operators are responsible for communicating during planes' approaching with the ramp personnel, crews, and air traffic control operators so as to instruct crews about where to stop and ramp personnel about where to converge in order to handle each plane properly,[4] given the duration of the turnaround times defined by each airline company.

RCT operators are also required to ensure that each aircraft on the ground has an appropriate parking area at its disposal for the length of its stay on ground. To this end, RCT operators plan the use of stands twice a day, monitor whether these planned solutions remain useful despite last-minute changes in the number and/or timetable of scheduled flights, and modify the plans as necessary. The plan setup is organised in stages of necessity in that the operators access the necessary information at different times of the day. As a result, the stand allocation plan setup can be defined as a distributed activity as the plan is the result of layers of decisions made by several actors in due time while managing several other activities.

Planning the Stand Allocation

The stand allocation plan is defined when the operators know the exact number of planes that need to be parked, their dimensions, their arrival and landing time, and how long they will stay on the ground. RCT operators receive such information twice daily from cargo and passenger airlines; the information is shared in the form of "rotation lists". The rotation lists are documents in which each airline company matches aircrafts with the flights to be carried out the next day. This information enables the RCT operators to determine not only the number of planes to be parked and the time of their arrival and departure, but also how flights are assigned to planes. Thus, they can assess how long each plane will stay on the ground (see Fig. 1).

For the stand allocation plan to be set up, the RCT operators have to consider the number of stands and gates at their disposal as well as the stands' technical features. Stands' features allow their exploitation in different ways so that possibilities and constraints in their use emerge as a consequence of the planning itself. Stands are delineated according to their maximum capacity (which, in turn, is defined on the basis of the length of the fuselage and the wingspan of the biggest

---

[4] Handling activities on the ground comprise aircraft fuelling, luggage loading and unloading, and passenger assistance during boarding and disembarkation procedures. The apron tower operators coordinate the activities on the ground by means of both radios and mobiles, with which they are in touch with all the operators on the ramp (ramp agents, bus drivers, marshalers, follow-me truck drivers, etc.).

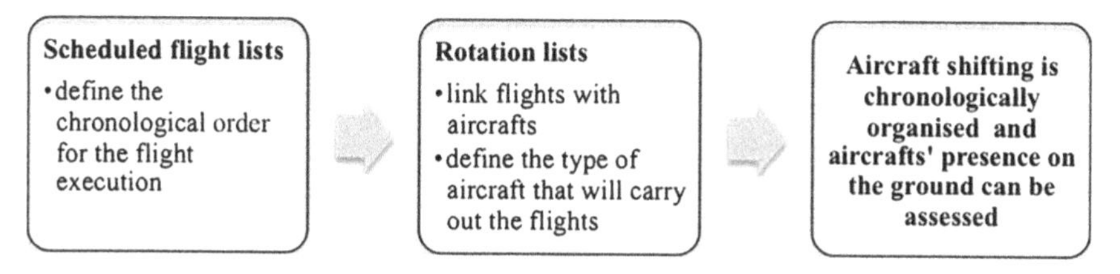

Fig. 1 Matching schedules with rotation lists

aircraft that can be parked there), the manoeuvres allowed to reach and leave them, and the number of parking areas that cannot be used simultaneously (see Fig. 2).

Parking areas for aircrafts have different dimensions to appropriately accommodate the various planes, whose sizes vary considerably. Each stand can accommodate different types of aircraft as they can be used to park planes whose size does not exceed the maximum capacity of the stand. It is important to understand the manoeuvres required for each type of plane to leave the stand as different types of aircrafts' manoeuvring requires a different amount of space when moving into and out of the stand. Stands might also overlap exit ways, so their use might be limited during the planes' manoeuvring. Stands are distributed over the ramp and the apron space. The ramp space is the airside area next to the terminal building, while the apron is an area far from the terminal building.

Like stands, not all gates are equal. Gates, which have different features, can be directly connected with stands by means of fixed jet bridges (structures the RCT operators call "fingers"); thus, the use of stands and gates has to match. In other words, once a stand is assigned to a certain flight, the boarding procedures of that flight have to take place at the gate structurally linked to that stand. In addition, whereas some stands allow for passengers' boarding on foot, others do not, meaning that buses have to be provided for the latter group. RCT operators plan the use of stands and gates while considering flights' scheduled times. The operators set up the stand allocation plan based on the premise that flights will be carried out as expected according to the schedule, working sequentially on the plan set up.

Although software devoted to the determination of stand allocation is available, RCT operators never use it for the automatic allocation of stands; rather, they use to aid in the manual allocation of stands, exploiting the fact that the software highlights conflicts during the stand allocation. The software presents stands in a

Stand number	1	2	3
Capacity	Up to B757	Up to B747	Up to B737
Manoeuvres	Push back	Self-manoeuvring	Push back Self-manoeuvring
Inhibitions	2 3 4	1 3 4	2 4 5

Fig. 2 Technical features of stands

Gantt's chart that allows for the visualisation of stand allocation over time. Operators drag and drop flight numbers on the chart, and icons that represent the length of planes' stay on the ground appear; a colour code system alerts the operators whenever conflicts in the stand allocation emerge. For example, the alarm colour code would signal a mismatch between the size of the stand and the size of the plane.

Managing Time When Planning in the RCT

When planning, the RCT operators do more than solve space allocation problems as they not only match stands with planes' dimensions, but also—by allocating stands and gates—contribute significantly to the coordination of handling activities. The careful exploitation of gates and stands allows for the convergence of passengers, equipment, and personnel when necessary, thereby ensuring the timely execution of handling activities and ultimately maintaining the coordination of the activities necessary for flight execution. Yet to achieve such a result, the RCT operators have to address three main problems connected with temporality: ensuring the stands' availability over time, monitoring the duration of handling activities, and keeping delays under control.

Ensuring the Stands' Availability Over Time

The objective of planning in the RCT is to ensure the necessary stands are available to accommodate arriving planes for the entire duration of their stop. To achieve such a goal, the RCT operators have to set up the stand and gate allocation plans within fixed deadlines even if they neither receive all the rotation lists simultaneously nor receive them in time to set up the plan. This implies that the RCT operators often have to plan in relatively uncertain conditions. In addition when the RCT operators establish their plans, they never have empty bays to fill as they always have planes on the ground whose allocation was defined by the previous planners

> If three airbuses are going to arrive, I have to put them at 37, 40, and 42, respectively, and this inhibits the use of several stands: 36, 38, and 39. In the evening, 14 Redair planes are going to arrive, then we could have the Blueair and perhaps the Pinkair, so we have to study how to assign stands (Track 2 10/05/2011).

RCT operators not only have to ensure appropriate gate and stand allocation within the planned lapse of time, but they also have to consider that their planning has effects that overcome each lapse of time planned, thereby undermining stand availability over time. It is therefore strategically relevant for RCT operators to plan in such a way that it does not threaten their ability—or that of the next planners—to allocate stands effectively.

Practically speaking, the operators succeed in preventing planning from negatively impacting the maintenance of the stand availability by drawing on practices that allow for the identification of usable spaces. The identification of usable space consists of evaluating whether stands free at a certain moment correspond with the need for usable spaces. The identification of usable space mostly draws on operators' knowledge of recurring patterns in schedules and is devoted to defining stands that—even in the absence of certain information about the number, movements, and dimensions of the incoming planes—should be kept free as it is likely that they will be needed for planes arriving in the upcoming hours. For example, RCT operators who plan the evening allocation—even if they do not know the number of cargo flights that will arrive that night—reserve an area of the ramp for cargo flights when planning to ensure that stands for those possible flights are available for the next colleagues. At night, arriving planes often remain on ground overnight; without the reservation of some stands, it would not be possible to find parking areas suitable for the incoming cargo flights, which are usually wide-bodied aircrafts and for which it is particularly difficult to find appropriate stands as large stands are limited in number.

The adoption of such planning practice usually makes operators' own planning more difficult: the higher the number of usable stands, the less complex the stand allocation process is because the distribution of aircrafts over several stands facilitates the synchronisation of the use of stands with departures and arrivals. A similar situation occurs when information about the arrival of charter flights is certain.

> Today we know that tomorrow a Tupolev will arrive and that we have to park it at stand 2. The use of stand 2 inhibits the use of all these other stands so we and our colleagues will never assign, for example, stand 1 to another aircraft (Track 6; 10/07/2011).

As such, regardless of whether the information about the movements of planes is certain or not, RCT operators consider the free stands usable as long as this assumption does not interfere with the forthcoming planning, either definitively or potentially.

The RCT operators not only plan to prevent stand unavailability, but also to ensure the availability of stands on the ramp in particular as assisting aircraft on the ramp is less complex in terms of organisation and less time consuming. The RCT operators' planning ensures ramp availability in terms of both planes length on the ground and the ordered use of stands. For example, RCT operators usually assign stands on the apron to planes that stay on the ground for long periods of time. This does not mean that the operators' choices about where to park aircrafts are standardised. If, in fact, an aircraft is expected to stay on ground for several hours but RCT operators consider it likely that the aircraft will be used ahead of schedule, despite the information available to them showing the contrary, they might decide not to park that aircraft on the apron.

> It's the case of Sxxair. Yesterday evening we had a plane that would have remained the whole next day on ground. We know that, if an aircraft needs to be replaced, the Sxxair staff uses the aircraft that is already on ground, so instead of parking the aircraft on the apron to have a stand free on the ramp, we decided to park it on the ramp. This morning,

> when Sxxair changed the rotation list, we already had the plane on the ramp and were able to board on time (Track 6; 10/07/2011).

In addition, the RCT operators allocate stands for maximum capacity as much as possible so as to keep the biggest parking bays, which are limited in number, free for aircraft that need them.

> I try to use stands for their capacity. I do not park aircrafts in stands that have a bigger capacity because it is not advantageous in terms of space use. As you can see, I can use this self-manoeuvring stand for an airbus but this way we would lose the use of these other stands and this is nonsense. You have to know the stand capacity and to work as the others do (Track 6; 10/07/2011).

Monitoring the Duration of Handling Activities

The RCT operators not only plan so as to prevent stands' unavailability, but also with the aim of keeping the duration of handling activities under control so as not to cause delays in planes' departures. RCT operators do not decide the amount of time necessary for handling planes; the airline companies fix the duration of the turnaround time, although they also recognise that the allocation of stands and gates is essential for contributing to the timely execution of flights. Indeed, the allocation of stands can impact on both the duration of the turnaround activities and the convergence of ramp personnel necessary for the timely assistance of planes on ground to get started.

The methods adopted by RCT operators during the stand allocation for the timely execution of handling activities include measures for both the promotion of the immediate execution of handling activities when necessary and the prevention of circumstances that could increase the time necessary for their execution. The promotion of the timely execution of handling activities is characterised by "time-saving practices"—namely, planning measures that aim to reduce the time necessary for the execution of some of the turnaround activities and for the convergence of ramp personnel at stands when their presence is necessary. The timely convergence of personnel at stands is achieved by minimising occasions that require the personnel's movement on the apron and ramp space as well as reducing the distances that they have to cross. Meanwhile, the prevention of delays is pursued by assigning stands and/or gates with the aim of shortening the time necessary for the execution of specific handling activities as well as by planning to avoid conditions that produce delays in the execution of the handling activities.

Operators promote the timely execution of handling activities by assigning stands so that planes are next to the equipment necessary for their handling. The use of the ramp and apron is arranged among the four handler companies that work in the analysed airport. A specific area of the ramp space is dedicated to each company, and they keep their own equipment for assisting planes in a timely manner in their dedicated space. Although such equipment is movable for the most part, handlers prefer to maintain it in the same place for several reasons. Vehicles can move on the ramp using predefined routes, but the continuous transfer of vehicles exposes them to damage, is expensive, creates traffic jams, and is time consuming. In addition, the continuous movement of supplies increases costs and the risk that handlers will not have them ready when and where necessary. For these reasons, RCT operators usually try not to park aircrafts handled by one company on the ramp space assigned to another company, especially as the airline companies have flights scheduled in the same period of time.

Operators prevent circumstances that could increase the time necessary for the execution of the handling activities through the careful allocation of gates to flights. They try not to assign flights directed to similar destinations in adjacent stands during the same period of time. This approach to planning the use of gates draws on the RCT operators' knowledge of passengers' behaviour. Passengers might be late or misread the monitors, causing them arrive at the wrong gate. The contiguity of boarding of flights with similar destinations can increase such confusion and passengers' mistakes, thereby creating more disruptions in the boarding process. In such cases, passengers can complain, and the operators at the gates have to spend time instructing them, which can slow down the boarding process. Increased boarding time negatively impacts turnaround procedures and, consequently, the possibility for the plane to depart on time. Thus, RCT operators try not to create such unfavourable conditions.

RCT operators also contribute to the timely execution of handling activities through the intensive use of gates connected with stands via fingers instead of those gates which require boarding by bus. Boarding on foot is quicker than boarding by bus. Time saved in passengers' movements can compensate for delays in the execution of other activities, such as passengers' seating. In addition, boarding by foot allows for the containment of the use of buses—a limited resource—and ultimately of the costs of each handling procedure.

Keeping Delays Under Control

Stand allocation can be used to keep delays under control thanks to the adoption of methods for planning that allow for limiting delays when it is foreseeable that temporal boundaries for handling will be exceeded. Ideal conditions for RCT operators' planning are those in which they can allocate stands so as to park all the scheduled aircrafts on the ramp while also respecting safety and security requirements, ensuring the timely execution of handling activities, and meeting airline companies' preferences about the allocation of stands.

However, when the number of flights to park is high, this is not possible, and the operators have to assign planes to stands on the apron. As previously explained, organising assistance for planes on the apron is a complex process as both the equipment and personnel necessary for handling the planes have to be transferred from the ramp to the apron. In addition, such transfers backfire on the organisation of the ramp activities as the time required for ground operators to move back and forth between these two areas increases, making it more likely for delays to occur in aircraft assistance as a whole. Thus, when operators have to plan in less-than-ideal conditions—that is, conditions that will probably cause delays—they allocate planes in such a way to minimise delays, such as by assigning stands on the apron to those passenger flights with the fewest passengers to board or disembark or to cargo flights that only have to load or unload parcels. In this way, the RCT operators succeed in maintaining good relations with all the parties involved in handling planes and with airline companies in particular.

Discussion

As previously mentioned, the careful exploitation of gates and stands allows for the convergence of passengers, equipment, and personnel at gates and stands when necessary. Even if stand allocation involves the organisation of seemingly simple changes in the use of the field (stands, as well as gates, may be free or occupied), the process actually embodies the possibility for handling to take place as expected. Thus, it can be concluded that stands, as well as gates, are not equivalent structures, not only because of their distinct technical features and different positions in the airport space, but also because the allocation of such areas assumes different relevance in terms of their position in the airport space, given the typologies and numbers of flights scheduled in certain periods of time.

As the previous discussion indicated, RCT operators have to deploy a specific corpus of knowledge to deal with problems that emerge during planning in order to ensure the timely execution of handling. The operators' local expertise (Carassa 2000; Normark and Randall 2005) related to "how things usually go"—whether in terms of knowing how passengers behave, how flights are usually planned, how changes in the rotation lists are managed by airline companies, or how operators on the ramp deal with the accomplishment of the aircraft assistance—plays a central role in stand and gate allocation. In particular it is our contention that the operators' knowledge of temporality in planning is organised in terms of knowledge of the temporal horizon of planning, the span of planning, and the management of temporal ambiguity.

Temporal Horizon and Temporal Span in Planning

The term "temporal horizon" refers to people's use of their knowledge of likely future events for the organisation of their current activities in the absence of protocols that have to be followed in "lock step" (Reddy et al. 2006; p. 42). Reddy et al. developed such a concept primarily to highlight how individuals perceive their own activities as temporally organised, showing how people increase or decrease the pace in the execution of their own activities in order to comply with deadlines. We contend that the concept of temporal horizons can be effectively used to focus on the nature and complexity of problems that people expect to arise when meeting deadlines as well as the modality by which they address such problems.

The temporal horizon of planning refers to the fact that the RCT operators know that the plan setup has temporal deadlines that cannot be exceeded and that they have to arrange their planning to comply with such requirements despite the actual circumstances. The RCT operators' main difficulty in complying with these temporal requirements does not depend on finishing the plan setup in due time, but rather in setting up the plan despite the lack of certain information about flight rotations.

We refer to the operators' knowledge of the duration of the effects of planning in terms of the "temporal span of planning". The temporal span of planning does not correspond with a precise prediction of the effects of planning over time; thus, the evaluation of the impact of one operator's planning can be better described in terms of approximate estimations to which methods for planning correspond. The operators manage both the temporal horizon of planning and its temporal span, drawing on practices that allow for the identification of the usable space and the maintenance of ramp space usability.

Recasting the operators' local knowledge on temporality in terms of the temporal horizon and span of planning allows for a better understanding of the types of problems that planning as a distributed activity imposes on planners, who have to articulate (Schmidt and Simone 1996) their planning over time. The distinction between horizon and span of planning highlights that the continuity of proper stand allocation cannot be taken for granted; it has to be actively pursued and is achievable only by means of the application of precise planning practices. The operators' practices for the identification of the usable space, in particular, restrict the number of usable stands; although this makes their own planning more difficult, it facilitates their colleagues' subsequent stand allocation. This also means that the practices for planning that make efficient stand allocation possible are the same that allow for the connection of planning over subsequent shifts.[5]

It is also worth noting that all the practices for the management of horizons in the stand allocation optimise the use of the resources at operators' disposal, thereby contributing to the complexity of colleagues' planning as well. If delays occur in the execution of handling activities due to improper planning and flights are not carried out as scheduled, reasonable expectations about plane departures—and thus about the availability of stands—are no longer possible.

[5] In air traffic control, cooperative functions are embedded in the execution of work in a similar way (see: Berndtsson and Normark 1999).

Managing Temporal Ambiguity

Egger and Wagner (1993) defined temporal ambiguity as the effect of the impossibility for organisations to respect temporal boundaries in which work activities are organised. Temporal ambiguity refers to the difficulty organisations face in keeping orderliness and predictability in the execution of work activities. According to Egger and Wagner's definition, organisations face temporal ambiguity by means of scheduling. We contend that the RCT operators are aware of the temporal ambiguity that an improper stand allocation might cause; as such, they adopt measures to both avoid and contain the temporal ambiguity as much as possible when planning.

Stand allocation can be used to prevent temporal ambiguity thanks to the planning methods adopted that allow for handling to be executed in a timely manner. However, it can also contribute to the control of temporal ambiguity when it is foreseeable that temporal boundaries for handling will be exceeded, as previously explained. The focus on temporal ambiguity highlights how planning can contribute to maintaining order at work, thereby enriching our understanding of the use of plans in workplace settings. In addition the description of operators' planning practices for keeping delays under control by controlling the temporal ambiguity indicates how planning methods allow them to comply with contingent situations and identify which changes in work circumstances trigger such modification in planning methods.

The Features of Temporal Allocation of Stands

The analysis of planning practices not only allows for a deeper understanding of planning as situated practice, but also for the revision of the existing definitions of "allocation".

As previously explained, the RCT operators allocate stands with the aim of keeping the duration of handling activities under control so as not to cause delays in planes' departure. However, none of the existing definitions of "allocation" gives an account of what "allocation" consists of for the RCT operators. Malone and Crowston (1994) recognised allocation as a basic process for coordination—namely, for the management of interdependent work activities. They concluded that allocation consists of the process necessary for the organised use of shared resources among different users who often have conflicting interests. Meanwhile, Bardram (2000) suggested that allocation consists of deciding the amount of time to dedicate to various activities according to temporal priorities.

We suggest that theoretical approaches to the study of allocation processes might be inadequate for the comprehension of what allocation consists of in situated contexts and, thus, for the understanding of how people deal with the problems that specific forms of allocation raise. As such, considering the study of "allocation" as a situated phenomenon in order to understand what people mean when using such a term allows for a deeper understanding of how it is related with the solution of time management problems. A definition of "allocation" that better describes RCT operators' practice is the organisation of resources among different users following temporal priorities for the promotion of the timely execution of work activities within certain periods of time.

Deficiencies of Constraint Programming Techniques Applied to Stand Allocation

Existing stand allocation software is based on constraint programming techniques (Hon Wai Chun et al. 2000). Although such software provides the automatic generation of the stand allocation plan, as previously indicated, RCT operators do not rely on the automatic allocation of stands as they consider the software to be inadequate. Such inadequacy stems from the fact that the software is ineffective in sustaining planners' articulations and evaluating the effects of the stand allocation on the coordination of the handling activities. The software does not favour the efficient connection between stages of plans in that it cannot create plans in the absence of certain information about the flight rotations. In addition, automatic stand allocation based on constraint programming techniques fails to consider the effects of the stand allocation on the timely execution of the handling activities. Thus, it seems reasonable to say that, when several solutions to the same stand allocation problem are possible, the operators are better able than the software to choose the stand coherently given their orientation towards the allocation of stands for the timely execution of handling. Ultimately, software for the stand allocation should be interpreted as an "affording mechanism" (Cabitza and Simone 2012) that, for example, provides alarm codes whenever the stand allocation is inappropriate rather than as a tool that can be used to replace humans in carrying out tasks.

Sustaining the Essential Coordinative Functions of Planning the Stand Allocation

Crabtree et al. (2000) asserted that the main objective of an ethnographic study of work settings for system design should be to understand what to automate and what to leave to human expertise. This research is not oriented to software design; nevertheless, it allows some considerations for the improvement of the system for stand allocation. In fact, even if software for automatic stand allocation can be improved by incorporating the evaluation of further constraints so as to support the plan setup in a more consistent way, it seems unlikely that such software could substitute for humans in the management of stand allocation due to the strong impact of local knowledge on time management in planning.

Instead, we suggest that software should be designed to support planners' articulation of work. This could be achieved by facilitating operators' sharing all information regarding colleagues' planning and the changing state of work useful for the maintenance of the stand availability. In addition, inspired by the RCT operators' practices—and differently from what current research shows—we argue the need to develop software that conceptualises the problems of gate/stand allocation and planes' handling as integrated rather than separated phenomena. This, in fact, could contribute to minimise flight delays and optimise the use of airport's facilities and handlers' resources. Our research highlights the necessity of increasing the integration of airport operations (by increasing the integration of airport operations; see: Atkin et al. 2010; Kelemen 2005).

Concluding Remarks

The successfulness of planning in the RCT depends on the interplay between shared methods for the plan production that allow for both the allocation of resources and the management of temporal constraints while maintaining orderliness and predictability in the execution of work activities. As discussed herein, such a definition of allocation does not correspond with definitions of the same process developed from theoretical points of view—namely, that of coordination theory and activity theory—but rather emerges from the situated study of the setting. We do not contend that this definition of allocation should replace existing ones; instead, we suggest that theoretical approaches to the study of allocation processes might be inadequate for comprehending what allocation consists of in situated contexts and, consequently, how people deal with problems that specific forms of allocation raise, thereby impeding the implementation of software for the coordination of work activities by means of resource allocation. We also suggest that the exclusive automation of stand allocation is insufficient for ensuring the smooth execution of aircraft assistance, which draws heavily on the situated relevance of the operators' local knowledge.

Our analysis of planning enriches our understanding of the use of plans as organisational artefacts in that our study shows how planning can simultaneously impact coordination in time and space by managing the substantive contents of the field. As such, our study enables CSCW scholars to determine how temporality and distance affect coordination as intertwined phenomena that future empirical research can help further clarify.

Acknowledgments Thanks to Dave Randall with whom we discussed the role of plans in workplace settings.

References

Amerine, R., & Bilmes, J. (1988). Following instructions. *Human Studies, 11*(2–3), 327–339.

Atkin, J. A. D., Burke, E. K., Ravizza, S. (2010). The airport ground movement problem: Past and current research and future directions. In *Procedings of the 4th International Conference on Research in Air Transportation* (pp. 131–138). Busapest: CATSR.

Bardram, J. E. (1997). Plans as situated action: An activity theory approach to workflow systems. In *Proceedings of ECSCW'97* (pp. 17–34). Netherlands: Kluwer Academic.

Bardram, J. E. (2000). Temporal coordination. *Computer Supported Cooperative Work, 9*(2), 157–187.

Bardram, J. E., & Hansen, T. R. (2010). Why the plan doesn't hold- a study of situated planning, articulation and coordination work in a surgical ward. In K. I. Quinn, C. Gutwin, J. C. Tang (Eds.), *Proceedings of the 2010 ACM Conference on Computer Supported Cooperative Work, CSCW 2010* (pp. 331–340). Savannah: ACM.

Berndtsson, J., & Normark, M. (1999). The coordinative functions of flight strips: air traffic control work revised. In *Proceedings of the International ACM SIGGROUP Conference on Supporting Group Work 1999* (pp. 101–110). Phoenix: ACM.

Bossen, C., & Markussen, R. (2010). Infrastructuring and ordering devices in health care: Medication plans and practices on a hospital ward. *Computer Supported Cooperative Work, 19*(6), 615–637.

Button, G., & Sharrock, W. (1996). Project work: the organization of collaborative design and development in software engineering. *Computer Supported Cooperative Work, 5*(4), 369–386.

Button, G., & Sharrock, W. (1998). The organizational accountability of technological work. *Social Studies of Science 28*(1), 73–102.

Cabitza, F., & Simone, C. (2012). Affording mechanisms: an integrated view of coordination and knowledge management. *Computer Supported Cooperative Work 21*(2–3), 227–260.

Carassa, A. (2000). La conoscenza entra in azione. In G. Mantovani (Ed.), *Ergonomia* (pp. 123–150). Bologna: Il Mulino.

Ciborra, C. (2002). *The labyrinths of information*. NY: Oxford University Press.

Crabtree, A., Nichols, S. M., O'Brien, J., Rouncefield, M., & Twidale, M. B. (2000). Ethnomethodologically informed ethnography and information system design. *Journal of the American Society for Information Science, 51*(7), 666–682.

Dant, T., & Francis D. (1998). Planning in organisations: Rational control or contingent activity? *Sociological Research Online, 3*(2). http://www.socresonline.org.uk/3/2/4.html.

Egger, E., & Wagner, I. (1993). Negotiating temporal orders. *Computer Supported Cooperative Work, 1*(4), 255–275.

Garfinkel, H. (1967). *Studies in ethnomethodology*. Englewood Cliffs: Prentice Hall.

Garfinkel, H. (2002). *Ethnomethodology' s program: working out Durkheim' s aphorism*. Lanham: Rowman and Littlefield.

Hon Wai Chun, A., Ho Chuen Chan, S., Ming Fai Tsang, F., & Wai Ming Yeung, D. (2000). Stand-allocation system. *AI Magazine, 21*(4), 63–74.

Karasti, H., Baker, K. S., & Millerand F. (2010). Infrastructure time: long-term matters in collaborative development. *Computer Supported Cooperative Work, 19*(3–4), 377–415.

Kelemen, Z. (2005). Resource management system—The first step to the airport information system integration. *Periodica Polytechnica Transportation Engineering, 33*(1–2), 15–24.

Koskinen, I. (2000). Plans, evaluation, and accountability at the workplace. *Sociological Research Online, 4*(4), http://www.socresonline.org.uk/4/4/koskinen.html.

Llewellyn, N. (2008). Organization in actual episodes of work: Harvey sacks and organization studies. *Organization Studies, 29*(5), 763–791.

Llewellyn, N., & Spence, L. (2009). Practice as a members' phenomenon. *Organization Studies, 30*(12): 1419–1439.

Malone, T., & Crowston, K (1994). The interdisciplinary study of coordination. *ACM Computing Surveys, 26*(1), 87–119.

Nilsson, M., & Hertzum, M. (2005). Negotiated rhythms of mobile work: time, place, and work schedules. In *Proceedings of GROUP'05* (pp. 148–157). Sanibel Island: ACM.

Normark M., & Randall, D. (2005). Local expertise at an emergency call centre. In H. Gellersen et al. (Eds.), *ECSCW 2005: Proceedings of the Ninth European Conference on Computer-Supported Cooperative Work* (pp. 347–366). Paris: Springer.

Orlikowski, W., & Yates, J. (2002). It's about time: Temporal structuring in organizations. *Organization Science, 13*(6), 684–700.

Randall, D., O'Brien, J., Rouncefield, M., & Hughes, J. A. (1996). Organizational memory and CSCW: Supporting the 'Mavis' Phenomenon. In J. Grundy, M. Apperley (Eds.), *Proceedings of the Sixth Australian Conference on HCI (OzCHI'96)* (pp. 26–35). IEEE.

Randall, D., Harper, R., & Rouncefield, M. (2007). *Fieldwork for design*. London: Springer.

Randall, D., & Rouncefield, M. (2011). Plans and planning: Conceptual confusions and empirical investigations'. In M. Rouncefield & P. Tolmie (Eds.), *Ethomethodology at work* (pp. 73–89). Farnham: Ashgate.

Reddy, M., & Doursih, P. (2002). A finger on the pulse: Temporal rhythms and information seeking in medical work. In *Proceedings of CSCW'02* (pp. 344–353). New Orleans: ACM.

Reddy, M., Dourish, P., & Pratt, W. (2006). Temporality in medical work: time also matters. *Computer Supported Cooperative Work, 15*(1), 29–53.

Rönkkö, K., Dittrich, Y., Randall, D. (2005). When plans do not work out: How plans are used in software development projects. *Computer Supported Cooperative Work, 14*(5), 433–468.

Schmidt, K., Simone, C. (1996). Coordination mechanisms: Towards a conceptual foundation of CSCW systems design. *Computer Supported Cooperative Work (CSCW): The Journal of Collaborative Computing*, *5*(2–3), 155–200.

Schmidt, K. (1999). Of maps and scripts: The status of formal constructs in cooperative work. *Information Software Technology, 41*(6), 319–329.

Schmidt, K. (2011). Frail foundation. In K. Schmidt (Ed.), *Cooperative Work and Coordinative Practices* (pp. 359–389). Spinger: London.

Sharroch, W., & Button, G. (2003). Plans and situated action 10 years on. *The Journal of the Learning Science*, *12*(2), 259–264.

Sherman Heyl, B. (2001). Ethnographic interviewing. In P. Atkinson, A. Coffey, S. Delamont, J. Lofland, & L. Lofland (Eds.), *Handbook of Ethnography* (pp. 369–383). London: Sage.

Suchman, L. A. (1987). *Plans and situated actions: The problem of human-machine communication*. New York: Cambridge University Press.

Suchman, L. A. (1997). Centres of coordination: A case and some themes. In L. B. Resnick, R. Säljö, C. Pontecorvo, & B. Burge (Eds.), *Discourse, Tools, and Reasoning: Essays on Situated Cognition* (pp. 41–62). Berlin: Springer-Verlag.

Vera, A., & Simon, H. (1993). Situated action: A symbolic interpretation. *Cognitive Science, 17*, 7–48.

Whittaker, S., & Schwartz, H. (1999). Meetings of the board: The impact of scheduling medium on long term group coordination in software development. *Computer supported Cooperative Work*, *8*(3), 175–205.

Zimmerman, D. (1971). The practicalities of rule use. In J. Douglas (Ed.), *Understanding Everyday Life*. London: Routledge and Kegan Paul.

Calendars: Time Coordination and Overview in Families and Beyond

Susanne Bødker and Erik Grönvall

Abstract This paper discusses how calendars and time coordination can be used across social and organizational borders, bridging between work and non-work, and between family coordination and external collaborators. The paper moves beyond family on-line calendars towards coordination and collaboration with professional caregivers and public authorities, and discusses how such shared calendars revitalize some of the very basic discussions of CSCW: The notion of shared goals in cooperative activities, the understanding of time and time-granularity in cooperation, common information spaces, and in particular boundary-crossing capacities and the holding back of information for fragmented exchange. Based on two cases, in which we have worked with sharing and coordination of time-resources in families on the one hand, and external parties such as external caregivers, employers and municipal authorities on the other, this paper will reopen these old CSCW debates. This paper questions if calendars, in particular family calendars should be designed based on shared goals and common interests. We argue that collaboration needs to be supported, even when families and their professional and amateur collaborators do not share the same goals, rhythms and routines.

Introduction

This paper will discuss how calendars and time coordination are and can be used across social and organizational settings, bridging between work and non-work, and between the much-hyped area of family coordination and external

S. Bødker (✉) · E. Grönvall
Department of Computer Science, Aarhus University, Aarhus, Denmark
e-mail: bodker@cs.au.dk

E. Grönvall
e-mail: gronvall@cs.au.dk

O. W. Bertelsen et al. (eds.), *ECSCW 2013: Proceedings of the 13th European Conference on Computer Supported Cooperative Work, 21–25 September 2013, Paphos, Cyprus*, DOI: 10.1007/978-1-4471-5346-7_4,

collaborators. Family on-line calendars are a somewhat new topic that we find is treated somewhat naively as seen from the point of view of CSCW. In this paper we will revitalize some of the very basic discussions of CSCW in order to provide a less naïve view on family calendars. We will discuss the notion of shared goals in relation to cooperative activities (Bødker et al. 1988; Raeithel 1992; Bardram 1998), the understanding of time, time rhythms and time granularity and its relationship to the cooperation (Egger and Wagner 1992), boundaries, boundary-crossing capacities (Star and Griesemer 1989) and fragmented exchange (Clement and Wagner 1995). All of this with a view towards family calendars and how such time resources are shared within families and across boundaries to a network of other amateur and professional communities.

The paper is based on two cases in which we have worked with sharing and coordination of time-resources in activities involving families on the one hand, and external parties such as external caregivers, employers and municipal authorities on the other (Bohøj et al. 2010; Borchorst and Bødker 2011; Bossen et al. 2012). Through two calendars, built intentionally to support different forms of collaboration across organizational and social settings, this article will examine and discuss the calendar as a collaborative tool that spans from families across to organisations and non-professional constellations such as a municipality.

Calendars and Cooperation

A calendar is a common tool for planning, communication and collaboration. Calendars are used by individuals to organize and document one's life. Calendars are used within defined groups, such as families or at workplaces, and can there enable collaboration as one can locate people, see their availability and book them. In the words of Crabtree et al. (2003), calendars represent "*temporal plans of coordinate action (…) and may be characterised as temporal maps constructed by users to coordinate events with others*"—(Crabtree et al. 2003, p. 120).

Calendars are one of the most successful collaborative tools in existence (Palen and Grudin 2003) and the use of calendars has been investigated extensively for many years within CSCW. Family calendars have been designed to support (temporarily) separated families (Markopoulos et al. 2004; Saslis-Lagoudakis et al. 2006; Neustaedter et al. 2009; Yarosh and Abowd 2011), or divorced families (Yarosh et al. 2009; Odom et al. 2010). The increased popularity of cross-group coordination support such as Doodle (2012) indicates a need and benefit for allowing diverse groups to coordinate and collaborate around certain activities without giving unlimited access for others to one's calendar.

Calendars have for long been recognized as an important coordination artefact in the home setting (Venkatesh 1996). Elliot and Carpendale (2005) discuss the use of family calendars, and put emphasis on three major activities supported through family calendars: (1) *Coordination and Negotiation*—to work out a shared understanding of what, when and by whom something should be performed, (2) *Review and reminders*—to provide an overview (short-term and future) of what activities will take place and act as a to-do list and finally (3) *Awareness*—provide and understand what other people within a family are doing and where. Neustaedter et al. (2009) discuss different calendaring practices within families, focusing on who is in control, and whether one or several calendars are involved.

Crabtree et al. (ibid.) propose that to move from the workplace and into the home, calendars should be made available at home as well as elsewhere; they should devise negotiation protocols to enable users to negotiate their schedules, and support the development of distributed collaborative access models. "*The domestic calendar is a personal object, not in the sense that it belongs to one individual, but in the sense that it belongs to a very small collection of individuals to organize and coordinate what can only be described as their intimate affairs.*"—(Crabtree et al. 2003, p. 134).

The two cases we present in this article, in each their way, live up to the requirements outlined, and we will return to the challenges of *how they are made available outside the family; how they set up negotiation protocols and how they support the development of shared access models.* Lee (2005) points out how artefacts that live within organizational and activity boundaries are constantly developed, both through the development of local uses (in the dialectical manner), and because there are many situations where the standardized methods and forms need to be negotiated across activity boundaries, in continuation of Crabtree et al. (2003)'s demand for development of shared access models.

Ganoe et al. (2003) stress the need to provide awareness of the 'overall situation' including dependencies and shared task goals within a collaborative group. In other words, adding to Crabtree et al. (ibid.), *calendars must share and give access to rhythms of activity and they need to provide awareness to the overall situation, or overview.* Star and Griesemer (1989) analyse in detail the design and use of various artefacts as boundary objects in and around a zoological museum. The setting of family calendars resembles the work of Star and Griesemer (ibid.) in that *boundary objects such as calendars are shaped by professionals to support participation by professionals and amateurs* (in this case parents, children, and various kinds of volunteers) in sharing information and duties. However, it is also a case of the opposite, namely *amateurs shaping boundary objects to be shared with professionals.* If we think about how family calendars may be used to reduce complexity across boundaries we need to look for how amateurs and professionals alike limit information that is provided for boundary crossing, in our case calendar entries and information.

Clement and Wagner (1995) describe fragmented exchange across organizational boundaries. As we shall discuss for family calendars, like the work of (Reddy et al. 2006), they challenge different needs of privacy, and diverse temporal trajectories among the collaborators. Grönvall et al. (2005) describe a calendar/timeline based system where opportunities to communicate are set by different actors in a healthcare scenario. They discuss the value of being able to restrict bandwidth or services available (e.g. only allowing audio, even if video could be possible) in specific collaborative care situations and by that introducing granularity to handle specific privacy and filtering-concerns exiting in their case. In this paper we will discuss *if and how it makes sense to provide equal access or if there is a need to support fragmented exchange through different granularity.*

In divorced families, collaboration (e.g. concerning the shared care for a child) can be challenging. Divorced families challenge collaboration as they often are distributed, may not like each other and have a need to retain privacy while still collaborating. Odom et al. (2010) describe challenges and opportunities in how technology and electronic calendars can be used to support the joint care of a child in divorced families. Yarosh et al. (2009) describe communication challenges arising from the physical separation, different rhythms and lack of subtle cues to detect activities (e.g. might a child's dirty shoes for example indicate a trip through the forest or a football game?).

Bødker et al. (1988) discuss how CSCW had, in its early days, adapted the small research group as ideal for cooperative work. They point out that this ideal leads to a rationality that is naïve and limited, and suggest that there are other forms of rationality at stake. In (Noddings 1984), they find a philosophical alternative, *caring* or "the Mother's voice." In contrast to the authoritative "Father's voice", a person cares about somebody by taking on this person's situation, based on her former experiences with caring. For example is it not uncommon that adult children provide assistance to their older parents, seeing this as a way to 'pay back' for previously received help or care when they were young, rather as 'work' (Schulz 2010; Christensen and Grönvall 2011). Where work calendars may be viewed from a classical rationality, the notion of care rationality provides a challenge for family calendars.

There is an additional difference between private and shared work calendars: At work, time fundamentally belongs to the employer, who can make decisions, e.g. for everybody to use and share calendars and for the time rhythms as such (Begole et al. 2002), whether this happens or not (Palen and Grudin 2003). In the private sphere there are no instrumental incentives like salary or straight-forward demands from management to enforce a shared calendar use. Without outside push it is even more important that the users can see an immediate benefit themselves of doing the work to share information with others (Grudin 1994).

(Bardram 1998), as well as Clases and Wehner (2002) use Raeithel's categorization of cooperation in relation to shared goals and identity, in the context of CSCW. This model illustrates that there is no simple way in which a common goal is the precondition for cooperation. At one end of the spectrum, actors are gathered to act on a common object, but their individual actions are externally related to each other through scripts and routines, which is why Raeithel (1992) talks about how people in this type of coordination see themselves as 'me-and-the-others'. At the other extreme, the actors focus on re-conceptualizing their doing in relation to their shared objects. Both the object and the script are re-conceptualized, and people according to Raeithel (ibid.) see themselves as belonging together as 'we-in-the-world'. This kind of perspective may be used to further discuss the assumption made regarding family calendars; that they deal with *the family as a group of equal peers with joint interests.* Calendars, and other coordination artifacts are needed as much for 'me-and-the-others' setting as they are for 'we-in-the-world'. However, the scripted gathering around a shared object, may point towards different needs than the open sharing. Accordingly simpler means of cooperation are needed, where each party can to a large extent mind their own business. We will return to this discussion later.

Two Family Calendar Cases

In the following section we present two cases where we have been involved in understanding and designing family-related calendars. We shall look at how our two cases address the challenges of shared calendars, in particular how these cases deal with the concerns for shared interests within the families, how they deal with access to rhythms of activity, their attention to awareness to the overall situation, or overview, to how calendars were made available outside the family; how they dealt with negotiation protocols and shared access models across families and outside collaborators.

CareCoor: Supporting Homecare-referred Older Adults' Care Networks

CareCoor was developed in a research project based on ethnographic field studies and a participatory design process, involving mainly care-workers, a care-worker team-leader and family members. The purpose of CareCoor was to address a number of collaborative challenges in referred, home-based care, especially in those situations where the referred, older adult could not be an active partner in the collaboration—for example due to dementia. The following case description represents a condensed version of previously published work. For details regarding the study background, design rational and method, the developed system and test results the reader is advised to consult the following two works (Christensen and Grönvall 2011; Bossen et al. 2013).

Homecare work is to a large degree a cooperative effort. Numerous home care-workers, relatives, friends and others all contribute to the care of an older adult. All these actors provide care from different perspectives and with different goals and motivations while following their own temporal rhythms. While all partners like to provide the 'best possible care' for the older adult, they do this from different stances as these actors all have their own individual roles, goals, rhythms, time to invest and relations to the other actors. For example, the professional care-workers provide care as part of their job, and based on a need-assessment (i.e. the referral process). Relatives on the other hand rarely see their contribution as 'work' or home care, but rather as acts of love or giving back care received earlier, for example as a child (Schulz 2010). Also, a professional care-worker may have to attend ten different clients a day whereas a family member only has one or two older relatives to care for. We observed that these diversities at times challenged a, for all parties, fruitful collaboration. Usually it is the close family members and the care-workers who are the most active care-providers. However, other parties are involved such as friends of the elderly, volunteers from NGOs and other professional actors. CareCoor accordingly was designed to support communication and collaboration among these diverse actors, i.e. the Care Network, supporting an older adult.

Without the CareCoor technology, the collaborative activities depend on the use of a paper-based care-binder placed in each referred person's home, face-to-face communication, phone calls and letters. The paper-based care binder contains information such as the referred activities (i.e. when and what referred tasks will be done) and a message-exchange area where care-workers and family members can exchange information and communicate. Typically several care-workers work with the elderly, due to their internal work shifts. At times the referred work schedule in the care binder is not up-to-date (i.e. being paper-based, someone must remember to print, bring and change the care-plan when the referred tasks change) and the message-exchange is not optimal: One have to be in the apartment and look through the whole care-binder in order to learn if someone has written a message or the care-plan has been updated. Alternatives such as face-to-face or telephone conversations between carers require both parties' availability and attention. Many relatives have the telephone number, and sometimes even the private number, of one or two care-workers. As the relatives do not have access to the work rhythm and schedules of the care-workers it is, however, difficult to know when to call. In our studies, the care-workers mention that such calls are often disruptive because they are attending other care-receivers, are in other problematic situations or simply not attuned with the discussed situation. Accordingly, providing *a better overview, or understanding, of these time rhythms* is an essential part of CareCoor.

CareCoor is, in its simplest form, a digital implementation (on a Samsung Galaxy Tab) of the paper-based care-binder connected to an internet database through the mobile 3G network (see Fig. 1).

Through web and app-based calendar-based interfaces, CareCoor provides an awareness and collaboration platform that allows family members and the municipal care-workers and team-leaders to collaborate in the care of an older adult. In CareCoor, the referred care plan, medication information etc. is always up-to-date and CareCoor indicates when someone has left a new message. Furthermore, CareCoor extends the paper-based care binder's functionality by allowing all actors to (1) insert non-referred care activities in the calendar and (2) allow collaboration around the listed activities. For example a son visiting his older mother on a Sunday can decide to clean up his mother's apartment. Through CareCoor he can see that his mother's apartment is scheduled for cleaning Monday afternoon. Without CareCoor, there is no effective way for him to 'take over' the cleaning and

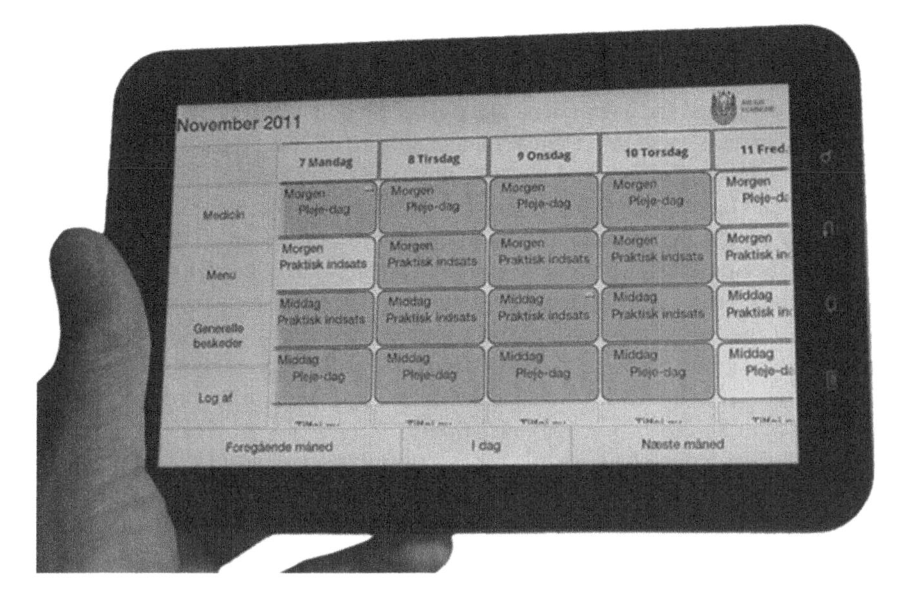

Fig. 1 The matrix-based CareCoor calendar interface running on a tablet

the care-workers will clean the apartment even if this is not needed. With Care-Coor the son can 'take over' the referred task of cleaning by acknowledging this using the tablet. The care-workers and their team leader will obtain this 'transfer of responsibility of a referred activity' and can hence plan other activities. The son can also propose a new (but not referred) task, such as buying some milk to his mother. Since the son cleaned the apartment, the care workers can now have time to buy the milk and have a chat with the old mother. The acceptance of tasks, proposed new activities and messages, and the acceptance of messages are all documented through CareCoor. The set of rules in which the different actors act, for example when taking over a referred task must be negotiated to maintain a clear definition of responsibilities, etc. The documentation of these tasks as they are carried out can be seen as an ad-hoc contract between the municipality and a non-professional care-provider such as next-of-kin. Accordingly the challenges of providing shared calendars in this setting include:

- Providing a shared overview across carers in the Care Network.
- Yielding time rhythms visible at levels that support sharing of routines at granularities that are suited for the various practices.
- Facilitating negotiation of rules and contracts.

The latter two, in particular are challenges of potential tension and conflict between parties.

CaseLine: Couples Planning Parental Leave

This study addressed the interaction and collaboration involved in the planning and control of parental leave in a Danish municipality. The planning involves several citizens, a municipal office and several other stakeholders such as the parents' employers and labor unions. We developed CaseLine in a research through design process, involving initial field studies and participatory design. CaseLine prototypes have been tried out in various workshop settings, and our findings are based on data from these and the initial field studies. The following case description represents a condensed version of previously published work. For details regarding the study background, design rational and method, the system as such and test results the reader is advised to consult the following three works (Borchorst et al. 2009; Bohøj et al. 2010; Borchorst and Bødker 2011).

This parental leave planning process is typically a product of the negotiation between the parents and the surrounding stakeholders, focusing on how the parents may use their rights for parental leave, as determined by national legislation and managed by the municipality, while making the most of the payment that either parent get from their employers. The legislation constrains this planning in particular since the rights of the parents are interwoven with one-another, as do e.g. the parents' vacation rights and agreements with each employer, if there is one. Establishing the best possible solution, in terms of total leave-time, split between mother and father, total income during the leave period, the possibility of spending leave-time together, and saving leave-time for later, calls for the consideration of various "what-if" scenarios. Parents often do not have all the information necessary to calculate these scenarios, and the legislation is difficult to work with due to its inherent flexibility. The municipal office is an important source of advice on this as well as it is approving the final plan. As part of the counseling process the "what-if" scenario can be explicitly shared with a caseworker (see Fig. 2).

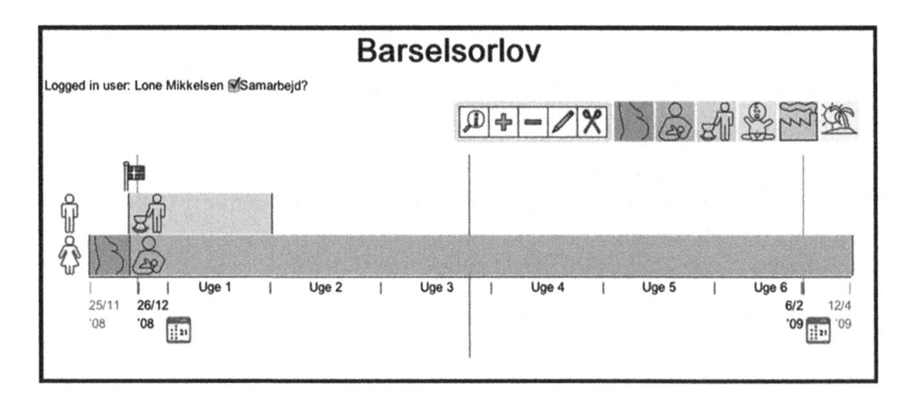

Fig. 2 The timeline based CaseLine calendar (Sandbox mode, the tick-box makes explicit sharing with caseworker possible)

The planning period for parental leave is up to nine years, which is the child-age when all parental leaves should have been used. Even when parents have decided on the best solution, this has to be *communicated to, and negotiated with* the respective employers. Moreover, despite having settled on even the best of plans, parents may desire to *change their plan*. Often, when the time comes for the child to start daycare, the parents need to adjust their plans e.g. to the actual starting date of the daycare. Over the nine-year period, many events may happen that makes a change of plans necessary: New jobs, additional children, etc. Consequential changes need to be reiterated with all of the above stakeholders.

As a consequence of the above complexity, friends become an important source of inspiration and advice. However, sharing experiences is also complicated and often the municipal office gets questions from expecting parents, who cannot understand why and how their situation differs from that of their friends and relatives. This is also true for parents who search for information in the limited, available Internet sources.

Bohøj et al. (2010) describe the many challenges of joint parental leave planning, suggest a design concept and present some early prototypes for CaseLine, a timeline/calendar based planning and overview tool to be shared between parents, and towards employers and public authorities (Fig. 2).

The design concept supports the enabling of citizens to help themselves and each other in understanding, planning, and applying for parental leave funding through a timeline-design. CaseLine is designed to facilitate the communication and collaboration between citizens and municipal caseworkers, and ultimately also between the parents and e.g. their employers and unions. Simplified, CaseLine provides a timeline-based interface to parental leave plan objects. This supports and facilitates sharing and open exploration between parents, at the same time as it supports controlled sharing with the municipality, when parents allow access to their plan. In addition, the municipality can provide general plan elements on-line. These latter elements may be tailored by e.g. employers and unions, and used by parents as basis for their agreement with the municipality, or by each parent in their agreement with their employer. However, a shared timeline poses a number of concerns even among the parents: "*Do parents of a child wish to share with each other all information about their interaction with employers, and government? Even if this is the case, can such openness also be assumed if the parents are divorced, but share joint custody over the child? (…) Who gets to decide which information is shared? Should the consent of information sharing expire after a certain period of time, and how is this visualized?*"—(Bohøj et al. 2010).

It is important for all parties to be explicitly aware of when a certain timeline gets shared, and when it is approved and hence binding. Such sharing of information only takes place when a formal application is generated. Indeed, both citizens as well as the municipality need to withhold information from each other, not sharing "everything". Consequently, the citizen needs to be able to make a clear distinction between exploring possibilities and sharing information with other stakeholders such as employers and the municipality.

CaseLine contains both an experimental 'sandbox' and a more formal part where the actual agreements are made visible. The formal part can be seen as a contract between parents and the municipality (and the employers). The parent's motive for using CaseLine is to get as much out of the parental leave as possible as the system helps them to experiment and learn about different parental leave configurations and their short-, and long-term effects.

CaseLine helps families manage and visualize shared time resources. It does so on a time-scale that may be a bit unusual to family calendars, but perhaps for this reason it helps challenge what shared family calendars are.

In terms of the time coordination and calendars, this case has the following main challenges:

- Supporting both a 'sandbox'-mode and a formal contract mode.
- Sharing of plans with many parties supporting different granularities in time and personal information (sharing the time rhythm independent of personal information, or with only the personal information of one of the parents).
- Accommodating change and control over sharing over an extensive time period.

As with CareCoor, these are areas of different interests and potential conflict.

Through the implementation of CareCoor and CaseLine, the nature of collaboration changed (see Fig. 3). In CareCoor, the focus shifted from care providers acting to a large degree in isolation, to an actively collaborating Care Network. In CaseLine, parental leave planning went from being parent-initiated communication to collaboration around the CaseLine tool. The two cases present the starting point for exploring (time) coordination within families and across to public offices, wider networks of professional and non-professional actors, etc.

Similarities and Differences Between the Cases

On an overall level CareCoor is addressing the existing coordination needs between care-workers and next of kin in relation to an older adult's referred home care. CaseLine is addressing the parental leave pertaining to one child and the therefore needed collaboration between mainly the parents and the municipality.

The two cases directly target collaboration, negotiation and shared access between different primary and secondary actors, considering both the professional and amateur set of users (see Table 1).

Both cases are developed for their primary users, but support and benefit from when used also by the secondary users. While highly depending on the non-professional users, it is the primary professional user (i.e. the municipality) that controls, and has set up the rules and space for interaction.

The two cases bear resemblance in how they orchestrate private–public communication and collaboration (i.e. in our two cases primarily family-municipality communication and collaboration) and similarity with other (calendar-based) collaborative tools. However when further exploring the cases they present important

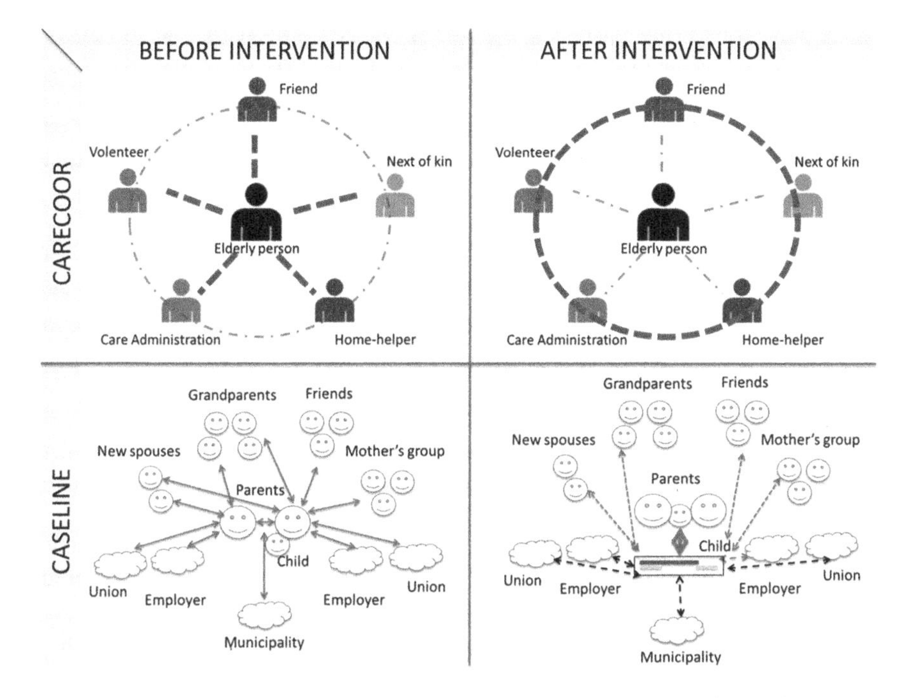

Fig. 3 The two settings, the involved actors and their modus operandi before (*left*) and after (*right*) the implementation of the calendar-based, collaborative tools. In both cases there is a change of focus through which the complexity of the coordination is reduced

Table 1 The different actors in the two cases

	CareCoor	CaseLine
Primary professional users	Workers	Municipal office
	Care worker's team leader	Employers of mother and father
Primary amateur users	Adult children to older adult	Parents
Secondary professional users	Municipality	Previous employers
	The general practitioner	
Secondary amateur users	Friends and neighbours	Grandparents
	Volunteers (from NGOs etc.)	Mother's support group

differences that emphasize diverse aspects of collaboration and set them off from other work. In this section we will highlight and discuss some of these differences.

Caring or Sharing Goals

CareCoor and CaseLine distinguish themselves from the literature on family calendars on the one hand, and that of professional shared calendars on the other, in that they both bridge between one or more professional communities and amateurs, in particular the family, in addition to various forms of extended families, groups, friends, and NGOs. In both our cases the planning and coordination activity is triggered by, and centred on, a person being either a child or an older adult. The family-municipality collaboration and communication are the starting point, but is on neither side of the collaboration a simple and open relationship. Families are complicated as are municipal bureaucracies, and there is a tendency for each side to not fully understand the other. Additionally, other parties can participate in the collaboration as well (Table 1), further complicating the matter.

Membership in different groups (as in these cases e.g. the municipality workers group and the municipality-family group) is known to create tension (Mark and Poltrock 2003), especially if different goals and collaborative systems exist within these groups and are not outspoken and shared. This is one of the places where families don't necessarily share a goal, being "we-in-the-world" to use Raeithel's term, with the municipality. This phenomenon is discussed for the parental leave situation in (Borchorst and Bødker 2011) where suspicion, or lack of understanding of the goals of the municipal office, leads to a number of workarounds and information filtering strategies used by the citizens in their communication with the municipality.

Even if the set of actors is rather well defined in both cases, and both having the municipality and family members as part of the primary user set, a large variation exists in each actor's motivation, needs and temporal scope. CareCoor illustrates that even among the professional actors there are different interests and goals that are only to some extent related to the rationality and goals of the family members: For the care-workers, ease of communication with relatives and documentation are the main concerns. With CareCoor, the care-workers move from a synchronous telephone communication to a chat-based, asynchronous communication model that can easier be integrated into their individual work rhythms. For the team-leader managing the municipal care-workers is a matter of resource planning and quality-assurance through e.g. always updated care plans as these can get automatically updated over the 3G network rather than manually carried out to each care receiver. For the municipality, the concern is to provide better and even-quality services, for better flexibility in the care situation and for sharing care responsibility with other parties. CaseLine provides further examples; while the parents like to get the most out of their parental leave, the municipality's role is to educate and make sure that regulation and rules are followed.

With family calendars in general and with our two examples here, it may make more sense to see the rationality as related to the caring of the particular child/children or an elderly relative, than to shared purposes, a contrast to e.g. Neustaedter et al's. (2009) calendars within families. This does not mean that the numerous practical tasks should be ignored, but rather that they are not pending on a shared motive. They often can and will be pendent on the caring-relation with the child or elderly being cared for. This relationship and its practical tasks can still function even if the actors see themselves without a common goal and motive, in a "me-and-the-others" relationship (Raeithel 1992). Characteristic to such a relationship is exactly, according to Bardram (1998), that it is about coordination of routines, and not about sharing an understanding of motives, and in this type of case, insight into the lives of others. Indeed some of the professional actors in particular still act from a more classical, "Father's voice" rationality, emphasizing rules, etc.

The two cases explore a design axis where collaboration on one side takes place among equal peers with joint interests, whereas on the other side collaboration takes place among diverse actors with diverse interests and scope. Accordingly, in the situations we have analysed, there are three ways in which we are not dealing with calendars from the perspective of a common goal: That different rationalities are at stake, that the actors do not see themselves as being "we-in-the-world" and that they have different purposes or motives, even as seen from a more classical rationalism.

Time, Granularity and Rhythms

The essence of calendars is sharing of temporal plans and temporal rhythms. When describing the "we-and-the-others" perspective we emphasized that the sharing of these time rhythms is not a matter of an open sharing of 'everything'. We pointed out that it makes sense to look at the activities being coordinated through the shared calendar as scripted gatherings around an object, this being the care of an elderly or the parental leave regarding a particular child. The time rhythms are in both instances plans, i.e. they are resources for action (Bardram 1998). They script the actions that go into the caring for the older adult, or the leave periods, which are also actions from this perspective. There are behind these shared rhythms many levels where the actors follow their own rhythms, as discussed below. The rhythms as such address the shifts: When is somebody with the elderly, when not? What overall activities are being performed? Which parent is home with the child? When is he or she going back to work, and the child going off to day care? They provide overview and awareness, both of what is happening, and what is not.

The two cases work with different levels of time granularity. In CareCoor, both the care-workers and next-of-kin use the system ranging from some days or weeks up to years. The use of CareCoor is discontinued if the care-receiver moves (e.g. to a nursing home) or passes away. CaseLine is generally used in family-municipality collaboration for up to nine years. However, in both cases the amateur users (i.e. the family) only have to consider the own family and its situation, while the professional users (i.e. the municipality and its employees) tend to a large number of clients (i.e. older adults and parents on parental leave).

While CaseLine provides a tool for a family and the municipality to jointly project and plan activities some months into the future and even years, CareCoor works more on a day-to-day and week-to-week basis. What assistance an older adult will need in a year or even six months' time are in most circumstances considered irrelevant as no-one can foresee the future situation, while what help will be required in two days can be a main concern. The two systems' graphical representation mirror these diverse user needs. In CareCoor a matrix-based time representation is applied, where the detail-level is on activity and task level where one can navigate back and forth between different weeks and days. In CaseLine, time has been zoomed, or dragged, out to become a timeline that can be manipulated on a week, month and even year basis.

Another aspect of time-granularity can be observed in CareCoor where the care-workers did not like to communicate exact 'planned' time of arrival at an older adult's apartment to the relatives and other stakeholders but rather just 'morning', 'lunchtime', 'afternoon' etc. as they saw problems in giving away this precise information. The care-workers were concerned with making too specific promises in terms of time, and pushing their own work processes more than necessary. To the extent that the appointment involve other actors, such as volunteers or relatives, this perception of time points towards a general perspective on the side of the professional, that the time of these other actors, and not only the elderly, is worth less. It is, however, also a simple example of the kind of work that one group does to control the boundaries vis-à-vis other groups. And it simply reduces the complexity of what one group needs to know about the other. Obviously it is a specific challenge for each calendar design on such boundaries to identify what is needed and not needed in terms of granularity on the boundaries, as we discuss further below.

However, the timescale is not the only dimension of granularity. Neale et al. (2004) discuss work coupling and the granularity of dependencies and the amount of communication needed to complete a specific task. Our cases differ as CaseLine per se requires interaction, and hence has dependences with the municipality seen from a family perspective. Homecare-work in Denmark is however not (yet) designed to rely on the involvement of next-of-kin, and even if often perceived as something positive, we have encountered examples where care-workers prefer less involvement of family members in the day-to-day care of an older adult.

Sharing Across Community Boundaries

The shared, democratic approach to care made possible by CareCoor, where family members and others can assist in performing refereed care tasks can support the professional actors by for example enable a higher level of freedom in day-to-day reallocation of the care-workers in respect to emerging situations such as illness. Also, if tasks are shared and hence other actors than the homecare-workers can assist with referred tasks, this can give care-workers the time to provide other forms of support, e.g. having a cup of coffee and a chat with the older adult or preparing a meal together. The primary amateur user, the next-of-kin's, motive is mainly different forms of 'peace of mind'. This can be achieved for example through knowing that someone has been visiting one's older parent during the day, a better communication with care-workers and the possibility to help, or assist, meaningfully with the everyday care of their family member.

In CaseLine the municipal office and caseworkers represent the primary professional users, who get better control and overview of the parents' worktime and corresponding payments. A better control can help to secure law and rule compliance. This is independent of the citizens' willingness to share information (Borchorst and Bødker (2011)). However, the way in which the sandbox may be opened to a specific caseworker for a controlled time, as well as the notion of being able to share the plan/time line without fiscal and other information are examples of ways in which CaseLine supports sharing beyond the direct and open involvement of all parties.

It is evident that while the benefit or success of a particular parental leave plan is highly dependent on very specific details of e.g. ones individual's income, this kind of detail is rarely what anybody would like to share with acquaintances, whether these are in the same room or on-line. Still, sharing of experiences is happening extensively in mothers' groups and on Facebook and specialized webpages. Hence it is part of the idea to be able to share the plan with CaseLine, without personal details, for others to pick-up and use as part of a 'best practice' or for e.g. the municipality to be able to put certain recommended trajectories online. It is one of the still underexplored issues how these boundaries are drawn, and how information are controlled so that privacy is protected, and the information that is put online can be understood and used by others. With the divorce rate in e.g. Denmark, being tied to share with a spouse-turn-ex-spouse and his or her new family, detailed personal information provides similar challenges of boundary control that touches upon complicated issues of privacy, and of understanding what other users see and don't see.

Over a period of time when the two systems are in use, a range of secondary users may interact with, and/or benefit from its presence. Among the professional users that directly access the systems, are the older adult's general practitioner (CareCoor) and parents' previous employers (CaseLine). Potential secondary amateur users in CareCoor are friends and neighbours to the older adult and volunteers from different NGOs' or other organizations that assist older adults in their home. Looking at parental leave, grandparents, friends to the parents and the 'mother group' can from time to time be involved in the use of CaseLine. In both cases, it can be observed that the secondary professional users have other functions, provide and require other information from the systems compared with the primary professional users. In order to provide a coherent system, it is important that they are involved in an effective manner when this is needed. The secondary amateur users, such as neighbours, NGO's and mothers' groups to a large extent share the primary amateur users' needs and requirements, such as peace of mind, communication and learning about the situation from the systems. While exceptions exist, like a very engaged neighbour to an older adult, the secondary actors' use of the systems is mostly more ephemeral compared with the primary actors. Rogers et al. (2004) state that collaborative decision-making can be promoted through allowing stakeholder equal access to information. However, in our cases there are situations (e.g. in CaseLine where the parents are divorced or in Care-Coor where the relationship between an adult child and older parent is not harmonic) where information filters, and different granularities should be applied. In such situations, the openness and closedness of information spaces become relevant system design elements to consider (Bannon and Bødker 1997).

Drawing boundaries between places, activities, etc. is a way of reducing complexity (Star and Griesemer 1989). In the beginning of the CareCoor project, most relatives wanted to have 'ALL' information more or less real time, but many of them later started to perceive problems in a constant 'information overload'. In the design process, this led to a discussion of different message types and levels of importance. There is a need for relatives to maintain their own lives even if they have to step in and take over parts of the care for their parents. Also, as the older adult gets frailer and in need of regular, more demanding care for example due to dementia, the closest relatives might live with much fear and need 'peace of mind'-support, for example to understand what is going on in the older adults home when they are not there (Christensen and Grönvall 2011). In CaseLine, we observed that divorced parents may actually not want to know quite as much about what happens in the other home, they may prefer to rest assured that the child gets cared for when it is away, and it is indeed often part of the process of divorcing to draw such boundaries, based on a combination of trust and need-to-know-information. From both cases there was a wish for boundary control and reduced complexity. As we move outside a strict group, such as two divorced families, collaboration among diverse companies or as in our two cases—family-municipality collaboration—the notion of 'the more information the better' is challenged by the respective collaborative entities and their need or will to sometimes restrict the information provided.

In our two cases the collaboration and coordination often involve external parties such as municipal workers of various kinds, other caregivers, employers, etc. with whom it is necessary and often straight forward to share some information elements, but not all. In the case of CaseLine it was for example discussed that ex-spouse's income is not something that one might want to share with one's own current employer, even if it is relevant to the couple's (and both employer's) joint planning of the parental leave. It is also an issue for the families what kind of information and how much they want to give to the municipal case-workers, because they are not certain how their own situation will be presented best to these case-workers. The approaches used by citizens essentially relate to whether they are able to define the constellation of collaborating actors and their respective motives and artifacts.

Depending on the situation at hand, the involved stakeholders, their former experiences and current needs, the use of the two systems will be dynamic and constantly developed, similar to the observations by Lee (2005). Indeed, the same system setup deployed within different family-municipality configurations will create different system use practices over time.

Framing our discussions in this paper as primarily family calendars, is indeed not telling the whole truth. We have pointed out that there is a need for a less naïve understanding of the family calendar as such. However, our cases work entirely with calendars that are *also* work calendars. We know from the past that there are many challenges pertaining to such calendars without the complexity of having to share content with amateurs/families. However, in this paper we have chosen to focus mainly on the challenges for work calendars that arise from their function on the boundaries between work and non-work.

Conclusion and Outlook

In this paper we have used a number of perspectives and concepts coming out of computer supported cooperative *work* to address time coordination in, and with families. Our way to this has been via calendars on the boundaries between professionals, families and other amateur actors. Through this path we have come to a profound critique of many of the attempts to work with family calendars as such and the assumptions behind them: That modern family calendars, like classical groupware before them, are sometimes designed based on overly naïve assumptions regarding shared goals and common interests. We have even discussed how a different kind of rationality may be needed to understand these situations and how *cutting off*, and having peace of mind, knowing that somebody else it caring, may be just as important as knowing what is happening for these kind of calendars.

With a revitalization of other concepts and assumptions from CSCW, we have discussed how time coordination and overview can be supported, in families and on the boundaries between families and other professional and amateur actors. We have illustrated how such calendars support, share and give access to rhythms of the diverse actors' core activities at a level of granularity that may vary, depending on the involved actors. Awareness to the overall situation is the essence of the two calendar-based systems and this overview is made meaningful for all actors without being dependent on the rhythms and routines of either actor. The development of shared access models is very much a matter of negotiation on the boundaries of various activities.

Looking beyond the two cases towards the many known calendar systems, for example Outlook, allows people to send an email containing a meeting proposal, but there is no way of learning if the other person is indeed available or not. For this, telephone calls, Doodle or other tools must be used. Accordingly, across calendar systems as we know them, we envision a calendar implementation that could be enhanced if it was possible to invite 'friends' to see, and make booking requests in, an online calendar. To be able to control the sharing of one's calendar with different people over time (share for a day, a week, etc.), and with different granularity (e.g. one person can see the whole calendar and the activities at hand while other external partners can just see availability-status (i.e. busy or free) on a particular day or week) could promote collaboration, with different partners and scope over time. Additionally, to allow people to discuss activities (proposed and accepted), e.g. as a chat connected to each calendar element would allow negotiations directly related to the specific activity.

Acknowledgments We thank our collaborators and users in eGov+ and BDSI/CareCoor, Marianne Dammand Iversen and Liam Bannon for comments, CfPH and the AU center PIT.

References

Bannon, L., & Bødker S. (1997). Constructing common information spaces. In *Proceedings of the 1997 European Conference on Computer Supported Cooperative Work* (pp. 81–96). Netherlands: Kluwer.

Bardram, J. (1998). Collaboration, coordination and computer support: An activity theoretical approach to the design of computer supported cooperative work. *Ph. D. thesis*'. 27(533). (DAIMI PB).

Begole, J. B., Tang, J. C., Smith, R. B., & Yankelovich, N. (2002). Work rhythms: analyzing visualizations of awareness histories of distributed groups. In *Proceedings of the 2002 ACM Conference on Computer Supported Cooperative Work* (pp. 334–343). ACM Press.

Bødker, S., Ehn, P., Knudsen, J., Kyng, M., & Madsen, K. (1988). Computer support for cooperative design (invited paper). In *Proceedings of the 1988 ACM Conference on Computer-Supported Cooperative Work* (pp. 377–394). ACM Press.

Bohøj, M., Borchorst, N. G., Bouvin, N. O., Bødker, S., & Zander, P.-O. (2010). Timeline collaboration. In *Proceedings of the 2010 SIGCHI Conference on Human Factors in Computing Systems* (pp. 523–532). ACM Press.

Borchorst, N., & Bødker, S. (2011). You probably shouldn't give them too much information—Supporting citizen-government collaboration. In *Proceedings of the 2011 European Conference on Computer Supported Cooperative Work* (pp. 173–192), London: Springer.

Borchorst, N., Bødker, S., & Zander, P.-O. (2009). The boundaries of participatory citizenship. In *Proceedings of the 2009 European Conference on Computer Supported Cooperative Work* (pp. 1–20), London: Springer.

Bossen, C., Christensen, L. R., Grönvall, E., & Vestergaard, L. S. (2013). CareCoor: Augmenting the coordination of cooperative home care work. *International Journal of Medical Informatics*, *82*(5), 189–199. doi:10.1016/j.ijmedinf.2012.10.005.

Christensen, L. R., & Grönvall, E. (2011). Challenges and opportunities for collaborative technologies for home care work. In *Proceedings of the 2011 European Conference on Computer Supported Cooperative Work* (pp. 61–80), London: Springer.

Clases, C., & Wehner, T. (2002). Steps across the border—cooperation, knowledge production and systems design. *Computer Supported Cooperative Work (CSCW)*, *11*(1–2), 39–54.

Clement, A., & Wagner, I. (1995). Fragmented exchange: disarticulation and the need for regionalized communication spaces. In *Proceedings of the 1995 European Conference on Computer-Supported Cooperative Work* (pp. 33–49), Kluwer.

Crabtree, A., Hemmings, T., Rodden, T., & Mariani, J. (2003). Informing the development of calendar systems for domestic use. In *Proceedings of the 2003 European Conference on Computer Supported Cooperative Work* (pp. 119–138), London: Springer.

Doodle (2012). Doodle Webpage. Retrieved 8 Nov, 2012, from http://doodle.com/.

Egger, E., & Wagner, I. (1992). Time-management: a case for CSCW. In *Proceedings of the 1992 ACM Conference on Computer-Supported Cooperative Work* (pp. 249–256), ACM Press.

Elliot, K., & Carpendale, S. (2005). *Awareness and coordination: A calendar for families*. Calgary: University of Calgary.

Ganoe, C. H., Somervell, J. P., Neale, D. C., Isenhour, P. L., Carroll, J. M., Rosson, M. B., & McCrickard, D. S. (2003). Classroom BRIDGE: Using collaborative public and desktop timelines to support activity awareness. In *Proceedings of the ACM symposium on User interface software and technology* (pp. 21–30), ACM Press.

Grönvall, E., Marti, P., Pollini, A., Rullo, A., & Bertelsen, O. W. (2005). Palpable time for heterogeneous care communities. In *Proceedings of the 4th Decennial Conference on Critical Computing: Between Sense and Sensibility* (pp. 149–152), ACM Press.

Grudin, J. (1994). Groupware and social dynamics: Eight challenges for developers. *Communications of ACM, 37*(1), 92–105.

Lee, C. (2005). Between chaos and routine: Boundary negotiating artifacts in collaboration. In *Proceedings of the 2005 European Conference on Computer Supported Cooperative Work*, (pp. 387–406), Netherlands: Springer.

Mark, G., & Poltrock, S. (2003). Shaping technology across social worlds: Groupware adoption in a distributed organization. In *Proceedings of the 2003 ACM SIGGROUP Conference on Supporting Group Work* (pp. 284–293), ACM Press.

Markopoulos, P., Romero, N., Baren, J. v., IJsselsteijn, W., Ruyter, B. d., & Farshchian, B. (2004). Keeping in touch with the family: home and away with the ASTRA awareness system. In *Proceedings of the CHI '04 EA on Human Factors in Computing Systems* (pp. 1351–1354), ACM Press.

Neale, D. C., Carroll, J. M., & Rosson, M. B. (2004). Evaluating computer-supported cooperative work: models and frameworks. In *Proceedings of the 2004 ACM Conference on Computer Supported Cooperative Work* (pp. 112–121), ACM Press.

Neustaedter, C., Brush, A. J. B., & Greenberg, S. (2009). The calendar is crucial: Coordination and awareness through the family calendar. *ACM Transactions on Computer-Human Interaction, 16*(1), 1–48.

Noddings, N. (1984). *Caring: A feminine approach to ethics and moral education*. Berkeley: University of California Press.

Odom, W., Zimmerman, J., & Forlizzi, J. (2010). Designing for dynamic family structures: Divorced families and interactive systems. In *Proceedings of the 2010 ACM Conference on Designing Interactive Systems* (pp. 151–160), ACM Press.

Palen, L., & Grudin, J. (2003). Discretionary adoption of group support software: Lessons from calendar applications. In: *Implementing Collaboration Technologies in Industry* (pp. 159–180), Springer.

Raeithel, A. (1992). Semiotic self-regulation and work. An activity-theoretical foundation for design. In C. Floyd, H. Züllighoven, R. Budde, & R. Kiel-Slawik (Eds.), *Software Development and Reality Construction* (pp. 391–415), Cambridge: Cambridge University Press.

Reddy, M., Dourish, P., & Pratt, W. (2006). Temporality in medical work: Time also matters. *Computer Supported Cooperative Work (CSCW), 15*(1), 29–53.

Rogers, Y., Hazlewood, W., Blevis, E., & Lim, Y.-K. (2004). Finger talk: Collaborative decision-making using talk and fingertip interaction around a tabletop display. In *CHI '04 EA on Human Factors in Computing Systems* (pp. 1271–1274), ACM Press.

Saslis-Lagoudakis, G., Cheverst, K., Dix, A., Fitton, D., & Rouncefield, M. (2006). Hermes@Home: Supporting awareness and intimacy between distant family members. In *Proceedings of the 2006 Australia conference on Computer-Human Interaction* (pp. 23–30), ACM Press.

Schulz, E. (2010). The long-term care system for the elderly in Denmark. ENEPRI Research Report, 73.

Star, S. L., & Griesemer, J. R. (1989). Institutional ecology, 'translations' and boundary objects: Amateurs and professionals in Berkeley's Museum of Vertebrate Zoology, 1907–1939. *Social Studies of Science, 19*(3), 387–420.

Venkatesh, A. (1996). Computers and other interactive technologies for the home. *Communications of ACM, 39*(12), 47–54.

Yarosh, S., & Abowd, G. D. (2011). Mediated parent-child contact in work-separated families. In *Proceedings of the SIGCHI Conference on Human Factors in Computing Systems* (pp. 1185–1194), ACM Press.

Yarosh, S., Chew, Y. C., & Abowd, G. D. (2009). Supporting parent–child communication in divorced families. *International Journal of Human-Computer Studies, 67*(2), 192–203.

The Collaborative Work of Heritage: Open Challenges for CSCW

Luigina Ciolfi

Abstract This paper discusses seminal contributions by and current open challenges for CSCW in the study of cultural heritage practices. It provides an overview of key issues relating to social and cooperative interactions—particularly around the design and use of technology—at heritage sites that have emerged in CSCW, and pertaining the conduct of visitors, the design and evaluation of interactive installations for guidance and access, and the creation of novel artistic performances. The paper then presents a set of open challenges for future CSCW work, particularly regarding the very re-definition of heritage in light of the social and collaborative practices that have arisen in recent years within the museum and heritage professionals community, and the emergence of new roles and practices for organisations, staff, visitors and related stakeholders. The paper aims at consolidating the range of contributions that CSCW has made to cultural heritage and at outlining key issues and challenges for future research in this domain.

Introduction

Cultural heritage institutions, museums in particular, have long been a domain of study in human-centred computing from a variety of different perspectives: from usability studies of museum technologies, to the design of innovative interactive exhibits, information displays and fully immersive installations. Within this landscape, cultural heritage has been a relevant domain for CSCW as well, with particular regard for how groups and communities approach heritage sites and for how technology can mediate this. The relevance of cultural heritage for CSCW researchers has further increased as the identity of heritage institutions as

L. Ciolfi (✉)
Communication and Computing Research Centre,
Sheffield Hallam University, Sheffield, UK
e-mail: L.Ciolfi@shu.ac.uk

O. W. Bertelsen et al. (eds.), *ECSCW 2013: Proceedings of the 13th European Conference on Computer Supported Cooperative Work, 21–25 September 2013, Paphos, Cyprus*, DOI: 10.1007/978-1-4471-5346-7_5,

information collection and delivery units began to be questioned and challenged, and a new socially inclusive and participative idea of heritage became widespread (Simon 2010).

Museums, in particular, were seen in the past as didactic institutions allowing for very limited overt interactivity and focusing more on their holdings than on their visitors (Hooper-Greenhill 1992). The tradition of visitor studies contributed to change this mindset by actually investigating what people did in museums, and how an exhibit was perceived and understood, thus acknowledging the importance of visitors in the life of heritage institutions. CSCW researchers further developed this work by conducting in-depth studies of museums as settings for social interaction, collaboration and co-participation, whereby visitors' practices are illuminated and detailed with regard to their relationship with each other and with what is exhibited (see for example vom Lehn et al. 2001, which we will discuss in greater detail in the following section).

However, museums and exhibitions are only one example of cultural heritage institutions where a CSCW focus can unearth knowledge: if we think of heritage as the domain that collects and preserves what people and communities value as representative of their history, identity and values (Giaccardi 2011), the range of places of heritage worthy of investigation extends to cities, historic buildings, open-air parks and other sites, that groups and communities visit and frequent for leisure, study or work. Other heritage sites, such as city quarters, landmark buildings and outdoor sites also represent historical, political and social values, therefore practices of sharing and collaborative creation and interpretation occur there. In this light, several examples of CSCW research in these settings are undoubtedly of relevance to the heritage domain.

Whereas CSCW has produced key contributions to understanding and defining cultural heritage, it is not quite continuing to do so at a time when heritage is being redefined in social terms, and when conceptual and practical approaches to curating and communicating heritage have developed a distinct affinity with themes of coordination, awareness and cooperative sense-making that are core to. In recent years, much CSCW work in and for heritage sites has largely being limited to case-study exercises whereby themes that have previously been unearthed within the discipline, for example the nuances of instances of social interactions in experiencing heritage, are echoed and/or confirmed through new empirical data sets. Other exemplars of work simply utilize heritage sites as a backdrop for the evaluation of multi-user technologies, however without delivering novel contributions to the understanding of heritage and of novel social and collaborative dynamics occurring.

While much of this body of work is well executed and adds knowledge to the existing stream of research, it has not produced significant new insights on heritage itself: how is the notion of heritage changing in light of new organisational approaches to involving visitors? How is technology playing a different role in this respect?

We do feel that the scope for CSCW for producing novel and seminal work in the heritage domain is greater even than it has been in the past, and that some current themes of research on social and cooperative work in curating, presenting and interpreting heritage being explored in related disciplines should feature also in CSCW and be approached through the field's concepts and sensitivities.

Museum professionals themselves have developed sensitivities for audience-centric work in museums with the goal of increasing participation. As Simon puts it:

> [An audience-centric approach] requires staff members to trust that visitors can and will find the content that is most useful to them. When staff members put their confidence in visitors in this way, it signals that visitors' preconceptions, interests, and choices are good and valid in the world of the museum. And that makes visitors feel like the owners of their experiences (Simon 2010).

This perspective on the relationship between heritage institutions, their staff and their visitors opens a wide range of possibilities for the study of how complex ecologies of collaboration are currently redefining our very notion of heritage. Very little work thus far has studied this in depth, and a great many issues are left to be investigated. We believe that this very reconfiguration of heritage offers CSCW open challenges and opportunities for providing in-depth accounts of such practices in ways that have not been adopted by other disciplines.

From this premise, the goal of this paper is twofold: firstly, to highlight and consolidate through a review the significant contributions made thus far by CSCW with regard to cultural heritage and to reflect on the potential of other current work to be developed further, and secondly—and most importantly—to propose a set of future challenges linked to current developments in heritage studies and heritage management practice that can inspire and encourage novel developments within our field.

In the following sections, we present a review of seminal CSCW contributions to cultural heritage, discussing their importance in defining an understanding of the domain. We will then propose a set of current and future heritage themes and, finally, a discussion of the challenges and open questions linked to them.

CSCW and Cultural Heritage: Key Contributions

In this section we provide an overview of key CSCW contributions to the cultural heritage domain, highlighting how this research has helped shed light on crucial issues such as visitor experience and the potential of interactive technology in developing our very understanding of heritage.

We see this work as addressing three major interconnected themes: firstly, visitor activities and social interactions at heritage sites; secondly, the design, deployment and evaluation of heritage technologies in 'companion' roles, such as aiding the interpretation of an exhibit or site and for visitor guidance; thirdly, the creation of interactive artistic installations that are not mediating access to existing museum or exhibition holdings, but that are themselves newly realised heritage artefacts (e.g. interactive art and performance).

These three themes of CSCW research are quite distinct given that they concentrate on different issues, questions and goals, and as to where the main contribution lies (e.g. documentation of practices versus design guidelines, for example), although they are closely interlinked for they are often connected by conceptual and methodological approaches and together they depict the multi-faceted aspects of experiencing heritage.

Visitor Practices

The work conducted on understanding visitor conduct at heritage sites and the social and collaborative aspect of experiencing heritage unearthed the nuances of social interactions, communication and cooperation within groups and between individual visitors (vom Lehn et al. 2001). Visitors were observed in naturalistic situations while exploring exhibits either alone or in groups, and their physical and communicative activities detailed. These studies largely utilised the technique of video-based observations, allowing for the subsequent moment-by-moment analysis of data capturing visitors' activities (vom Lehn 2010).

One of the key findings in this body of work is that, even if a certain museum or gallery did not explicitly encourage social interaction and participation, these occurred naturally in visitor practices. Museums, exhibitions and other heritage sites are therefore inherently social and a focus on lone actors, without considering the broader physical and social context of their actions, is limited when attempting to truly understand the visitor experience of exhibits.

Not only interpersonal interaction takes place regularly in heritage settings, but others are essential part of how the experience of heritage is configured: "The visual, vocal, and tactile conduct of others provides resources for looking, seeing, and experiencing the various exhibits" (vom Lehn et al. 2001, p. 206).

Moreover, behaviours emerging among groups of visitors aim at both maintaining coherence to the visit as an individual pursuit and at supporting the group experience: work is put in by group members in exploring exhibits in a desired way, but also in keeping group cohesion and in keeping interpersonal interaction at a desirable level while visiting.

Visitors pay attention to exhibits but also to others, and key to a positive experience for them is the possibility to gain access both to exhibits and to others for conversations, and to maintain awareness of the overall environment and of other people.

In other words, visitors 'work' to keep things social and endeavour to make interpretation social through verbal discussions, gestural illustrations, show and tell-like interactions, etc. This happens also with strangers when casual encounters and casual interactions occur both verbally and non-verbally (through hand gestures, positioning of one's body, gaze, etc.).

Another finding is that dwell time in itself is an incomplete indicator of engagement, although it had been utilized as key measure of engagement with exhibits (and often in isolation) in early literature in both HCI and museum studies. Longer dwell time in front of an exhibit does not necessarily equal to positive and prolonged engagement with it; conversely, short dwell time does not equal to lack of engagement. Social and contextual factors need to be considered as well as dwell time for understanding how visitors establish connections with what is on display. Similarly, that of engagement with heritage is a nuanced notion: as length of time is not a univocal measure, engagement can also be more or less active (e.g. certain "passive" visitors approaching exhibits are differently engaged with them), central or peripheral, etc. (Heath et al. 2002).

These insights significantly moved beyond the body of work on visitor studies that was very much focused on single instances of behavior rather than socially situated conduct, such as—for example—Veron and Levasseur's framework of visitor typologies entirely based on spatial movement and on "boxing" visitors into fixed and strictly individual models (Veron and Levasseur 1983) that has influenced the design of model-based technologies such as certain types of adaptive guides (see for example, Marti 2001): similar instances feature in a lot of HCI research but were never truly successfully deployed in heritage settings.

A particular aspect of heritage experience is its educational value. Structured and informal in museums and other heritage sites have been important topics in the literature, particularly within Computer-Supported Collaborative Learning, with particular attention to understanding how learning occurs and can be facilitated in heritage settings and to how educational activities take place (Marr et al. 2003; Hemmings et al. 1997; see also Hornecker 2010). From this body of empirical work, implications have been drawn particularly for the design of educational technologies.

The findings of the CSCW body of research on visitor practices have been influential specifically to the design and deployment of interactive technology for heritage settings. The nuanced understanding of how heritage is experienced provides guidance on what technology design should be mindful and supportive of. Conversely, a detailed understanding of how technology can interplay with a visitor's interpersonal interactions and relationships with an exhibit is essential for good heritage experiences.

A crucial insight from studies of visitor activities in terms of technology design is how interactions around exhibits are more successful whereby there are opportunities for people to be "drawn in", possibilities of physical accommodation around an exhibit, and an open nature of the exhibition itself in terms of commentary and interpretation. Opportunities for interactions with companions and strangers should be supported and encouraged. Overall, variable and contingent forms of interaction around an exhibit should be facilitated (Heath et al. 2002).

Tightly linked with this work is the stream of research on how technology mediates the visitor experience. Technology (when present) at a heritage site can play an ambiguous role: that of facilitating such interactions, but also that of encumbering them. Therefore, many of the findings and design sensibilities from visitor practices studies are resonated in research regarding the evaluation and/or introduction of heritage technologies.

Heritage Technologies in Use

Another set of significant CSCW contributions regards the study of technology use in heritage settings, whether an extant technology or a newly designed one. This work is focused on the socio-technical aspects of the use of individual and collaborative technologies (e.g. audioguides, touch screens, etc.) and on the design of intentionally collaborative technologies that encourage and often reward cooperative interaction. In the latter case, the research features a specific effort to *design* collaborative technologies and understanding of their use.

An important difference from the previous theme, although equal attention to visitor practices can be found in this body of work—and indeed there are many connections between the two themes of research in terms of agenda, authorship and approach—is a greater attention to technological mediation, and also a stronger focus on the potential for visitors to take on not just the role of spectators of heritage sites, but also that of active participants by providing them with a range of opportunities for interaction with the exhibits and with others: for example, the interactive guidebook "Sotto Voce" (Grinter et al. 2002) provided visitors to a historic house with additional content and the opportunity of sharing it with others via a shared audio mechanism. In certain cases, visitors are also allowed to make direct contributions to an exhibit, for example by means of written comments, audio recordings, photos, etc.: in an exhibition at the Hunt Museum (Ireland) called "Re-Tracing the Past" (Ferris et al. 2004), visitors were invited to record interpretations of museum objects that were never conclusively interpreted; in the "Secret Life of Objects" at the Helsinki Design Museum (Finland), visitors and staff were invited to leave annotations on digital representations of a set of historic Finnish design pieces (Salgado et al. 2009).

Researchers have studied the physical engagement with technology (for example the effectiveness or engagement value of certain interaction styles and modalities versus others), have developed the know-how on how to augment a heritage site through technology in mindful ways, and also have evaluated how different technologies (e.g. desktop, mobile, tangible, etc.) can be of use in particular settings, from enclosed galleries to historic buildings and outdoor sites. Many examples feature studies of novel technologies that have then become commercially widely available, from touch screens and interactive projections, to—more recently—mobile devices, mixed and augmented reality, and multi-touch tabletops (Grinter et al. 2002; Schnädelbach et al. 2002; Galani 2003; Hornecker 2008).

Such studies of collaborative use of novel and existing technologies in situ have also led to detailed guidelines for the design of in-gallery systems and other public interactive systems and, importantly, have demonstrated through empirical evidence the shortcomings of technology introduced without careful consideration of the social nature, use and physical qualities of a particular heritage environment (Hornecker and Stifter 2006). Moreover, this work furthered understanding of collaborative interactions around heritage as mediated and not by technology and of the re-configurations around technology use and appropriation (Heath and vom Lehn 2010; vom Lehn et al. 2007).

A main finding is that physical design of technologies—similarly to that of exhibitions—affects group experience in terms of accommodation and access points and therefore in terms of social interaction. In her study of visitor interactions with the "Jurascopes" at the Berlin Museum of Natural History (periscope-like devices overlaying digital 3D animations over real-life dinosaur skeletons and linked to a related multi-touch screen console), Hornecker observed how the physical accommodation of hands-on interactions by more than one individual is linked significantly to dwell time and to spontaneous social interactions, and there is a balance struck between the occurrence of cooperative interactions versus lone ones, and trade offs of collaboration versus individual use (Hornecker 2010). Conversely, in studies of multi-touch tabletop installations (such as Hinrichs and Carpendale's field study of the "Collection Viewer" at Vancouver Aquarium) it has been shown that physical interaction is influenced by the social context, the presence of others and the opportunities for non technologically-mediated interaction (Hinrichs and Carpendale 2011).

Furthermore, group interactions can present very different qualities: for example in the case of families where complex practices of directing, scaffolding and facilitation take place between parents and children in ways that would not occur within groups of a different nature (Hornecker and Nicol 2012). Encouraging these types of interaction by means of technology can also be part of broader cultural and social policy relating to heritage, as it happens for example in Japan where family visits to museums are seen as ways to build cultural capital and technology support to them is encouraged (Hope et al. 2009).

Collaborative interactions vary not only depending on the type of visitors and groups, but also on the specific configuration of technology: for example, in mixed reality visiting co-experiences involving both located and co-located visitors, interactions are co-present but also remote, occurring within a digital space representing certain features of the heritage setting as well as in the physical world. The "George Square" system allowed visitors exploring a city to share their location and media annotations to others, both co-located and distant (Brown et al. 2005); the co-visiting system deployed at the Mackintosh Interpretation Centre at the Lighthouse in Glasgow (Brown et al. 2003) allowed physical visitors to interact with "digital" visitors exploring online a VR representation of the exhibit. These examples of literature have thus explored issues of awareness of others, casual interaction with strangers and accommodation of collaborative actions both between co-located and remote visitors.

Another significant body of CSCW work documents the design of and instances of interaction around multiple technological components that are distributed within a heritage environment (Fraser et al. 2003; Hindmarsh et al. 2005; Ciolfi and

McLoughlin 2012). In particular settings, "assemblies" of interlinked interactive artefacts, rather than standalone installations or independent mobile applications, can best sustain how visitors explore, make sense and relate to a heritage site. Besides the challenges of technically realizing an engaging assembly, this work investigates how coherence in the visit is achieved, and sustained engagement and group cohesion can be supported by facilitating the awareness of others across assembly components and by understanding the relationship the visitors establish with the components, with the assembly as a whole and with the site.

Yet another subset of research pays particular attention to technological guides (the study and design of which is a long-standing exercise also in the field of HCI), one of the longest-living types of technology to be used at heritage sites. Findings on the effects of individual guides (particularly audio guides) in disrupting social aspects of the visitor experience and in forcefully shaping the trajectory of the visit have been widely documented in museum studies literature (see for example Gammon and Burch 2008), and have been addressed within CSCW through designs including social elements to the interaction such as "eavesdropping", e.g. allowing pairs of visitors to hear the audio selected by their companion (Aoki et al. 2002), and tagging and sharing facilities of what the guide provides individual visitors to companions and larger groups (Cosley et al. 2009; O'Hara et al. 2007).

A final subset of contributions worth mentioning focuses on collaborative interactions in online heritage resources, particularly regarding practices of information retrieval and exchange. Digital repositories of heritage content can be seen as "virtual exhibits" that can be visited without a physical presence, with Second Life having been one of the early platforms to experiment with "virtual" displays of collections (Urban et al. 2007), as well as enhanced tools for archiving and recording used by visitors and by heritage staff alike, as adopted by the Spurlock Museum (USA) since the mid 1990's (Marty 1999). This body of work is significant as heritage institutions are increasingly offering to the public digital exhibitions as well as their physical holdings.

Interactive Installations as Heritage Artefacts

A third and final theme we review here is that of the creation of technologically-enhanced art and performance pieces, whereby the technology is not aimed simply at the interpretation or documentation of what is displayed in an exhibit, a building or a museum room, but it is part of the exhibit itself—for example in the case of interactive art and performance.

In this case, the technology is (part of) the heritage artifact that people come to experience, and this heritage artefact *per se* embodies digital and interactive elements. Here the focus of CSCW research is on the relationship not only between visitors and between visitors and exhibits, but also between the artist/creator and the public: issues referring to the artist's practice are paramount when studying the role of the artist/designer in engendering particular interactions and experiences.

Seminal CSCW research on this theme is represented, for example, by studies of the low-tech artistic pieces created by artist Jason Cleverly that have been exhibited at several galleries worldwide (Hindmarsh et al. 2005). The "Ghost Ship" installation presented the painted scene of an ocean cruise liner with a wooden façade. Video-linked portholes on the ship featured the faces of visitors that were captured on a "deck" situated in another area of the exhibition. In their study of "Ghost Ship" during its exhibition at the SOFA fair in Chicago, Hindmarsh et al. observed how, through its own creative design, the piece facilitated the visitors' own creative practices—such as planned pictures of themselves aboard the Ship to show others—as well as social interactions in the proximity of the exhibit. The artist can design to provide engagement, surprise and humour for individual visitors and groups.

Another significant contribution relating to this theme is Benford et al. (2011) framework for orchestrating performance and spectator experience with the creation of artistic technological interventions. By ethnographically examining the practice of the professional artist group Blast Theory in creating and exhibiting interactive installations such as "Day of the Figurines" (a multi-media experience involving participants in the life of a fictional down over 24 days), the authors argue that the orchestration of positive visitor experiences should be mindful of issues of time around the discovery of a piece and the revelation of aspects of the piece itself, the trajectories of these discoveries, and the transitions among different parts of the exhibits (Benford et al. 2011).

Other studies have been conducted on drawing insights from interactive exhibitions for designing the spectator experience (Reeves 2011), public leisure indoors and outdoors (Flintham et al. 2011; O'Hara et al. 2007), and immersive experiences in general (Robertson et al. 2006).

These examples feature interactive collaborative technology that constitutes a newly created, purposely designed interactive heritage artifact for public and social use. This links to current discussions on heritage that is "born digital" and open questions on its authorship, status and preservation challenges (Kalay et al. 2008), as well as on heritage that is seen as "natively" created by visitors and participants by means of extensive use of media platforms (Iversen and Smith 2011).

Through this review of key CSCW contributions to the domain of cultural heritage, we can see how the focus of our field has spanned from describing the finer details of visitor experiences in heritage settings, to introducing design approaches and guidelines, to other issues including artistic performance and digital heritage. These substantial contributions have been produced alongside countless other exemplars of work focused on technology development and deployment and on a small scale case-study format, rather than on high level issues, of which a full review would be beyond the scope of this paper (see, for example, Simarro Cabrera et al. 2005; Fuks et al. 2012).

The work that we have chosen to review in this paper constitutes in our opinion the main body of foundational CSCW knowledge on heritage, for it illuminates fundamental issues that must be understood when studying the domain and the role and potential of technology there. Although some of the examples discussed above are rather situated by their authors within a "leisure" framework, they do however provide key insights on heritage in our opinion, and particularly on informal settings that are less frequently studied than museums and galleries.

Despite the significant contributions outlined above, the stream of seminal research on defining and articulating new heritage practices has recently somewhat "disappeared" from CSCW, or rather it has not maintained the same level of conceptual development that can be seen in previous work, being more focused on small scale case-studies of technology introduction and evaluation. In other words, studies of collaborative uses of heritage technologies are still being conducted, but the furthering of CSCW-relevant themes in heritage has become less substantial. While the number of technology designs to be deployed and tested in heritage settings (museums, galleries, city spaces, etc.) is constant if not increasing, we see little in this work as yet that is aimed at furthering the understanding and re-definition of collaborative heritage practices beyond the simple recognition of heritage sites as a useful setting for the deployment of collaborative technology.

Nonetheless, if we compare this current work on heritage produced within CSCW to ongoing research in heritage and museum studies, we can see that there is greater potential for the exploration of current issues from a CSCW frame and that this potential should be embraced.

Recently, a notable surge of interest has emerged from the museum management and education community regarding social and collaborative technologies in museums, also due to the low costs and minimal technical training needed to employ social media platforms for blogging, social networking and crowdsourcing that have become widely available and well known by visitors and staff alike. The number of initiatives led by heritage institutions and interest groups involving the public in collaborative activities both offline and online has increased very significantly. Researchers at the boundary between heritage studies and technology design have explored emergent issues of cooperative authorship, shared interpretation and collaborative design that are also important to CSCW (see Petrelli et al. 2013); Giaccardi 2012.

In this current scenario, more work is needed in understanding the ecologies of collaborative practices in heritage that have emerged of late by the initiative of both institutions and visitors, and that have led to complex patterns of collaboration and cooperation in interpreting, communicating and creating heritage.

Reviewing existing work and pointing out how CSCW has filled gaps in the knowledge and understanding of heritage practices indicates where further work is needed, moreover an awareness of current work in heritage studies points out new areas where significant contributions can be made.

In the following section we will discuss in greater detail what we identify as the open challenges that CSCW can and should embrace more thoroughly in future research.

Discussing Open Challenges for CSCW

What can CSCW bring to the current lively area of research on the social and collaborative aspects of heritage? To give a better sense of what kind of activities are currently taking place in the heritage domain (and thus to articulate current challenges), we will illustrate one example of the work that a major museum is conducting through collaborative and social technologies.

The Victoria & Albert (V&A) decorative arts Museum in London, one of the world's most important heritage institutions in terms of holdings and number of visitors,[1] has developed for many years a dedicated media strategy to regularly involve communities of decorative arts enthusiasts and of passionate museum visitors into their exhibits (V&A 2010). This has been extended beyond a rich web presence and accessible on-line catalogues (that have been maintained by the museum for over a decade and are used by approximately 25 million visitors a year) by the embracing of approaches such as crowdsourcing through social media to drive some of their flagship exhibitions.

One such recent initiative is "V&A Weddings",[2] whereby the V&A's existing collection of wedding dresses, ornaments and wedding-related objects currently scattered across different departments of the museum (fashion, jewellery, etc.) got to be exhibited from 2009 in a "themed" way online (e.g. before any such physical exhibition yet existed). As well as having curated and created the online exhibition, the V&A has made "Weddings" open to contributors by means of public social media platforms, such as for example the photo sharing service Flickr, where people have been submitting their wedding images to the V&A "Weddings" pool for years. The museum had been recruiting participants in this initiative throughout the web, on both personal websites/blogs and mainstream media.[3] The material submitted by the public is curated online by museum staff, but also open to commentary by visitors,[4] and made available for fair re-use by other not for profit initiatives.

The most interesting contributions provided by online visitors were, after negotiation, acquired by the museum for their online collection catalogue (Fig. 1).

Finally, "Weddings" has become an actual physical exhibition, titled "Unveiled", that has travelled in Australia, New Zealand and Singapore during 2012 with plans for the exhibition final homecoming in London in the near future. "Weddings" is now a permanent microsite on the V&A main website, together with other similar projects that the museum has spearheaded over the years.

---

[1] http://www.vam.ac.uk

[2] http://www.vam.ac.uk/page/w/weddings

[3] See for example: http://www.wornthrough.com/2009/04/17/va-wedding-photos-site-needs-you/ and http://www.dailymail.co.uk/home/you/article-1285624/The-V-A-launched-database-wedding-fashion.html.

[4] http://www.flickr.com/groups/va_museum

Fig. 1 Contributions by online visitors now feature in the "V&A Weddings" photo gallery, besides V&A holdings (*Source* http://www.vam.ac.uk/page/w/weddings/)

This simple example shows how a strategy for collaboratively accessing, exhibiting and opening up heritage holdings and collections to visitors and contributors online and offline has been deployed by the V&A as part of a larger vision for public engagement and collaboration with stakeholders, that includes online communication and other resources (such as, for example, open source labels[5]) for certain parts of their collection.

This initiative is not an exception: many other heritage institutions (museums, historical sites, industrial heritage institutions, city and town centres, etc.) have adopted similar ways of cooperatively building and documenting their holdings. Other examples include the Brooklyn Museum's "Split Second—Indian Paintings" exhibition,[6] whereby visitors were invited to explore the museum's collection of Indian paintings online and were asked to express their reaction to what

---

[5] http://www.vam.ac.uk/b/blog/digital-media-va/open-sourcing-digital-labels

[6] https://www.brooklynmuseum.org/opencollection/labs/splitsecond/

they saw by commenting on a painting in their own words, rating its appeal and choosing one over another. This open-access activity online was followed by a physical exhibition at the museum of the set of paintings that generated the most dynamic responses together with a visualization of the accompanying data. Thus, the online visitors' reactions became part of the exhibition as well.

A final example we bring to bear is "It's Elemental",[7] an online community heritage initiative promoted by the Chemical Heritage Foundation, a small museum in Philadelphia (USA), where students were invited to submit short videos linked to each element of the periodic table. Almost 700 videos are now stored in an online archive that is open to comments. In this case, the collection and the discussion are housed completely online and not on the physical premises of the museum, although this resource is being used for educational activities that the Chemical Heritage Foundation conducts in schools and community centres.

The strategies put in place by many institutions and community groups to foster the social aspect of heritage access and interpretation lead in our opinion to several important open challenges for CSCW research. First of all, we must refer back to the notion of "work", and to the detailed articulation of what happens in the interaction within socio technical systems that is core to CSCW: the work performed by heritage professionals in coordinating, mediating and facilitating online and offline interactions, such as those occurring in the example of "Weddings", requires detailed study and a focus on unearthing situated practices in a changing organizational, physical and cultural context. While much work has been done on understanding visitors, there is a need to focus also on staff and to study their practices in depth. Curating an exhibition, presenting opportunities for visitor engagement, creating educational activities in heritage institutions have acquired different connotations with a view of heritage that is open and participative: the dialogue and interaction between museum professionals and visitors needs investigation and CSCW is ideally placed to gain a deep understanding of such work in the new reality of participative heritage.

Some work within the broader human-centred computing field has begun to explore the role of visitor contributions, albeit a limited way, through the use of interactive technology. While Cosley et al. (2009) see such forms of visitor participation akin to guestbook entries, in our opinion they can be seen as attempts to build on the re-conceptualisation of heritage as being cooperatively created as observed by, among others, Giaccardi and Palen (2008) and Oomen and Arovo (2011). Crucially, this view of heritage is not only open to visitors' dialogical interaction with heritage, but to co-creation. Further work should be conducted with attention to the reconfiguration of roles and organisations in this context. As the possibilities for visitor interactions with heritage have broadened, there is also a need to extend CSCW's nuanced understanding of visitors to include practices of study, work, apprenticeship, voluntary participation, etc., and not simply leisure or informal learning.

[7] http://www.chemheritage.org/discover/online-resources/its-elemental/index.aspx

Furthermore, it is important to pay attention to the formal and informal communities that are created around heritage, to how they come together (whether, for example, following local initiatives in support of a heritage site, or bottom-up through online participation) and to how they take advantage of, share and create heritage. Studying how the material that comes to document a collection or an exhibit is collaboratively generated by a community, with different perceptions of ownership, interpretation and meaning, is key in this respect. Related issues beginning to be recognized are how authority and expertise are perceived and sometimes challenged (Thom-Santelli et al. 2010), how value is attributed to newly-created heritage and embraced by a community (Giaccardi 2011), and how informal communities can generate alternative shared narratives around heritage holdings through the use of their own mobile phones and mainstream media platforms (see Weilenmann et al. 2013). All these issues have been touched upon by recent work, but they need to be substantially expanded and systematically investigated.

In this scenario of change in the heritage domain, we can see that a range of issues is open to investigation for CSCW researchers, studying the use of online and offline technological mediums, and also how communication unfolds between different groups and communities. Other strands of work that CSCW has produced on understanding ecologies of online and on-site collaboration can also be extended to the heritage domain, for example when investigating the transition from web platforms to a physical exhibition and vice versa. Existing studies of organisations at work can also be extended by looking at collaboration not just between visitors, but also between visitors, staff and other stakeholders.

We summarise the range of current open challenges for CSCW in studying cultural heritage alongside three interlinked strands:

- The work of visitors: the practice of visiting heritage sites has evolved, including also the presence of new technological tools for sensemaking and participation. Moreover, we see new forms of social visiting experiences. There is already a substantial body of knowledge on this in CSCW that, however, needs to be extended and expanded to investigate the new forms of interactions for visitors that the heritage domain is embracing. Visitors are also increasingly proactive contributors to heritage, and their new role needs understanding. Visitors are also not necessarily leisure-driven, as the range of activities made available to them is expanding, so our understanding of the visit needs greater specificity.
- The work of curators and facilitators: existing work does not offer much on this, it is thus a gap to be filled and particularly so as heritage professionals are becoming key in mediating communication and participation among different stakeholders. Their role has changed from that of providers of authoritative content, or simply that of guides, to that of conversation partners in the interpretation process. Curating is also becoming a collaborative practice online and offline, as we saw in "Weddings" and the other examples described earlier.

- The work of communities: communities of interest around heritage (with different degrees of formality and training) are increasingly defining and taking ownership of what is of value for them, thus defining and reconfiguring heritage. From cases where an established institution and a community of enthusiasts work together to consolidate and communicate heritage to a wider public—for example the successful "Saving Bletchley Park" campaign in the UK[8] where the work of the British codebreakers during the Second World War has been brought to public attention and recognition—to examples where ordinary citizens create an informal group for the preservation of what they consider to be of value, no matter how local or small—such as the Cassiar community initiative in Canada[9] for the preservation of the history of a now abandoned asbestos mining town and its people—we see that community work in heritage creates rich relationships between members and with other stakeholders. Conversely, established heritage institutions are increasingly open to community outreach, and may on occasion leave their physical premises to occupy other spaces where visiting and interpretation dynamics can be quite different from those occurring in traditional exhibit-based museums.[10] The CSCW body of knowledge on community dynamics and on organizational memory and practices constitutes a solid foundation for further studies.

Open questions across these three strands include: how are these new understandings of and practices around heritage negotiated? How are multiple forms of participation mediated? How do visitors, staff and other stakeholders coordinate understandings and meanings? How are their perceptions of theirs and others' contributions, of their roles or of their involvement emerging? What artefacts (technological and not) are central to mediate and assist in coordinating these practices?

In heritage studies, there is currently a widespread use of established social media platforms (e.g. Facebook, Twitter, Instagram, Flickr, etc.), however the exploration of a broader range of possibilities in technology design can be enriched by CSCW sensibilities and understanding. We have seen in previous sections how established heritage technologies—such as mobile guides and interactive displays—have been studied and evaluated in detail, and often re-designed with insights from the study of visitors in situ. Therefore, in the spirit of CSCW that sees technology as a medium and a facilitator, there is room to contribute to the design and development of novel technologies that are currently emerging as useful platforms in this new scenario of collaborative heritage: for example, DYI electronics, tangibles, lightweight and mobile AR, among others.

---

[8] http://savingbletchleypark.org/

[9] http://www.cassiar.ca/

[10] For example, the Walters Art Museum (USA) has held exhibitions of part of its collection and of reproductions outside of the museum and around the city of Baltimore.

Conclusions

In their 2005 paper published in the CSCW Journal, Hindmarsh et al. thus outlined some open challenges for CSCW and cultural heritage:

> The challenge is to consider how to adopt approaches common in CSCW to re-think museum technologies and provide museum designers, and indeed artists, with the tools and technologies to organise innovative collaborative experiences. Indeed, with its concern with understanding and designing for collaboration, CSCW would seem well placed to inform the development of exhibits and exhibitions which aim to enhance interaction and co-participation (…) One additional interest for CSCW in museums and galleries relates to the formidable problems of deploying prototype technologies in workplaces. (Hindmarsh et al. 2005, p. 3).

The authors advocated for CSCW to further its understanding of how heritage institutions foster collaboration and participation. They also recognized that the work of museum staff and also of artists could benefit from CSCW concerns.

In the first part of this paper, we have seen how CSCW has indeed made substantial contributions, and well beyond understanding visitor practices, by also focusing on the design of collaborative experiences and on the orchestration of inclusive artistic performances. The examples of work we have reviewed in this paper have tackled foundational issues in the understanding of heritage: the actual in situ practices of visitors, the social and collaborative nature of exhibits, the opportunities and risks offered by technology and the concerns in creating partially-digital heritage artefacts for public display.

In the second part of the paper, we have argued that, although we see a proliferation of case studies where technology is designed and then deployed in a heritage setting, it is crucial for CSCW to take on more substantial challenges in furthering research in the cultural heritage domain. This is strictly linked to current developments in heritage studies and heritage management practice, whereby we see an increasing interest for and adoption of participative and collaborative approaches to engaging visitors and other stakeholders. This interest is not only academic, it is in fact embodied by actual practical strategies for engagement put in place by heritage institutions around the world. We have argued that, firstly, CSCW can contribute meaningfully to current discourse surrounding heritage by extending its body of foundational research and insights on work settings, collaboration and co-participation in organisations, and on online and offline communication, to the heritage domain. Secondly, that new areas of investigation, such as the social co-creation of heritage, can be explored and understood by means of a CSCW approach to in-depth studies of situated practices and of related technologies and meditational tools. More specifically about heritage technologies, CSCW work has influenced their design to respond to crucial social concerns such as the support of more than one user and the support of interpersonal communication during the visit. It can undoubtedly extend this contribution to novel technologies that mediate the social production of heritage. In conclusion, the "work" of visitors, of museum professionals and of the communities that surround cultural heritage institutions are strands whereupon a CSCW focus could be enlightening, if not groundbreaking, if these open challenges are tackled in a timely way.

Acknowledgments This work is supported by the EU FP7 project "meSch" (grant agreement 600851)—http://mesch-project.eu. Thanks to Daniela Petrelli for her comments on earlier versions of this paper.

References

Aoki, P. M., Grinter, R. E., Hurst, A., Szymanski, M. H., Thornton, J. D., & Woodruff, A. (2002). Sotto voce: Exploring the interplay of conversation and mobile audio spaces. *Proceedings of CHI 2002* (pp. 431–438). New York: ACM.

Benford, S., Crabtree, A., Flintham, M., Greenhalgh, C., Koleva, B., Adams, M. et al. (2011). Creating the spectacle: Designing interactional trajectories through spectator interfaces. *TOCHI, 18*(3), Art 11, 1–28.

Brown, B., MacColl, I., Chalmers, M., Galani, A., Randell, C., & Steed, A. (2003). Lessons from the lighthouse: Collaboration in a shared mixed reality system. *Proceedings of CHI 2003*, Ft. Lauderdale. New York: ACM.

Brown, B., Chalmers, M., Bell, M., Hall, M., MacColl, I., & Rudman, P. (2005). Sharing the square: Collaborative leisure in the city streets. *Proceedings of ECSCW 2005* (pp. 427–447). London: Springer.

Ciolfi, L. & McLoughlin, M. (2012). Designing for meaningful visitor engagement at a living history museum. *Proceedings of NordiCHI 2012* (pp. 69–78). New York: ACM.

Cosley, D., Baxter, J., Lee, S., Alson, B., Nomura, S., Adams, P. et al. (2009). A tag in the hand: supporting semantic, social, and spatial navigation in museums. *Proceedings of CHI '09* (pp. 1953–1962). New York: ACM.

Ferris, K., Bannon, L., Ciolfi, L., Gallagher, P., Hall, T., & M. Lennon (2004). Shaping experiences in the hunt museum: A design case study. *Proceedings of DIS04*, pp. 205–214. New York: ACM.

Flintham, M., Reeves, S., Brundell, P., Glover, T., Benford, S., Rowland, D. et al. (2011). Flypad: Designing trajectories in a large-scale permanent augmented reality installation. *Proceedings of ECSCW 2011* (pp. 233–252). London: Springer.

Fraser, M., Stanton, D., Ng, K. H., Benford, S., O'Malley, C., Bowers, J., Taxén, G., Ferris, K., & Hindmarsh, J. (2003). Assembling history: Achieving coherent experiences with diverse technologies. *Proceedings of ECSCW 2003*. London: Kluwer.

Fuks, H., Moura, H., Cardador, D., Vega, K., Ugulino, W., & Barbato, M. (2012). Collaborative museums: An approach to co-design. *Proceedings of CSCW, 2012*, 681–684.

Galani, A. (2003). Mixed reality museum visits: Using new technologies to support co-visiting for local and remote visitors. Museological Review, No. 10.

Gammon, B., & Burch, A. (2008). Designing mobile digital experiences. In L. Tallon & K. Walker (Eds.), *Digital technologies and the museum experience: Handheld guides and other media* (pp. 35–62). London: AltaMira.

Giaccardi, E. (2011). Things we value. *Interactions 18*(1), 17–21. (New York: ACM).

Giaccardi, E. (Ed.). (2012). *Heritage and social media*. London: Routledge.

Giaccardi, E., & Palen, L. (2008). The social production of heritage through cross-media interaction: making place for place-making. *International Journal of Heritage Studies, 14*(3), 289–298.

Grinter, R. E., Aoki, P. M., Hurst, A., Symanski, M. H., Thornton, J. D. & Woodruff, A. (2002). Revisiting the visit: Understanding how technology can shape the museum visit. *Proceedings of CSCW 2002*, pp. 146–155.

Heath, C., Luff, P., Vom Lehn, D., & Hindmarsh, J. (2002). Crafting participation: Designing ecologies, configuring experience. *Visual Communication, 1*(1), 9–33.

Hemmings, T., Randall, D., Marr, L., & Francis, D. (1997). Situated knowledge and the virtual science and industry museum. *Journal of Archive and Museum Informatics, 11*(2), 147–164 (Vol II, Kluwer)

Hindmarsh, J., Heath, C., vom Lehn, D., Cleverly. J. (2005). Creating assemblies in public environments: Social interaction, interactive exhibits and CSCW. *CSCW Journal, 14*(1), 1–41 (London: Springer).

Hinrichs, U., & Carpendale, S. (2011). Gestures in the wild: studying multi-touch gesture sequences on interactive tabletop exhibits. *Proceedings of CHI 2011* (pp. 3023–3032), New York: ACM.

Hooper-Greenhill, E. (1992). *Museums and the shaping of knowledge*. London: Routledge.

Hope, T., Nakamura Y., Takahashi, T., Nobayashi, A., Fukuoka, S., Hamasaki, M., & Nishimura, T. (2009). Familial collaborations in a museum. *Proceedings of CHI 2009*. New York: ACM.

Hornecker, E. (2008). "I don't understand it either, but it is cool" Visitor Interactions with a Multi-Touch Table in a Museum. *Proceedings of IEEE Tabletop, 2008*, 121–128.

Hornecker, E. (2010). Interactions around a contextually embedded system. *Proceedings of TEI, 2010*, 169–176.

Hornecker, E., & Nicol, E. (2012). What do lab-based studies tell us about in-the-wild behavior? Insights from a study of museum interactives. *Proceedings of DIS 2012* (pp. 358–368), Newcastle UK, New York: ACM.

Hornecker, E., & Stifter, M. (2006). Learning from interactive museum installations about interaction design for public settings. *Proceedings of OZCHI, 2006*, 135–142.

Iversen, O. S., & Smith, R. C. When the museum goes native. *Interactions, 18,* 15–19.

Kalay, Y., Kvan, T., & Affleck, J. (Eds.). (2008). *New media and cultural heritage*. London: Routledge.

Marr, L., Randall, D., Mitchell, W. L. (2003). Coming off the rails: Evaluation and the design process. In C. Ghaoui (Ed.), *Usability evaluation of online learning programs* (pp. 110–127). IDEA Group 2003.

Marti, P. (2001). Design for art and leisure. *Proceedings of ICHIM 2001* (pp. 387–397), Pittsburgh: Archives and Museum Informatics.

Marty, P. F. (1999). Museum informatics and collaborative technologies: The emerging socio-technological dimension of information science in museum environments. *Journal of the American Society for Information Science, 50*(12), 1083–1091.

O'Hara, K., Kindberg, T., Glancy, M., Baptista, L., Sukumaran, B., Kahana, G., & Rowbotham, J. (2007). Collecting and sharing location-based content on mobile phones in a zoo visitor experience. *Computer-Supported Cooperative Work, 16* (1–2), 11–44. (London: Springer).

Oomen, J., & Arovo, L. (2011). Crowdsourcing in the cultural heritage domain: opportunities and challenges. *C&T'11: Proceedings of the 5th International Conference on Communities and Technologies 2011.*

Petrelli, D., Ciolfi, L., van Dijk, D., Hornecker, E., Not, E. and Schmidt, A. (2013), "Integrating Material and Digital: A New Way for Cultural Heritage", ACM Interactions, July + August 2013 (pp. 58–63). New York: ACM

Reeves, S. (2011). *Designing interfaces in public settings: Understanding the role of the spectator in human-computer interaction*. London: Springer.

Robertson, T., Mansfield, T., & Loke, L. (2006). Designing an immersive environment for public use. *Proceedings of PDC 2006.*

Salgado, M., Saad-Sulonen, J., & Díaz, L. (2009). Using online maps for community-generated content in museums. *Proceedings of Museums and the Web 2009*. Toronto: Archives & Museum Informatics.

Schnädelbach, H., Koleva, B., Flintham, M., Fraser, M., Izadi, S., Chandler, P., Foster, M., Benford, S., Greenhalgh, C., & Rodden, T. (2002). The Augurscope: A mixed reality interface for outdoors. *Proceedings of CHI 2002* (pp. 9–16). New York: ACM.

Simarro Cabrera, J., Frutos, H. M., Stoica, A. G., Avouris, N., Dimitriadis, Y., Fiotakis, G. (2005). Mystery in the museum: Collaborative learning activities using handheld devices. *Proceedings of Mobile HCI 2005* (pp. 315–318). New York: ACM.

Simon, N. (2010). *The Participatory Museum,* Museums 2.0. Retrieved January 01, 2013, from http://www.participatorymuseum.org/.

Thom-Santelli, J., Cosley, D., & Gay, G. (2010). What do you know?: Experts, novices and territoriality in collaborative systems. *Proceedings of CHI 2010* (pp. 1685–1694). New York: ACM.

Urban, R., Marty, P., & Twidale, M.B. (2007). A second life for your museum: 3D multi-user virtual environments and museums. *Proceedings Museums and the Web 2007.* San Francisco, CA.

V&A (2010): *V&A Strategic Plan 2010-2015 2010/2011*, London: Victoria and Albert Museum. Retrieved January 01, 2013 from http://media.vam.ac.uk/media/documents/about-us/2010/v&a-strategicplan2010-15.pdf.

Veron, E., & Levasseur, M. (1983). *Ethnographie de l'Exposition.* Paris: Bibliothque Publique d'Information, Centre Georges Pompidou.

vom Lehn, D. (2010): Examining response: Video-based studies in museums and galleries. *International Journal of Culture, Tourism and Hospitality Research*, *4*(1), 33–43.

vom Lehn, D., Heath, C., & Hindmarsh, J. (2001). Exhibiting interaction: Conduct and collaboration in museums and galleries. *Symbolic Interaction*, *24*(2), 189–216.

vom Lehn, D., Hindmarsh, J., Luff, P. and Heath, C. (2007). Engaging Constable: revealing art with new technology, Proc. Of CHI 2007 (pp. 1485–1494), New York: ACM.

Weilenmann, A., Hillman, T., & Jungselius, B. (2013). Instagram at the museum: Communicating the museum experience through social photo sharing. *Proceedings of CHI 2013.* New York: ACM.

Drops Hollowing the Stone: Workarounds as Resources for Better Task-Artifact Fit

Federico Cabitza and Carla Simone

Abstract The paper reports on a systematic survey of the literature around the manifold theme of workarounds in CSCW and in so doing presents a range of definitions that focus on different aspects of this phenomenon. We also report a case study in a large hospital where we discussed with some key users the opportunity of a tool that could promote awareness of existing workarounds, as a way to provide feedback on the actual use of an IT application in a bottom-up fashion. This case study led to the design of a simple process annotation tool, where users could distinguish between different kinds of workarounds: either as misalignments with respect to the organization procedures, or circumventions of the technology supporting them, or both.

Background and Motivations

In December 2011, we began a research-oriented partnership with the IT department of a large hospital in Northern Italy that employs approximately 1,500 nurses and 600 doctors and that in 2011 admitted 45,000 inpatients, 8,000 outpatients and over 4 million ambulatory patients. The common idea shared by the research group and directly endorsed by the Chief Information Officer (CIO) of the hospital was to assess the impact of an articulated Electronic Patient Record (EPR), which had been awarded in 2004, 2009 and 2010 as the most innovative and impressive project of hospital digitization in Italy, on patient safety and the daily work of the

F. Cabitza (✉) · C. Simone
Universitá degli Studi di Milano-Bicocca, Milan, Italy
e-mail: cabitza@disco.unimib.it

C. Simone
e-mail: simone@disco.unimib.it

O. W. Bertelsen et al. (eds.), *ECSCW 2013: Proceedings of the 13th European Conference on Computer Supported Cooperative Work, 21–25 September 2013, Paphos, Cyprus*, DOI: 10.1007/978-1-4471-5346-7_6,

so called *frontline users* (Tucker and Edmonson 2007) of this application, that is nurses and doctors.

Everything was going well, until the CIO must have realized that we were going to involve frontline users *directly*, partly with a closed-ended questionnaire to administer to the whole clinical workforce, and partly through a series of focused semi-structured interviews on a convenience basis. This roadmap was never officially forbidden, but the initial enthusiasm began waning considerably, more and more perplexities were raised by the IT Department, and the research seemed to take out a new "one step forward, two steps back" policy. We even began thinking that in that hospital the level of acceptance of the EPR and related satisfaction could be epitomized by rephrasing a CSCW title from the 90s: "I love the system—THEY just don't use it". Probably as an attempt to remove this increasing suspicion of ours, the CIO invited us to attend one of the periodic, approximately monthly, meetings that were organized between him and some nurse representatives to collect observations, issue reports and enhancement requests related to the EPR usage in their wards.

> The meeting was informal and friendly, and nurses seemed glad to share their issues also with us, i.e., external persons that had been presented to them as "*consultants from the University who have come here to study how well our EPR has come to fit our work practices and routines*" in the CIO's words, "*also thanks to your great work of analysis, and continuous feedback!*", as he was pleased to add before letting the nurses have the floor.

The main thing that struck our attention in this meeting was that several times the issues, misfits and shortcomings that were reported by the nurses (be these about either the graphical interface, functional aspects or the application workflow) were interpreted by the CIO as actually a *misuse* of the system: "*this is not a bug, the EPR is supposed to do that*"; or also "*yes, you get stuck, but it's because you haven't done this and that before, and the EPR is expecting you do that instead*"; or "*yes, probably this could have been made more clear, but you should have used the other command, and then opened the other dialog box… in this way, look, there you go!*". In some cases, the CIO was genuinely surprised that certain ways to get things done with the EPR—like printing a report before completion, proceeding to the next available screen without a validation, or checking a medication without the related prescription—did even exist, i.e., that some unanticipated operation was possible *at all*, or that two alternative ways to complete a task were equally feasible, one being completely undocumented and much more error-prone than the other: "*I'll have this fixed soon, don't worry, and remember that you have to do like I've just told you now, not in the other way*" was a typical way he addressed those "discoveries". This left the nurses often in a state of bewilderment mixed to an ineffable feeling of having done something wrong, as well as with a slight touch of optimism that the IT supplier (i.e., the vendor of the EPR, probably the largest health IT company in Italy) could do something to improve their record, *sooner or later*.

As one of the nurses told us at the coffee machine after the meeting: "*we know that only a small portion of our reports are passed on to the vendor…*" (she said that so much alike a teenager would have said that she *knows* that Santa Claus does not exist) "*… either because we are to change our habits [with the EPR], or we were doing something the wrong way, or because some things are really trifles with respect to other due updates and important improvements. Yet, we are happy that someone is listening to us, and that our efforts to systematically collect our troubles with the EPR and take part in the changes of the next releases of the system are acknowledged eventually; it's a way to mould the system, if you will, so that it fits better our practices here. It's like the proverbial small drops that hollow the stone: our periodic reports are the drops. And of course the EPR is the Stone!*" While we were jotting down this evocative remark, another nurse abruptly threw in sarcastically: "*And yet, sometimes we would prefer having a good pneumatic drill!!*". A general laughter ensued (but undoubtedly that remark was aimed at IT people and also at us…).

In this paper we report an informal *side* research with respect to the main project on the impact of the EPR on hospital work mentioned above; a study that stemmed from those meetings and small talks at the coffee machine about the nurses' inchoate quasi-bugs, imperfect issues, misbugs and miswarts and their *translation* to the supplier through the IT Department. Taking our word that we would reconsider the methodological approach to assess the degree of user acceptance and satisfaction of the current EPR in the whole hospital (that is that we would give it up), the CIO organized a short series of individual meetings with some of the head nurses involved in the project where to address the patient safety dimension only. Thus, partly for contrived serendipity and partly for dogged resolution, in those interviews we also focused on those peculiar ways nurses and doctors achieve their tasks by coming to break, either intentionally or unintentionally, with intended or specified practices and technologies, i.e., on what in the specialist literature is usually denoted with the term *workaround* (Wimelius 2011).

Working Around and Working Through

We consulted a number of literature contributions to get a picture of the concept of workaround in order to better focus on the subject during our field study.[1] Workarounds are mentioned in many research papers from several different research areas, especially those related to health information technology and organizations. Most of the recent contributions, especially from the workflow-related literature, declare to be motivated in trying to understand how to minimize the risk of workaround occurrence, as a symptom of workflow inadequacy (e.g. Kobayashi et al. 2005), while others (a large minority, but yet the most interesting

[1] We report some of the definitions we collected in our survey in the shared resource that is available on ResearchGate at http://goo.gl/BUKDJ.

ones to our aims) focus on this subject to exploit their existence as signs of appropriation and drivers for change (VV.AA. 2005; Vassilakopoulou et al. 2012).

Irrespective of their motivations, the number of research contributions that use this expression is growing at a steady rate: in 2002, PubMed indexed approximately 20 papers containing this word, while in 2011 they were more than 180. Despite this increasingly broader interest, few researches have been so far explicitly aimed at studying this phenomenon thoroughly (e.g., Gasser 1986; Ferneley and Sobreperez 2006; Wilkerson 2009; Wimelius 2011). This can be traced back to at least two main criticalities: first, workarounds must be observed "in vivo", that is in the situated unfolding of work practices and technology use, which requires direct and expensive observational studies (e.g., Bowers et al. 1995; Obradovich and Woods 1996; Phillips and Berner 2004; Patterson et al. 2006; Koppel et al. 2008); moreover, as we also can report from direct experience, workarounds regard a kind of "invisible work" that users could not have any interest in making explicit in interviews, nor other IT project stakeholders be willing to acknowledge: it is a sort of dark side of the IT deployment, or open secret, that the involved stakeholders could like to keep a lid on, for almost the same reasons IT researchers would like to peek below that lid, i.e., because "finding device deficiencies and exposing error traps is a politically, legally, and financially charged enterprise" (Obradovich and Woods 1996). Focusing on workarounds as a first-class concept could also clash with the pervasive custom to evaluate the acceptance of a technology, and the success of the related digitization project, in terms of whether an important number of people use it regularly or not: for instance, the fact that the electronic medical record was used in almost all the departments of the hospital that hosted our field study was, for the CIO of that hospital, a sufficient reason not to "waste precious resources" in deploying a user satisfaction questionnaire for such application. Yet, when coping with collaborative, and more specifically workflow-based, applications, usage is not always an option and other dimensions should be considered, such as reluctance and satisfaction of end-users, the degree of "distributed viscosity" (Rogers 1994) that is perceived by end-users (i.e., the extra efforts introduced by the computer-based support that they do not feel contributing to their goals), and their level of compliance with the intended use of the system and the related procedures, and hence whether workarounds are applied, and which ones (Poelmans 1999).

The main difficulty in unravelling the true nature of workarounds lies in the truism that such a true nature does not exist, as what a workaround is arises from the concurrence of particular "characteristics of the material artifact, the characteristics of the human agents who use it, and the nature of the context in which it is used" (Wimelius 2011, p. 48). In other words, workarounds are to be discovered (or, better yet, uncovered) at the meeting point, so to say, of technology and users, that is where the technological component of a socio-technical setting meets the social and human side of such setting, when the "technological artifact" is put "in use" and becomes a "technology-in-practice" (Orlikowski 2000). This point of intersection of different trajectories, i.e., the product life cycle trajectory of the technological artifact on one hand, and the continuous evolution of the social context on the other, is difficult to frame and pinpoint in a detailed manner and it has been the object of appropriation analysis, which is aimed at studying how technologies "are used, misused, or not used by people in various contexts" (Orlikowski 2000, p. 407), and of other analyses aimed at understanding how users interpret technology in use, i.e., what meanings users assign to the artifacts embedded in their situated lives, and to what extent these meanings are consistent with the designers' intended interpretative scheme (Pipek 2005); in other words, the extent these technologies provide the necessary "slack" or leeway for a workaround. In one of these analyses (Koopman and Hoffman 2003) make the interesting point that workarounds should be clearly distinguished from kludges, that is any awkward or clumsy fix that are temporarily effective, because workarounds rather concern procedural variations or adaptations in the use of some system, i.e., a behavior, rather than a physical hacking and tweaking of a system. In the same vein, (Halbesleben and Wakefield 2008) propose to differentiate workarounds from errors ("occasions where one fails to achieve the intended outcome"), mistakes (deficiencies or failures in cognitive processes), and especially from deviations, as the former ones "have a very specific motive (to complete a task by getting around a block), whereas deviance tends to have a wider variety of motives [... and most of the times] the goal of the workaround is to get the work done, with the self-serving benefit a secondary gain" (p. 5).

Beyond Good and Evil

Taken all together, these proposals, from one hand provide a rich conceptual background for any research interested in this topic; on the other hand they also lead researchers confronting a fuzzy and fragmented picture, which can undermine any attempt to extract precise requirements for the computational support of the emergence of this phenomenon with a coherent set of tools or practices. Notably, these many contributions, although they agree upon the pervasiveness and almost unavoidability of this phenomenon, do not converge on a quite basic element, i.e., whether workarounds should be considered as a positive, neutral or negative phenomenon, and therefore whether they should be computationally supported or prevented.

On a common sense level, workarounds are perceived as positive whenever the intentions lying behind are recognized aimed at overcoming the (perceived) shortcomings of a technology (Joshi 1991; Bain and Taylor 2000; Button et al. 2003), or at pragmatically managing unusual circumstances and problem situations that always occur even in the most accurate workflow (Kobayashi et al. 2005); conversely, workarounds are perceived as negative, when they seem to be motivated by an ungrounded intention to resist the technology (or "inertia" as called in Boudreau and Robey 2005), or as resulting from underrating the potential negative consequences deriving from the misuse, non use or even sabotage (Ferneley and Sobreperez 2006) of the supportive technology (e.g., Marakas and Hornik 1996;Bain and Taylor 2000;

Lapointe and Rivard 2005). Obviously, this approach focuses on causes (e.g., perceived inadequacies, blocks, inefficiencies) and motivations (e.g., appropriation, resistance, opportunism) and disregards the criterion to assess the impact and effect of workarounds, on collaboration, data quality, task completion, business unit performance, and the like, as this is much more difficult (e.g., for the cascading effect by which a workaround may raise the need to perform other patching workarounds and so on, cf. Kobayashi et al. 2005), and controversial (Obradovich and Woods 1996; Martin and Koopman 2004; Petrides 2004; Patterson et al. 2006; Vogelsmeier et al. 2007).

Ferneley and Sobreperez (2006) propose to go beyond the mere positive–negative dichotomy mentioned above: they follow the notion submitted by Kobayashi et al. (2005); Petrides (2004), which relates workarounds to either an "action ensuing from resistance" for both "good" or "bad" organizational reasons, or to an engagement with the system that yet fails to conform to the prescribed "rules of engagement"; yet, they also distinguish between: "hindrance workarounds", which are undertaken to circumvent system procedures or processes that are perceived to be too time consuming ("viscous" in the sense hinted above), onerous or difficult (Prasad and Prasad 2000); harmless workarounds, which do not significantly affect the flow of work or the quality of the involved information (Button et al. 2003; Lapointe and Rivard 2005); and lastly, essential workarounds, that is actions that are necessary to complete a task or reach a goal (Kobayashi et al. 2005). Similarly, Wilkin and Davern (2012) have recently proposed to distinguish between all system usages that are unfaith with respect to the design's spirit denoting as "circumventions" any potentially harmful actions with respect to both collaboration and information quality; and as "user innovation" those workarounds that, although produce outcomes that are inconsistent with system design, nevertheless "meet common goals", possibly even more efficiently than the system.

While those taxonomies (and any other effort in this direction) can be useful for analytical purposes, caution should be adopted in applying them too rigidly: indeed, the positive and negative nature of a workaround is inextricably bound to the observer's perspective and judgement (the same idea is conveyed in the attribute *distributed* in the expression "distributed viscosity" mentioned above); for instance, the same behavior can be traced back either to an hindrance or to an advantage according to the users' idea of what is necessary to achieve their goals; to their familiarity with the structures that are inscribed in the technology (Orlikowski 2000); or to their capability to imagine and foresee at least some of all the possible consequences deriving from such a behavior.

These behaviors can originate from multiple causes: a steep learning curve requested to users to master the system complexity; users' ignorance of the system's proper use (Boudreau and Robey 2005); either grounded or ungrounded (namely false) perception of limitations of the technology by users (Wilkin and Davern 2012); poor user interfaces leading to unproper use by users (intentionally or unintentionally) (Kushniruk et al. 2005); discrepancies between the application workflow and existing operating procedures or cooperative conventions, be them either intentional, e.g., related to some process redesign initiative (Halbesleben and Wakefield 2008), or unintentional, i.e., due to poorly conducted business analysis, requirement elicitation or process modelling activities (Pan et al. 2008); user hostility and resistance towards tools that are imposed from above or that disrupt existing power relations (Ferneley and Sobreperez 2006); their will to react to a perceived lack of responsibility and identity, or to a perceived reduction of their skills and competencies caused by digitization within their organization (Alvarez 2008).

Moreover, two further interesting aspects of workarounds are worth being isolated, at least to the aims of our research: their *collective*, almost collaborative, nature, and their *evolutionary* characteristics, a sort of "regional metamorphism" that can transform their status from reproachful deeds to even ordinary features of a next release of a system. In regard to the former dimension, it is clear that any single worker can perform a workaround on the basis of her autonomy and power; yet, as also noted by (Wilkin and Davern 2012), it would be improper to define the extempore single action of an individual working around an official application as an "innovative workaround": speaking of "innovation" requires that a group of "users at the worksite have agreed that system functionality is unsatisfactory and have *implemented* an alternative usage that *meets* the defined needs of *at least some* key users" (emphasis added). This does not mean that such workarounds are necessarily planned, devised or even designed "on paper", but rather that they can emerge from the spontaneous agreement of peers (instead of been given from above as a standard operating procedure) and "stabilize" into socially acceptable conventions of use (Cabitza et al. 2009a); or into something even further. This brings us to the latter aspect: their metamorphism; this regards how the temporary and informal nature of a workaround can evolve into a persistent structure and flank the solutions devised in the traditional approach (i.e., analysis-design-development cycle). To this regard, Tyre and Orlikowski (1994) have pointed out how extempore, but to some extent, appreciated workarounds conceived as a temporary adjustment to technology misfit (cf. Gasser) can become, incrementally or by simple repetition, a permanent solution and accepted practice over time, and even persist and outlive the system shortcoming or perceived block that originated them. This phenomenon has been observed frequently (most recently also by Zhou et al. 2011) and can be suggestively depicted in terms of the natural phenomenon known as "social trails", i.e., in terms of those traces of collective and repeated crossing that wear down unpaved paths over time, e.g., in public meadows between regular paved paths (which would represent the intended workflows, in a way).[2] These "social trails", once carried to the IT domain can bring both risks and opportunities. From the negative side, consolidated but unanticipated usages can jeopardise the full capacity of the IT system, which most of the times evolves from the interventions of people that are fully unaware of these local and yet effective workarounds (e.g., CIOs, IT designers, developers): what develops over

---

[2] Some nice examples are available at http://goo.gl/X42TW.

time and in bottom-up manner as an "essential workaround" (see above) can become a harmful one, when the system has been changed and thus the surrounding conditions that let the former thrive. On the other hand, it is known that harmless workarounds have sometimes evolved in extremely popular features (e.g., hashtags in Twitter[3]), and that similar concepts developed in ethnoclassification and psychogeography have recently been absorbed also in the Web page design principle of "paving the cowpaths".[4] Workarounds, as expressions of unanticipated and situated use, are in these cases a powerful source for the meliorative change of artifacts, in terms of their "better fit" with the tasks at hand (Carroll et al. 1991).

A Matter of Perspective

Thus, for summary's sake, most of literature contributions can be put along two main perspectives: first, those authors that see workarounds as mainly *deviations* that go astray from an ideal path or course of action, and that metaphorically "move around" a system that is supposed to support that course of action in a cooperative setting (and which, conversely, is perceived as a block or obstacle by the involved agents): in this mold, Azad and King (2008) describe workarounds as "[...] non-compliant user behaviors vis-à-vis the intended system design".

On the other hand, a complementary way to see workarounds is to conceive them as alternative, ad-hoc, creative ways by which practitioners reach a goal, *irrespective* and *in spite of* any perceived inadequacy or shortcoming of the means that should support them in their tasks (Ash et al. 2004; Tucker and Edmonson 2007); this stance sees those phenomena more like *work-through* than work-*around*, as users involved therein could be said to *go straight to their goal*, by more or less metaphorically overriding the system and its embedded policies. In this latter line, the first and probably most influential contribution is by Gasser (1986). Gasser defines workarounds as one of the specific strategies that users adopt "for accommodating to the misfit" of their computational resource "to the work it is intended to support": it's a sort of adaptation or accommodation (Bowers et al. 1995) where both users and the system is likely to change. Gasser starts from the consideration that all organizations are open systems subjected to unpredictable contingencies, to which users have to respond in extempore manners and *readjust* their work activities to accommodate the "qualitative misalignment of resources needed or expected for carrying out a task". To this aim, he enumerates the strategies of *fitting*, i.e., either making changes to the "computing

[3] See e.g., the discussion at http://goo.gl/HPkno.

[4] "2.4. When a practice is already widespread among authors, consider adopting it rather than forbidding it or inventing something new", from the HTML Design Principles issued by the W3C Working Draft (2007).

arrangement" or, the other way round, "adjusting work schedules and commitments"; *augmenting*, i.e., undertaking additional work to make up for misfits (e.g., by additional training); and *working around*. This activity is defined as "intentionally using computing in ways for which it was not designed or avoiding its use and relying on an alternative means of accomplishing work" (p. 216). Moreover, Gasser distinguishes between different types of workarounds: "data adjustment" regards making up input data to get the system produce the desired response or, in other terms, gaming the system with wrong data to get the right response: for instance, filling in an input field of a form with some nonsensical character just to avoid a mandatory check for complete forms that blocks the application; "procedural adjustment", or hacking the procedure by knowing how to get the same results faster: for instance, asking the right person to do something, bypassing some necessary steps or verifications, or gaming the system by post hoc corrections; lastly, backup systems, i.e., the use of alternative, also paper-based or "pretechnology" ones (Vogelsmeier et al. 2007), systems, which are also called "duplicate systems" (Wimelius 2011), or "shadow tools" (Boudreau and Robey 2005; Handel and Poltrock 2011), that coexist in tension with the legitimate and formally sanctioned system.

The two perspectives mentioned above, namely the *work-around* and the *work-through* oriented ones, stress each a different, but not necessarily exclusive, idea of the inherent main reason behind this phenomenon, i.e., either the existence of "flaws in the technological solutions" or the will of "users not adhering to procedures defined by the technology" (Wimelius 2011, p. 186) (or by its designer, cf. Pipek 2005), respectively. Consequently, discourses on workarounds and workthroughs also reflect two different stances on the role of technology in managing cooperative organizational work and on the capability of users to cope with contingencies and breakdowns (Tyre and Orlikowski 1994), possibly generated by an inadequate, or so perceived, technology. Yet, both views in some way subscribe the general idea that workarounds are a kind of unintended consequence of digitization (Ash et al. 2004; Boudreau and Robey 2005), and one of its inescapable "side effects" (Pipek 2005; Wilkin and Davern 2012): as noted by Azad and King (2008), automating for sake of better standardization, reduction of process variation and hence better quality can lead to the paradoxical consequence of having more variability, that is introduced by "user behaviors [...] which may go so far as to bypass the formal system entirely" (p. 264).

In light of all these considerations, for the rest of the paper we restrain from giving yet another original definition of workaround; we rather adopt the essential elements of the Gasserian perspective to denote as workaround *any behavior end-users of a technology, or the members of an organization, intentionally exhibit, also on a regular basis, to reach a legitimate and agreed goal (such as completing a work item or task), in spite of either the technology or an organizational procedure*; in the former case we speak of *system workaround*, while in the latter we speak of *process workaround*.

The Case Study

As anticipated in the Introduction, we had the opportunity to discuss with some key users of a complex EPR of the idiosyncratic behaviors that they and their colleagues adopt to have their work done even *in spite of* formal procedures and dedicated applications. More specifically, we report here on the interviews we had with: a head nurse (HN) who was responsible of several groups of nurses in four different units; a nurse working in the inpatient ward (IWN); a nurse working in the Day Hospital Unit (DHN); and a Head Physician (HP) who worked in both wards. These roles covered different kinds of work experiences that were anyway strongly correlated, and possessed complementary perspectives on the impact of the EPR on daily care, and yet all equally grounded, as all the practitioners involved were using the system since its first deployment, years before. More precisely, the EPR had been in standard use for three years to the date of the interviews: this allowed us to collect experiences of usage and opinions well after the initial phase of appropriation, which usually affects the stability and validity of users' perceptions.

In those interviews the word "workaround", or any close phrasing, was never used, as we did not want to bias the discussion by hinting at any shrewd way to game or circumvent the system; yet, we often sided with end-users in assenting to little "stretches" or tricks that they could perform in spite of official procedures to convey a sort of complicity and make those little admissions, if any, easier. We purposely adopted a low profile and avoided direct questions to understand how *deep* in situated practice these little "detours" were; how practitioners perceived these liberties (e.g., awareness, guilt, satisfaction, overindulgence), and their impact on preexisting work practices. The interviews were all tape recorded, but recording was stopped whenever the interviewees asked for a more confidential observation (that happened twice); one of us participated as silent observer with the task to take notes during the talk to facilitate later keyword analysis, thematic analysis and passage retrieval (Seidman 2006). The average length of the interviews was 44 min; the total recording was of 176 min. In the next section we will outline the main relevant behaviors our interviewees described to us.

Chronicles from the Frontline

All key actors agreed that the introduction of the EPR had been useful, especially for its potential role in improving patient safety and reducing errors in drug management. They also agreed that the system was not difficult to appropriate, after the necessary initial period of training and adaptation (which lasted approximately 2–3 months). Yet, quite surprisingly, we were told that while the order entry feature of the system was used regularly (also because highly pushed by the Hospital Pharmacy for legal and inventory reasons), the system was scarcely or not at all used to support the phase of drug administration at the patients' bed. The main reason for this *system workaround* (see above) was simply that the disposition of the beds and armchairs both in the ordinary admission ward and in the Day Hospital rooms did not allow the drug cart, on which to put a PC connected to the hospital network, to move among the patient's beds or chairs: EPR-supported drug administration would require nurses (and sometimes doctors) to move back and forth from the bed/chair to the cart, a condition that was shortly rejected, as impracticable and leading to even more potential risks and errors. DHN said that *"the distance is not a problem per se, as it is approximately five meters or so, but we have to cover that short way many many times everyday. [...] Some patients lie in beds, while others are seated in special armchairs and attached to an infusion pump in different rooms [...] when they sound their little alarm to notify us that the their infusion is finished, we have to run to them, then to the cart, and then back again to them: we would have little time to log in the EPR and use it in this frantic activity as we were told to do, to check every administered medication"*. DHN was aware that the EPR was supposed to be used to check that the right drug would be administered to the right person by means of a barcode scanner, as well in the right order according to a detailed drug protocol defined by the physician for that particular patient; that notwithstanding, the physical (although relatively short) distance between the PC and the actual "point of care" prevented Day Hospital nurses from using the system: *"we ask our patients first name and family name twice, and then administer the drug; indeed some of them respond quite absent minded, or weary for the medication, but that's the kind of control we can afford right now, at our current work rates"*. She added: *" I would like to use the EPR, I would feel safer, or comforted that everything is all right. Indeed, we used it for about six months at the beginning and it was fine, although quite cumbersome [...] but then we had to increase our pace and serve more outpatients per day, I suppose for economic reasons [...]"*.

The system workaround described above can also generate correlated process workarounds. For instance, in the inpatient ward, also the IWN told us to systematically bypass the patient-drug-patient check, but for an opposite reason with respect to the Day Hospital case: *"every day we come to handle few patients, the same ones for quite long stays [...] we come to know our patients very well, it would be weird and alienating to double check everything with the EPR: [...] just imagine the worst case: even in a case of bone marrow transplantation between twins, I would administer the right drugs to the right person even without really looking at the person [...] I'd go straight to the right person, as we really come to know them, they are not just bed numbers, if you get what I mean [...]"*. Also the HN raised a similar concern *"we cannot ask to the same patient her name and family name for each drug in the drug protocol [...], paradoxically, this would give her a bad impression and make her think we don't know what we're doing there"*.

The situation described above and the obligation to keep both the electronic and paper based information up to date required nurses to duplicate their work, a situation that have been described several times (e.g., Cabitza et al. 2005;

Munkvold et al. 2006). This redundancy of data and effort was mentioned by all the interviewees as time consuming and error-prone. Some of them recognized the necessity of this additional effort as a consequence of not using the EPR as prescribed, while the IWN emphasized that she would prefer to work only on the EPR, but the others would do differently and this leads to nasty situations: the best tool is the one chosen by the majority of the colleagues, not the best one "in se": *"they [the management] do not fully support the system adoption, or just do not consider whether it is used at the 100 % of its capabilities or not […] the data in the EPR are always correct in my experience, but in regard to currency, I would have some doubt […]"* he said.

Another workaround was reported when the drugs are delivered from the Hospital Pharmacy to the ward where they are to be administered to the patients. The procedure and the EPR require nurses to check if all the drugs that had been prescribed are delivered as expected. This should be made through the system, by ticking off the items shown in a drug list one by one with a barcode scanner that yet was seldom employed for technical problems of hardware compatibility; therefore, since this check would require the time to compare the barcode of each drug with a corresponding item in the drug list "by hand", this operation was generally performed later at the end of the shift, and not exactly when the drugs arrive at the ward. Yet, in order to cope with this process workaround at the ward side, the hospital pharmacy pushed for a corresponding system workaround, that is requiring the nurse on duty to sign a paper-based delivery note to acknowledge receipt of the drugs, whatever the shipment. Obviously, this might cause a potential mismatch between the current step in the EPR workflow and the actual task, until the ticking off is performed, as well as more serious data-related misalignments whenever nurses realize at the end of their shift that some drug had not been dispatched (a rare event, though). These workarounds are considered harmless, at least from the perspective of the pharmacy, as they have a regular receipt (although on paper) and this can enable them to trigger the stock depletion and replenishment procedures; yet, all the interviewees agreed upon the fact that if administration were supported by the EPR, as it should, everything would be stuck irremediable, as the system would not allow for the administration of drugs that have not yet been officially dispatched from the pharmacy.

The lack of investments that is due to current economic restrictions and that our interviewees recognized as the main reason behind some misuses of the system (e.g., the cumbersome cart and the faulty barcode scanner) has an impact also on the phase of drug prescription. As the HP told us *"the lack of a digital signature system forces us to keep and sign a paper copy of each drug prescription […] this has to be faxed to the pharmacy as soon as possible so that they can allocate the materials and prepare the necessary drugs […] this of course does not exempt us from filling in all the details also on the EPR, because in short what we sign and fax is a printed screenshot of one of its pages."* This system workaround is the source of another process workaround. When doctors complete the prescription of a protocol for a given patient, the EPR makes this information immediately available to the pharmacists; these latter start the preparation of the drugs before receiving the fax with the handwritten signature of the doctor (that comes after that a specific page of the application has been printed by a nurse, usually checked and signed by a doctor and finally faxed by a nurse again to the Pharmacy). This lapse of time can rarely generate a mismatch between what has been prepared and the actual formal prescription, as this latter can be modified before the paper-based prescription has been signed. The modification of a prescription is not an arbitrary and meaningless action, but rather is something that allows doctors to cope with exceptional cases (e.g., patient's allergies, rare adverse reactions, drug shortage): however, the above mentioned workaround can generate mismatches also in those rare cases where the due modifications occur during the "grey zone interval" between these two events. It is easy to understand that any mismatch consumes time to be caught and properly handled by either the nurses at the ward or the pharmacists, either separately or within an interaction between these two roles that is usually mediated by phone.

The HP mentioned another situation where a system workaround occurred for what could be related to an analysis or design mistake. In case of protocols containing expensive drugs, it is necessary to associate each of those drugs with a specific document, that contains information about the drug administration sequence; this information is monthly delivered to the regional health authority that uses it to monitor drug usage across the territory and allow for its reimbursement. In some protocols, one of the drugs might be not very expensive and could be used in other protocols: in these second contexts *"the document does not make any sense [...] but it has to be produced the same, otherwise the EPR would prevent us from any other action [Thus] we tell the system to create a copy of it, we even have to open it, and then throw it away and forget about it [...] so the EPR will allow us to proceed and do our work"*. On the one hand, the EPR considers the simple fact that users have opened the file as a validation of its content; on the other hand, the EPR designers did not consider that what makes sense in a department (e.g., in haematology where the cheap drug is used within a crucial and expensive protocol) generates a useless redundancy in another department.

The definition of the therapy protocols is problematic since, to prevent unwanted modifications, any change generates a new protocol that has to be filled in from scratch. For this reason the definition of complex protocols requires time and concentration, two scarce resources for doctors. This fact generated an odd form of workaround, a role-based workaround in-between the system and the official procedure: the doctors proposed to the hospital management that they would still be in charge of defining and validating the protocol on paper, also to exploit the natural flexibility of this medium; but also that later someone else would have to put all the paper-based protocols into the system, someone "*who does not need to be a doctor [...] as they have only to copy our files into the system, one character after one character*". Doctors experimented this solution for a certain period of time, but their protest led only to multiple typos in the protocols imputed into the system, to the suspicion that some typo could also lead to some serious misnomer, and hence to wrong drug administrations, and they had to choke down their protest for silly data entry duties and work again *with* the system.

Reflections on Experience

The interviewed key actors emphasized several times that they would like to use the EPR more, and in all its capabilities, "*provided that [...] some contextual conditions are satisfied*". This recalls a similar argumentation proposed by Bowers et al. (1995): a system is never good or bad *per se*, rather it has to be evaluated in relation to its context of use. This issue emerged during the interviews as a side effect of the main theme related to the workarounds, nevertheless it was discussed with high ardour by the interviewees as they felt that they could contribute in a factual way to the establishment of these enabling conditions. For example, the HP mentioned that the EPR requires him to perform the modification of any protocol modification by hand, for example when the same therapy is administered during two or more days or when the pharmacy substitutes an equivalent drug for another. Doctors have often reported this problem to the Hospital CIO "*from the very beginning*" and asked for a modification that from the programming point of view has always seemed almost trivial, "*[...] but then they [the vendor's developers] must have forgotten to make the modification we asked for, or something went wrong in the passing on...*". Paradoxically, then, the few doctors that are able to perform these manual changes have never taught the others doctors how to perform this operation, in order to avoid that "*too many doctors change the protocols they could introduce errors and misalignments*": thus doctors were complaining for a cumbersome and difficult procedure but, at the same time, they were also happy of these hurdles, and jealous of their capability to modify the protocol, although extremely time consuming.

The study shows that also in the case in which the technology is welcome for its positive effects on some aspects of the work practices, e.g., an increased patient safety in some phases of their caring process, the practitioners can feel necessary to adopt workarounds to reach their primary goal, i.e., the patient care and recovery, irrespective of the limits of the technology involved, or of the general policies and procedures that such technology enacts and enforces. Our study confirms the findings reported also elsewhere, and notably in (Zhou et al. 2011) that workarounds might concern problems that could be (and sometimes are) solved by either a stronger adaptation of users to their computational system, or by usually small adjustments of the system's functionalities by its developers, or of the related organizational procedures; or they might concern problems that are related to more complex situations that require more demanding efforts to be dealt with. However, in both cases the voice of the frontline users of the system deployed in an organization, in this case doctors and nurses in a hospital, does not easily reach the people that can actually solve the problems detected at the shop floor: i.e., either the organization top management (including the CIO), or the system developers (usually a third-party vendor). The reasons for that can be diverse and range from time pressure, to more political or strategic concerns, often related to the relationships between the IT Department, the other departments and (external) IT suppliers. Our interviewees admitted that "*often the IT Department is a useful filter, that is a refiner which sifts improper reports from real bugs, and that prioritizes multiple internal reports into a single, coherent set of evolutionary requests, also in light of precise and urgent budget constraints [...] but other times it also acts as a deafening barrier, which provides external stakeholders with a simplistic picture of the internal process of technology appropriation and acceptance, [...] also because they want the digitization project be a success at any price"* and this prevents the end-users' voice to reach both the top management and the supplier timely, systematically, or just faithfully.

Unlike the findings reported by Tucker and Edmonson (2007), the practitioners involved in our study were in favour of letting a persistent record of their problems, proposals and partial solutions—among which those essential workarounds that they had devised to reach their goals better—be preserved by some computational tool, and promoted, so that their contributions could be taken in consideration more likely than being forgot, disregarded or underestimated. This tool, the "pneumatic drill" hinted at by the nurses in front of the coffee machine, would not substitute already established occasions in which "due feedback is collected", nor let end-users bypass the IT Department in making sense of their troubles with the system. Far from it, such a recording tool was envisioned to help collect feedback also by whom has little time to organize her interactions with the system in a systematic report, or that does not have any particular inclination in analysing the intended behavior of the system and comparing it with her working habits; such a tool should provide a lightweight communication channel between stakeholders, by creating new opportunities for confrontation and discussion, both in an inter-department context, and when the whole organization has to negotiate maintenance contracts and change requests with the IT supplier. Lightweight in this case would mean that such a tool should not be either demanding nor binding in terms of use, but also contextual with respect to the work practices, and flexible in the amount of information that it manages so as to be usable (and possibly useful) in different working contexts. On the basis of these informal requirements, we developed a prototype that is described in the next section.

The ProAnnoto Prototype

On the basis of the findings of the field study and inspired by the idea to let workarounds emerge in an almost stigmergically manner from work practice, we conceived a functionality, that we called ProAnnoto (Process Annotation), as a supportive means for end-users to visually represent upon an official workflow (possibly enacted by a computational system) the limitations and blocks they encounter in the use of such a workflow: to this aim, users are asked to leave a sign on the process maps that could evoke in their mind the workarounds they adopt to circumvent or avoid those shortcomings.

Since the Business Process Modeling Notation (BPMN[5]) is considered as sufficiently powerful to express ideal models of work processes (and workflows), as well as relatively easy to appropriate by end-users (Wohed et al. 2006), we decided to build the ProAnnoto functionality on the basis of a BPMN(-like) description of the work protocols that are enacted in the considered setting.

In order to have an agile tool that could be discussed with prospective users in terms of potential usefulness and applicability irrespective of the real existence of an automated workflow, ProAnnoto has been developed with the collaboration of Davide Saronni as a stencil of Oryx; Oryx is a common Web platform for process modelling (Decker et al. 2008) that allows for the collaborative editing of process models and that stores those protocols in an online repository that can be shared within a group of users.

This means that each user can generate its own copy of the protocol (e.g., a different copy for each patient) or, likewise, on the basis of a simple parametrization and access rights, the same copy of a protocol can be shared within a group of users (e.g., an hospital unit, that shares the same model to treat a specific disease, without differentiating according to the patient). More specifically, the basic BPMN editor of Oryx has been extended with a symbol stencil that users can use to annotate their protocols with three specific icons: one denoting what we called *system workaround* occurring during the execution of the protocol; one denoting what we called *process workaround* (see above); and a third icon to denote those cases where it is not easy to distinguish between system or process workarounds (or there is no reason to), but yet the user wants to convey the idea that a workaround *is* in place. In this way, the users can use a process model as a simple report form to record extempore anomalies and inadequacies that they detected in a real situation. When the protocol is shared and at a certain point in the process a single user experiences a workaround that has been already signaled by another users, she can access a dialog box associated with the related existing icon and increment the number of occurrences of the detected workaround, as it were a sort of "I agree" counter. Users can also leave an anonymous comment where to characterize their annotation with some further details related to the situation in which the workaround occurred.

The functionality is purposely left as simple as it looks: ProAnnoto does not ask users to appropriate a complex taxonomy to annotate critically a workflow instance, but rather it offers them the opportunity to record and report that the intended process (or enacting system) was found inadequate (in a particular point) and that some action had to be done to move on. On the other hand, ProAnnoto allows for the extraction of simple statistics from the accumulation of several reports: this information can be accessed by the interested people (e.g., the CIO of an organization or the project manager of the supplier) who can understand that some further inquiry is necessary and that something (that usually is irremediably) "off the record" is going on.

[5] http://www.omg.org/spec/BPMN

Some years ago, we prototyped an innovative EPR, called ProDoc (Cabitza et al. 2009b), whose main feature was offering, for each patient record, a contextual BPMN representation of the current clinical pathway associated with the patient at hand in terms of a "process map", which affords next due activities, as well as provides a process-aware access to the whole medical documentation. The future development of ProDoc will encompass the logical and technical integration of the ProAnnoto functionality: this activity will be scheduled after that (and if) the initial positive reactions, which we collected from the key users when we showed them the Oryx editor augmented with ProAnnoto on a tablet, will be confirmed in some more thorough validation sessions.

Conclusions

The paper reports on a systematic survey of the literature concerning the general concept of workaround, and in so doing it presents a range of definitions that focus on different aspects of this phenomenon. In particular, we shed light on the idea that workarounds are not always considered as harmful anomalies but *also* as resources for a better task-artifact fit, as well as for the evolution of the computational system *itself*, especially when they regard what we called "system workarounds". Yet, these insights have not yet been translated into any computational tool aimed at helping end-users let their workarounds emerge as a way to "put pressure" on whom it may concern to improve their digital tools.

To close this gap, in this paper we envision the utility of a lightweight tool called ProAnnoto by which practitioners can collaboratively annotate visual representations, or "maps", of their processes, and in doing so indicate either any deviation from the official organization procedure ("process workaround"), or any circumvention of the technology that enacts those procedures ("system workaround"), or both, with specific iconic symbols (whose shape or characteristics are of secondary importance at best). Notwithstanding its computational simplicity, this solution is the first one to address the problem of involving frontline users in reporting their own workarounds at the degree of detail they deem as useful in a possible communication with the IT department of an organization and/or the provider of its IT solution as a means in their full control to prompt evolutionary maintenance of their appropriated artifacts towards a better fit of these with their situated work practices.

As anticipated in the Introduction, we are aware that the theme of workaround is a delicate one as their elicitation could raise conflicts among different stakeholders, like the users, the management and the IT providers, who might have different goals and perspectives with respect to the IT; we are also aware that the users themselves could prefer not to make visible those workarounds that make their daily professional life easier as outing them could make the system become just more difficult to game, not better. However, the voluntary (and anonymous) elicitation that is allowed by our system is only one of the means that users could exploit to break the barrier between them and those who do not perceive that the process of IT adoption is problematic and that an intervention is needed.

After decades of speculations about the need to have users participate in the conception and introduction of the technologies they are going to use, the most recurrent situation is still characterized by their *de facto* exclusion from this process for the inability of management and IT professionals to leverage the work experience of frontline users. The research efforts that aim to change these situations (e.g., Hartswood et al. 2008) sometimes look for complex solutions that encompass methodologies, methods, tools and technologies aimed at taking all aspects of these problematic situations into account (e.g., Fischer and Giaccardi 2006; Stevens et al. 2009) On the other hand, we observed that users put to work simple strategies to take an active role in the development/refinement process of the IT they use and in the improvement of the task-artifact fit, and probably they only need more friendly environments to make these strategies more effective and "visible". The prototype proposed in this paper goes in this second direction, as it facilitates the user-driven and bottom-up definition of those strategies towards a better fit, and allows multiple stakeholders to find situated ways to support the users' workflow "from within" (Bowers et al. 1995).

References

Alvarez, R. (2008). Examining technology, structure and identity during an Enterprise System implementation. *Information Systems Journal, 18*(2), 203–224.

Ash, J. S., Berg, M., & Coiera, E. (2004). Some unintended consequences of information technology in health care: The nature of patient care information system-related errors. *JAMIA, 11*(2), 104–112.

Azad, B., & King, N. (2008). Enacting computer workaround practices within a medication dispensing system. *European Journal of Information Systems, 17*(3), 264–278.

Bain, P., & Taylor, P. (2000). Entrapped by the 'electronic panopticon'? Worker resistance in the call centre. *New Technology, Work and Employment, 1*(15), 2–18.

Boudreau, M.-C., & Robey, D. (2005). Enacting integrated information technology: A human agency perspective. *Organization Science, 16*(1), 3–18.

Bowers, J., Button, G., & Sharrock, W. (1995). Workflow from within and without: Technology and cooperative work on the print industry shopfloor. In *ECSCW'95: Proceedings of the 4th European Conference on Computer-Supported Cooperative Work* (pp. 51–66). Kluwer Academic.

Button, G., Mason, D., & Sharrock, W. (2003). Disempowerment and resistance in the print industry? Reactions to surveillance-capable technology. *New Technology, Work and Employment, 1*(18), 50–61.

Cabitza, F., Sarini, M., Simone, C., & Telaro, M. (2005). When once is not enough: The role of redundancy in a hospital ward setting. In *GROUP'05: Proceedings of the 2005 International ACM SIGGROUP Conference on Supporting Group Work* (pp. 158–167). ACM Press.

Cabitza, F., Simone, C., & Sarini, M. (2009a). Leveraging coordinative conventions to promote collaboration awareness. *Computer Supported Cooperative Work (CSCW), 18*(4), 301–330.

Cabitza, F., Simone, C., & Zorzato, G. (2009b). ProDoc: An electronic patient record to foster process-oriented practices. In *ECSCW'09: Proceedings of the European Conference on Computer Supported Cooperative Work* (pp. 85–104). Springer.

Carroll, J. M., Kellogg, W. A., & Rosson, M. B. (1991). The task-artifact cycle. In J. M. Carroll (Ed.), *Designing interaction: Psychology at the human-computer interface* (pp. 74–102). New York, NY, USA: Cambridge University Press.

Decker, G., Overdick, H., & Weske, M. (2008). Oryx—an open modeling platform for the BPM community. In: M. Dumas, M. Reichert, and M.-C. Shan (Eds.), *Business process management, Lecture Notes in Computer Science* (Vol. 5240, pp. 382–385). Berlin: Springer.

Ferneley, E. H., & Sobreperez, P. (2006). Resist, comply or workaround? An examination of different facets of user engagement with information systems. *European Journal of Information Systems, 15*(4), 345–356.

Fischer, G., & Giaccardi, E. (2006). Meta-design: A framework for the future of end-user development. In H. Lieberman (Ed.), *End user development* (pp. 427–457). Dordrecht, NL: Kluwer Academic.

Gasser, L. (1986). The integration of computing and routine work. *ACM Transactions on Information Systems, 4*(3), 205–225.

Halbesleben, J. R. B., & Wakefield, D. S. (2008). Workarounds in health care settings: Literature review and research agenda. *Healthcare Management Review, 33*(1), 2–12.

Handel, M. J. & Poltrock, S. (2011). Working around official applications: Experiences from a large engineering project. In *CSCW'11: Proceedings of the ACM 2011 Conference on Computer Supported Cooperative Work* (pp. 309–312). ACM.

Hartswood, M., Procter, R., Slack, R., Voß, A., Büscher, M., Rouncefield, M., et al. (2008). Co-realization: Toward a principled synthesis of ethnomethodology and participatory design. In *Resources, co-evolution and artifacts*, CSCW (pp. 59–94). Berlin: Springer.

Joshi, K. D. (1991). A model of user's perspective on change: The case of information systems technology implementation. *MIS Quarterly, 15*(2), 229–240.

Kobayashi, M., Fussell, S. R., Xiao, Y. & Seagull, F. J. (2005). Work coordination, workflow, and workarounds in a medical context. In *CHI '05 extended abstracts on Human factors in computing systems*, New York, NY, USA (pp. 1561–1564). ACM.

Koopman, P., & Hoffman, R. (2003). Work-arounds, make-work, and kludges. *IEEE Intelligent Systems, 18*(6), 70–75.

Koppel, R., Wetterneck, T., Telles, J. L., & Karsh, B.-T. (2008). Workarounds to barcode medication administration systems: Their occurrences, causes, and threats to patient safety. *JAMIA, 15*(4), 408–423.

Kushniruk, A. W., Triola, M. M., Borycki, E. M., Stein, B., & Kannry, J. L. (2005). Technology induced error and usability: The relationship between usability problems and prescription errors. *International Journal of Medical Informatics, 74*(7–8), 519–526.

Lapointe, L., & Rivard, S. (2005). A multilevel model of resistance to information technology implementation. *MIS Quarterly, 1*(29), 461–491.

Marakas, G., & Hornik, S. (1996). Passive resistance misuse: overt support and covert recalcitrance in IS implementation. *European Journal of Information Systems, 1*(5), 208–219.

Martin, C., & Koopman, P. (2004). Representing user workarounds as a component of system dependability. In *PRDC '04: Proceedings of the 10th IEEE Pacific Rim International Symposium on Dependable Computing* (pp. 353–362). IEEE Computer Society.

Munkvold, G., Ellingsen, G., & Koksvik, H. (2006). Formalizing work: Reallocating redundancy. In *CSCW'06 Proceedings of the 20th Conference on CSCW* (pp. 59–68). ACM Press.

Obradovich, J. H., & Woods, D. D. (1996). Users as designers: How people cope with poor HCI design in computer-based medical devices. *Human factors, 38*(4), 574–592.

Orlikowski, W. J. (2000). Using technology and constituting structures: A practice lens for studying technology in organizations. *Organization Science, 11*(4), 404–428.

Pan, G., Hackney, R., & Pan, S. L. (2008). Information systems implementation failure: Insights from prism. *International Journal of Information Management, 28*(4), 259–269.

Patterson, E. S., Rogers, M. L., Chapman, R. J., & Render, M. L. (2006). Compliance with intended use of Bar Code Medication Administration in acute and long-term care: An observational study. *Human Factors, 48*(1), 15–22.

Petrides, L. A. (2004). Costs and benefits of the workaround: Inventive solution or costly alternative. *International Journal of Educational Management, 18*(2), 100–108.

Phillips, M. T., & Berner, E. S. (2004). Beating the system-pitfalls of bar code medication administration. *Journal of Healthcare Information Management: JHIM, 18*(4), 16–18.

Pipek, V. (2005). From tailoring to appropriation support: Negotiating groupware usage. Doctoral thesis, Faculty of Science, Department of Information Processing Science, University of Oulu, Finland, Oulu, Finland.

Poelmans, S. (1999). Workarounds and distributed viscosity in a workflow system: A case study. *ACM SIGGROUP Bulletin, 20*(3), 11–12.

Prasad, P., & Prasad, A. (2000). Stretching the Iron cage: The constitution and implications of routine workplace resistance. *Organization Science, 1*(11), 387–403.

Rogers, Y. (1994). Exploring obstacles: Integrating CSCW in evolving organisations. In *CSCW'94 Proceedings of the 1994 ACM Conference on Computer Supported Cooperative Work* (pp. 67–77). ACM Press.

Seidman, I. (2006). *Interviewing as qualitative research: A guide for researchers in education and the social sciences*. New York: Teachers College Press.

Stevens, G., Pipek, V., & Wulf, V. (2009). Appropriation infrastructure: Supporting the design of usages. In V. Pipek, M. B. Rosson, B. Ruyter, & V. Wulf (Eds.), *End-user development* (Vol. 5435, pp. 50–69). Berlin: Springer.

Tucker, A. L., & Edmonson, A. C. (2007). Why hospitals don't learn from failures: organizational and psychological dynamics that inhibit system change. *California Management Review, 42*(2), 55–72.

Tyre, M. J., & Orlikowski, W. J. (1994). Windows of opportunity: temporal patterns of technological adaptation in organizations. *Organization Science, 5*(1), 98–118.

VV.AA., Patient Safety Authority. (2005). Workarounds: A sign of opportunity knocking. *Pennsylvania Patient Safety Advisory, 2*(4), 25–28.

Vassilakopoulou, P., Tsagkas, V., & Marmaras, N. (2012). Workaround identification as an instrument for work analysis and design: a case study on ePrescription. *Work: A Journal of Prevention Assessment and Rehabilitation, 41*, 1805–1810.

Vogelsmeier, A. A., Halbesleben, J. R., & Scott-Cawiezell, J. R. (2007). Technology implementation and workarounds in the nursing home. *JAMIA, 15*(1), 114–119.

Wohed, P., Van Der Aalst, W. M. P., Dumas, M., ter Hofstede, A. H. M., & Russell, N. (2006). On the suitability of BPMN for business process modelling. In *Business process management, Lecture Notes in Computer Science* (Vol. 4102, pp. 161–176). Berlin: Springer.

Wilkerson, T. W. (2009). An exploratory study of the perceived use of workarounds utilized during the prescription preparation process of pharmacies in alabama. Master thesis, Auburn University, Auburn, ALabama, USA.

Wilkin, C. L., & Davern, M. J. (2012). Acceptance of post-adoption unanticipated is usage: towards a taxonomy. *ACM SIGMIS Database, 43*(3), 9–25.

Wimelius, H. (2011). Duplicate systems: investigating unintended consequences of information technology in organizations. Doctoral thesis, Umeå University, Umeå, Sweden.

Zhou, X., Ackerman, M. S. & Zheng, K. (2011). CPOE workarounds, boundary objects, and assemblages. In *CHI'11: Proceedings of the ACM Conference on Human Factors in Computing Systems* (pp. 3353–3362).

Physicians' Progress Notes

The Integrative Core of the Medical Record

Jørgen Bansler, Erling Havn, Troels Mønsted, Kjeld Schmidt and Jesper Hastrup Svendsen

Abstract This paper examines physicians' progress notes, an artifact that, in spite of its obvious importance in the coordination of cooperative work in clinical settings, has not been subjected to systematic study under CSCW auspices. While several studies have addressed the role of the medical record in patient care, they have not dealt specifically with the role, structure, and content of the progress notes. As a consequence, CSCW research has not yet taken fully into account the fact that progress notes are coordinative artifacts of a rather special kind, an open-ended chain of prose texts, written sequentially by cooperating physicians for their own use as well as for that of their colleagues. We argue that progress notes are the core of the medical record, in that they marshal and summarize the overwhelming amount of data that is available in the modern hospital environment, and that their narrative format is uniquely adequate for the pivotal epistemic aspect of cooperative clinical work: the narrative format enables physicians to not only record 'facts' but also—by filtering, interpreting, organizing, and qualifying information—to make sense and act concertedly under conditions of uncertainty and contingency.

J. Bansler · T. Mønsted
University of Copenhagen, Copenhagen, Denmark
e-mail: bansler@diku.dk

T. Mønsted
e-mail: monsted@diku.dk

E. Havn (✉)
Technical University of Denmark, Copenhagen, Denmark
e-mail: havn@dtu.dk

K. Schmidt
Copenhagen Business School, Copenhagen, Denmark
e-mail: schmidt@cscw.dk

J. H. Svendsen
Rigshospitalet, Copenhagen, Denmark
e-mail: jesper.hastrup.svendsen@regionh.dk

O. W. Bertelsen et al. (eds.), *ECSCW 2013: Proceedings of the 13th European Conference on Computer Supported Cooperative Work, 21–25 September 2013, Paphos, Cyprus*, DOI: 10.1007/978-1-4471-5346-7_7,

Introduction

The institution of the medical record is under increasing pressure. Driven by advances in pharmaceutical, diagnostic, surgical, anesthetic, clinical, prosthetic, physiotherapeutic, and other technologies, the clinical profession is undergoing a process of radical specialization. At the same time, as a result of the very same advances in medical technologies people live longer and the percentage of patients with chronic diseases is consequently rising steadily (Strauss et al. 1985; Parekh and Barton 2007). The combined effect of these developments is that the medical record becomes bloated and fragmented: (a) the sheer volume and heterogeneity of the record increases with the repertoire of diagnostic and therapeutic technologies; (b) the medical record becomes partially replicated as chronic patients are in the care of increasingly specialized medical professionals; (c) the rising prevalence of multimorbidity further exacerbates the growth and disintegration of the record, as many patients are being treated for multiple diseases at the same time (e.g., diabetes and heart disease). The result is that the cost of coordination increases and with that the risk of error (Hewett et al. 2009); and (d) these issues are again aggravated by increasing reliance on patient work, especially by moves towards telemedicine and other forms of patients' self-monitoring, which potentially will generate enormous volumes of data to be integrated into the medical record.

In view of these developments, it seems safe to state that the institution of the medical record is in a crisis (Bansler et al. 2011).

An obvious strategy in response to this calamity is to develop Electronic Patient Record systems (EPR) in the form of comprehensive computer-based documentation systems that prioritize standardized records (Rosenbloom et al. 2011). However, while notable progress has been made with respect to administrative patient records (i.e., repositories of data for purposes of bureaucratic accountability), when it comes to the medical record very little has been achieved in practice, in spite of enormous investments (e.g., Clarke et al. 2001; Stead and Lin 2009). The implicit assumption that the medical record can be subjected to digitalization in much the same way as administrative records have been, has turned out to be quite naive.

The idea of an EPR system is fraught with serious difficulties simply because the medical record is not just any organizational record. As pointed out already 50 years ago by Garfinkel and Bittner, in their study of psychiatric records, administrative and clinical records are organized by entirely different kinds of logic. In an administrative record system 'information may be repeated for the sake of expediency', because 'the statement of a present state of a bank account does not add any information to what can be readily gathered from the account's earlier state and the subsequent deposits and withdrawals': 'If the two do not match, this points irrefutably to some omission. The record is governed by a principle of relevance with the use of which the reader can assess its completeness and adequacy at a glance'. In contrast, a clinical record works in a different way:

> A subsequent entry may be played off against a former one in such a way that what was known then, now changes complexion. The contents of a folder may jostle each other in bidding to play a part in a pending argument. It is an open question whether things said twice are repetitions, or whether the latter has the significance, say, of confirming the former. The same is true of omissions. Indeed, both come to view only in the context of some elected scheme of interpretation (Garfinkel and Bittner 1967, pp. 204 f.).

That is, to make progress we have to understand the specific ways in which the medical record is constructed in an ongoing process of aggregation and arrangement of test results and observations, of offering hypotheses and suggestions, of deduction and allusion, of explicit reference and tacit omission.

The point of departure in this line of research is to recognize that the medical record as an institutional practice is immensely complex and variegated. This has been brought home, quite cogently, in fact, by number of CSCW studies that have addressed the coordinative practices of clinical staff with special emphasis on the role of the medical record in these practices (e.g., Hartswood et al. 2003; Bossen 2006; Bansler and Kensing 2010; Fitzpatrick and Ellingsen 2013). A key finding emerging from these studies is that the medical record is better conceived of as a distributed system, an ecology of artifacts (Fitzpatrick 2004; Bardram and Bossen 2005; Schmidt et al. 2007). The medical record is a heterogeneous assembly of specialized representational and coordinative artifacts, typically spatially distributed and only occasionally and temporarily aligned spatially, and in any event only partially organized in a folder ('the working medical record', to borrow an apt phrase from Fitzpatrick 2004). That is, what has been established is that the medical record, as an 'ordering system', is adapted to support the high degree of specialization of clinical work.

However, in the analyses of the medical record, CSCW studies have generally treated the progress notes as just one entity among many. As a result, CSCW research in this area has not yet taken fully into account the fact that progress notes are a coordinative artifact of a rather special kind, a complex artifact consisting of a series of prose texts, written sequentially by doctors to facilitate and document their collaborative process of medical reasoning (as well as for administrative, legal, and research purposes). It is, if such a metaphor can be allowed, the black hole at the center of the galaxy of a multitude of coordinative and representational artifacts and practices.

Now, a body of literature outside of CSCW has undertaken what has so far not been done in CSCW, namely, to investigate the discursive nature of medical work by employing the notion of 'narration' in order to express an essential characteristic of the practices to which progress notes belong (e.g., Montgomery Hunter 1991; Atkinson 1995; Montgomery Hunter 1996, 2006; Greenhalgh et al., 2009). So far, this literature has provided a very important contribution to our understanding of the medical record in general and the progress notes in particular—by grasping their role against the background of the nature of medical reasoning. Montgomery Hunter refers to this as narrative case-based reasoning:

> Case narratives supplies a workable medium for representing knowledge that is time- and context-dependent […]. Physicians must know the facts of pathophysiology, the biological

> 'laws', but they cannot start there. They start instead with the individual patient: the symptoms and signs and answers to questions that fill out the story of the illness presented to medical attention [...]. Narrative's sequential presentation unfolds the tactful, tactical deployment of knowledge and experience relevant to determining what is wrong with one particular patient and deciding what action to take on her behalf (Montgomery Hunter 2006, p. 46).

That is, the challenge the physician faces is to understand what is wrong with a particular patient in light of general knowledge obtained from medical textbooks, scientific papers, and electronic media as well as clinical experience and available epidemiological evidence. This poses a challenge not just because of the incompleteness of medical knowledge but also because each patient has particular characteristics and because the available patient-related evidence in many cases is ambiguous and incomplete (Berg 1992). Under these circumstances, narrative provides a means for physicians to make sense of the patient's situation, impose some order on events, and explore possible cause-effect relationships:

> From the designation of certain details as relevant 'facts' and certain occurrences as 'events' to the use of rhetorical strategies in the representation and description of those facts and events, story-telling is concerned with the construction and interpretation of meaning (Montgomery Hunter1996).

The narrative aspect of medical discourse, and of the progress notes, is embedded within an overall interventionist logic, a logic of—possibly ongoing—diagnostic work and treatment. When a patient presents with a complaint, the physician will listen to the patient's story, ask questions, possibly conduct a physical examination, and in doing so transform the patient's initial story into a *medical* narrative emphasizing possible diagnosis and action (Berg 1992; Davenport 2011). At morning Conf.s this tentative medical narrative ('the case') will be shared with other members of the medical team, discussed, elaborated and perhaps compared with other similar cases (Atkinson 1995); and at every hand-over—e.g., when a patient is transferred to another ward—the story is retold, albeit often in a highly abbreviated version, but always with a view to possible diagnosis and action. Further versions or excerpts of this story may be shared with nurses, laboratory technicians, radiologists, and other clinicians who, in turn, may construct their own narratives which interpret and make sense of the data they produce (e.g., X-ray images) in light of the overall medical narrative (Rooksby and Kay 2003). The point here is that images and laboratory data require an appropriate context to be meaningful: 'the lab data, so to speak, never speak for themselves. Those various data are delivered framed by some sort of narrative about this patient, however truncated, however impersonalized a form it might take' (Waymack 2009, p. 220).

The notion of 'narration' has been very productive and illuminating, in bringing out and emphasizing the deeply narrative character of clinical discourse and reasoning. Surprisingly, however, the narrative approach has so far focused on oral communication among physicians, with a few notable exceptions, especially Pamela Hobbs' sociolinguistic study of the use of evidential markers in progress notes (2003).[1] This research suggests that progress notes are written in a discursive manner that allows authors to not only record data but to determine what is taken to be 'fact'; to select what is considered pertinent data; to qualify data in terms of certainty; to relate, aggregate, and organize data into a coherent exposition; and to make observations and suggestions in the infinitely subtle syntactic affordances offered by the prose genre (e.g., Poirier and Brauner 1990; Hobbs 2003). It is equally surprising, if not more, that the fact that physicians' progress notes are produced in a cooperative effort, as an integral part of coordinating and integrating the cooperative effort of providing medical treatment, has hardly been investigated (for an exception, cf. Svenningsen 2004). The purpose of the present study is to begin to unpack this strategically important coordinative practice.

Method and Data

The study we present in the following developed as a thread within a rather large four-year research project conducted in collaboration with physicians and lab technicians at the cardiology clinic of Rigshospitalet, the university hospital of Copenhagen. The focal point of the project was the treatment of patients with chronic heart failure by means of Implantable Cardioverter Defibrillators (ICDs), an advanced type of pacemaker that uses electrical pulses or shocks to help control life-threatening arrhythmias, especially those that can cause sudden cardiac arrest. Furthermore, it can store data about events that in turn can be downloaded wirelessly and transmitted to the hospital. The project involved, first of all, in-depth field studies to investigate existing documentation practices: observing the downloading of data from devices, tracing interpretation and migration of ICD data within the clinic, observing the use of medical records in consultations and interventions (Mønsted et al. 2011). Moreover, the project aimed at and involved the design and experimentation with prototypes for enhanced cooperation and information sharing among clinicians and between clinicians and patients (Bansler et al. 2010).

It was evident from the outset that ICDs and similar implanted monitoring technologies already had had significant impact on the medical record as an institution, in that it had become further fragmented, while the network of clinicians in need of being able to access the data, at some level of aggregation and interpretation, had expanded. One of the key issues therefore became to understand the ways in which medical records, both at the cardiology clinic of Rigshospitalet and at a major regional hospital, were structured, maintained, aligned, and used. A selection of ten patient records (the central patient folders as well as 'satellite' archives, altogether about 5,000 pages) were examined and from that study, as well as from observations of consultations, the pivotal role of the progress notes in

[1] For a kindred study of the discharge letter, cf. Winthereik and Vikkelsø (2005).

the medical record became obvious. A subset of medical records concerning five patients was therefore selected and the progress notes in these subjected to systematic scrutiny in order to understand their dual role as a coordinative and representational artifact. The present paper reports on the investigation of just one of these, namely, a series of progress notes concerning one patient. It was chosen because it was the most rich or complex and therefore the most telling. In other words, the case is exemplary.

In order to bring out the role of the progress notes in physicians coordinative practices and the way in which the format of the notes affords that role, we focus on how the physicians use narrative to make sense of the available evidence, construct plausible cause-and-effect relationships, and express degrees of certainty and uncertainty in very nuanced ways, and in doing so, we attempt to identify the structural, linguistic, and substantive conventions that guide the composition of progress notes, that is, what JoAnne Yates and Wanda Orlikowski have termed 'genre rules' (1992).

Progress Notes: An Example

In order to study the structure and content of progress notes, we shall here follow the acute hospitalization of an elderly man, Mads Jensen,[2] for cardiac (heart) rhythm disturbances. He has a long history of heart disease and has been hospitalized several times in the past for heart failure (at different hospitals). Diagnosed with *paroxystic atrial fibrillation*, which is the most common cardiac arrhythmia and gives rise to irregular heart rhythm that occurs only occasionally, Mads Jensen takes several kinds of medicine for controlling his arrhythmia. In this case, the hospitalization lasted 29 days. He was first admitted to a local general hospital (referred to below as the 'General Hospital') for 5 days and later transferred to Rigshospitalet—We focus on the series of paper-based progress notes produced in the course of the 5 days he was at the General Hospital, altogether 13 pages of typewritten text.[3]

Acute Hospitalization

Mads Jensen is admitted to the cardiology department at the General Hospital by ambulance on 27 May, in the evening, with the diagnosis of *atrial fibrillation with increased heart rate* and promptly treated with an intravenous injection of

---

[2] All names, dates, and other identifying information have been changed.

[3] At the time of the study, progress notes at the hospital in question were dictated digitally by the physician, typically immediately after examining the patient, for instance upon admission or during a ward round, and later typed by a medical secretary, printed out, and added to the patient's medical record (today they are also available in electronic form). The notes are usually recorded daily, but for patients in critical care, notes are typically made several times a day.

Amiodarone (Cordarone[4])—an antiarrhythmic agent used for various types of tachyarrhythmias (cardiac arrhythmia which give rise to increased heart rate). This has an immediate positive effect and slows the ventricular frequency to about 80 beats per minute. However, very soon he develops sweating and seizures and has cardiac arrest. Resuscitation is initiated according to the hospital's guidelines for advanced life support[5] (ALS) and after 6 min treatment he has restoration of spontaneous circulation. He is still unconscious and the physicians decide to transfer him to the Intensive Care Unit (ICU) for therapeutic cooling to reduce the risk of brain injury. The admission note reports[6]:

27.05.2009 21:15 CWARD

Admission
64 year old male admitted w.d. atrial fibrillation with rapid heart rate.
Previous
Known with paroxystic atrial fibrillation, treated with ablation in fall 2006.
30.01.07 CAG done at GH without indication for revascularization.
Ventriculography with normal LVEF.
Has reportedly mainly been treated at LOH, according to his son he has been hospitalized at LOH for most of 2006.
Furthermore had PCI.
Present
Is reported with fast atrial fibrillation, comes in with broad complex tachycardia, as mentioned known with left bundle branch block, in acutely bad shape, respiratorically and circulatory. Is awake and has communicated with the staff. Complains of nausea and would like a bag to throw up in. Due to fast, broad complex tachycardia there is given
rp. inj. Cordarone 300 mg as bolus IV
with good effect on the ventricular frequency, which falls to about 80. Continued broad QRS complexes. Pt becomes pale and cold sweating, gets seizure like twitches in the face and the extremities. Pt becomes unconcious and his respiration fails, cardiac arrest is diagnosed and basic resuscitation 30/2 is commenced. Scope shows bradycardia down to 30. There is given
rp. inj. Atropin 3 mg IV
and after 4 min inj. Adrenalin 1 mg IV
Pt has a decent systolic BP between 110 and 140. Does not wake up at all and is intubated. Has still has seizures with grimacing movements in the head-neck region, pt conferred with HM, pt is transferred to ICU for cooling.
There is an ABG with pH 6.9, PCO2 9.2, PO2 10, BE—16.9, N 138, K 3.8, glucose 15.6, lactate 9.5.
Provisional biochemistry: Leuc. 17.8, thromb. 220, Hb 8.3.
Christian Nielsen/gl

---

4 Amiodarone is the active ingredient in Cordarone (and other brand name drugs). In this context it is to be taken as a synonym of Cordarone.

5 Advanced Life Support (ALS) is an emergency procedure performed to manually support breathing and circulation with the aim of preserving intact brain function until the patient has a return of spontaneous circulation (ROSC) or is declared dead.

6 The excerpts from the progress notes have been translated from Danish by the authors.

This note recounts a quite dramatic episode, but is otherwise unremarkable in that it follows a fairly standard structure and is written in the usual format and style of progress notes in this hospital. It illustrates several important features of progress notes. First, we notice the standardized layout with headers and indentations that allow the reader to quickly locate information of interest. Second, the note is clearly identified by the acronym of the ward (CWARD, the cardiology department), the name of the dictating physician (Christian Nielsen), the initials of the medical secretary who typed it (gl), and date and time. Third, the note is written in a technical language using medical terms and standard abbreviations such as Pt (Patient) and PCI (Percutaneous Coronary Intervention). Furthermore, initials and local abbreviations are often used instead of the full names of people and organizational units (e.g., GH for General Hospital). Fourth, the note is written in a concise format and it relies heavily on the reader's background knowledge, both of medicine and of local circumstances such as the organization of the region's hospital system. For instance, no reason is given for the decision to cool down the patient, because this is a standard procedure for patients with cardiac arrest.

The structure of the note follows a common pattern: chief complaint, typically one sentence that introduces the patient and the principal reason for the admission; the medical history prior to the current admission (under the heading 'Previous'); a short account of the current admission (under the heading 'Present'); the physical examination of the patient, which in this case is quite rudimentary and leads directly to the initiation of treatment; and finally a rather truncated assessment and plan, which simply states that the patient should be cooled down. Quite unusually, however, the note ends by listing a number of laboratory findings.

It is characteristic that the account given in the note locates the current episode in the temporal framework of the overall illness trajectory of the patient and constructs a chronology that identifies significant events and arranges them in a logical order. The turning point in the narrative is the sudden onset of sweating and seizures leading to cardiac arrest, which is described quite graphically. No explanation for the cardiac arrest is given, but the narrative hints at the possibility that it is caused by the injection of Cordarone (Amiodarone).

Transfer to the Intensive Care Unit

Mads Jensen is then transferred to the Intensive Care Unit (ICU) at the hospital where therapeutic hypothermia (cooling) treatment is initiated. After the transfer, a new admission note is added to his medical record, this time composed by an intensive care physician. This admission note has many similarities with the previous one. The layout and style of writing is the same and it follows the same overall structure, beginning with the chief complaint and ending with the assessment and plan.

This admission note recounts the story of how Mads Jensen was admitted to the hospital with atrial fibrillation, how he developed cardiac arrest after treatment with Amiodarone IV, and how he was resuscitated and transferred to the ICU. But this time the story is retold with more emphasis on the patient's neurological state and the risk of brain damage due to insufficient oxygen supply during the cardiac arrest and less emphasis on the patient's cardiological problems:

> **Present**
> Pt admitted tonight by ambulance due to AF with 1:1 conduction. General condition affected by this. In addition dilated unresponsive pupils observed. In the admission room at C 23, Cordarone is given and pt becomes momentarily unresponsive, has generalized tonic–clonic seizures and goes into clinical cardiac arrest. In the beginning what looks like VT, but before we get to give a shock, then asystole. Pt is given chest compressions, ventilated and atropin 3 mg and adrenalin 1 + 1 mg are administered. Pt is intubated. After 6 min. of ALS pt has spontaneous circulation again. GCS 3. Gets intermittent jerks, is grimacing on the tube and increases to GCS 6. First ABG with pH 6.92, PCO2 9.21, PO2 10.1, BE 16.9, lac. 9.5. Infusion with bicarbobate 100 ml. is administered. Transferred to ICU, where cooling, sedation is commenced. Bladder catheter and an arterial line are inserted and a 5-lumen CVC is placed in the right sided external jugular vein (right side due to marevan[7]).

First, it is noted that the patient had 'dilated unresponsive pupils' when admitted to the hospital, which can be a sign of brain injury. Second, it is recorded that 'GCS [is] 3′ immediately after the successful resuscitation and that it later increases to 6. GCS is an acronym for the *Glasgow Coma Scale,* a neurological scale that aims to give a reliable, objective way of assessing the state of consciousness of a person.[8] Third, many of the specific cardiological data, such as information about EKG readings, blood pressure and heart rate, are omitted from this version of the story, and the evocative account of how the patient starts sweating and develops severe muscle seizures is replaced by the matter-of-fact statement that the patient develops 'generalized tonic–clonic seizures'.

During the night the ICU staff succeeds in stabilizing the patient, but he is still sedated and cooled down to 32 °C. At midnight, after 24 h of hypothermia treatment, they begin slowly warming him up again and the next morning (29 May) he is awake and able to communicate by nodding his head as sign of yes or no, although still partially sedated. However, the ICU physicians now have a new worry: the patient's white blood cell count is rising (sign of infection) and he has developed a pleural effusion (accumulation of water in the chest cavity) that could be caused by pneumonia. They decide to immediately start antibiotic treatment.

The cause of his heart arrest is also still unresolved and therefore they send for a cardiologist to perform an echocardiography (a cardiac ultrasound) and assess the patient's cardiac condition. The cardiologist arrives at noon and after examining the patient, he dictates a comprehensive progress note.

The note starts, once again, by reviewing the patient's history—but this time the primary focus is on his heart troubles, which are discussed in much more detail

---

[7] An oral anticoagulant. Marevan is the Danish brand name for this drug (Warfarin).

[8] The scale provides a score in the range 3–15, in which progressively higher scores indicate higher levels of consciousness. Patients with scores of 3–8 are usually said to be in a coma.

than before. The note confirms some information, for instance that Mads Jensen, according to his family, took Cordarone tablets for his atrial fibrillation, but it also questions previous information about his having a coronary angioplasty at some point (referred to as a PCI, percutaneous coronary intervention, in the progress notes).

Furthermore, the note adds two new pieces of information about his heart problems. It describes how he has been free of symptoms until 4 months ago, but then began having episodes of difficulty breathing and rapid heart beating, and it discusses in detail an ECG printout from the ambulance, which has not been mentioned before.

After the review of the patient's recent medical history follows a discussion of the most likely reason for the heart arrest. First, it is pointed out that cardiac telemetry (i.e., long term in-hospital monitoring of the heart rhythm) conducted after the cardiac arrest shows 'severe prolongation of the QT interval,[9] up to 600 ms, which confirms the suspicion of an acute Amiodarone effect'. Second, it is noted that a test carried out the same morning shows that the level of troponin T (a cardiac protein which is leaked into blood during cardiac injury) is normal, 'which weighs against the suspicion of acute ischaemic genesis and consequently against the suspicion of ventricular arrhythmia'. However, no firm conclusion is reached:

> On ward C23 perceived as circulatory instable, which is why IV Amiodarone was administered. At first, it apparently stopped the SVT, but also caused SA block leading to severe bradycardia and clinical cardiac arrest.
> Subsequent telemetry shows severe prolongation of the QT interval, up to 600 ms, which confirms the suspicion of an acute Amiodarone effect.
> Biochemical measures this morning show normal troponin T, which weighs against the suspicion of acute ischaemic genesis and consequently against the suspicion of ventricular arrhythmia.

The note ends with a cardiological assessment and plan. The 'most probable' diagnosis is recorded as 'paroxystic atrial fibrillation and atrial flutter that despite Cordarone are being conducted with a high rate to the ventricles'. Consequently, the cardiologist recommends that the patient resumes taking his usual Amiodarone (Cordarone) tablets as soon as possible. At the same time, he warns against giving more bolus injections (the injection of a drug in a high quantity, called a bolus) of Amiodarone.

Life Threatening Crisis

Mads Jensen's condition seems to be improving and the expectation is that he can be discharged from the ICU and transferred back to the cardiology ward within a day or two. However, after the morning round the next day (30 May), the

---

[9] The QT interval is measured on an electrocardiogram (ECG).

physician is very concerned about his infection. She notes that 'Pt has rapidly increasing biochemical markers of infection, possibly stemming from pneumonia', despite treatment with antibiotics. She decides to call for a microbiological specialist, who thinks it is too early to tell whether the antibiotics are effective or not and advises to 'wait and see'.

The next morning (1 June), Mads Jensen has difficulties breathing and his condition deteriorates rapidly. The physician has a strong suspicion that the patient in fact has pneumonia and that it is getting out of control.

Four hours later, the same physician notes that Mads Jensen has developed atrial fibrillation and speculates whether the underlying cause is heart failure or sepsis, a severe, potentially fatal complication to bacterial infections where the infection triggers a variety of delirious disease processes causing manifestations such as bleeding, coagulation and shock:

01.06.2009 14:00 ICU

Increasingly circulatory unstable, AF 130-150. Could be caused by worsening heart failure, but it could also be due to worsening septic condition.

[...]

He decides to call for a cardiologist. The cardiologist tries three times to restore a normal heart rhythm with DC cardioversion,[10] but without success, and then recommends trying to regulate the atrial fibrillation (i.e., decrease the pulse rate) by giving three IV injections of Digoxin at 6 h intervals—despite the bad experience with the Amiodarone bolus 4 days earlier, which led to his cardiac arrest.

The digitalization is without effect and the next morning (2 June), after consultations with a cardiologist, the ICU physician decides to transfer Mads Jensen to Rigshospitalet, which is better equipped to treat heart failure and sepsis.

Functions and Genre-characteristics of Progress Notes

As the case should show, the medical record should be conceived of as far more than a set of records, or an 'ecology' of artifacts, but rather as a rather special ordering system in which the progress notes perform an essentially epistemic function and in that capacity serve as the integrative force at the center of the cloud of orbiting inscriptions and artifacts.

Physicians' progress notes are produced in an open-ended, enormously variegated, and essentially contingent, epistemic process (Strauss et al. 1985; Atkinson 1995; Montgomery Hunter 2006). The notes concerning a particular patient constitute a working document that 'records the core narrative of the patient's medical

[10] DC (Direct Current) cardioversion is a medical procedure by which a cardiac arrhythmia is converted to a normal rhythm, using electricity. It is performed by giving the heart an electric shock, at a specific moment in the cardiac cycle. In contrast, pharmacologic cardioversion, uses antiarrhythmia medication instead of an electrical shock.

care' as it unfolds over time (Hobbs 2003, p. 454). They serve both as a tool for thinking for the individual physician, enabling him or her to make sense of the patient's past history and current condition, and as a coordinative artifact used by physicians, nurses, and other health care professionals.

In a way that is similar to a scientific community's evolving repertoire of papers (apart from the imperative to act that is defining of clinical work), some entries serve to present bits of fact (similar to research notes), other entries serve to outline treatment plans or strategies (research problems and hypotheses), while other entries again serve to review what has been learned so far. Written over time by several clinicians, often from different specialisms, in a highly distributed process, the progress notes serve to reflect ongoing external developments, to select and counterpose bits of data, to formulate hypotheses as to causation, to suggest lines of action, etc. The epistemic function of the progress notes is clearly reflected in the way progress notes are composed and formatted. The conventions guiding their form and substance have developed over more than a century and today play a cardinal role in medical practice. It is therefore useful to conceive of the format of progress notes as a specific 'genre' of clinical communication (next to discharge letters, lab reports, etc.). In the words of Yates and Orlikowski, a 'genre' functions in a given community as an 'institutionalized template' (2002, p. 15) for communicative action, by establishing a set of taken-for-granted expectations that influence both how communicative artifacts are routinely composed, interpreted, and understood. In fact, and as illustrated in the previous section, physicians' progress notes constitute an established and well-defined genre of clinical communication, with a wide normative scope, governing how physicians organize, record, and share their observations and thoughts (Hobbs 2003). From the case we can distill a set of important genre-specific features of the progress notes are:

(1) The format is concise. The notes are written in medical language using highly specialized terminology as well as shorthand, acronyms and abbreviations—some of which are standardized and common while others are more local and idiosyncratic. Therefore, understanding the text requires a great deal of background knowledge concerning not only common medical terms and procedures, but also local circumstances and resources. As pointed out by Hobbs (2003), a progress note is a 'condensed text' in which 'the reader's background knowledge supplies the cohesion that is provided by explicit linkage in other contexts' (Hobbs 2003).
(2) The notes have a standardized layout and are clearly identified by date and time, author, and transcriber. The main body of the note is divided into sections with relatively standardized headings as a guide for readers and indentations are used to accentuate prescriptions and orders and make it easy to spot them in text.
(3) The composition of the notes follows a common pattern. They are typically organized into the following sections: (a) past medical history, (b) history of present illness, (c) laboratory data, images and results from the physical examination of the patient, (d) assessment, and (e) plan. However, progress

notes are written in a variety of formats and vary much in length and detail. Admission notes are quite comprehensive and, in addition to the above mentioned sections, they usually also contain sections that describe the chief complaint (i.e., the reason for hospitalization or for transfer to another ward or hospital), allergies, medications on admission, tobacco and alcohol use. The daily progress notes, on the other hand, may vary from lengthy and very thorough to rather short or even quite rudimentary, depending on the clinical situation or task at hand.

(4) Substance, organization and style varies from one medical specialism to another. Each group of specialists addresses 'concerns that reflect the unique philosophy and skills of that professional group' (Poirier and Brauner 1990). The cardiologists, for instance, focus on cardiovascular disease and hone in on such issues as blood pressure, heart rate and stroke volume, while the ICU physicians usually have a broader perspective, taking a more systemic approach to treatment. In other words, the progress notes embody the complexity of medical work in the hospital setting and, consequently, they lack 'the ultimate cohesiveness of a *single* author or point of view' (Poirier and Brauner 1990). For instance, in the previous section, we saw how different specialists—while adhering to the conventions of the progress note genre—construct noticeably different clinical narratives, each foregrounding certain events and types of data.

(5) It is characteristic of the progress notes we have analyzed that doubt, uncertainty, and ambiguity are very much present in them. Physicians must regularly act upon uncertain, incomplete, and even contradictory evidence, and the process of diagnosis and treatment is therefore, in the words of Poirier and Brauner, often 'fraught with ambiguity and inconclusiveness' (Poirier and Brauner 1990). This essential uncertainty of medical practice is reflected in the physicians' writing. They are clearly wary of drawing unfounded or premature conclusions about the source of the patient's problems and, consequently, they often present their hypotheses and conclusions as tentative and provisional, for instance by hedging their statements with adverbs such as 'possibly', 'probably', and 'presumably'. Furthermore, the physicians carefully express their degree of trust in the recorded information by marking it for both source and mode of knowing (factual, firsthand, or reported) and, sometimes, even by explicitly questioning its trustworthiness. They do so by following writing conventions that 'key grammatical forms to the sources of information' (Hobbs 2003). The patient's own report of his or her symptoms is, for instance, marked as indirect discourse, while information stemming from other health professionals is reported in the agentless passive voice. So-called objective information, that is, information which is 'deemed to be directly observable or independently verifiable', is conventionally reported as facts (Hobbs 2003).

The progress notes mediate the integrative discourse in which the ensemble of clinicians collectively make sense of the myriad inscriptions on multitudes of artifacts associated with the medical record and express what they collectively take to be the state of the world at the time of writing.

Of course, the progress notes do not stand alone. They only make sense as part of the ongoing conversation and coordination among physicians (and other clinicians) about possible diagnosis, treatment options and prescribed therapies (Garfinkel and Bittner 1967; Conn, et al. 2009). As Atkinson (1995) has pointed out, the practice of medicine constitutes to a large extent an oral culture. Physicians constantly talk with each other, with other health professionals, and with patients—in clinical Conf.s, during ward rounds, in the hallway, by telephone, and so on. Nevertheless, the written progress notes provide a common point of reference, which is of crucial importance given the highly distributed and around-the-clock nature of hospital work. They serve as the 'primary means of communication among treaters who are not co-present with each other' and allow them not only to coordinate their actions but also to share their thoughts and observations concerning diagnosis and treatment (Hobbs 2003). According to Atkinson (1995), there is a 'close relationship between written and oral accounts' (Atkinson 1995, p. 91) of patient care constructed by physicians. Physicians refer to the progress notes (and other written materials) when discussing the patient with their colleagues and the outcome of these discussions may in turn be recorded in subsequent progress notes. Several examples of this are present in Mads Jensen's medical record. Finally, physicians share vast amounts of medical knowledge and they rely heavily on this background knowledge when dictating and reading progress notes: 'Background knowledge operates as a reciprocally shared resource, with speakers assuming its availability to recipients in designing their utterances, and recipients assuming that this assumption has in fact been made, and interpreting the message accordingly' (Hobbs 2002, p. 267).

Discussion

As we have shown in the previous sections, progress notes are far from being idiosyncratic scribbles or 'glob[s] of free text' (McDonald 1997) as one medical informatics researcher disdainfully has put it. On the contrary, they constitute a well-defined genre, with elaborate rules for composing different kinds of notes (e.g., admission notes) and for conveying attitudes towards recorded information (e.g., degree of reliability). This is not to say that there is no variation in how different physicians dictate their notes. Although genres shape communicative action in organizations, genre rules are not rigid and they do not create a 'binding constraint' on the substance and form of the progress notes (Yates and Orlikowski 1992, p. 306). As we have seen, the genre rules are flexible enough to allow for significant and systematic differences in both content and structure of progress notes from one specialism to another. Furthermore, there are also individual variations in how physicians dictate their notes, and the rules can always be bent or broken, dependent on the circumstances and the information the physician may wish to convey.

Nevertheless, progress notes have their own distinctive format and style that enable experienced physicians to exchange information and thoughts efficiently. The genre rules guide authors in composing notes and they orient readers to how they should read and what they should look for and expect to find where. Thus, in a study of physicians' ways of reading medical records, Nygren and Henriksson (1992) found that the 'format, layout and other textural features' provided 'effective guidance in the process of searching, reading and assessing the relevance of different items of information in the record' and allowed them to skim through even quite voluminous notes rather easily (Nygren and Henriksson 1992, p. 1).[11] This is presumably not just because the conventions of the genre impose a certain degree of standardization, but also because they, as Hobbs has put it, promote an 'economy of form' (2003, p. 471) without superfluous details or explanations, which allows physicians to convey a great deal of information in a few words.

The progress notes articulate the 'core narrative' of the patient's illness and medical care (Kay and Purves 1996; Hobbs 2003). It is not the patient's story, but a medical case narrative, authored by the involved physicians as part of their effort to diagnose and treat the patient's illness: 'The medical record contains the medical discourse of at least one physician talking, so to speak, to him- or herself about the possibilities of diagnosis and treatment, a process which can be fraught with ambiguity and inconclusiveness' (Poirier and Brauner 1990, p. 31).

The construction of a case narrative necessarily implies a selection and ordering process, and this can only be done from a certain perspective and for a specific purpose. During the reasoning process, the physician sifts through the available evidence in the form of the patient's own account of the course of illness, the results from the physical examination, biochemical laboratory results, X-rays, pathology reports, etc., assesses its credibility, identifies important 'events', 'signs', and 'symptoms', and arranges them in a certain order to construct a recognizable medical story. The function of the case narrative is to give meaning to an otherwise intractable collection of data by establishing causal relations between selected events, signs, and symptoms, thereby allowing these to 'take their meaning by belonging to, and contributing to, the story as a whole' (Mattingly 1998, p. 46). The structure of the narrative serves to: 'emphasize or de-emphasize certain story-events, to interpret some and to leave others to inference, to show or to tell, to comment or to remain silent, to focus on this or that aspect of an event or character' (King 1992. Cited in Kay and Purves, 1996, p. 76).

In sum, progress notes are not a literal recording of what happened along the patient's illness trajectory, but rather a highly selective account of events, findings, and thoughts, as seen from a certain—interventionist—perspective. They function as a cognitive artifact that facilitates memory and recall and they enable

[11] The study did not focus exclusively on the progress notes, but on the traditional medical record as a whole, that is, including lab reports, X-rays, etc. contained in the patient's folder.

collaborative sense-making and coordination of actions in a highly complex, distributed work practice.

This insight has important implications for the design of electronic patient record systems. To be truly useful in clinical practice, such technologies must accommodate physicians' need for composing and sharing medical narratives, hypotheses, reflections, elaborations, plans of action, etc. in a straightforward and flexible way. However, the dominant design philosophy runs counter to this requirement. Extending the database technologies that were developed for administrative record systems, it emphasizes structured data capture at the expense of flexibility and expressivity, because data standardization according to a pre-defined scheme of types is a prerequisite for computer facilities such as decision support, quality assurance, workflow automation, as well as secondary use of data for research and administrative purposes.

On the other hand, as argued earlier, current coordinative practices in clinical settings, based on paper-based medical records, are not sustainable. They are crumbling under their own weight. Nor is it a tenable strategy to replicate the flexibility of the conventional practices of composing progress notes by offering 'free text'. This approach risks under-exploiting the potential of computing technology, for instance capabilities for creating hypertext links to laboratory tests or diagnostic images, for setting up notifications and automatic alerts, for presenting data in different ways dependent on the user's perspective, and for easy lookup of information, keywords or codes while entering data (cf., e.g., Wilcox et al. 2010). Worse, as pointed out in a recent editorial in *The American Journal of Medicine*, a simple replication of traditional practices combined with the copy-and-paste function of EPR may have the 'insidious consequence' that 'the narrative' is lost: 'Because charts have become capacious warehouses of disorganized, irrelevant, or erroneous data, the story of the patient and the patient's illness is no longer easy to read or likely to be read. In a most compelling and perhaps unintended way, we are witnessing the "death" of the health record narrative, as many of us have known it' (Siegler and Adelman 2009, p. 495). This may lead to frustrated physicians and the creation of informal records, sometimes referred to as 'parallel charts' (Siegler and Adelman 2009), 'shadow charts' (Wears 2008), or 'cheat sheets' (Varpio et al. 2006), and even, in the worst case, to medical errors and patient harm.

Moreover, the existing progress notes genre has its own weaknesses. The genre was created at a time when the division of labor in medicine was less developed and typical illness trajectories were shorter and less complicated. Thus, originally, progress notes were primarily meant to support communication and collaboration within small, relatively homogeneous groups of physicians for a comparatively short period of time. In the hospital of today, this situation is radically changed because of the increasing prevalence of chronic diseases and the continued growth of specialization in medicine. Patients with chronic diseases often have complicated, protracted courses of illness and require treatment from multiple medical specialists. The result is that a typical patient's progress notes may span years or even decades and contain hundreds of entries from different medical experts.

When the notes swell to such proportions, they become quite unmanageable and nearly impossible to browse, read, and absorb in any meaningful way—not just because of their sheer size and number of entries, but because of the diversity of content and authorship, and the fact that physicians from different medical specialties speak different languages, both literally and figuratively. This is not an entirely new development (cf. Poirier and Brauner 1990), but it has accelerated markedly over the past decades due to the rapid growth in medical technology and knowledge, which has spurred specialization and challenges the implicit assumption of 'background knowledge' (Hobbs 2002, 2003). Thus, physicians from different specialisms may have trouble understanding each others' progress notes (Bansler et al. 2010).

The obvious route to explore is to impose a certain degree of structure on the notes by dividing them into labeled and standardized segments, e.g., sections, fields, and paragraphs (Tange et al. 1998; Tange 1999; Johnson et al. 2008). Such documents are sometimes referred to as 'semi-structured', indicating that they impose certain 'restrictions on the clinician (standard fields for data entry), while allowing freedom of expression within those units (free text paragraphs)' (Johnson, et al. 2008, p. 55). According to Johnson et al., such an approach may 'improve completeness and accuracy of clinical narrative'; it may help physicians 'to locate data efficiently' by 'displaying documents in labeled chunks or paragraphs'; and it may allow for the construction of new documents, e.g., summaries or overviews, by reusing data and text from designated fields of existing documents. Imposing a higher degree of structure on the progress notes may thus both improve the quality of the narrative and make it easier to navigate and browse long documents (Johnson et al. 2008, p. 55). It does not, however, solve the problem of communication between different medical specialisms.

Yet another approach might be to aim for a much deeper integration of computational functionality in the design of the progress notes editor, for instance, by providing dynamic support to the physicians in their task of composing progress notes in the form of an underlying computational interpreter that, based on a nomenclature and possibly a classification scheme, recognizes key terms as they are being types, offers possible synonyms, and allows the physician to confirm or disconfirm the interpretation. Such interpreter facilities are well-known from text-composition technologies as exemplified by online spelling checkers and dictionaries, as well as by the 'autocompletion' and semi-automatic formatting facilities of advanced text editors such as source code editors. The potential advantage would be to retain the current degree of expressivity and flexibility while at the same time providing for cross-indexation with other forms of documentation (e.g., links) and facilitating rigorous indexation and classification of clinical data, for instance for secondary use. The challenge here lies in making the coordinative protocols, in the form of the underlying nomenclature and classification scheme, accessible for cooperative maintenance. That is, it must be possible for physicians at a particular clinic (or at a given hospital, or at some higher organizational level) to negotiate and maintain the standard nomenclature or classification scheme. However, these ideas are simply just ideas.

The overall conclusion must be that there is still much we do not know about the role of narratives in clinical discourse and that there are still many open questions about how to incorporate medical narratives in the EPR. Although the paper-based progress notes genre is widespread today, it is difficult to see what the electronic equivalent should look like and what exactly its role should be in relation to the structured or coded data in the record. Consequently, there is a strong need for more field-based innovation and experimentation to develop and test new approaches to the design of EPR systems.

Acknowledgments The research was supported by the Danish Council for Strategic Research as part of the CITH project (2008–2012). Technicians and cardiologists at Rigshospitalet and Bispebjerg Hospital participated in the project, and their essential contribution is gratefully acknowledged.

References

Atkinson, P. (1995). *Medical talk and medical work: The liturgy of the clinic*. London: SAGE.

J. P. Bansler & F. Kensing (Eds.). (2010). Information infrastructures for healthcare. [Special theme of] *Computer Supported Cooperative Work (CSCW): The Journal of Collaborative Computing, 19*(6), 519–520.

J. P Bansler, E. C. Havn, & T. Mønsted. (2010). Designing shared electronic records for chronic care. In C. Nøhr & J. E. C. M. Aarts (Eds.), *ITHC 2010: Information technology in healthcare: Sociotechnical approaches, Aalborg, Denmark, 23–24 June 2010* (pp. 53–58). Amsterdam: IOS Press.

J. P. Bansler et al. (2011). A study of the fragmentation of the medical record. In P. Bjørn et al. (Eds.), *Infrastructures for healthcare 2011, 23–24 June 2011* (pp. 94–97). Copenhagen: IT University of Copenhagen.

J. E. Bardram & C. Bossen. (2005). A web of coordinative artifacts: Collaborative work at a hospital ward. In K. Schmidt, et al. (Eds.), *GROUP'05: International conference on supporting group work 6–9 November 2005, Sanibel Island, Florida* (pp. 168–176). New York: ACM Press.

Berg, Marc. (1992). The construction of medical disposals: Medical sociology and medical problem solving in clinical practice. *Sociology of Health and Illness, 14*(2), 151–180.

C. Bossen. (2006). Representations at work: A national standard for electronic health records. In P. J. Hinds, et al. (Eds.), *CSCW 2006: ACM conference on computer supported cooperative work, 4–8 November 2006, Banff, Alberta, Canada* (pp. 69–78). New York: ACM Press.

Clarke, K., et al. (2001). The electronic medical record and everyday medical work. *Health Informatics Journal, 7*, 168–170.

L. G. Conn, et al. (2009) Communication channels in general internal medicine: A description of baseline patterns for improved interprofessional collaboration. *Qualitative Health Research, 19*(7), 943–953.

N. H. M. Davenport. (2011). Medical residents' use of narrative templates in storytelling and diagnosis. *Social Science and Medicine, 73*(6), 873–881.

Fitzpatrick, G. (2004). Integrated care and the working record. *Health Informatics Journal, 10*(4), 291–302.

G. Fitzpatrick & G. Ellingsen. (2013). A review of 25 years of CSCW research in healthcare: Contributions, challenges and future agendas. *Computer Supported Cooperative Work (CSCW): The Journal of Collaborative Computing and Work Practices, 22*(4–6). http://link.springer.com/article/10.1007/s10606-012-9168-0 (in press).

H. Garfinkel, E.Bittner. (1967). "Good" organizational reasons for "bad" clinic records. In H. Garfinkel (Ed.), *Studies in ethnomethodology* (pp. 186–207). Englewood-Cliffs:Prentice-Hall.

Greenhalgh, T., et al. (2009). Tensions and paradoxes in electronic patient record research: A systematic literature review using the meta-narrative method. *The Milbank Quarterly, 87*(4), 729–788.

Hartswood, M., et al. (2003). Making a case in medical work: Implications for the electronic medical record. *Computer Supported Cooperative Work (CSCW): The Journal of Collaborative Computing, 12*(3), 241–266.

Hewett, D. G., et al. (2009). Communication in medical records: Intergroup language and patient care. *Journal of Language and Social Psychology, 28*(2), 119–138.

Hobbs, P. (2002). Islands in a string: The use of background knowledge in an obstetrical resident's notes. *Journal of Sociolinguistics, 6*(2), 267–274.

Hobbs, P. (2003). The use of evidentiality in physicians' progress notes. *Discourse Studies, 5*(4), 451–478.

S. B. Johnson,, et al.(2008) An electronic health record based on structured narrative. *Journal of the American Medical Informatics Association, 15*(1), 54–64.

S. Kay & I. N. Purves. (1996). Medical records and other stories: A narratological framework. *Methods of Information in Medicine, 35*(2), 72–87.

Mattingly, C.l. (1998). *Healing dramas and clinical plots: The narrative structure of experience.* Cambridge: Cambridge University Press.

C. J. McDonald. (1997). The barriers to electronic medical record systems and how to overcome them. *Journal of the American Medical Informatics Association, 4*(3), 213–221.

Kathryn, M. H. (1991). *Doctors' stories: The narrative structure of medical knowledge.* Princeton: Princeton University Press.

Kathryn, M. H. (1996). Narrative, literature, and the clinical exercise of practical reason. *The Journal of Medicine and Philosophy, 21*, 303–320.

M. H. Kathryn [K. Montgomery]. (1992). *How Doctors Think: Clinical Judgment and the Practice of Medicine.* Oxford: Oxford at the Clarendon Press.

T. Mønsted, M. C. Reddy, & J. P. Bansler. (2011). The use of narratives in medical work: A field study of physician-patient consultations. In S. Bødker, et al. (Eds.), *ECSCW 2011: Proceedings of the 12th European conference on computer supported cooperative work, 24–28 September 2011* (pp. 81–100). Aarhus: Springer.

E. Nygren, & P. Henriksson. (1992). Reading the medical record. I: Analysis of physicians' ways of reading the medical record. *Computer Methods and Programs in Biomedicine, 39*, 1–12.

A. K. Parekh, & M. B. Barton. (2007, April 7). The challenge of multiple comorbidity for the US health care system. *The Journal of the American Medical Association, 303*(13), 1303–1304.

S. Poirier, & D. J. Brauner. (1990). The voices of the medical record. *Theoretical Medicine, 1*(1), 29–39.

J. Rooksby, & S. Kay. (2003). 'Patient reports as stories of clinical work: Narrative and work in neuroradiology. *Methods of Information in Medicine, 42*, 445–450.

Rosenbloom, S. T., et al. (2011). Data from clinical notes: A perspective on the tension between structure and flexible documentation. *Journal of the American Medical Informatics Association, 18*, 181–186.

K. Schmidt, I. Wagner, & M. Tolar. (2007). Permutations of cooperative work practices: A study of two oncology clinics. In T. Gross, et al. (Eds.), *GROUP international conference on supporting group work, 4–7 November 2007, Sanibel Island, Florida* (pp. 1–10) New York: ACM Press.

E. L. Siegler, & R. Adelman. (2009). Copy and paste: A remediable hazard of electronic health records. *The American Journal of Medicine, 122*(6), 495–496.

A. L. Strauss, et al. (1985). *Social organization of medical work.* Chicago: University of Chicago Press.

Svenningsen, S. (2004). *Den elektroniske patientjournal og medicinsk arbejde: reorganisering af roller, ansvar og risici på sygehuse.* København: Handelshøjskolens Forlag.

Tange, H. J. (1999). Consultation of medical narratives in the electronic medical record. *Methods of Information in Medicine, 38*, 289–293.

H. J. Tange, et al. (1998). 'The granularity of medical narratives and its effect on the speed and completeness of information retrieval. *Journal of the American Medical Informatics Association, 5*(6) 571–582.

Varpio, L., et al. (2006). Working off the record: Physicians' and nurses' transformations of electronic patient record-based patient information. *Academic Medicine, 81*(10), S35–S39.

Waymack, M. H. (2009). Yearning for certainty and the critique of medicine as "science". *Theoretical Medicine and Bioethics, 30*(3), 215–229.

Wears, R. L. (2008). The chart is dead—long live the chart. *Annals of Emergency Medicine, 52*(4), 390–391.

L. Wilcox, et al. (2010). Physician-driven management of patient progress notes in an intensive care unit. In *CHI 2010: Proceedings of the SIGCHI conference on human factors in computing systems, 10–15 April, 2010, Atlanta, Georgia* (pp. 1879–1888). New York: ACM Press.

B. R. Winthereik & S. Vikkelsø. (2005). ICT and integrated care: Some dilemmas of standardising inter-organisational communication. *Computer Supported Cooperative Work (CSCW): The Journal of Collaborative Computing, 14*(1), 43–67.

Stead, W.W. & H. S. Lin (Eds.), *Computational technology for effective health care: Immediate steps and strategic directions*. Washington, D.C: National Academies Press.

J. Yates & W. J. Orlikowski. (1992). Genres of organizational communication: a structurational approach to studying communication and media. *The Academy of Management Review, 17*(2), pp. 299–326.

J. Yates & W. J. Orlikowski. (2002). Genre systems: Structuring interaction through communicative norms. *The Journal of Business Communication, 39*(1), 13–35.

Moving Healthcare to the Home: The Work to Make Homecare Work

Tone Bratteteig and Ina Wagner

Abstract The paper discusses the work of care recipients, informal caregivers, and the larger networks that are involved in homecare work. It discusses different kinds of work, and also if all the tasks involved in homecare could and should be labeled work. Finally, the paper looks into what kinds of work is delegated to machines and how this affects the work performed by people. One of the main conclusions from this analysis is that seeing the many different kinds of work that go into making homecare work is a good basis for designing alternative solutions.

Introduction

Many countries worry about their health care system not being able to handle an increasingly ageing population with a decreasing number of health careers to implement the system. A common solution in line with New Public Management is to move health care to the home to be carried out by care workers and the care recipients themselves (e.g., EU's Ambient Assisted Living (AAL) initiatives). In this paper we critically reflect on how healthcare is moved to the home and delegated to the people living in the home, their relatives and neighbours, as well as to a range of technical devices and systems. We particularly focus on elderly people living independently in their own homes, which is at the heart of the AAL initiatives. Activities that used to be paid work tasks are 'translated' into tasks to be carried out by the care recipients themselves and those who support them assisted by 'homecare technologies'. We examine and reflect on the ways in which

T. Bratteteig (✉) · I. Wagner
University of Oslo, Oslo, Norway
e-mail: tone@ifi.uio.no

I. Wagner
e-mail: ina.wagner@tuwien.ac.at

O. W. Bertelsen et al. (eds.), *ECSCW 2013: Proceedings of the 13th European Conference on Computer Supported Cooperative Work, 21–25 September 2013, Paphos, Cyprus*, DOI: 10.1007/978-1-4471-5346-7_8, © Springer-Verlag London 2013

caregiving in a home environment can be considered work and on who are the people involved in doing this work.

Translating Healthcare into Smart Homes

The development of homecare technologies today seems to concentrate on the delegation of work to machines: AAL envisions the intelligent technical home environment looking after people (e.g. van der Broek et al. 2010; AALIANCE). However, just like much of technical development in general, it seems that the focus is on tasks that are possible for machines to perform rather than on a comprehensive understanding of the homecare situation. In many cases 'smart homes' for elderly people only add features such as automatic doors, window lockers, stove alarm and flood sensors to a more general solution that provides for e.g. power saving and fire alarm. The idea is to have the inhabitant feel safe in the sense of being 'watched' and not left alone if helpless. The automatic door locker can close if a dement person walks out in the middle of the night and open if the fire alarm rings. The smart home enables surveillance of the inhabitant without a relative or paid carer being present (and is just as welcome by the family as by the elderly person her/himself). Care is, however, more than 'watching'.

In general, experience shows that the partition of care work into work that can be carried out by artefacts and work that cannot be automated may present the human with a incoherent set of tasks detached from its contextual meaning (Bainbridge 1983) and hence contribute to isolating the automated tasks from the care context. For example, monitoring a person's physical condition (blood sugar, heart rhythm) and monitoring safety issues (fire, flood, fall accidents) remove the social aspects of watching over a person to the task of detecting pre-defined dangerous states (Roberts and Mort 2009). Moreover, cases of false or 'uncooperative' alarms abound, such as too sensitive fire alarms or heat sensors on a stove, which may weaken the awareness of risk (Miller and Parasuraman 2007).

However, there is also an increasing body of research that takes account of the reality of homecare, trying to design technologies that support or augment current practices, partially also involving care recipients and caretakers in their work. With our analysis of 'the work to make homecare work' we seek to enrich researcher's and technology developer's understanding of the complexity and collaborative character of homecare.

The Home as a Place in a Care Network

The home as a place for caregiving is an enormously variegated phenomenon. It becomes a place where the work of different types of 'workers' is carried out and needs to be coordinated internally, as well as with the outside world. There is a diversity of people in need of support at home. Among the elderly the kind and severity of impairment varies: old people who need support with day-to-day activities, such as shopping, preparing a meal or bathing and want to feel safe, socialize and be mobile; old people with a medical condition that requires specialized machines, regimes and care; as well as old people with different degrees of dementia. Their needs vary largely and they also vary with time. Accordingly, the technologies that are being developed for their support range from smart home devices that assist in small ways to healthcare technologies (in support of people with heart problems, diabetes, respiratory problems, etc.) to 'persuasive technologies' that encourage people to lead healthy lives.

Living at home and needing support of some kind is dependent on sometimes extensive 'care networks'. They consist of 'informal carers': family members, friends, and neighbours. In addition, many have paid help for support with day-to-day activities (house cleaning, shopping) or professional care (nurses, physiotherapists, dieticians). The wider network of carers can also include pharmacists, doctors and technicians (Consolvo et al. 2004). The care network consists of people of varying skills who provide assistance ranging from day-to-day activities and specialized medical services to social support. Beyond individual people the home becomes connected to healthcare institutions, community care centres, call centres, and providers of social and technical services of different kinds. In this paper we are particularly interested in discussing how homecare technologies change the work of informal carers and of the recipients of their care, and how their work relates to the work of professional carers and other types of providers. In sum, we are interested in understanding the collaborative nature of caretaking in the home.

Our interest in understanding the 'work to make home care work' is driven by our own research on the installation of a smart home solution implemented in a housing complex for 90 elderly people in Oslo municipality (Culén et al. 2013). As much of this research is still at beginning, we decided to base our analysis on a growing body of literature on homecare technologies. We focus on studies that are of an ethnographic nature or that at least provide descriptions of the practice of caregiving. Our main interest is in accounts of the work of care recipients and informal caregivers. Much of the available literature refers to chronically ill people who need continuous attention and care to prevent the outbreak of an acute episode. There are also studies on taking care of people with cognitive impairments, in particular dementia.

The paper starts with a discussion of the work of care recipients, informal caregivers, and the larger networks that are involved in this work, to then ask the question: 'Is this work?' It discusses different kinds of work, and also draws on some central CSCW concepts characterizing homecare work. Finally, it looks into what and how work is delegated to machines and discusses what and how the machines support care work.

The Home as a Workplace for Caregiving

The concept of 'work' has been and still is of general concern within the CSCW community. Schmidt (2011a) makes an elaborate argument advocating its central position in CSCW: work is not just 'any kind of socially organized activity' but refers 'to purpose and circumstance' (p. 373). Arguing that 'work' is a polymorphous concept Schmidt discusses work as particular activities that are considered 'necessary or useful in a practical way' (Schmidt 2011a, p. 375) either in terms of what the work produces or in terms of other kinds of rewards. He goes on to discuss the distinction made by James Urmson in an essay 'Polymorphous concepts' (1970) between activities that 'would be counted as "work" in all standard contexts and those, which would be called "work" only for some purposes' (Schmidt 2011a, p. 374): for the gardener gardening is work, however, for the garden owner gardening can be a hobby or just recreation—should we then call gardening work? In our analysis we will reflect on this distinction.

Apart from Schmidt's definition of work, we draw on Strauss and colleagues' classic studies of work in the hospital (Strauss et al. 1985) and at home (Corbin and Strauss 1985). Strauss understands work at many analytical levels, emphasizing the 'trajectory' and 'arc of work', paving the way for distinguishing between 'primary work' and 'articulation work':

> Any endeavor requires planning and coordination if the work is to proceed smoothly and to completion. That work we shall refer to as "articulation work" (Strauss et al. 1985), to denote the planning and coordination necessary to operationalize *any* associated set of tasks (Corbin and Strauss 1985, p. 243).

Corbin and Strauss (1985) argue that homecare involves two types of work:

> … *illness-related work* and *everyday life work*. Each line of work is made up of different types of work. For instance, illness-related work consists of regimen work, crisis prevention and management, symptom management, and diagnostic-related work. Everyday life work refers to the essentially daily round of tasks that keep the household going. It includes housekeeping and repairing, occupational work, marital work, child rearing, sentimental work (Strauss et al. 1985), and activities such as eating. Implicated in each of these two main types of work are interactions with spouse, children, friends, health professionals and others in the gathering and dispersing of information, expressions of concern, caring, and the division of tasks (ibid, p. 226).

They also describe as a third type of work: biographical work, coming to terms with one's illness or impairment. According to Strauss et al. (1985) learning to manage one's life in the face of impairments *is* work but much of this work remains invisible (Star and Strauss 1999) and is not recognized as such. Strauss and colleagues use a great variety of terms for characterizing the kinds of work performed in healthcare settings, for describing and capturing the variegated nature of the work—machine work, safety work, comfort work, and body work—concepts that we will take up in our analysis.

Places for Caregiving

The home is often portrayed as a place that facilitates privacy and intimacy and is designed for comfort and sensory enjoyment. It is contrasted with dedicated healthcare spaces, such as a hospital ward, in which concern for cleanliness, functional efficiency and standardization prevail. Materials in these spaces are durable and easy to clean and maintain. In contrast, a personal space, such as the home, may be small and cluttered, as their inhabitants cannot afford a larger living space; it may be filled with souvenirs, books, cushions, embroideries and other objects. Also the location of furniture reflects particular preferences and habits. In sum, the home is an expression of its inhabitants' biography and aesthetic preferences; but it is precisely this, which may make it difficult to maintain the level of accessibility and cleanliness required to perform medical and nursing interventions. In addition, finding suitable places for technologies in ordinary homes may be challenging (Axelrod et al. 2009).

Moving healthcare into the home is not only about placing equipment. The home is a place of 'ingrained practices' where particular norms of conduct have to be observed:

> The structures and spaces of the home are arranged to facilitate privacy and intimacy, and visitors are selectively screened before they are permitted access to front hallways, living/dining rooms, bedrooms and bathrooms [...]. The social practices associated with guest/host relationships are integral to privacy and impression management. Even in the closest quarters, privacy is constructed through social conventions such as averting eyes and controlling the volume of speech (Angus et al. 2005, p. 163).

Caregivers who are invited into the private space of a home are confronted with contradictory expectations: although expected to behave like a 'guest' they have to negotiate spaces for doing their work. Some of this work may be intrusive and may disturb its inhabitants' feeling of identity and their control over what they want to happen in their personal space. When the home becomes increasingly 'institutionalized', those living in it may experience stress and ambivalence. Under certain circumstances a private home may offer less privacy and less comfort, make it more difficult to establish boundaries, and impose stronger rules of conduct on an individual than a hospital or nursing home (Ruddick 1994): '[I]llnesses and treatments can make familiar domestic settings alien, or they can confuse family roles and foster mutual deception, detachment, and resentment, even (or especially) in well-ordered families' (ibid).

We can say that the private home frames the working conditions for caregiving in particular ways. In contrast to a hospital or nursing home the private home with its routines and dedicated spaces for activities has not been designed for delivering more specialized medical and nursing care. How to arrange for caregiving in the home raises many 'classical' issues (Bannon et al. 2011) concerned with workload and stress, dependability and safety, the temporal structure of work and the 'margins of disposition' for care recipients and their informal carers.

Moving technologies away from the hospital may mean moving them not just to the home but to many places:

> … they will be used in the kitchen or bedroom, transported in a car or train, brought over to a friend's place, carried around a shopping mall or the office. These places, in which different social rules and norms apply, are all likely differentially to modulate the meaning and use of health technologies (Lehoux et al. 2004, p. 623).

Indeed, some technologies are designed to support more mobile forms of social aging and to help elderly people in maintaining or even extending their personal communities of friends, neighbours, and leisure associates. The outside of their home—its 'physical and social landscapes'—is important for elderly people (Phillipson 2007). Navigation tools seek to respond to the fact that navigating in complex physical spaces may be difficult for elderly people. They may lose their to recognize places, and to understand and navigate in (complex) spaces using abstract representations (like maps). Another currently debated issue is to make the 'wandering' of people with dementia safe by incorporating technologies 'that monitor but do not confine residents' (Wigg 2010).

The Recipients of Care: What is Their Work?

Care recipients are part and parcel of the total organization of work that needs to be done and their contribution is necessary if they want to stay in their own homes. Looking at homecare in a modern context we see that care recipients perform different types of machine work, safety work, and bodywork (Strauss et al. 1985), and that much of this work is collaborative. Lehoux et al. (2004) provide two examples of homecare technologies that involve considerable input from care recipients: antibiotic intravenous therapy (IV) and parenteral nutrition (PN).

> IV therapy is typically used for a short period (10 days), although patients with recurring infections (e.g. cystic fibrosis) may use it repeatedly and for longer periods. Tasks delegated to the patient are kept to a minimum, and involve connecting the catheter to reservoirs and, in the case of the programmable pump, pressing on/off keys, managing alarms and changing batteries. Users are asked to monitor the catheter site and use aseptic procedures. They should follow a pre-defined schedule and take the drug out of the fridge 4–6 hours before administering the treatment (ibid, p. 629).

'Tasks are kept to a minimum' but still, the authors mention high levels of stress and anxieties on the side of care recipients connected to, for example, 'an uncooperative alarm system, a catheter threatening to dislodge or a heavy shoulder bag' (ibid, p. 632). Parenteral nutrition (PN) requires even more manipulations, since the vitamins, drugs and fluids that have to be added to a solution are based on a regimen that varies from individual to individual. Also the aseptic procedures are more demanding.

The machine work that care recipients engage in does not only include using a technical device for diagnosis, therapy, or maintenance of life (as in these two cases); it involves doing this with regard to clinical safety and accuracy; and may require tending the machine and monitoring it for various features. For example, in the study of IV therapy managing the auditory alarms by adjusting the placement of the tubes was identified as a major problem. Failing eyesight may turn monitoring the programmable pump or manipulating needles into a challenge. Also, seemingly simple maintenance work, such as changing batteries, can become a problem. 'Hidden interfaces' may make 'simple' tasks difficult to carry out and require workarounds. And what happens when the machine does not work? While more complex tasks are usually not within the competence of care recipients themselves, they clearly perform the work of making the IV or PN equipment function correctly and safely and many of them seem to be able to after a period of training.

An even more 'direct' example of care recipients engaging in machine work is provided by Winance (2010) who describes how users test and trial wheelchairs, seeking to find the right wheelchair or improve its comfort, making 'compromises between the wheelchair's material obduracies and the possibilities of its redesign'. A lot of machine work has to be carried out by the care recipients, including the 'tinkering' some of them may have to perform to make things work: 'To care is to tinker, i.e. to meticulously explore, 'quibble', test, touch, adapt, adjust, pay attention to details and change them, until a suitable arrangement (material, emotional, relational) has been reached' (Winance 2010, p. 111).

This resonates with the notion of 'patient-as technologist', which Strauss et al. (1982) evoked already 30 years ago in the face of the increasing complexity of medical devices and of the regimens care recipients have to comply with when sent home from a hospital.

The two examples also illustrate what Strauss et al. refer to as body work: adjusting and connecting the body to a machine; assuming a particular posture for a test or treatment to happen properly; or, in the case of rehabilitative care, performing exercises in the correct way. Strauss et al. give an example of a patient who had to spend considerable time under a 'nuclear tracer machine', struggling with discomforting pressures on his neck and back and having to prevent himself from coughing: 'Except for the body positioning, none of this work was visible to the technician, physician or nurse—[...]—but it was all relevant to the success of the machine's accurate recording' (ibid, p. 982).

Much of the work that care recipients do is collaborative. One example is how patients using cardiac telemonitoring technology are expected 'to play an active role in the diagnosis of their heart problems':

> When patients experience symptoms, they have to manually activate the ambulatory ECG recorder to retain the current contents of the memory buffer, along with an additional post-event portion of the ECG signal. When patients have stored one ECG recording or more (with a maximum of four) they have to contact a special medical centre. After a short anamnesis by the contacted physician, the patient has to send his or her recordings to the telemedical centre, where the ECGs emerge on a computer screen. In combination with the anamnesis the ECG is interpreted by the physician. This interpretation is directly passed

> on to the patient, and later, together with (parts of) the ECG, faxed to the patient's general practitioner who has prescribed the device (Oudshoorn 2007, p. 274).

Care recipients' work in this example is crucial, as they have to decide on the moment when their heart rate is irregular—something they have to do 'without clear guidance'. They participate in the diagnostic process. Many people are involved in the monitoring of the patient's heart condition: home-care nurses, general practitioners, heart specialists, and a newly created telemedical service centre (Oudshoorn 2007). The diagnosis of a problem with the patient's heart thus becomes distributed over an extensive network of actors.

We can say that care recipients contribute to what Strauss et al. (1982, 1985) have termed trajectory work:

> We have coined the term 'trajectory' to refer not only to the physiological unfolding of the patient's disease but to the *total organization of work* done over that course of illness, plus the *impact* on those involved in that work and its organization. For different illnesses, the trajectory will involve different medical and nursing actions, different kinds of skills and other resources, a different parcelling out of tasks among the workers, and involve two quite different relationships—instrumental and expressive—among the workers (including patients) (Strauss et al. 1982, p. 983).

The Work of Informal Caregivers

In most of the work we described so far, informal caregivers, be it family, kin, friends or neighbours, have a share; in many cases living at home would not be possible without their help. They often collaborate in the machine work, safety work, and bodywork required making the technologies work. Moreover, informal caregivers are often the ones who manage those aspects of everyday life that the care recipients are no longer able to do entirely by themselves; this includes cleaning, shopping, cooking, washing. They perform basic nursing care, such as helping to take a bath and dress or going to the toilet. Another classical nursing task that informal carers perform is comfort work, which aims at preventing, minimalizing or relieving discomfort. Comfort work, although supported by particular devices (e.g. special beds), techniques and drugs, relies on empathy with the care recipient's situation, on common sense and also often requires physical engagement with the care recipient's body.

A lot of the work of informal carers do is trajectory work. They coordinate healthcare services by scheduling appointments, requesting/providing documents, and arranging transportation. In a study on the home-based management of chronic heart failure (CHF) Clark et al. (2007) describe how the informal carers performed trajectory work like monitoring care recipients' limbs for signs of fluid retentions or adjusting the medication dose. They paid attention to subtle bodily changes (of complexion, facial expression, appearance, and mood) and this surveillance of the care recipient was often carried out as a continuous task, even when s/he was asleep. Due to their engagement in symptom assessment and management the informal carers had an important role in decision-making, discussing their observations and judgments with the care recipient as well as with the formal carers. Clark et al. (2007) emphasize the semi-professional character of the work of informal carers in as these looked beyond the immediate problem, expressing their commitment to larger goals, 'such as maintaining independence and normality while managing a disruptive and unpredictable illness' (ibid, p. 380).

The literature also provides insight into the work of informal carers of people with dementia, acknowledging the special challenges connected with it. It is well known that when left alone with the burden of coping with a relative's behaviours, such as wandering, aggression, anxiety, delusions, hallucinations, eating and sleeping disorders and the like, informal carers may experience depression and role overload. In a study of family care of people with advanced dementia De la Cuesta (2005) gives a lively account of what this requires and how informal carers cope. Communication, understanding a person's needs and wishes, is a problem but not the most pressing one, given the demands and pressures of the care situation as such. Caregivers seem to use all kinds of tricks or ruses to deal with stubborn relatives who refuse to eat, take medicine, go to the toilet, who get upset upon not recognizing their home, or blankly refuse to cooperate. Her respondents stressed that 'there is no magic formula' and that 'one has to invent so many things' (ibid, p. 885). She compares caretaking to the work of artists, characterizing it as crafting care in creative ways, a very 'practical intelligence' that 'is applied to realities that are unexpected, ambiguous, and unstable …' (ibid, p. 886). De la Cuesta (2005) also points at the resourcefulness of caregivers in turning objects in the home into useful devices, 'for instance, baby alarms to monitor relatives' sleep, syringes to give fluids, or a bicycle to rehabilitate the relative' (ibid, p. 891).

Agrawal (2002) has pointed out that 'all practical knowledge, although the application of some familiar or unrecognized principle, is useful precisely because of the experience gained in the use of that knowledge' (ibid, p. 292). The account provided by De la Cuesta suggests that in a homecare situation such practical knowledge may complement the more formalized procedures connected with specific devices and therapies in ways that make homecare feasible. It is also important to note that the practical knowledge informal carers apply is deeply rooted in their knowledge of the care recipient and the home, as well as the objects that populate it.

The Larger Network of Care

As mentioned above, most homecare situations involve an extensive network of formal carers and other people whose assistance is needed to make the homecare situation function. In many countries mobile community nurses have the responsibility to support care recipients and their families with tasks they cannot carry out themselves. In case the person has been hospitalized, information transfer and coordination involves planning before discharge. Even trained nurses may encounter difficulties when having to deal with new devices and procedures, because there are so many different technologies and procedures involved and some of them may be used only by a few care recipients:

> What kind of tube it is, there are different models and I feel my knowledge of that is very vague, how often they are supposed to be changed and so on… If I used them [feeding tubes] more often I would try harder to get that information, I believe. I might have received information about this button model a long time ago, but you know… I do understand that they insert a kind of tube in different ways in the patient's stomach… (Bjuresäter et al. 2008, p. 3025).

Nurses in this study also felt some insecurity about who was responsible for changing the 'button' and some lacked knowledge about complications such as infections, leakage, incorrect position of the tube, aspiration or pneumonia.

When comparing the study by Bjuresäter and colleagues (2008) to the one carried out by Oudshoorn (2007) we can see that the care recipients, who are fit to do so, perform exactly the same work that in other cases mobile nurses carry out. This shows how care technologies enable a shift of some procedures and tasks from highly specialized environments and professional workers to the home. This of course requires careful planning and training. For the case of heart patients Oudshoorn (2007) describes this need:

> This instruction work consists of several actions nurses have to perform when patients come to their office to collect the ambulatory ECG recorder. Nurses have to explain how the technology works, including an explanation of the whole procedure from putting the band aids to the chest, fixing the electrodes to the band aids and the recorder, and making and sending an ECG. The instructions nurses have to give are not restricted to verbal explanations but also include a demonstration to give patients a first hands-on experience with the new technology (ibid, p. 279).

In addition to the visible work of instructing professional nurses often have to provide comfort and reassurance to care recipients who feel overwhelmed by, for example, the expectation to carry an ECG recorder day and night and who have difficulties to accept the responsibility this entails. The home environment may encourage nurses to engage in types of comfort work that a nurse in a hospital probably would not have the time to do, such as making the care recipient feel better by preparing a nice meal: 'We can enhance the patient's well-being with simple measures if one's aware about it, maybe give a sensation of taste in the mouth at the same time as the patient receives nutrition via the PEG or button' (Bjuresäter et al. 2008, p. 3026).

With complex technologies entering the home, care becomes increasingly on technical support. A lot of the maintenance and calibration work needed to make technologies function smoothly is beyond the skill level even of a professional nurse that comes to visit. Studies show a desire for technology that is just there, reliable, portable, and simple: easy to learn and to configure (e.g. Sohlberg et al. 2005). But experience tells that technologies often do not work properly and/or may break down frequently. Stringer et al. (2006) show that these problems tend to occur even in households with relatively 'fit' old people with all kinds of technologies that were already in place. They refer in particular to the problems that sensor-based technologies created, including false alarms. Grinter et al. (2005) report on problems surrounding the set up, administration and troubleshooting of networks in families, pointing at the complications resulting from 'the tension between invisibility and comprehensibility', as well as from the fact that so many outside parties may be involved in fixing problem.

Is it Work? What Kind of Work is it?

In our description of what caregiving in the home entails we have assumed that what care recipients, informal caregivers and the larger network engage in *is* work. Schmidt (2011a) distinction between primary and secondary cases of work: characteristic of *'primary cases of work'* is their

> practical necessity or usefulness: the necessity of having to deal with all sorts of imposed relevances, constraints and requirements, priorities and urgencies, and what flows from that: mastery of technicalities, ability to make do with available resources and to persevere, and so on. Not only that. In a system of social division of labor, constraints and requirements, etc. are typically externally defined, by other parties.
>
> The *'secondary cases of work'*, by contrast, can be considered work because they are also serious affairs in that they too require 'effort and concentration' ... the secondary cases are considered work, in particular situations, not in virtue of the circumstances but in virtue of the similarity of the particular activities with prototypical work activities.

We argue that those involved in homecare do 'serious stuff' also in the sense that the activity faces 'serious complexities'. It is this latter part we want to elaborate.

'Work', Schmidt argues, is related to the concept of 'practice'; and a practice is more than the 'situated doing' of something. A practice is shared; may require collaboration with others; and multiple perspectives may come into play. Moreover, as Kant (1793) argued, 'one does not call just any operation a *praxis*; rather, only such a purposive endeavour is considered a *praxis* that is taken to be attained by following certain generally accepted principles of procedure' (quoted in Schmidt 2011b). The modern notion of practice is not only connected with the concepts of experience, techniques, skills, and knowledge. It is also related to the notion of 'rule' in the sense Wittgenstein used it: 'descriptively, to indicate *regularity* or as a criterion of *correct* conduct' (Schmidt 2011b). Care work needs to be done 'correctly' and properly in a technical sense, as does 'self-care'. Rogers et al. (2011), in a study of care recipients with different chronic conditions maintain that 'as professional work becomes more protocol based, so too does the "work" of patients' (ibid, p. 1078). Homecare technologies have to be operated with regard to clinical safety and accuracy. These technologies are therefore accompanied by standards of e.g. cleanliness, correct procedure, etc. originating from professional practice, now introduced into the home.

A practice also has a normative dimension in the sense of doing things in a 'caring way' and with heed so that e.g. a person's vulnerability is not exposed and her/his feelings are respected. Also care recipients themselves are subject to notions of 'correct conduct':

> The most obvious mode is that staff expects patients to work (whether staff calls it work or not). Reluctant or recalcitrant patients are subject to the demand that they bear their responsibilities; and get scolded or otherwise punished when they will not do their jobs—as with patients who fight the respirator or rehab patients who will not 'put out'. Patients who honestly attempt to do their tasks but have difficulty—as with one who kept ruining a breathing test on a respirator machine by choking up and coughing—may eventually arouse some annoyance, but at least they are trying their best (Strauss et al. 1982, p. 983).

Another important element of a practice is the skills and mastery of technology required in the work. The literature is somewhat inconclusive here. For example, Rogers et al. (2011) argue that technical devices brought into the home offer little room for tailoring and that they are 'not explicitly made to engage potential patient expertise to self-monitor and self-manage' (ibid, p. 1081). They emphasize the limited nature of many homecare technologies, the fact that the technical skills their operation requires may not be highly specialized. Still, we maintain that operating them efficiently and safely requires some degree of practice, effort, and attention to detail (see Edwards and Grinter 2001); hence the need for instructions or training by a professional (e.g. a nurse).

Another key characteristic of work is that 'in a system of social division of labour, constraints and requirements, etc. are typically externally defined, by other parties' (Schmidt 2011a). This also applies to the home. However, the home offers a more open framework for practicing care with more possibilities for care recipients to decide for themselves. In a study of patients with hepatitis C Perzynski et al. (2012) observed that 'in their stories, the patients described their decisions to begin, delay or stop treatment and developed strategies to alter their diet, exercise and use alternative therapies according to changes in their test result' (ibid, p. 1). Decisions on the use of resources are in the hands of care recipients and their families, as is the responsibility to find those resources.

What makes the collaborative work of homecare different from care in a hospital or nursing home? Strauss et al. (1982) define the work of patients in hospitals as complementing and enhancing the work of healthcare professionals in various ways: it can be a 'mirror image' of staff's work (e.g. giving urine that staff transports to and analyses in a lab); supplementary to staff's work (like maintaining composure during a painful procedure): or a substitute. Patients also perform work they believe necessary: they may rectify staff error, do work that staff cannot possibly do (for lack of time) or that is outside of what they think their work is. An issue raised by Strauss and colleagues is that in the hospital context care recipients (or patients) are perceived as performing 'contributory actions' of various kinds, 'filling in the gaps', although they actually carry out 'work':

> … patients are being judged on their carrying out of *tasks*. These are not usually conceived of by staff as tasks (or jobs, or work) but in terms of patients' participation in the staff's work—contributory actions rather than work … (ibid, p. 979).

This brings us to a key point: in a homecare situation professional work and the responsibility that goes with it is shifted to care recipients and informal carers in the expectation that these develop and master the practice of (more or less specialized) caregiving, which, as we have argued may require considerable learning and 'practical intelligence' in solving problems as they arise. They do not 'fill in the gaps' but 'take over', at least to some extent. Moreover, they have to fit the activities into a context that they have not been designed for. Corbin and Strauss (1985) mention some of the challenges this implies, describing the difficulties of keeping the lines of information flowing, to negotiate divisions of labour, or to establish a workflow in the home when 'intruded on by contingencies flowing from the nature of illness, biographies, and daily life that disrupt the normal flow of work' (ibid, p. 237). In addition to participating in the care, care recipients have to contribute to making their condition and the attention it requires compatible with a 'mosaic of people, objects, and activities' (Aarhus and Ballegard 2010, p. 1230) that have nothing to do with their impairment or illness.

Moreover, the possibilities of shifting care to the home and supporting 'independent living' have increased the pressure and responsibility to live in a healthy way on elderly people (and not only on them). No doubt, 'healthy ageing' is a socially relevant goal worthwhile to pursue. However, the duty to be active (in contrast to 'idle' or even 'lazy') and the ways that activity is promoted and measured and individuals are made responsible are subject to ethical considerations (Katz 2000). Not only that: our point here is that the possibilities homecare technologies have created turn some everyday practices into 'work': 'serious' activities that require additional skills, training, and resources and are deemed of 'practical necessity', such as for example following measures to lower one's cholesterol level.

The 'Work' Things Do

Studying the potential application of technologies in cooperative work settings as well as contributing to the design of such technologies is a core issue of CSCW research and CSCW concepts have been developed with design in mind. Not surprisingly some of the technologies we encounter in ordinary work settings have entered the home-turned-workplace for caregiving, with attention to the special needs of people in need of care.

The home has become a place for technologies of all sorts that support the coordination work required in homecare, such as making arrangements, as with a laboratory; 'managing time, including its planning, scheduling, pacing, fitting together'; and 'establishing routines by scheduling tasks, equipment, and people, by becoming familiar with the work, and by streamlining the work to eliminate busy work' (Corbin and Strauss 1985, p. 243). These include coordinative artefacts, such as shared calendars, electronic diaries reports, medication control. Some of these artefacts aim at users with decreased cognitive functioning. Technologies that provide and strengthen awareness have been introduced in the home, for example technologies that present signals in ways easily by the user: as auditory signals for blind people, visual signals for hearing-impaired people. Sensor-based alarm systems are supposed to replace an attentive caretaker by calling attention to a human when action is needed (heart stop, fall accident, fire, flood). Embedded into or connected with these technologies are all kinds of medical devices.

We can say that today much homecare involves delegating tasks to an artefact of some sort. Paying attention to the work these 'things' do is important. A useful and much used concept for exploring this potential is the notion of articulation work. Articulation work is involved in both, the everyday work as well as the 'trajectory work' concerned with the care recipient's impairments, and takes place at three levels (Corbin and Strauss 1985). The first level is the task and the other tasks that it is intertwined with. The second level is the articulation between different lines of work, such as coordinating two different tests or filling in the gaps between two caretakers' work. The third level of articulation is planning and coordinating resources between the lines of work. Corbin and Strauss argue that a lot of coordination of lines of work is needed and that care work is never routine.

> Doing information work including networking, scouting out, coaching and training, providing and clarifying instructions, distinguishing between needs and wants, searching for people, places, and necessary things. For instance, calling a restaurant ahead of time to determine if salt-free food is available or if there are accommodations for a person in a wheelchair (Corbin and Strauss 1985, p. 244).

A 'classical' argument in CSCW is that well designed technologies reduce the articulation work necessary to get work done cooperatively. A good example is the old-fashioned pill organizer, where the medication for a certain time period is sorted so that the right number of the right pills is grouped into portions to be consumed at particular times. The pill organizer supports the memory both for which pills to take at a particular point in time and also whether the pills have been taken (or at least removed from the box). A well functioning memory artefact like this reduces the amount of everyday articulation work. Placing the artefact in a particular place e.g., by the coffee maker in the kitchen (Ballegaard et al. 2006) enables it to do memory work.

Homecare technologies also include artefacts that do things: automatons and machines. We have described examples of homecare technologies performing work, such as the IV programmable pump or the ECG recorder. Machines that do work are normally accompanied by people doing machine work: connecting the machine with the body, calibrating, programming, cleaning, repairing, etc. These work tasks require competence about the technology as well as about the overall work trajectory of which the automated tasks are part. Moreover, machines often involve new forms of collaboration for care recipients and informal carers as in the case of the ECG recorder, where the care recipient activates the recorder, stores the recordings, contacts a special medical centre, to which it sends the recordings, to finally receive an 'interpretation' and eventually discuss it with her/his general practitioner. The delegation of work to artefacts often creates new and additional forms of articulation work for those involved in caregiving. One type of articulation work that is deemed crucial but is often neglected, is teaching or training. A study of mobile nurses' work concludes that 'it was striking that very few included a family-oriented approach also including support and education for informal caregivers' (Hallberg and Kristensson 2004, p. 12).

There are different 'margins of disposition' (Volpert 1985) for people when (parts of) work gets delegated to a machine. In the example of the ECG recorder these margins are particularly large, since apart from operating the recorder correctly, the care recipient, although there is an 'arc of work' to complete in case of irregular heart beat, has some space for deciding himself if and when exactly she or he will start action. In the case of IV therapy there is s strict script to follow for the therapy to be performed correctly.

Delegation of work to machinery can also be a means for delegating work to 'new' people, making the machine act as tool and structure for the work and guide the user in doing things right. Many of the examples described above tell about the work people do to adjust to the machines and to interpret the machines correctly (i.e., to follow a professional standard that the informal caretaker does not share). Making sure that the machine gets the necessary working conditions is also a kind of care work—caring for the machine (Ciborra 1996; Finken 2012).

The Work to Make Homecare Work

In this paper we have discussed a variety of issues concerned with the ways in which caregiving in a home environment can be considered work and who are doing this work. We have built our argumentation for the variety of work carried out by care recipients and caregivers on theories of work known to the CSCW field. Of the many different kinds of work that care recipients and (informal) care givers carry out we have emphasized the 'serious' work that contributes to the care and is shaped by concerns and standards that come from professional practice. In fact, all the examples of work we described in this paper are 'primary' rather than 'secondary' cases of work. They do not just resemble 'prototypical work activities' (Schmidt 2011a) but *are* work. However, we find that the same activity may sometimes be considered work and sometimes not, depending on the context in which it takes place. What is not work and when? And what should be considered 'secondary cases of work'? And, last but not least: why do these distinctions matter?

Homecare is Many Different Kinds of Work

It is interesting to see why it may be difficult to draw clear boundaries between work and non-work, primary and secondary cases of work in homecare settings. Let us go back to the definition of everyday life work, as given by Corbin and Strauss et al. (1985):

> Everyday life work refers to the essentially daily round of tasks that keep the household going. It includes housekeeping and repairing, occupational work, marital work, child rearing, sentimental work (Strauss et al. 1985), and activities such as eating (ibid, p. 226).

This includes some prototypal work activities but also activities, such as for example marital work, sentimental work and eating, that under 'normal' circumstances would not or only partially be considered work even though they may require 'effort and concentration'. In a homecare setting the same activities may be considered work as they are essential to the care and may even require additional training and coordinative effort to be managed properly. When eating is no longer or temporarily not possible, it becomes the task of preparing the right kind of fluid (instead of a meal) and manipulating a programmable pump to deliver nutritive solutions into the patient's vein. A similar argument may be made with respect to the psychological and identity work of having to cope with the discomfort, pain, and anxieties a chronic illness or the decline of a person's capabilities implies. In a homecare setting this may, like in a hospital, turn into work required to have caregiving function properly, without disruptions.

On the other side, we may argue with Gaver (2001) that people in their homes 'do not just pursue tasks and solve problems, they also explore, wonder, love, worship, and waste time'. In contrast to a hospital or nursing home, a homecare setting may provide more space to explore emotional connections, make certain activities be performed in a playful way, allow for ample time, and so forth—all conditions that we will normally not find in a work context. However, they may also be 'necessary and useful' for healthy ageing and recovering from illness.

One point of reflection here is the shift of responsibility to care recipients and to their informal caregivers. It begs questions such as:

> Which aspects of a task can be entrusted to technologies or to informal caregivers? How does life change, not just for the patients, but also for their informal caregivers? Under which circumstances may they initiate measures which are legally reserved to physicians? To what extent can informal caregivers be held to account for the consequences of errors when interpreting and operating complex technologies? What forms of personal care and contact and the holistic view of the patient's situation and emotional state that can be obtained from them are surrendered with the use of AT? (Austrian Bioethics Committee 2009, p. 16).

As we have seen, this shifting of responsibility to the individual has many facets: the homecare technologies introduce machine and body work but in many cases the skills required for operating the machinery are not known (well) by the care recipients or informal care givers; illness-related articulation work is added onto the everyday living work; professional rule-based work entangled with everyday living may result in unclear responsibilities and duties blended with the emotions involved in caring and living at home.

The Work of CSCW

A second point of reflection concerns the design of supportive technologies for the different kinds of work homecare entails. What is it that is supported—and how? An important insight here is that health-related homecare technologies need to be based on realistic assumptions about their users and use contexts, rather than inheriting their preconditions-for-use from other care contexts (like clean, spacious hospitals) or from contexts characterized by skilled maintenance staffing or stable, non-negotiable, ever-lasting everyday routines.

A central point in what we perceive as problematic in the current AAL initiatives is that 'support' often means delegating a task to a piece of machinery rather than designing a tool to enhance the human capacity. To give an example: while automation in the home replaces tasks like washing, cleaning, keeping food fresh etc., automation of caregiving in the home replaces or better 'splits' and distributes complex activities, such as 'watching over' (monitoring a person's health status). 'Watching over' becomes partitioned into an automatable part, which is 'faceless' and disembodied, leaving the social part of 'watching over' to become a task of its own. The distinctions introduced by Strauss et al. are of relevance for understanding that this 'social part' may consist of different kinds of work that are not just 'add-ons' but crucial for the 'watching over' to be done in a caring, safe and heedful way. To add to this complexity: there are an increasing number of incidents of abuse against elderly people reported in the media. As such abuse may be difficult to detect in private homes, 'watching over' may include surveillance equipment that is normally considered intrusive and inappropriate for a private space but in this case offers the possibility to document abusive behaviour.

As CSCW researchers are moving into the field of homecare technologies, they take a critical position and carefully look into the practices of homecare, unraveling complexities such as the ones we describe in this paper *before* suggesting technical solutions. Still, most of this work focuses on specific aspects of homecare only, developing, for example: a scheduling tool (Bossen et al. in press); an application that 'enhance the awareness of rhythms and routines among elderly peers' (Riche and MacCay 2010); a tool in support of personalized medication management (Verdezoto and Olsen 2012); just to mention a few. While we see an increasing number of useful and useable artfacts being created, we want to argue here that much more work is needed that looks at homecare settings as a whole: at the web of different types of spaces, artfacts, work tasks, people, and collaborative patterns that make up these settings. This would allow CSCW researchers to contribute to radically re-thinking smart homes.

Care should be taken to design for better care trajectories. For example, artifacts developed for single activities may contribute to the workload of the care workers even if each of these artfacts is well designed as an independent device. It is the larger network of care that makes the work—and makes up the work. Designing AAL solutions that work therefore requires addressing several levels and kinds of work and see them as parts of the same solution.

References

Aarhus, R., & Ballegard, S. A. (2010). Negotiating boundaries: Managing disease at home. In *Proceedings of CHI 2010*, Atlanta, Georgia, USA, ACM, pp. 1223–1232.

Agrawal, A. (2002). Indigenous knowledge and the politics of classification. *International Social Science Journal, 54*(173), 277–281.

Angus, J., Kontos, P., et al. (2005). The personal significance of home: Habitus and the experience of receiving long-term homecare. *Sociology of Health & Illness, 27*(2), 161–187.

Austrian Federal Chancellery (2009) Ethical aspects of the development and use of assistive technologies. Opinion of the Bioethics Commission, Opinion 13, Wien, Austria, July.

Axelrod, L., Fitzpatrick, G., et al. (2009). The reality of homes fit for heroes: Design challenges for rehabilitation technology at home. *Journal of Assistive Technologies, 3*(2), 35–43.

Bainbridge, L. (1983). Ironies of Automation. *Automatica, 19*(6), 775–779.

Ballegard, S. A., Bunde-Pedersen, J., & Bardram, J. E. (2006). Where to, Roberta? Reflecting on the role of technology in assisted living. In *Proceedings of NordiCHI* 2006, Oslo, Norway, ACM, pp. 373–376.

Bannon, L., Schmidt, K., & Wagner, I. (2011). Lest we forget. The European field study tradition and the issue of conditions of work in CSCW research. In *Proceedings of ECSCW 2011*, Aarhus University, DK, 24–28 September, pp. 213–232.

Bjuresäter, K., Larsson, M., et al. (2008). Cooperation in the care for patients with home enteral tube feeding throughout the care trajectory: Nurses' perspectives. *Journal of Clinical Nursing, 17*, 3021–3029.

Bossen, C., et al. (In Press). CareCoor: Augmenting the coordination of cooperative home care work. *International Journal of Medical Informatics.*

Ciborra, C. (1996). *Groupware & teamwork: Invisible aid or technical hindrance?*. Hoboken, NJ: John Wiley & Sons.

Clark, A. M., Reid, M. E., et al. (2007). The complex nature of informal care in home-based heart failure management. *Journal of Advanced Nursing, 61*(4), 373–383.

Consolvo, S., Roessler, P., et al. (2004). Technology for care networks of elders. *IEEE Pervasive Computing, 3*(2), 22–29.

Corbin, J., & Strauss, A. (1985). Managing chronic illness at home: Three lines of work. *Qualitative Sociology, 8*(3), 224–247.

Culén, A., Finken, S., & Bratteteig, T. (2013). Design and interaction in a smart gym: Cognitive and bodily mastering. In *Proceedings of SouthCHI'13*, July 1–3, 2013.

De la Cuesta, C. (2005). The craft of care: Family care of relatives with advanced dementia. *Qualitative Health Research, 15*(7), 881–896.

Edwards, W. K., & Grinter,R. E. (2001). At home with ubiquitous computing: Seven challenges. In: G. D Abowd, et al. (Eds.), *Ubicomp 2001, LNCS* (Vol. 2201, pp. 256–272). Heidelberg: Springer.

Finken, S. (2012). Homework: When home becomes workplace in the very upholding of 'home': On public care services and care technology in private homes. In J. Chandler, J. Barry, & E.

Berg (Eds.), *Dilemmas for human services. Papers from the 15th research conference 2011* (pp. 32–39). London: Royal Docks Business School University of East London.

Gaver, W. (2001). Designing for ludic aspects of everyday life. *ERCIM News*, Online edition, no. 47, 2001. http://www.ercim.org/publication/Ercim_News/enw47/gaver.html.

Grinter, R. E., Edwards, W. K., et al. (2005). The work to make a home network work. In H. Gellersen, et al. (Eds.), *ECSCW 2005*, Paris (pp. 469–488). Paris: Springer.

Hallberg, I. R., Kristensson, J. (2004). Preventive homecare of frail older people: A review of recent case management studies. *Journal of Clinical Nursing, 13*(6b), 122–120.

Katz, S. (2000). Busy bodies: Activity, aging, and the management of everyday life. *Journal of Aging Studies, 14*(2), 135–152.

Lehoux, P., Saint-Arnaud, J., et al. (2004). The use of technology at home: What patient manuals say and sell vs. what patients face and fear. *Sociology of Health & Illness, 6*(5), 617–644.

Miller, C. A., & Parasuraman, R. (2007). Designing flexible interaction between humans and automation: Delegation interfaces for supervisory control. *Human Factors, 49*(1), 57–75.

Oudshoorn, N. (2007). Diagnosis at a distance: The invisible work of patients and healthcare professionals in cardiac telemonitoring technology. *Sociology of Health & Illness, 30*(2), 271–288.

Perzynski, A. T., Terchek, J. J., et al. (2012). Playing the numbers: How hepatitis C patients create meaning and make healthcare decisions from medical test results. *Sociology of Health & Illness, 20*(2), 1–18.

Phillipson, C. (2007). The 'elected' and the 'excluded': Sociological perspectives on the experience of place and community in old age. *Ageing & Society, 27*, 321–342.

Riche, Y., & Mackay, W. (2010). PeerCare: Supporting awareness of rhythms and routines for better aging in place. *Computer Supported Cooperative Work, 19*(1), 73–104.

Roberts, C. and Mort, M. (2009). Reshaping what counts as care: Older people, work and new technologies. ALTER, European Journal of Disability Research, (3), 138–158.

Rogers, A., et al. (2011). Established users and the making of telecare work in long term condition management: Implications for health policy. *Social Science & Medicine, 72*(7), 1077–1084.

Ruddick, W. (1994). Transforming homes and hospitals. *Hastings Center Report*, *24*(5) (Special Supplement pS11), 4ff.

Schmidt, Kjeld. (2011a). The concept of 'work' in CSCW. *Computer-Supported Cooperative Work, 20*, 341–401.

Schmidt, K. (2011b). *Computer supported cooperative work: Cooperative Work and coordinative practices: Contributions to the conceptual foundations of computer-supported cooperative work*. New York: Springer.

Sohlberg, M. M., Todis, B., et al. (2005). A profile of community navigation in adults with chronic cognitive impairments. *Brain Injury*, *20*/*19*(14), 1249–1259.

Star, S. L., & Strauss, A. (1999). Layers of silence, arenas of voice: The ecology of visible and invisible work. *Computer Supported Cooperative Work, 8*(1–2), 9–30.

Strauss, A., Fagerhaugh, S., et al. (1982). The work of hospitalized patients. *Social Science and Medicine, 16*, 977–986.

Strauss, A., Fagerhaugh, S., et al. (1985). *Social organization of medical work*. Chicago: The University of Chicago Press.

Stringer, M., Fitzpatrick, G., & Harris, E. (2006). Lessons for the future: Experiences with the installation and use of today's domestic sensors and technologies. In K. P. Fishkin, et al. (Eds.), *Pervasive computing* (pp. 383–399). Berlin: Springer.

Van der Broek, G., Cavallo, F., Wehrmann, C. (Eds.). (2010). *Ambient intelligence and smart environments: Ambient assisted living roadmap*. http://ebooks.iospress.nl/volume/aaliance-ambient-assisted-living-roadmap.

Verdezoto, N. X., & Olsen, J. W. (2012). Personalized medication management: Towards a design of individualized support for elderly citizens at home. In *Proceedings of the 2nd ACM SIGHIT International Health Informatics Symposium* (pp. 813–817). New York: ACM Press.

Volpert, W. (1985). Psychologische Aspekte industrieller Arbeit. In W. Georg, L. Kißler, & U. Sattel (Eds.). *Arbeit und Wissenschaft: Arbeitswissenschaft?* Bonn: Neue Gesekkschaft.
Wigg, J. M. (2010). Liberating the wanderers: Using technology to unlock doors for those living with dementia. *Sociology of Health & Illness, 32*(2), 288–303.
Winnace, M. (2010). Care and disability. Practices of experimenting, tinkering with, and arranging people and technical aids. In. A. Mol, I. Moser, & J. Pols (Eds.), *Care in practice: On tinkering in clinics, homes and farms*. Bielefeld: Transcript Verlag.
AALIANCE: 7th Framework Programme of the European Union on Ambient Assisted Living. http://www.aaliance.eu

Dwelling in Software: Aspects of the Felt-Life of Engineers in Large Software Projects

Richard Harper, Christian Bird, Thomas Zimmermann and Brendan Murphy

Abstract The organizational and social aspects of software engineering (SE) are now increasingly well investigated. This paper proposes that there are a number of approaches taken in research that can be distinguished not by their method or topic but by the different views they construct of the human agent acting in SE. These views have implications for the pragmatic outcome of the research, such as whether systems design suggestions are made, proposals for the development of practical reasoning tools or the effect of Social Network Systems on engineer's sociability. This paper suggests that these studies tend to underemphasize the felt-life of engineers, a felt-life that is profoundly emotional though played in reference to ideas of moral propriety and ethics. This paper will present a study of this felt-life, suggesting it consists of a form of digital dwelling. The perspective this view affords are contrasted with process and 'scientific' approaches to the human agent in SE, and with the more humanistic studies of SE reasoning common in CSCW.

R. Harper (✉) · B. Murphy
Microsoft Research, Cambridge, UK
e-mail: r.harper@microsoft.com

B. Murphy
e-mail: bmurphy@microsoft.com

C. Bird (✉) · T. Zimmermann
Microsoft Research, Redmond, USA
e-mail: christian.bird@microsoft.com

T. Zimmermann
e-mail: tzimmer@microsoft.com

O. W. Bertelsen et al. (eds.), *ECSCW 2013: Proceedings of the 13th European Conference on Computer Supported Cooperative Work, 21–25 September 2013, Paphos, Cyprus*, DOI: 10.1007/978-1-4471-5346-7_9,

Setting the Scene

A recent paper in *Communications of the ACM* asks whether changes in software engineering (SE) represented under the moniker 'agile computing' are as applicable today as they were in the middle of the 1990s. The changes exemplified by agile computing—and various other approaches of that time (such as 'Xtreme programming', and sometimes by the more prosaic sounding 'End User Programming')—all turned around the realization that SE required more flexible processes to requirements capture and coding (Williams 2012). Adherence to a plan came to be seen as something that should always be subordinate to the development of a product that worked and appealed even if this violated aspects of the plan. Bitter and expensive failures in the SE industry up to that time had made it clear that the right products could only be devised through constant iteration of the design and associated software engineering; this meant that plans had to be looser and made flexible, and this in turn meant that coding itself had to be more dynamic in tempo, more 'agile' as the saying had it. Though the ACM article focuses on Agile SE, it notes that the basic need to be more flexible in design and development has become more or less the norm, certainly in the engineering of consumer products, even to some extent in open-source activities. Another recent paper, this time in the *IEEE Transactions on S.E.*, de Souza et al. (2011) *The Awareness Network*, examines three different contexts of software development and finds that whatever the moniker given to the engineering process, coordination and change is the fundamental contradiction whose 'solution' needs to be ensured to deliver the product.

If one accepts this, and it seems reasonable to do so, then what these authors are arguing is that doing SE requires balancing of the relationship between plans, the ways that engineers orient to and used these plans, and the coding itself. Coding has to be done in a fashion that allows revision, and sometimes concurrency of revision in different places in the overall code base. This has to be achieved while the code remains of sufficiently good quality to be (easily) 'reconciled with' and 'fitted into' what comes to be the 'emerging plan' or 'evolving spec'. The relationship between tools of coordination (like plans) and actual instances of action (such as writing a line of code) are then complex, fraught with difficulties of comprehension and overview (De Souza 2011; Ronkko et al. 2005). Processes need to ensure that engineers 'program to plan' but at the same time can alter their coding when a new plan comes into play, whenever that might happen, without the quality of coding diminishing—though there is always a cost of some form in terms of delay or even in the quality of the code—leaving aside the question of what measures can be applied to such notions (see Nagappan et al. 2008).

All SE involves such problems. Very large scale SE development programs (sometimes involving hundreds, even thousands of individuals) have these problems in even larger scale. Coding is typically undertaken in 'branches' or in discrete units. Changing code is ring fenced and only reinserted into the 'code base' once complete. Such branching creates costs however: coders in one branch can lose sight of what is happening elsewhere and so even though their coding might fit the requirements of their 'own' branch, the overall goal of the application (or product) itself might be undermined. Considerable effort has been put into researching where these instances occur as well as to suggest ways of alleviating them (Philips et al. 2011). Key to this has been the development of coordination tools of particular kinds. Amongst the most important of these are Software Configuration Management (SCM) tools which allow communications and documentation of coding practices in different branches in an overall engineering program. These documentation practices can take various forms, some of which can be overly burdensome. Annotation of changes is obviously important, but this takes many forms and is often affected by the attitudes of those doing the annotation (Storey et al. 2008). Besides, annotation tools are more than just methods of documenting; they are also articulation devices, and so need especial care in design and use (Storey et al. 2008; de Souza et al. 2011). Just how to support 'mutual awareness' and articulation work through such tools is now an increasingly fertile area; suggestive of new theoretical constructs as well as empirical findings (de Souza et al. 2008). The emergence of Social Networking Systems (SNS), a technology that is essentially about sociability rather than the division of labour, has been of particular interest recently.

One could go on; this is just to sketch of the scene of contemporary software engineering research and the particular features of research in large-scale SE. The research agendas in question are in many ways straightforward and clear. What we would like to suggest, however, is that answers to the question of balance one finds in the literature are often coloured by assumptions made by researchers. The assumptions we have in mind are not to do with choices between method; say between quantitative or qualitative, between statistical technique, interviewing protocol or sample size, or between ethnographic and other data collection modalities. They often have to do with how the human actor in the software engineering setting (the coder if you like), the relationship between the structures that constrain and guide this individual, and the form of the actor's actions (their reasoning or predicted behavior, say) are construed from the outset. This in turn drives or determines which analytical perspectives are chosen that deliver 'data' of a particular kind; these choices too are made at the outset before data is gathered. When these are put altogether (these assumptions, tools of analysis and forms of data collection), a certain picture of the individual at the heart of this view is thereby constructed.

What we are thinking of here is Foucault's insight that institutionally organised research always emphasises particular aspects of human agency and exclude others (see in particular his 1966 book, *The Order of Things*). Different disciplinary perspectives don't simply offer diverse views on the same animal, like the proverbial blind men grasping the elephant. In Foucault's view, disciplines create the creatures they investigate. Taken to extreme, Foucault's view can be thought of as offering the most ardent relativism. We certainly want to avoid some of the exaggerated claims associated with his view, but we do want to preserve some of the merits that it affords. We are thinking of Rorty's (1979) interpretation of

Foucault in *The Mirror of Nature*. Rorty argues that one ought to judge the value of any particular rendering of human agency by the practical implications that the view generates. In this way one can also assess any claims it makes about empirical validity. Rorty argues this is particularly important when different methods and assumptions are used, implying a kind of internal interdisciplinarity within a domain; it is also important when diverse approaches are being deployed to address apparently similar topics.

We have both these manifest in the SE research: certainly the list above viz-à-viz SCM tools, branching structures and coding practices, annotation and articulation, and so on, would seem to suggest so. In each instance—or set of instances—certain type of creature, an instantiation of the species named a software engineer, is cast. As a result, there is more than one type of animal described within the SE literature: the species generalis, *homo softwarus*, in other words, is made up of many kinds.

And yet given this, it also seems to us that the creatures presented in this literature are notice-able for the lack of attention they give to the felt-experience of software engineers—to describing and exploring the form of life constitutive of what Ingold calls 'dwelling' (see his *Being Alive* 2011). Certainly there seems little interest in this felt-life and more shown in topics that seem too vague to be tractable, like 'culture', or, as in a recent case, to ideas that pertain to psychology rather than consciousness and experience. One thinks of the idea that cognitive abilities of coders are being affected by social networks, drawing them out of their somewhat private forms of reason to more public ones (Storey et al. 2010). These perspectives do not look at how engineers enact their selves through the mixtures of sense, feeling and compression that we noted in our research with SE; that resonate with the 'praxis of living', as Ingold puts it.

Our claim is not that our findings are any more correct than any other, but that we focus on aspects of 'being' that other approaches need to neglect by dint of their analytic assumptions. We approached our software engineers with a view for 'dwelling' not for, say, situated 'reason' or 'objective fact'. An important corollary of our argument is that other approaches are likely to have their own merits, focusing as they do on different concerns and thus producing a different sense of the software engineer and their practices. Having a sensibility for all these views is likely to be hard, we believe, but ought to be sought, so that appropriate evaluations of different ways of constructing the animal at the heart of SE can be done. One set of criteria has to do with empirical merit, another set should be in terms of what each view leads one to do.

It is our purpose in this paper to justify these claims: specifically that, (a), there are different species of software engineer in the literature; (b) to show one that we do not think has been looked at greatly before, namely some aspects of dwelling in software engineering; (c) and to make some suggestive remarks about how this and other views might be judged by their utility and empirical merits.

Overview of the Evidence

With this in mind we present, in the body of the paper, two views already common in the literature. We then present a differing perspective. The two extant views are, respectively, from what we will call, for the purposes of exposition, the objective science of SE and, second, the view from the humanistic perspective, one quite often taken in CSCW. As we explain and analyze each view, and to some extent we do this by showing each view in extremis, so we will also explain the benefits that each affords. Both views we present here lead to very practical suggestions, we shall show, some for design, others for learning and training, but both offering practical benefits for the subjects rendered in the analysis itself. We shall then explore our own set of data and convey what 'dwelling in software engineering' might look like (or be experienced as). Having completed our exposition we shall offer some remarks in conclusion that point towards how this sensibility for a Foucaultian understanding of the output of SE research might be leveraged in the future, as well as some comments on 'inter' and 'multi-disciplinarity' both within CSCW and other domains that treat SE as a topic.

View 1: The Animal in the 'Scientific Vision' of SE

The first approach we want to talk about is one that could be illustrated with more papers than any other, we think, for no other reason than because most of the software engineering research we are familiar with is produced under its auspices. We don't want to get into the process of quantifying this view since it adds nothing to our argument, nor are we saying that other views are less important, or even whether there is a shift towards other views (for discussion see Somerville 2007). The studies we have in mind tend to have an engineering science background and thus emphasise the processual, the quantitative, the 'objective' over the 'subjective'. It is with these concerns in mind that research from this view addresses the processual efficacy and use of SCM tools, the quantitative efficiency of different branch structures, and the relationship between these structures and pre-existing organizational forms.

A paper that illustrates this view well is Bird and Zimmerman (2012; see also Bird, Nagaappan et al. 2009a, b; Bird et al. 2011). This reports on the values that different braches offer in a large scale SE program, namely Windows. Its premise is that some branches will be more useful than others. Data for this study was collected through a mixed method, though garnering data through survey was central. Survey data included engineers own calculation of the time they give to dealing with code changes in some branch, similarly their own judgment of the difficulties entailed doing code rewrites, and the perceived burdens that dealing with the branching placed on their work. This is juxtaposed with simulations and testing against objective data stored in the SCM tool used in Windows. This allows modeling that identifies whether the files amended in some branch are the same as in some other branch and if so, whether the teams that undertake the changes in question are one and the same. The analysis offered in the paper suggests that the coding work will be more efficient, with less likelihood of code conflicts, when code is reinserted into the code base, if the teams working on the same code are the same, or rather if it is the same people who are modifying the same files albeit in different branches. If the teams are different, there can be potential problems between a pair of branches, as different people modify the same files and they are likely less coordinated. As it happens, this latter situation is less common, but the analysis helps identify where this is likely to be the case and makes suggestion as to how to alter the branch structure to minimise it.

Without wanting to comment on the empirical merits of the paper—it seems persuasive in its analysis—the view it offers entails understanding the software engineer in a particular way. To put it very simply, it treats the research problem as one of uncovering and understanding the overall SE process, the one into which the software engineer 'fits'. This picture is produced through corroborating findings, statistical investigations and hard facts. As we have remarked, one might say that it is a 'scientific-like' approach—and this is indeed the kind of nomenclature than the authors use. By dint of this orientation, the software engineer constructed creature at the heart of the analysis is a creature that is 'lacking'. It is lacking particularly in objective knowledge and it is not fully aware of all the considerations that affect its own behaviour. The view of this creature, the engineer, contrasts with the wisdom of the researcher, wisdom produced by the method of inquiries. The software engineer is not devoid of knowledge in this view, but when compared to the analysis, theirs is only a partial view, parochial at best.

Before we go any further, it is very important to bear in mind that we are not suggesting that this view, the one that casts the software engineer this way, is incorrect. As we allude above, this (and any other view) is to be judged by what it leads to, what actions that result, as well as in terms of evidence. In the case of this paper, the approach it embodies (and represents) has the great benefit of pointing out the ways understandings of the software engineer can be enhanced. If the engineer is parochial, the output of this research can be used to provide insights and tools that can educate and correct that parochialism. The empirical adequacy of the paper are to be judged in part by whether its insights do in fact lead to better reasoning about the relationship between branches and bug fixes.

Second, the construction of the software animal at the heart of this view are not necessarily bound to the method used, though the choice of method and the construction of the animal might appear to go hand in hand. This is not necessary, we do not believe. The fact that, for example, the authors of the branchmania paper use quite sophisticated statistical techniques to weigh the evidence does not mean they could not have supplemented that material with say, 'ethnographic' type evidence. There might be difficulties bringing the qualitative and the quantitative together but we do not think these are epistemic, so much as practical: so much of the stuff that comes from ethnographic evidence is orthogonal to processual matters for example and so needs sifting out. The important point is the presumption that research adds understanding to the somehow deficient software engineer. All sorts of information can benefit these impoverished animals, quantitative and qualitative.

View 2: The Engineer as 'Creative Reasoner'

The second view we want to highlight casts the engineer in quite a different light to the one mentioned above, in the scientific vision of the engineer. The long held emphasis on the ethnomethodological concern with reasoning in CSCW (Button and Sharrock 1994; Schmidt and Bannon 1992) has led to an approach to SE research that emphasizes and investigates how engineers 'work through' and 'work up' particular software concerns into solvable problems (see for example, the de Souza et al. paper mentioned above, 2011). That this is so does not always show itself in remarks on the premises of the research, however; it is, rather, simply often a characteristic of CSCW-type papers.

The paper that Phillips et al. (2011) provides a good illustration of how this view casts the engineer in this special way. This reports a study of the informational needs of those about to reinsert 'fixed' code back into the code database. Here the research does not assume that the software engineer is 'lacking'; rather, it shows that they have rich resources at hand which can be built upon and extended, made more general and made richer. The study uses evidence gathered through semi-structured interviews of seven individuals who, like the Bird et al. study, worked in a development team on the West Coast. These included release managers, two team 'leads' and two developers—coders in other words. Data from these interviews were coded against a predefined set of topics, generated by a prior survey of branching activities in the SCM tool used in Windows.

More specifically, the study identifies ten 'rules' (or maxims) that are used by a sample of software engineers to determine what is an optimal time for submitting revised code into the code base. One rule holds that the number of lines of code being altered in a branch can be used to predict the likelihood of the difficulty that the engineers addressing that code will face. Thus the number of lines can act as a predictor of the likelihood that the branch in question will produce code later than planned. By the same token, differences in the number of lines between branches may also indicate the likelihood that branches will deliver their code changes on time. Another rule has to do with the ordering of branch integration or the sequence of different code 'reinserts'. Concurrent activities do not always lead to identical times of merging but a sequence—some are upload-able before others and others later. Knowing which, knowing the rule that determines which goes first, and which is dependent upon another, can allow engineers to predict the likely order of problems that will happen when code inserts happen. This sequencing can indicate the likelihood of problems and dependencies that arise after code is put back into the main code base. Another rule has to do with distinguishing between 'bugs' and 'features': the latter are nearly always subject to 'agile iteration' and change and hence can take longer than predicted whereas the former, bugs, are more likely to have pre-determinable timelines, how long they take can be fixed as it were.

One could go on. The important point is that this approach, then, paints the engineer in quite a different light to view in Bird et al.: here it is their capacity and ability that is celebrated, not the contrast between 'the facts' and 'their knowledge'. Research in this vein tends to offer guidance for new kinds of information and data that will provide engineers with tools that refine their ability to use their rich knowledge (see also Martin et al. 2007; also the considerable corpus of research by de Souza and his colleagues). Thus, and for example, Phillips et al. propose that more information about the actual timelines of code reinserts be made clearly visible in the SCM tools; engineers know how to use this information but simply need it to be better specified.

View 3: The Felt-Life: The 'Dwelling of Engineers'

One of the things we have remarked upon repeatedly is that those who deploy these various ways of looking at SE don't often see themselves as constructing a view of the human actor in the centre of their inquiries (the software engineer) in the way we have described. There may be a number of reasons for this, one being a lack of interest in this possibility—it may simply not concern them. Besides, there is also sometimes a conviction on the part of those doing research that their approach has a purity that would make any claims about it being constructive of the subject matter something to be resisted. One can readily imagine those who claim a scientific attitude and who deploy 'scientific methods' would hold this view. One might be more surprised that anthropologists hold it too, however, especially given the apparent affinity of their discipline to the soft sciences, and to the humanities in particular. But in fact this is often the case: anthropologists often claim that theirs is the ultimate arbiter of all studies of human action, the 'totalizing science' as one textbook writer on the anthropological method put it (see for example Sykes' *Arguing with Anthropology* of 2005).

We mention this now because it is apparently a form of anthropology (and its methods) that we need to bear in mind as we approach the third view we want to expound. This too constructs its subject. And the way this one does resonate with the style and techniques of anthropology, treating the interview between the fieldworker, the so-called ethnographer, and the subjects of the enquiries as the essential mechanism and topic of the research. In the view of many contemporary anthropologists (even if historically this might have been disputed), it is not the world at large that is at issue, it is not the world that exists outside of the interview that matters; it is the specific interlocution of the anthropologist with 'subjects' in those moments that does. To paraphrase David Mosse, it is the dialogue between the anthropologist and their subject and their subject's world that is the 'crucible' of the anthropological imagination (Mosse 2006): the site of anthropology is thus the interview.

This has all sorts of consequences. One is that it becomes very important 'just who' the fieldworker meets. It also becomes important to do multi-sited ethnography, when the interviews are undertaken in different parts of a subject world (Coleman and Hallerman 2011). This also begs questions as to what an ethnography might be if it is of the virtual world where the interaction between the anthropologist and that world happens: for this interaction might be with proxies, not real persons and so this might skew the data in certain kinds of ways (Hine 2000). Besides all this, and to refer to Mosse again, there is also the problem of what happens when those interviewed come to dispute with the researcher: what happens when interviews turn into arguments?

Be that as it may, the reason why we are spending some time on the problem of interview is that unlike the other two approaches we have sketched, the point at which data is gathered, in this case in and through qualitative interviewing, is fundamentally the source and province of inquiry. It is not, say, a largely taken for granted resource, or one that has to be treated with candid corroboration from other data sources. In the Bird et al. paper, for example, other data was gathered from a SCM tool; in the Phillips et al. paper the process of interviews was treated as a gathering resource that produced information that had to be reinterpreted, 'coded' in reference to other (as it happens unspecified) resources 'drawn from a survey'. The function of the interviews was then to provide evidence to characterise something else, the reasoning of software engineers, say, for corroboration of quantitative facts about bugs, perhaps.

We can illustrate what one focuses on when the topic is the interview with our own data. Like the authors of both the papers mentioned above, we were fortunate enough to get access to the Windows programming team in Microsoft. With this access we sought to interview a range of 'subjects' in this domain. And like them, to get a comprehensive sense of the domain we sent out requests to individuals in a variety of roles, and this resulted in 17 interviews with engineers, from product managers (in charge of several dozen coders), branch managers (who had responsibility for ensuring the development and testing of code before it is re-entered into the main code database), coders and testers. In this way we had access to at least some of the 'sites' of SE.

All the interviews were qualitative, with a simple list of initial topics being used to foster an open-ended, 'constructive' interview that encompassed all that subjects felt important, and which could be combined with discussion of the topics that we thought valuable. Each interview thus informed the next, such that the process resembled a voyage, where the understandings provided at the end built on those created at the outset. As with all such fieldwork, extensive notes were made in and after interviews, as well as transcripts made when participants allowed tape recordings.

The first thing that came out of the interviews—or rather was made visible in them—was not anything to do with things like 'what the engineer knows' or 'examples of algorithms', nor perhaps more pertinently given the Bird et al. and

Phillips et al. papers: how the branch structure is, say, misleading. Certainly branches were talked about but something else happened first.

What was made clear at the outset of the interaction between us and the subjects was that 'the information' that we were about to be provided with was 'dangerous'. All of the interviews commenced with discussions as to who we were and who might hear or worse 'read' what was shared with us. As these discussions unfolded in the first minutes of each interview, so it became clear that we could only be given information if we understood something about the 'specialness' of what was being given us. Doors were closed, voices hushed, queries made about the security of our recordings. One interview (#3) came to an abrupt end when the subject exclaimed that he 'wasn't going to tell everything'—as if he was releasing something dangerous, fearful, something that our levity made him think we did not fully appreciate; he came to doubt us.

These actions, these patternings in the interviews were not merely people judging whether they ought to allow strangers to pass the gate—into the world of Windows programmers. This is a classical problem in fieldwork (reported in papers that use a different approach such as the Bird et al. 2009a, b; see also Button and Sharrock 1994); rather we had to learn and acknowledge in the opening moments of the interview process—even during the interview as with #3—that we understood that information would be dangerous if it got to the wrong person. We came to learn this by questions posed to us by our subjects such as 'Who would see this work?', or 'Is this just for research, not for Windows?'; or 'Who else are you talking to?' Somehow danger arose when information and persons combined, we were being told. But in being told this we were also being told something about ourselves: if we were to have the information, no danger was implied; our use was neutral, sterile one might say. If we were to act as couriers, on the other hand, that was another matter. These concerns seemed designed to evoke 'fear' in our part. Certainly, they did make us more timid, more respectful, keener to show silence.

What these interlocutions with our subjects lead was to think on was not what they were hiding. We did not see their injunctions as devices to put us off from seeing the truth. On the contrary, the apparently sensitive topics made us think that our prior readings of research on SE had not conveyed the felt-life of SE very well. This life world seemed somewhat drained of colour, certainly when compared with what we were experiencing. This life world also seemed more passionate, volatile and tendentious than the descriptions of reasoning and accountability presented in the CSCW literature. What our interviews, or rather the experience of the interviews lead us to think of, was Ingold's claim (in *Being Alive* 2011) that human life entails forms of embodied praxis in particular sites of movement. By this he means that people do not simply react to situations but produce their reactions through confronting the possibilities presented to them and their own aspirations in a kind of dialogue. This mixes material constraints with the trajectories of human beings in rich, resonant and evocative ways: it is the weave of all this that produces the thing called experience.

So in Ingold's view, a real place such as, for example, a software engineers' office will have certain sensual features—a kind of light, an ambient sound, a physical form and each of these material phenomena will have their own properties and dynamics. These are combined with the human-sourced tensions that result when occupants of those offices, engineers, think about and engage with the work they need to do in those spaces, work that entails them sitting at in the light of the windows (where they quiet their minds) and where they gently tap their fingertips on a keyboard. An office may afford silences that allow an engineer to concentrate, but they might need to talk with people elsewhere and so must break those silences to get their engineering job done. They need to navigate these constraints, Ingold's view suggests; engineers need to judge when to work quietly or when to speak noisily. They need to 'dwell' in ways that makes their domain work for them. It was this that was brought to mind when we started our interviews: when we got the 'push back' after our opening remarks, once we had described our own trajectories and 'work'.

Delving into Software *Dwelling*

To access 'dwelling' Ingold proposes that the fieldworker participate in the experience of the contexts, not in the sense of being a participant observer but in the sense of feeling some of the lived vitality of the places in question. They need to grasp just what it feels like to dwell there. For example, we soon began to learn just how fraught SE can be, bound up with fears and navigated through with powerful notions of who should not be given knowledge and who should be. We were being instructed on the importance of recognizing the trajectories of those who pass by and come through SE dwellings. We were learning to attend to what other researchers had chosen to bypass or ignore.

So what was it that was being pointed to in our interviews that seemed to demand timidity on our part? Moreover, why did this concern, this worry, have an almost mystical quality? And besides who were the wrong persons? As we say, we weren't given information about algorithms.

One of our interviewees (#6) worked on the 'security handles' in the Windows kernel and so one might have imagined that descriptions of code in that context could indeed be dangerous stuff to know—we could have walked out of the room with ways of breaking the Windows security paradigms. But that was not the kind of stuff were we given. Nor, for that matter, were the persons that seemed implied as dangerous the kinds of individuals that one would imagine: when we listed bosses that had given us access the stating of their names did not get reacted to as if they were dangerous; the hierarchical location of these individuals didn't seem to drive a sense of danger for our interviewees.

What was mentioned continuously, however, and reasserted again and again, was the idea that their code revision decisions, their management of code inserts back into the branch system and so forth, was always motivated by what they wanted us to understand was 'good faith', a phrase used just in passing by two individuals. To paraphrase what we were being told by them and the others we met: the motivations we had described to us were meant to be embody or reflect sympathy, sympathy with and consideration for others. Good faith had to do with how individuals oriented to the problem of how their own work impacted on others. The tales we were presented with in interviews made it clear that behaving in good faith and, conversely, the presumption that others would behave with similar good faith, was something that was sought for and assumed but in practice chronically undermined and tested.

For example, subject #1 explained that, in one instance, the interdependency of his own team and that of another branch broke down. This was not because of poor faith by either party. It was due to poor understanding. As he put it, 'We didn't really take it seriously'. The 'it' he was talking about was a component in their code that turned out to be much more consequential for other branches than he and his colleagues had realized. When his team altered it they did not think it would affect their colleagues in another branch. He explained that they ought to have realized that it would have done so, but as he put it, they were too whimsical, not taking it seriously enough to find out how it had consequences until it was too late. The example was meant to show that it was not that our subjects acted in bad faith, or that their colleagues did so; it was rather that trying to act in good faith by our subjects was very hard work.

It was partly in this sense that the information being shared in the interviews was dangerous: it was dangerous because it begged questions as to whether we, us researchers, 'really wanted to find this out': the implication in this formulation being that we concocted a picture in our minds of a pure world of branched software engineering where decisions and practices were not sullied by the failures of engineers who didn't take everything seriously enough. This aspect of danger then was not pointing towards the danger of, say, managers 'finding this out'. It was not those who were the dangerous souls we had to avoid sharing our cargo with, it was us.

We shall come back to this concept of danger in a moment. But before we do so we want to note that in several interviews we were provided with examples not of passion and anger, but with tales about attempts to negotiate and bargain when the thing that was being bargained over was the right to adjust some code. 'We didn't own that problem' (#6), was a common phrase used to describe attempts. What was being illustrated was not giving work to others but taking on work for oneself. Individual decisions about how long some coding work would take, about the consequences of that work and so forth, were not simply questions about one's own activity but always and endemically about the implied work that this had for others.

Unfortunately, the decisions that an SE would make might not always have the interests of other SEs at heart; sometimes SE's had to look after 'themselves'. Sometimes 'one's own interest' had to take precedence. Just as our subjects recognised that they would be selfish, so they accepted that others would be too: 'they told us to politely go away' one subject told us when they had sought to have responsibility for some code given over to them. If 'they had been given it', he explained, the other group judged that their work would be made greater. There was no knowing whether this was 'objectively' true, of course, but it was assumed to be a reasonable possibility; thus they rejection was 'OK', the engineer explained.

At the same time, we were told that there was danger in the relationships those we were interviewing had with others, danger when these simple negotiations failed. We were told that those 'others' got frustrated and angry, and would sometimes find excuses like 'not taking it seriously' simply not good enough. Their reactions 'didn't leave a very good taste in my mouth as.. they jumped up and down' (#6).

So if one part of the danger had to do with whether 'we' (i.e. us researchers) could handle a real understanding of the world rather than a tidy 'researcher's vision', another aspect of the danger had to do with the fact that things talked about were things that caused friction between persons: there really was anger, resentment, fury. In this view, software engineering naturally led to 'dangerous situations'.

Were our subjects telling us that this organizational context was riven by ubiquitous personal animosity? Not at all; for our participant's were seeking to instruct us that the relationship between software practice and large scale programs of coding, manifest in this case in a vast branching structure, was not simply a question of schedules and planning; the relationship between action and system was not mechanical.

What we were being led to see was that the world of a programmer is a contested one, where the motivations and desires of one individual can come to be played out at the expense of another, and where the danger that we needed to acknowledge had to do with the fact that people 'naturally', sensibly and understandably get angry and resentful, bitter at the lack of good faith of others. At the same time as learning this, we were not being told that the overall system of which our subjects were a part was collapsing; quite the reverse: our subjects told us stories that not only instructed us to see the natural order of passion in software engineering, but also the fact that most often, and in most instances, targets were hit and deadlines met despite the tensions that arose in the work itself.

In this sense, our subjects were saying that although the maxim of having good faith in others might not be constantly abided by, the organisation itself could have faith that its workers would deliver the goods despite the stresses and strains. In sum, what our interviewees drew attention to is human passion. Their goal was to teach us, to instruct us to see, that SE is not a computational-like activity, it's about an activity that is all too human.

Conclusion

Our proposal has been that within the SE literature various kinds of human animal can be seen. These animals are created by a mix of assumptions about topic, choices about methods, and following on from that, treatments of evidence. Key to the perspective we have just presented is the way the subjects of it, in this case software engineers, do not simply act as conduits of the facts, conduits between their world and the world of the interviewer. Rather, interviews with these subjects were opportunities wherein the software engineer in question instructed us, the interviewers, on how to understand and orient to their world, the felt-life world of software engineer. As they did so, so the nature of themselves as engineers in their dwellings was, as it were, 'determined' in what Ingold would call 'the lived praxis of interlocution between interviewer and subject' (Ingold 2011, particularly 229–243).

One important distinction between this view and the prior views sketched is that here it is the engineer who was treated as the expert; the researcher is treated as parochial. Or rather, the researcher is treated as gauche—hence the concern about what the researcher wants to find out. The reason for this concern is that the software engineer, the animal at the heart of the world, is quite different from the one that the SE's think the researchers expect; this is particularly in what we have called, without any perjorative intent, the scientific view—the one in for example Bird et al.

A similar distinction is to be found between the view that the real, embodied, software engineer wants to convey about the 'human predicament' of their circumstances and the 'reasoned professional' described in what we called the CSCW-type view. This latter view is an approach that emphasises the creative, situated purposeful reasoning of engineers exemplified in Phillips' et al. This 'reasonable person' view is also exemplified in de Souza et al.'s rich and well-argued study of awareness (2011: pp 325–339); just as it is in, for example, Storey et al.'s *TODO or To Bug* paper (2008). But this is quite unlike the world as the subjects in our study wanted to convey.

The world that the view we have emphasised is populated with experts, to be sure, but these experts are of a particular kind, one that might frighten the researcher. For these individuals want to make sure that visitors to their space, to their dwellings, walk away with a sense of the heat within: SE is not about calm algorithmic reasoning alone; indeed that hardly conveys the sense of it. Those who dwell seem to want to highlight the structures of human passion within. Theirs is the world that looks, for all practical purposes, like the one the great Scottish philosopher Hume populated, one where the logical reason of the individual has to be understood as bound to the human nature that produces that reason: that is to say one where action is affected by anger, by choices about good faith, or coloured by resentment about the distribution of labour. In the world of Hume and so in the dwelling of software engineers, the animal at its heart is 'flesh and blood and reason'. Just as passion and logic are married for Hume in ways that appalled the eighteenth century rationalists, so it would appear that passion with coding is the key to be what can be seen when studying SE. In this view, SE is to be understood as an all too human affair; that is why it is dangerous to ask about and dangerous to know. Dwelling here is all too human.

How different this vision from Bird, from Phillips, from de Souza or Storey et al.; how particular its topics and insights. The discussions in this paper have suggested quite a different way of thinking about evidence about software engineering. This holds that we might well be able to merge views on some cases but we might also find that the kinds of views we are marshaling are seeing quite different phenomena, constituting different animals all called engineers. When we recognize this we might not be so easily persuaded to conclude that one view on this animal is 'righter' than another; nor might we be so keen to bring them together. When we are confronted by such possibilities, the suggestion put forth in this paper is not that they should be avoid doing this at all costs but rather that one should treat doing so with care—triangulating the arithmetic of branch costs with the sense of dwelling in SE seems a hard thing to do, perhaps not even a sensible thing to do.

Besides, a more important concern might be to investigate instead what a one of these approaches allows one to do alone. In the case of the last view we have presented, the view that emphasises the sense of dwelling articulated in interview, then a number of obvious implications follow on. One has to do with realisation that SE in large corporate enterprises (where the code base is also large) involves considerable interpersonal and organisational skill, skills it should be clear of a peculiar kind, 'human ones' we have said. This is not simply because there is a loose fit between branch structures and code elements; it is because of the felt-life of existence within such enterprises: to feel concern for an unknown other is surely a different feeling for those one knows; but to worry about the travelers who pass through one's office and their likely destination is another. Part of the sensibility required to leverage this view turns around the fact that what is a finding in other approaches is the assumed starting place here: those who dwell in the spaces described know that large code bases are not designed around nucleated elements and that there is an inevitable blurring between one component and another. They know too that even the most ardent branch design may well fail to ensure that the mapping between who does what can in all cases guarantee that what one person's code does cannot have (in some obscure way) an unexpected consequence for someone else's work. In this sense, the suggestion by the agile theorists like Williams mentioned at the outset (if theorists is the right word) that there needs to be a constant desire to communicate on the part of engineers, often face to face, is as true now as when the agile turn was first initiated all those years ago. But what the approach focused on dwelling highlights is how profoundly this is felt; how agitating of the spirit this can be. Those approaches that have looked at reason and accountability seem to eschew this very fact: just how communication is facilitated, managed, controlled, and acted upon in the dwellings of software engineers. If our characterisation has pointed the way, then much further consideration of these spaces is required. The view that the SE animal is passionate means that the human arts of reasoned negotiation are all the more important to enable but this may not be something that will only entail reasonableness. The turn to SNS may not lead to the more effective articulation of needs, as Storey, Treude, et al. imply (2010). It might also facilitate the vituperative and the ill-considered; off-the-cuff explosions of vented passion. As Rettberg notes in her book *Blogging*, this is certainly what appears to be the emergent norm in the blogosphere (2009). Harper (2011) confirms this view.

Another has to do with how attempts to theorise reasoning by software engineers need to recognise the importance of the dwellings in which it occurs. For what one can say about this last study, brief though it was, is that it highlights how software engineers undertake regular, continuous and often artful ethical decision making. This decision making looks nothing like the abstract rendering of reason one finds in, for example, philosophical studies of ethical choice, especially those that deploy the so-called trolley method of enquiry, where ethical questions are posed in a totally hypothetical manner. There is nothing hypothetical about ethics in SE. Nor does it look like those representations of human reasoning articulated in game theory which is increasingly popular. As O'Connor (2012) notes the trolley method is so devoid of linkages to real situations of choice that the kind of reasoning it does illuminate are almost completely egregious. This will apply to game theoretic models when attempts are made to apply them to abstract renderings of SE for the same reasons.

What this approach to SE brings to bear then is the kind of ethics that SE entails. Some years ago John Bowers made the claim SE in CSCW should become ethical. This assertion was evidently without any reference to what engineers actually do in organisational life, day in, day out. They make decisions not about what to code but about how their coding choices will affect others and how the choices will affect them in turn. This is endemic to SE practice.

That this is so should make it clear that a concern for dwelling does not make available the world of coding; it highlights how coding turns around relationships between organisational roles as kinds of identity, the community to which identities owe affiliation (the workgroups or gang in which an SE fits), such things as the moral rights to comment and act upon code elements and not others, as well as the felt-life of that ensemble.

As we conclude this paper, so one ought to be able to see now that one can see the analogies between the structures in the felt-life and such things as tribal structure, kinship systems, distributions of 'rights to know' and 'rights to act' in places far distant from the development offices of Windows. These analogous ensembles are most often to do with religious matters, with who has access to the inner sanctum of some holy place. But, here, we have seen through the casting light of a concern for dwelling that when it comes to the world of Windows software engineering on the 'West Coast', access to and control of bits of code is similarly drawn. Who can get to the code in the branch, who has access to that branch and who is prohibited are not strictly rational matters, we have seen. Like priests protecting the sanctum of their temples, those who dwell in software have much to protect. But whether it is software or theology, it is all the same from the analytic point of view used in this paper. As Foucault suggests, it's a question of how one constructs the human at the centre of the world one is interested in, and, as a consequence, what that world comes to look like given the human put in the heart of it.

References

Bird, C., & Zimmerman, T. (2012) Assessing the value of branches with what-if analysis In: *Proceedings of the 20th International Symposium on Foundations of Software Engineering* (FSE 2012), USA: Research Triangle Park.

Bird, C., Nagappan, N., Devanbu, H., Gall & Murphy, B. (2009a). Does distributed development affect software quality? an empirical case study of windows vista In: *Proceedings of the International Conference on Software Engineering.*

Bird, C. N., Nagappan, P., Devanbu, H., Gall & Murphy, B. (2009b). Putting it all together: using socio-technical networks to predict failures. In: *Proceedings of the 17th International Symposium on Software Reliability Engineering.* USA: IEEE Computer Society.

Bird, C., Gall, H., Hagappan, N., Devanbu, P., & Murphy, B. (2011) Don't touch my code!, *ESEC/FSE'11* (pp. 5–9).

Button, G., & Sharrock, W. W. (1994). Occasioned practices in the work of software engineers. In J. Goguen & M. Jirotka (Eds.), *Requirements engineering: social and technical issues.* San Diego: Academic Press.

Coleman, S., & Hellerman, P. (2011). *Multi-sited ethnography.* London: Routledge.

de Souza David, C R B., & Redmiles, F. (2008). An empirical study of software developers' management of dependencies and changes, In: *Proceeding ICSE* (pp. 241–250).

de Souza David, C R B, & Redmiles, F. (2011). The awareness network, to whom should i display my actions, and, whose actions should i monitor? *IEEE Transactions on* S.E, 37(3), 325–339.

Foucault, M. (1966). *The order of things.* Chicago: Chicago University Press.

Harper, R. (2011). *Texture: human expression in the age of communications overload.* Boson: MIT Press.

Hine, C. (2000). *Virtual ethnography.* London: Sage.

Ingold, T. (2011). *Being alive: essays on movement.* Routledge: Knowledge and Description.

Martin, D., Rooksby, J., Rouncefield, M., & Sommerville I. (2007). 'Good' organisational reasons for 'bad' software testing: An ethnographic study of testing in a small software company. In *Proceedings of ICSE* (pp. 602–611).

Mosse, D. (2006). Anti-social anthropology? objectivity, objection and the ethnography of public policy and professional communities. *Journal of the Royal Anthropological Institute, 12*(4), 935–956.

Nagappan, N., Murphy, B, & Basili, V. (2008). The influence of organizational structure on software quality: an empirical case study. In *Proceedings of the 30th international conference on software engineering.*

O'Connor, J. (2012) The trolley method of moral philosophy. *Essays in Philosophy, 13*(1), 14.

Phillips, S., Sillito, J., and Walker, R. (2011). Branching and merging: an investigation into current version control practices. In *International workshop on cooperative and human aspects of software engineering (CHASE'11),* ACM (9–15).

Rettberg, J. (2009). *Blogging.* Cambridge: Polity.

Rönkkö, K., Dittrich, Y., & Randall, D. (2005). When plans do not work out: how plans are used in software development projects. *Journal of Computer Supported Cooperative Work, 14*(5), 433–468.

Rorty, R (1979). *Philosophy and the mirror of nature.* Princeton: Princeton University Press.

Schmidt, K, & Bannon, L (1992). Taking CSCW seriously: supporting articulation work. *Journal of Computer Supported Cooperative Work, 1*(1–2), 7–40.

Sommerville, I (2007). *Software engineering* (8th ed.). England: Pearson Education.

Storey, M., Ryall, J., Bull, R., Myers, D., inger, J. (2008). TODO or to bug: exploring how task annotations play a role in the work practices of software developers, In *30th International conference on software engineering (ICSE).*

Storey, M., Treude, C., van Deursen, A., & Cheng, L. (2010). The impact of social media on software engineering practices and tools. *In Proceedings of the FSE/SDP workshop on the future of software engineering research (FOSER 2010)* (pp. 33–38).
Sykes, K. (2005). *Arguing with anthropology*. London: Routledge.
Williams, L. (2012). What agile teams think of agile principles. *Communications of ACM, 55*(4), 71–76.

What You See is What I Need: Mobile Reporting Practices in Emergencies

Thomas Ludwig, Christian Reuter and Volkmar Pipek

Abstract Decisions of emergency response organisations (police, fire fighters, infrastructure providers, etc.) rely on accurate and timely information. Some necessary information is integrated into control centre's IT (weather, availability of electricity, gauge information, etc.), but almost every decision needs to be based on very specific information of the current crisis situation. Due to the unpredictable nature of a crisis, gathering this kind of information requires much improvisation and articulation work which we aim to support. We present a study on how different emergency response organisations communicate with teams on-site to generate necessary information for the coordinating instances, and we described, implemented and evaluated an interaction concept as well as a prototype to support this communication by a semi-structured request-and-report system based on Android devices. We learned that (1) the accuracy of request and reports can be improved by using an appropriate metadata structure in addition to creating multimedia-based information content, (2) requirements of trusted and fast information need to be respected in support concepts although they may even be contradictory, and (3) the coordination strategy of the emergency response organisation also shapes the way this interaction needs to be designed.

T. Ludwig (✉) · C. Reuter · V. Pipek
Institute for Information Systems, University of Siegen, Siegen, Germany
e-mail: thomas.ludwig@uni-siegen.de

C. Reuter
e-mail: christian.reuter@uni-siegen.de

V. Pipek
e-mail: volkmar.pipek@uni-siegen.de

O. W. Bertelsen et al. (eds.), *ECSCW 2013: Proceedings of the 13th European Conference on Computer Supported Cooperative Work, 21–25 September 2013, Paphos, Cyprus*, DOI: 10.1007/978-1-4471-5346-7_10,

Introduction

Nowadays cooperation often goes beyond spatial and organisational boundaries. One challenge for cooperation in heterogeneous settings is to provide information in the appropriate amount, level of detail, format and point in time. In such settings, the sender is faced with the challenge of perceiving the outer context, as well as anticipating what the recipient already knows. If both are successful, communication can concentrate on the essentials, otherwise failures arise as a 'lack of information' or an 'information overload' (Toffler 1970). In CSCW a distinction between (mainly distributed) cooperative work, that covers the tasks itself, and articulation work, that includes all activities to coordinate the tasks among individuals, is common (Schmidt and Bannon 1992). Articulation work is necessary if one participant is not able to accomplish the whole task by himself. If we look at the case of emergency services, it is obvious that one unit cannot manage the situation alone, therefore collaboration and, consequently, articulation is required. In terms of emergency management, articulation work includes reports of on-site units to the control centre, information provided by the control centre or even communication between different units or organisations (Reuter et al. 2012). Emergency services face an "unlimited variety of incidents that require interpretation, decision and coordination" (Normark and Randall 2005). The increasing emergence of mobile devices, data flats and almost all-encompassing internet during the last years created new possibilities that allow communication and may support cooperation from anywhere. However, the dynamics and specifics of emergencies aggravate finding appropriate approaches to articulate information needs among all actors (Heath and Luff 1992).

In order to support articulation and reporting, we concentrate on a scenario, where on-site units and off-site units have to share a common understanding of a situation. The focus lies on preventing 'lack of information' as well as 'information overload', at the same time increasing the quality of information, which should ensure a better basis for cooperative decision-making. In a qualitative empirical study of emergency services we explored their mobile collaboration practices, as well as possibilities to support those practices via mobile devices and applications. From these pre-studies, we have summarized the requirements for a mobile interaction approach, which allows semi-structured information requests and corresponding reports to stimulate a high-quality information basis. After introducing the resulting Android application "MoRep", which is supposed to support communication among emergency services, it will be evaluated by emergency services representatives concerning its impact on working practices and potentials to support articulation work in emergencies.

Related Work

Unexpected problems, dynamic changes of situations or environmental and knowledge limitations lead to the need for improvisation (Stein 2011)—especially in crises and emergencies. To support improvisation during emergency management it is essential to know the characteristics of the field. Based on an analysis of the response to the 2001 World Trade Centre attack, the following characteristics of emergency management can be considered as reasons for improvisation (Mendonca 2007). Firstly, (a) *rarity* of incidences limits opportunities for training and learning. Furthermore, (b) *time pressure* forces a convergence of planning and execution. (c) *Uncertainty* is present because the development of an extreme incidence is hardly predictable. Furthermore, extreme events have (d) *high and broad consequences*, therefore there is a need to manage interdependencies among a wide range of physical and social systems. The (e) *complexity* of the event arises, partly due to the high and broad consequences. Finally, (f) *multiple decision makers* and responding organisations may negotiate while responding to the event. Nevertheless, all organisations that help guaranteeing civil security have developed systematic approaches to deal with these uncertainties and to allow for planned, coordinated activities in crises. Still, many situations require spontaneous, ad-hoc decisions and short-term (re-)planning. The collapse of role systems need not result in a disaster, if people develop skills in improvisation (Weick 1993). The ability to improvise remains a valuable asset for individuals and organisations, and is usually cultivated in crisis trainings and grows with experience (Ley et al. 2012). Computer-based systems can support these processes, if the design is informed by an understanding of the cognitive processes involved in responding to unanticipated contingencies (Mendonca 2007).

The type, quantity and quality of information, that an agent needs within a given decision making context to complete a specific task, is called information demand, whereas objective and subjective information demands are not always identical. The objective demand includes information, which should be available according to a specific task. The subjective demand includes all information that is relevant in the agents' opinion. The information supply includes all external and internal information to which an agent can access at a certain time. O'Reilly (1980) studied how the amount of information affects the quality of the decisions made. He shows that actors, who claimed not receiving enough information to complete the tasks, were less satisfied, but made better decisions. On the other side, actors, who claimed that they were overloaded, were more satisfied, but the decision quality was not as good. But the impression that the 'lack of information' has less negative effects than the 'information overload' is relativized by the finding that a lower satisfaction of actors is closely linked to an *"increased tendency by senders to distort information during transmission"* (O'Reilly 1980). Therefore both problems have the same relevance. They are characterized by subjectivity, which outlines one of our main argument: *"What one perceives as information overload, may be perfectly manageable to the other"* (Mulder et al.

2006). However, not only the amount of information plays an important role in decision making, but also the quality and the format (Ho and Tang 2001). Both are subjective as well and can vary according to the individual (Naumann and Rolker 2000) or scenario (Christofzik and Reuter 2013).

As already mentioned, in emergency management, decisions have an extensive impact. They are based on incremental information from on-site reports and messages. Especially the forces need to make decisions *under conditions of incomplete or inaccurate information in a context of changing and possibly ambiguous hazard consequences and response objectives [...] under considerable time pressure* (Paton 2003). Bharosa et al. (2009) showed that, during exercises, Commando Place Incident Team (COPI) leaders spent on average *30 min or more collecting information and directing the operations of their own agency, followed by a 15-min interaction with other COPI members*. Lundberg and Asplund (2011) analysed groups involved in regional and international operations, with regard to the flow and exchange of information and communication and found that these organisations mistrust their IT systems or do not accept them, because they do not want to pay for training as well as the proper equipment. To assure trust, acceptance and a safe handling of the systems, the systems should be used in the everyday work, not just in emergencies (Kyng et al. 2006). Further problems exist in the area of situation awareness. The lack of communicating task-oriented, dynamic information and the related 'information overload' lead to serious problems during the response phase (Prasanna et al. 2011). Further on, in collaborative environments, the different roles and expertise of group members make sense making even more challenging, because group members do not only need to understand task-related information but also need to comprehend the relative relevance of the information available (Paul and Reddy 2010). Other occurring problems concern the finding of a correct recipient, unclear channels of communication (Ley et al. 2012), time-consuming, ineffective forms of messages (Lundberg and Asplund 2011) and different interpretations of used terminologies (Reuter et al. 2012). Some of the problems could be solved by appropriate communication technologies albeit the main challenge is to articulate the individual information need in an easy way.

Information technology can support articulation work (Schmidt and Bannon 1992). Currently, radio is the most important communication technology for emergency services in Germany. The digital radio, which is presently being introduced, makes it possible to use a single shared nationwide network, which creates new forms of communication. In contrast to analogue, the digital radio enables to transmit data on a narrow-band, but the rate is limited to 3 kbit/s, which does not allow transmitting much data, like multimedia. Based on empirical studies Guerrero et al. (2006) and Peng et al. (2007) developed conception frameworks, which determine appropriate devices besides digital radio for certain cooperation contexts. Both frameworks deem tablet PCs and PDAs as the most suitable in terms of mobility. Since the frameworks release, smartphones and tablets have become more popular and powerful and combine the performance of PDAs with the multimedia support of mobile phones, where the integrated sensors will be extended in the future (Gomez and Bartolacci 2011). Both, smartphones and tablets meet the requirements of everyday using and are fundamental elements of CSCW technology for mobile workers (Tamaru et al. 2005). Besides the devices, the growing range of mobile technologies such as LTE creates new possibilities for transmitting big amounts of data.

Various approaches already focus on supporting cooperation with the additional help of mobile devices. There officers-in-charge are information providers and consumers, whereas units on-site are primarily information providers (Nilsson and Stølen 2010). The officers-in-charge, either on-site or in the control centre, are mainly decision makers, whose decisions result in actions performed by on-site units. Büscher and Mogensen (2007) present different prototypes to enable command centres capturing live information about on-site movements and situation assessment in order to be able to construct a better situation overview without having to disturb on-site units via verbal communication. Catarci et al. (2010) present a system, in which each on-site unit uses a PDA that was supervised by a process management system, which orchestrates the units and conducts external data services. The mobile devices are able to receive tasks, to add comments to captured pictures and videos, to share these and to display them on a map application. Another more content-oriented concept was introduced by Singh and Ableiter (2009). Their application 'TwiddleNet' makes it possible to send and receive multimedia data, where the smartphones took on the dual-role of a server and a client. These data are available as a feed and are accessible via 'pull' or 'push' service. Those applications, which allow almost real-time reports, including multimedia data with location information, are able to increase situation awareness (Betts et al. 2005). Bergstrand and Landgren (2011) analysed the communication impact of live videos from the incident place to the control centre and found, that the videos improved situation assessment in the control centre enormously. Due to the bottom-up flow of communication, the on-site units provided information driven by their own motivation or previous radio transmission, which led to problems with prioritization: *When you decide to use the camera, you also decide not to do other things* (Incident Commander in Bergstrand and Landgren 2011). Wu et al. (2011) presented, in contrast to Bergstrand and Landgren (2011), a 2-way system including top-down communication, which is based on CIVIL, a mobile application allowing up- and downloading geo-referenced data. Professionals as well as citizens can use the application, which means that citizens become an active part of crisis management. Problems arose due to the amount of data, because a majority of the pictures caused an overloaded map application. A suggested solution was a picture cluster, but the question remains of *"how to choose a representative photo to describe the entire group of pictures"* (Wu et al. 2011). Such a similar problem arose while using the application 'diretto' (Erb et al. 2011), which allows transferring images and other formats to a previously asked query. The system Ushahidi (Okolloh 2009) has a similar approach, but without previously asked questions. An application which is aimed at supporting collaborative situation awareness and decision making in the specialized case of a chemical industrial accident is 'DIADEM' (Winterboer et al. 2011). With

DIADEM, the control centre can ask selected agents to take pictures, which are automatically geo-tagged and displayed on a digital map in the control centre.

Most approaches pursue a kind of push mechanism, where the information is received in the form of notifications and the recipient has no option to articulate the information need or to specify the needed format. Apart from problems that occur with voice transmission (Schöning et al. 2009), Bergstrand and Landgren (2011) showed that—despite possible enhancements of situation awareness—already available photos from on-site response teams are not regularly used. Therefore, decision makers should have the possibility to improvise and articulate their individual information needs in an appropriated way. Prototypes of Büscher and Mogensen (2007) allow pulling information in an appropriate way, but these do not address directly improvisational activities and try to substitute verbal requests. Other existing systems (Catarci et al. 2010; Winterboer et al. 2011) allow to request information, where these requests are often merely text messages and the decision makers have no option to articulate or specify their information needs and formats in a further dynamic, fine-grained, but still simple way.

Taking the existing reporting practice and existing approaches into account the research question of this paper is: How should emergency services articulate their information needs and how can mobile applications support articulation work in emergencies? The following empirical study will explore mobile collaboration practices of emergency services, as well as possible means to support these practices via mobile devices and applications.

Research Field

The findings and the concept in this paper are derived from a study focusing on collaboration, situation assessment and decision-making practices during coping and recovery work at emergency response agencies in Germany. The study was conducted in two regions. County A is a densely wooded, hilly and rural county, whereas county B consists of 10 growing and urban communes. In both regions, we focus on several organisations affected: Infrastructure suppliers (e.g. power supplier), public strategic administration (e.g. crisis management, county administration), public operative administration (e.g. police, fire department) and citizens. The organization of police and fire fighter forces differ among the counties: County 2 provides professionals, whereas fire fighters of county 1 are mostly members of voluntary fire departments. Here, just members of the control centre have salaried positions.

Empirical Study

The basis for the data analysis was the result of various empirical works during the years 2010–2012 in the application field. The studies were embedded in a scenario framework, which was developed together with actors from police and fire department, county administration and an electricity provider. It includes a windstorm with many incidents and energy breakdowns. The purpose of the scenario was to be able to quickly create a common understanding of an occurring emergency and therefore it helped to increase the validity and comparability in our interviews. We conducted five inter-organisational group discussions, each lasted about 4 h. The aim of the group discussions was to understand communication practice of inter-organisational crisis management. Furthermore, we conducted 22 individual interviews with actors from the participating organisations (Table 1). Each interview lasted between 1 and 2 h and followed a guideline, which was separated into three parts. The first part focused on the participants' role, qualification, tasks and work activities under normal conditions. The second part covered the participants' tasks during emergencies in our developed scenario

Table 1 Interviewes of the empirical study (phase 1): information and collaborative practices

Number	County	Organisation	Role	Control centre	On-site	
					Leader	Other
I01	A	Administration	Regulatory Authority	X	X	
I02	A	Police Department	Head of Control Centre	X	X	
I03	A	Police Department	Head of Section	X	X	
I04	A	Police Department	Patrol Duty			X
I05	A	Fire Department	District Fire Chief	X		
I06	A	Fire Department	Deputy Head of Control Centre	X		
I07	A	Fire Department	Workmanship			X
I24	A	Fire Department	Head of Control Centre	X		
I08	B	Administration	Office Civil Protection	X		
I09	B	Fire Department	Chief Officer/Chief of Fire Dept.	X		
I10	B	Fire Department	Operation Controllers		X	
I11	B	Fire Department	Clerical Grade Watch Department			X
I12	B	Fire Department	Control Centre Dispatcher	X		
I13	B	Fire Department	Head of Control Centre	X	X	
I14	B	Police Department	Member of the Permanent Staff	X		
I15	B	Police Department	Head of Control Centre	X		
I16	B	Police Department	Head of Group		X	
I18	Both	Energy Network Operator	Higher Area, High Voltage	X		
I19	Both	Energy Network Operator	Operation Engineer, High Voltage		X	
I20	Both	Energy Network Operator	Operation Technician, Low Voltage		X	
I21	Both	Energy Network Operator	Dispatcher, Low Voltage	X		
I22	Both	Energy Network Operator	Workmanship Technical Incidents		X	

Table 2 Interviewes of the empirical study (phase 2): mobile collaboration practices

Number	County	Organisation	Role	Control centre	On-site	
					Leader	Other
IM01	A	Police Department	Head of Control Centre	X	X	
IM02	A	Fire Department	Administrator of the Control Centre	X	X	
IM03	A	Fire Department	Control Centre Data Support/ Digital Radio Coordinator	X	X	X
IM04	A	Police Department	Head of Police Station		X	
IM05	B	Fire Department	Department Chief Control Centre	X	X	X

framework. The third part covered applied information and communication systems and perceived problems with these tools. Group discussions and interviews were audio recorded and later transcribed for subsequent data analysis.

The empirical study showed that, especially in police and fire departments, decision makers depend on on-site information to be able to make appropriate decisions. Therefore, the organisations of the second empirical phase in 2012, which researches the effects of dynamic information requests and their fine-grained specifications to create a high qualitative base for making decisions, were fire and police department with their different management and lead structures. The police coordinate operations directly from the control centre *(lead from the behind)*, in the fire department, however, the officer-in-charge is on-site and the control centre only supports him *(lead from the front)*. To be able to study the mobile collaboration practices more closely, additional five partially structured interviews were conducted in 2012 which lasted in average 60 min, in which the current practices were analysed, also in regards to the creation, exchange and use of information by the response teams and the works in the control centre (see Table 2).

Results: Mobile Reporting Practices

In the following, the empirical results concerning the information and communication practices and the articulation of information needs are presented.

Information and Communication Practices

Emergency management requires making decisions in situ based on current conditions. Hence, it is necessary to keep track of the occurrences. Some of the information, which is used for the work tasks in operations management, is provided by "official" information systems. In major catastrophic events or in case of weather alerts these internal information resources are enriched by many external, *informal information resources*, which are necessary in various situations. Many actors individually collect supplementary information from various sources (e.g. the current weather condition outside the building, phone calls or webcams that are focused against the wind direction) to obtain a better overview of the situation: *"You need as much information as possible"* (I24). Or: *I need verified information for a decision about a particular situation* (I05), which needs to be *"as detailed and accurate as possible to give an exact representation of the situation"* (I06). Nevertheless information from own personnel is judged as being very valuable. The heads of control centres (I01, I09) mentioned that visual on-site impressions are crucial, because if you *explain to someone that there is an accident with 300 injured people, both of us have a very different imagination of the situation* (I09). Therefore, *the most reliable information is what I have seen myself* (I05), where the difficulty exists *that we can't look through the phone and we don't see how it looks like on-site*. (I06). The response team on-site already knows, that it can be important to send visual data to the control centre, because*if you've seen it yourself, you have a better overview of the situation* (I10). Currently verbal communication is executed via radio. In the control centre *the flood of communication kills us in our daily work* (I03), where the permanent risk of *"being overloaded by information"* (I03) exists, that *in the end you don't understand what's going on anymore, because there is too much input and you can't handle the information* (I03). On the other side, the on-site team complains about having not enough information: *It would be great to have more information on-site"* (I07), because currently *"the office-in-charge wants something done and then we have to understand what he means* (I07).

The information demand is very subjective:*What we need in order to be able to make a decision varies from individual to individual* (I03) and cannot be specified in advance. Nevertheless all agents agreed that particular criteria need to be met: (a) The emergency work is based on situation maps, therefore *the necessary GPS coordinates need to be included, so that you know the location the information comes from and don't have to guess* (IM05). (b) Sending and receiving information in different data formats is desirable (I05), while pictures and videos are seen as most relevant (IM04) and long text messages critical (IM03). (c) It is necessary that it is visible which user took the picture (IM03) and that (d) the information is time-stamped (IM01). The information between the control centre and on-site units' needs to be 100 % synchronized (IM05), because *during an operation there is nothing worse than talking about different things* (IM05).

When communicating no unit in the hierarchical structure may be left out, even if it means a larger amount of time (IM01), for example, a sub section leader will always communicate only with his section leader and not directly with the head of operations (IM01). The control centre always communicates at the level of section leaders (IM01), where information from the section leader does not need to be evaluated and can be used immediately (IM01). Involving citizen-generated information into crisis management is seen critical: *Someone who does not have a background in emergency services would hardly be able to deliver necessary information in such a situation* (I02). Sending pictures by citizens *will get out of control if everyone takes pictures. [...] If you've had an accident or anything else happened to you, you wouldn't want a stranger to take pictures* (I01). Of course scenarios exist where citizen-generated information might be useful and could contribute to situational awareness (Vieweg et al. 2010), but due to the interviewees mentioned that applications for supporting direct communication should only be available to emergency services, we blanked out the dimension of citizen-generated information in our paper.

Articulation of Information Needs

A wide range of emergency response actions show that situation assessment is often a collaborative task. To deal with the uncertain and changing environment during emergencies, usually a big number of people are involved in gathering or analysing data, decision making and monitoring of implementations and consequences. However, in order to articulate information needs, infrastructures are needed. Independent from knowledge about both frameworks for selecting devices for specific contexts (Guerrero et al. 2006; Peng et al. 2007) the interviewees confirmed: "*if we're talking about an ideal situation, then I have a smartphone in my patrol car and the officer-in-charge uses a different device that gives him even more functionality*" (IM04). Right now the communication path is still via radio, but smartphones are already used for purposes like using Google Maps for satellite views or navigation (I04), because the control centre gives an address and the on-site team often does not know the exact location. Moreover, mobile devices are not only interesting for the on-site units, but also for the actors in the control centre since they are not present 24/7 so that they have mobile access to information (I13). The participants asked for a simple and easy-to-use hardware *with as few features as possible, so that a unit, who has never used it before, can be trained quickly* (IM04) and it *should* be used almost daily to establish routines (I06). An important feature is to be able to take videos or photos quickly and record voice data and write short messages all without using a pen (IM03). The hardware needs to be quickly ready for use, *if we need to boot an additional notebook, then it won't be used* (I04).

Usually the on-site teams are responsible to deliver relevant information, so information is provided via push mechanisms. This practice has some disadvantages. One problem also occurred during our interviews: On-site teams often do not know which information they have to transmit or they prioritize outgoing reports very low, especially volunteer forces (IM01, IM02). Therefore the current control centre practice is to request information from the incident place actively (pull mechanism) and to not wait for appropriate reports. By requesting information actively, it is possible to prevent that *everybody just takes pictures and sends them back, without really knowing what is going on* (IM05). During the dynamic requests for information, the return format of information often needs to be specified (IM04). In case of such requests, the control centre *"should see the location of a unit and instruct him to take a picture"* (IM02). Currently the determination of the units' locations only works verbally via radio: *I take my radio and contact him: Where are you? At best he will answer: I'm here or there* (IM05). *Ideally, besides the location, you see whether the unit is busy or not* (I03). These articulations currently take a lot of time. Therefore the forces mentioned that, based on the location, there should be an option to navigate units remotely: *If I see their locations and also the plans on a map, I could say: Go five meters further, that's where the next hydrant should be* (IM02). Due to the high dynamics and improvisation within response teams, people can be spontaneously assigned to new roles. Therefore, requests need to be always assigned to roles, never to persons (IM01, IM03). Besides the influences from an incident itself, *organisational factors* and structures can bear unpredictable challenges. That is why each actor will have to be able to divert from given routines to be capable of acting even if the given structures and circumstances change: *If a system is strongly rigid and structured, and then one component is missing, mostly the whole system will collapse. For this, informal acting can be helpful.* (I01).

A Semi-structured Mobile Reporting Concept

Decision making in crisis management depends on incremental written or mostly verbal on-site reports. The empirical results on current practices of emergency services show a need for improvisational action in order to get appropriate reports. Information producers in the form of on-site units are not always able to anticipate the needs of their counterparts in the control centres, so arising 'information overload' or 'lack of information' negatively affect decisions.

Control centres are mainly interested in impressions from the incident place supported by visual multimedia data to get remotely a situation overview. The cycle of semi-structured information requests and reports (Fig. 1) visualizes the concept grounded on the empirically studied work practice. If the written or verbal on-site reports do not satisfy their needs, the control centre needs to have the option to actively articulate information needs. Currently this dynamic requesting activity is not supported: Using the radio verbally, the control centre complains about being flooded with information and the on-site units are left with much space for interpretations: *"The office-in-charge wants something done and then we have to understand what it means"* (I07). Therefore a mechanism which allows semi-structured information requests and does not leave space for interpretations could support their cooperation. Due to the fact that information needs vary from individual to individual, reports should be easy to specify for each user, and some context information always needs to be captured automatically: the coordinates of the location, the source and the time, which identify the information as a whole (IM03). These context data need to be available when looking at the information. By requesting or reporting information, the predefined hierarchical organisational

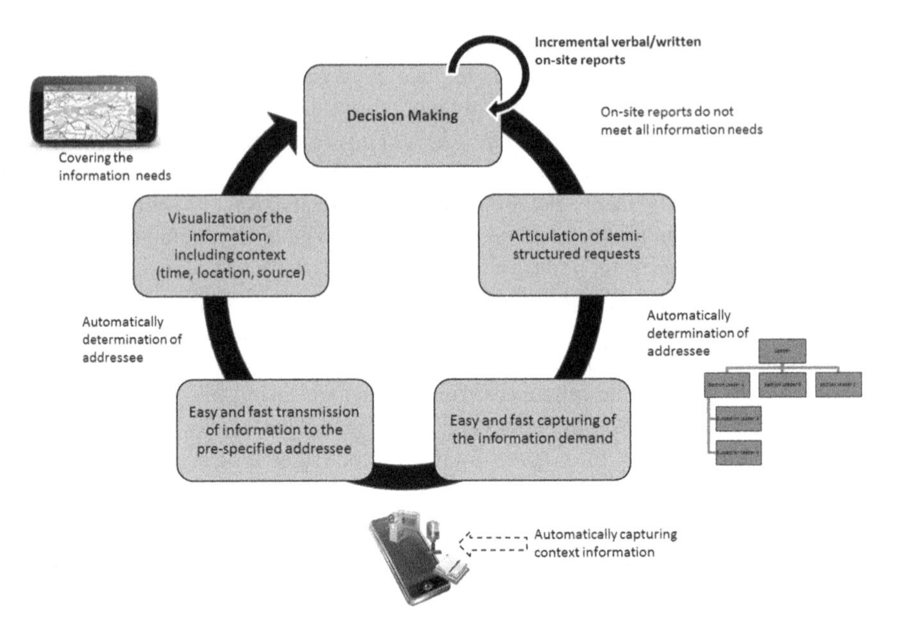

Fig. 1 Supporting decision making through mobile semi-structured information requests

structure has to be considered, for example, the sub section leader is not allowed to send information to the control centre directly, because otherwise the section leader is skipped. On the other hand, the control centre is not allowed to request information from the sub section leader directly, because otherwise the section leader is skipped again.

Determining addressees of requests needs to be possible by its location or role: Location-based requests give a location overview on all subordinates of which information can be requested, which enriches the awareness between the control centre and the on-site units. For role-based requests the addressee can be determined by its role (e.g. *sub section leader area 1*). A supportive mechanism must be applied to smartphones as well as tablets to guarantee a proficient handling including following rights:

- *Requesting information* allows a response unit to fine-specify and articulate the kind of information needed. At this, transmitting a destination location for a remote-navigation of the unit and setting the priority for a more appropriate assessment of the task's urgency must be possible.
- The *independent sending of information* allows authorized units to send information, directly, without previous requests. For instance, this permission is relevant for section leaders, as their information does not have to be authorized anymore.
- *Sending information by previous request* allows a unit to send information by himself, but only as an answer to a previous request. This restriction should help to avoid 'information overload' for decision makers due to information needs to be requested first.

Implementation of a Mobile Reporting Application

In order to verify the concept and research its effect we implemented a mobile application. By using Android 4 the application MoRep can be used on smartphones as well as tablets. The technical concept is based on REST architecture as form of the SOA-paradigm, where the services are implemented by HTTP-servlets. Using modern communication technologies, such as Google Cloud Messaging, innovative notification mechanisms are implemented that simplify communication and allow a parallel use to radio communication. In the following, the application MoRep will be briefly introduced.

Start up: After authentication, the user receives current information of his role and permissions. The main screen is designed according to these permissions. Figure 2 shows a user with all rights: Seeing reports, requesting reports from subordinates, answering requests made by superior as well as writing reports independent from previously request.

Requesting reports: When requesting reports, a location- and role-based determination of on-site units is possible. By the first option, the user can scan for subordinate response units (Fig. 3), where the unit is displayed on the map characterized by role and name. By selecting the unit, the request form is opened (Fig. 4). There the user has to enter specified characteristics and the desired format of a report. He has the option to define a destination location for the remote navigation (Fig. 5). Afterwards the request can be sent. For role-based requests the recipient can be chosen from a combo box, where all the possible recipients are listed, from whom information can be requested, no matter what their location is.

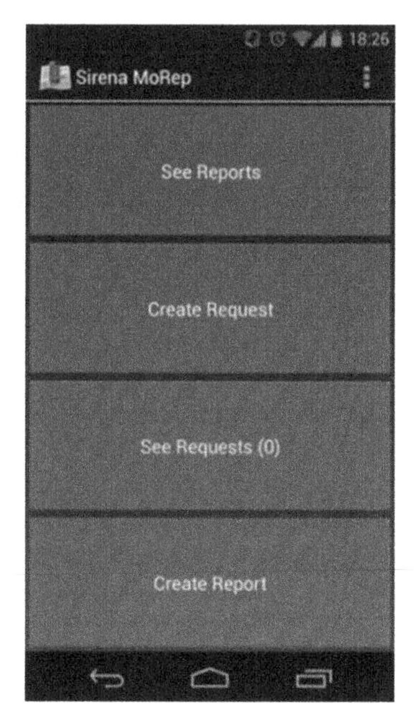

Fig. 2 Main screen

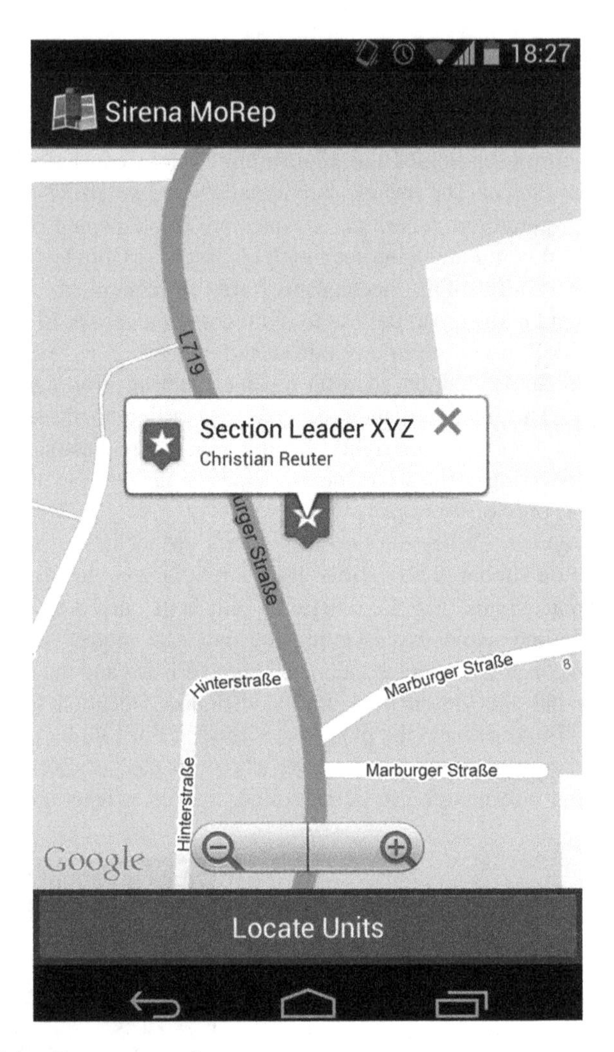

Fig. 3 Localizing the response units

See requests/creating report: In the request overview (Fig. 6) open requests are displayed for the user sorted by priority and time. A request can directly be answered with a report, where a form (Fig. 7) appears, in which the text fields have already been pre-determined by the creator of the request. If a target location was transmitted, the coordinates-button will be shown that offers the possibility of navigating to that location (Fig. 8). By entering the format button, the standard application for generating files is opened; subsequent the text button is activated to make an optional text input (Fig. 9). A report that is not based on a request can also be created from the main screen. In that form the recipient is immediately determined as the next superior unit.

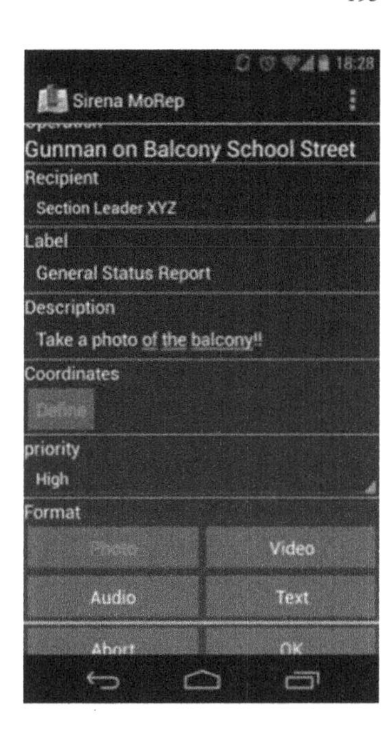

Fig. 4 Request form

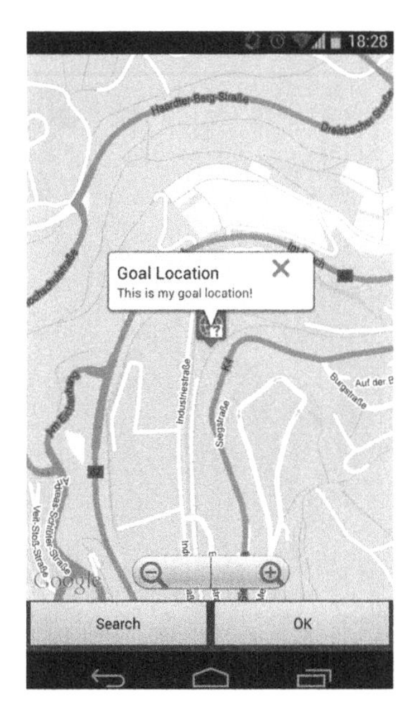

Fig. 5 Determining the location

See reports: The main element is a Google Maps map (Fig. 10), on which previously created reports are shown with icons that indicate the data format. The user can view all reports or only those he requested. It is also possible to add this

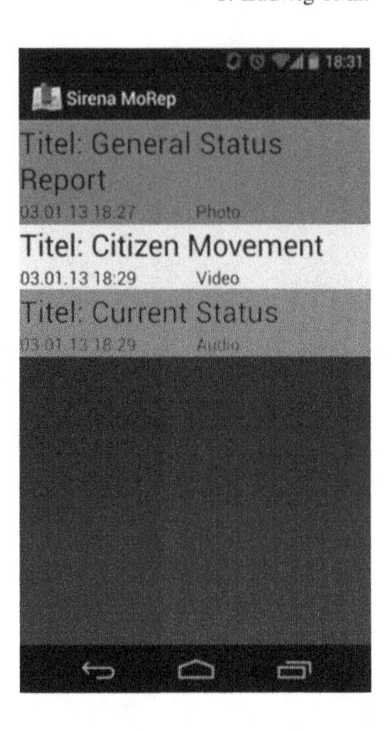

Fig. 6 Request overview

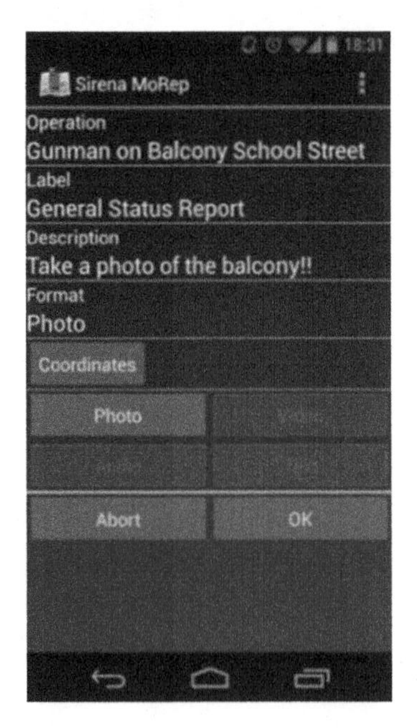

Fig. 7 Report on request (I)

view to any Geographical Information System using Web Map Services. In the information window the source and time are displayed that, in combination with the geo-location, meet the criteria specified for suitable information (IM05). If it is

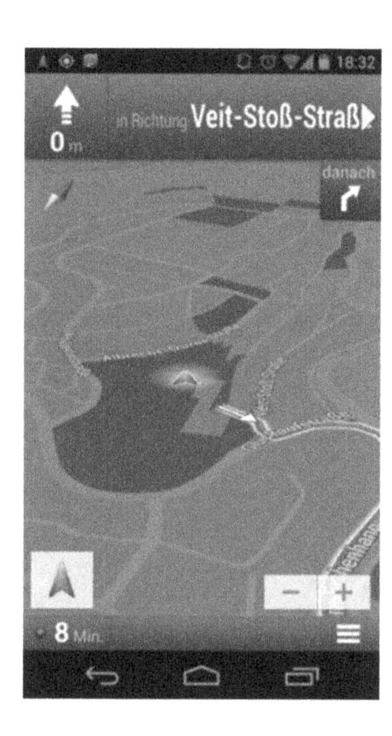

Fig. 8 Target navigation

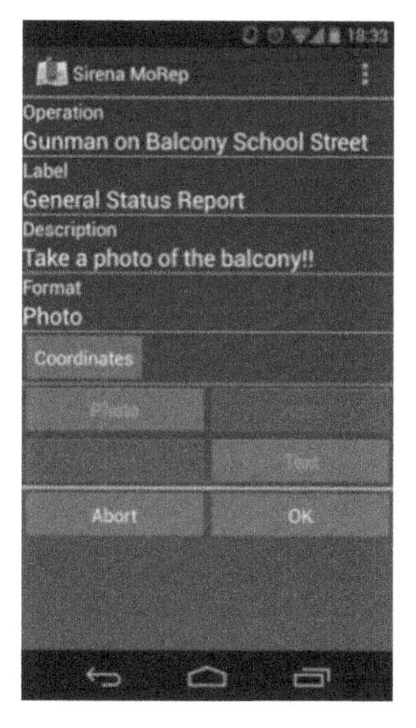

Fig. 9 Report on request (II)

entered, the content will show (Fig. 11).The text symbol on the left side of the window indicates an additional text (Fig. 12) the arrow symbol creates an easy forwarding of information to the superior.

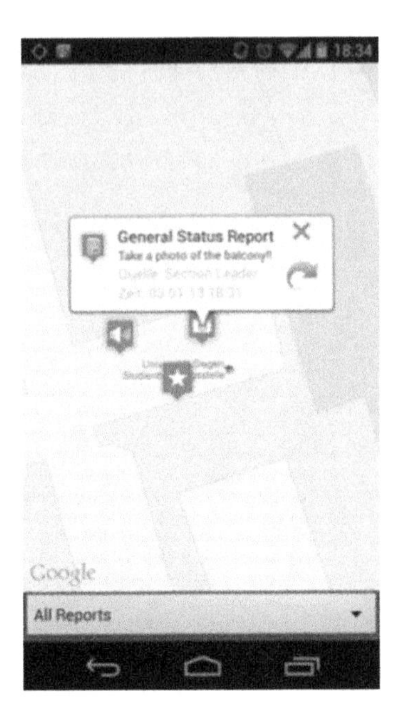

Fig. 10 See reports

Fig. 11 Content of report

Evaluation

Although our system had been fully implemented, IT security regulations and privacy and documentation concerns of the emergency response organisations prevented us from having an in-use evaluation. We evaluated with practitioners in police and fire stations how mobile dynamic semi-structured requests can support current decision processes by providing a high-quality information basis and avoiding 'information overload' as well as 'lack of information'. In order to evaluate the findings, concepts and our supporting tool related to the work practices we evaluated the prototype in a scenario-based walkthrough and following

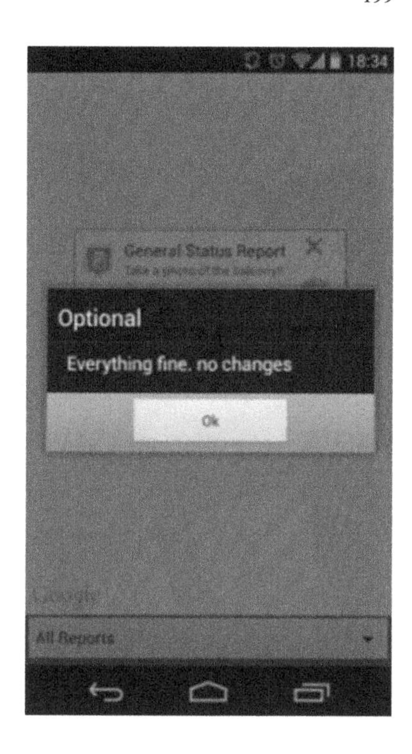

Fig. 12 Additional text

interviews. Again the participants were members of the police and fire department, but this time also volunteer emergency forces were included, due to these are potential end users as well (IM01, IM02). The evaluation sessions lasted in average 45 min and 11 persons from police and (professional and volunteer) fire departments participated in different sessions. With this selection of interview partners the impressions and experiences of communication partners on different levels within the chain of command could be gathered and evaluated.

Within each evaluation MoRep was introduced functionally and it was demonstrated how it could support in different situations by referring to operations mentioned by the interviewees in the empirical study. The demonstration was an interactive session, where the users directly explored the application. The participants were asked to make remarks using "thinking aloud" (Nielsen 1993). After the demonstration, the participants were asked questions regarding the practice-oriented use, e.g.: What are possible implications of using semi-structured requests in emergency response? Under what conditions can the concept and application support current working practices? What are limitations concerning the usage? The workshops were recorded and later transcribed (Fig. 13; Table 3).

Fig. 13 Evaluation of the mobile application in the fire department

Results

Using our design we were able to derive the impact of mobile dynamic semi-structured requests on improvisation work practices of decision makers and on-site units.

Extending Articulation Work with Semi-structured Mobile Requests

The concept of semi-specified mobile reports as a consequence of dynamic, semi-structured information requests cannot cover major emergencies over their entire time, but it can easily be used for "*basic information and a common understanding*

Table 3 Interviewees of the empirical study (phase 3): evaluation of the collaboration tool

Number	County	Organization	Role	Control centre	On-site	
					Leader	Other
IM06	A	Police Department	Head of Control Centre	X		
IM07	A	Police Department	Head of Section	X	X	
IM08	A	Police Department	Head of Section		X	X
IM09	A	Police Department	Executive Staff			X
IM10	A	Police Department	Executive Staff			X
IM11	A	Fire Department	Fire Chief, Administrator Control Centre	X	X	
IM12	A	Fire Department	Municipal Fire Inspector		X	
IM13	A	Fire Department	Volunteer Fire Chief		X	
IM14	A	Fire Department	Volunteer Workmanship			X
IM15	A	Fire Department	Volunteer Workmanship			X
IM16	A	Fire Department	Volunteer Workmanship			X

of the situation" (IM08). In contrast to phone calls, it is an additional way of communication and articulation, which can enrich reports with visual data (IM09). The mechanism of fine-specifying and requesting report demands was seen as very useful in case of insufficient reports. Therefore the decision makers have the option to enhance the routine reporting structure and informally request information. The on-site units have the duty to answer those requests (IM04). Requesting information by the units' localization as well as their role were important aspects to establish awareness between the spatially distributed units and to get an overview of the situation assignment of the units (IM07). By being able to determine units by their role was regarded as stress reducing, because the actors did not have to think about the correct addressee (IM08). Another important feature of applications that support the communication between on-site units and the control centre is the fast transmitting and forwarding of information. Being able to forward information to the superior was regarded as being one of the most important functionalities, which enriches the entire information flow (IM06, IM08).

Improving Situation Awareness Through Semi-structured Requests

The handling of semi-structured information requests as one of the core concepts has two supportive dimensions: First, it supports local volunteer fire fighters that indeed know the location of the incident place, but do not necessarily have the experience in judging the importance of information for the control centre respectively the officer-in-charge and which information needs to be reported (IM06). Therefore semi-structured information requests provide and foster training effects. Second, semi-structured information requests support professional units from other counties, who assess the importance of information better than volunteer units do, but who often—especially in large-scale emergencies—do not know the location. Therefore, the requests foster situational awareness of the units. For example, the head of the studied police station mentioned that they will have new recruits starting very soon and the majority of them are not familiar with the region. Thus, they will use their smartphones to navigate which is why transmitting locations is very important (IM06). They are already using GoogleMaps on private smartphones (IM10), wherefore "*introducing something different makes no sense, because everyone knows and uses GoogleMaps and it is up to date*" (IM11).

Taking Organizational Specifics and Improvisational Practice into Account

The different leading structures of the police ("from the behind") and the fire department ("from the front") have an important impact on using the concept in the work practices during emergencies. At the police department, the control centre has the entire responsibility for an operation. For this purpose it maintains software, which manages the included actors and their dynamically assigned roles. Through this matching they have always an overview of the command and reporting flow (IM06), wherefore an automatic connection between those control centre systems and the mobile applications could easily be implemented to guarantee up-to-date role assignments and correct command- and reporting flows in the applications like MoRep. In contrast to the police departments, the fire departments in our study do not maintain such software systems. The officer-in-charge on-site has the entire responsibility for an operation and the control centre has just supportive task to the officer-in-charge. The control centre has the problem *"if I send him coordinates, then it is a process, where I directly influence the operation and you need to decide if that makes sense and on which level you have the permission to do that"* (IM11). It's not the control centre, but the officer-in-charge would use such mobile systems to support the communication between the on-site units, because he stays at a location while the other units are distributed around the incident site (IM11).

Enhancing Debriefing with Multimedia-based Documentation

After an emergency the automatically saved requests and transmitted information can be used for the documentation *"where I need the timestamp and the content what happened. Right now there is no standard"* (IM03). This documentation could be the basis for debriefing of the past operations: *"Currently we use internet videos of photographers and information of journalists from the incident place for debriefing afterwards"* (IM11), because, except written reports, no other data for documentation or training exist.

Predefined Communication Path Versus Improvisation Work

Even though it was mentioned as very useful, that communication paths are predefined by the application, there were still doubts whether the on-site units will utilize this feature (IM07). Through the predefined command and reporting structure the concept is currently too static to cover all improvisational activities during emergencies. While on the one hand the hierarchy of the police could be easily adapted to the mobile applications, on the other hand, there are still open issues and a need for action to the technical implementation and to maintain the actuality of the organisational structure of the fire department. But all participants were aware that mobile applications like MoRep only *"support an additional way of communication and that in case of emergencies you can still make a call"* (IM09), to guarantee options for high-flexible extensive improvisation activities.

Discussion and Conclusion

In emergencies, gathering the necessary information to generate a situation overview is crucial for emergency services to make informed decisions. The interplay between control centres and on-site units is an important information chain that is shaped by legal regulations (e.g. on notification and documentation duties) and professional conventions (e.g. reporting agreements). But in crises, the routines connected with these regulations and conventions do not cover all information needs: Situational aspects connected with the crisis require stakeholders to improvise and to engage in articulation work about information needs and resources that emerge as the crisis goes on.

There has been previous research on the technical support of response units on-site to share reports with control centres including multimedia data. But in some situations those reports were ignored (Bergstrand and Landgren 2011) or disregarded, simply due to the sheer amount of incoming notifications (Wu et al. 2011). Applications such as DIADEM (Winterboer et al. 2011) or diretto (Erb et al. 2011) enabled the control centres to actively articulate information needs and request needed information. The requests were described by short text messages, which still left plenty of room for misunderstandings as with voice transmission.

In this paper, we explore the practice and necessities of articulation work with regard to the ad-hoc gathering of information in emergencies, and suggest and evaluate an interaction concept involving semi-structured multimedia reports. In our empirical study on current work practices of emergency services with regard to collaboration in situation assessment and decision-making activities, we could establish that the spontaneity and volatility of emerging information needs on all sides pose a significant challenge to communicate them accurately as well as to provide accurate feedback. Existing practices show that, in order to cope with requirements like time-criticalness of feedback or reliability of information, a set of framing conditions needs to be addressed when developing technological support:

- *Targeted requests:* The missing information in a decision situation is often very specific to a location, a critical infrastructure or another situational aspect. These specifics of information needs have to be articulated and understood.
- *Trusted reports:* Decisions in the control centre may affect lives of crisis victims and may have legal consequences. Therefore, staff members require high quality information for the specific decision in situ, which cannot be secured in terms of technical information quality only, but also in terms of trust, which is established through the professional expertise of the source creating the information.
- *Documented action:* To enable debriefing and provide material for training purposes the requests as well as the reports have to be documented.

It is important to note that these framing conditions may lead to conflicting information quality requirements in a concrete situation: The faster reports may come from an information source with a lower expertise, and the report from a trusted information source may not be available fast enough to inform the decision-maker at hand. As a result, not only time, location and content type of information are important metadata for requests as well as report interactions allowing an easy interpretation and assessment of the content, but also role, contact data, location and experience of the person providing the feedback. Documentation and interpretation needs may be addressed by establishing a content structure for request and report messages that relates to professional signs and languages of the emergency response service and that allows free comments. The interpretation of information in the context of a specific decision may turn out to be a collaborative effort requiring additional interactions.

We developed, implemented and evaluated an interaction concept using semi-structured request and reports based on Android devices, and allowing location-triggered as well as role-triggered interactions (MoRep). The feedback we got from practitioners using the prototype confirmed that the suggested content and metadata structures would improve the expected information accuracy and quality. But it also revealed further side aspects of organising this interaction, for instance the material that would be gathered may help improving debriefing processes and educational initiatives.

In particular, the organisational structures and coordination strategies influence information needs and interaction details. In some cases it is required to delegate and forward information requests to people who are even closer to the site of interest in a documented, traceable way. The police with their 'leading from behind' coordination strategy has a more static role and responsibility structure and the direction of the main information flow is towards the control centre, whereas fire fighters with their 'leading from the front' coordination strategy have changing roles and responsibilities on-site, and an information flow directed mainly to the on-site coordination. Request and report strategies of our prototype need to adapt to these differences by maintaining the organisational and information structure. In the long run, these predefined information structures also carry a notion of potential information needs to all forces involved in the interactions and may also raise the general awareness on information necessities.

Our research efforts described here are part of a larger research initiative to improve the *collaborative resilience* (Goldstein 2011) of and in critical infrastructures. In contrast to many crisis management approaches in the field of IS and HCI, we do not aim to further capture and refine holistic process representations or to extend sensor data collection and visualization to be better prepared for crises, but rather to improve improvisation capacities in crises by addressing smaller ad-hoc collaborations we found to be important to practitioners. We believe to have found an interesting one here, and would now further explore its integration into new emerging technological and organisational infrastructures like the German emergency service digital radio network ('BOS-Digitalfunk') or recent inter-organisational infrastructures for coordinating regional crisis management work (Ley et al. 2012).

Acknowledgments The project 'InfoStrom' is funded by the German Federal Ministry for Education and Research (No. 13N10712).

References

Bergstrand, F., & Landgren, J. (2011). Visual reporting in time-critical work: Exploring video use in emergency response Chalmers University of Technology. *Proceedings of the MobileHCI*, Stockholm (pp. 415–424).

Betts, B. J., Mah, R. W., Papasin, R., Del Mundo, R., McIntosh, D. M., & Jorgensen, C. (2005). *Improving situational awareness for first responders* via *mobile computing*. Moffett Field, CA: National Aeronautics and Space Administration Ames Research Center, Ed..

Bharosa, N., Lee, J., & Janssen, M. (2009). Challenges and obstacles in sharing and coordinating information during multi-agency disaster response: Propositions from field exercises. *Information Systems Frontiers, 12*(1), 49–65. doi:10.1007/s10796-009-9174-z.

Büscher, M., & Mogensen, P. H. (2007). Designing for material practices of coordinating emergency teamwork. In B. Van De Walle, P. Burghardt, & C. Nieuwenhuis (Eds.), *Proceedings of the* ISCRAM, Delft.

Catarci, T., De Leoni, M., Marrella, A., Mecella, M., Bortenschlager, M., & Steinmann, R. (2010). The WORKPAD project experience: Improving the disaster response through process management and geo collaboration. *Proceedings of the* ISCRAM, Seattle.

Christofzik, D., & Reuter, C. (2013). The aggregation of information qualities in collaborative software. *International Journal of Entrepreneurial Venturing (IJEV), 5*(3).

Erb, B., Kaufmann, S., Schlecht, T., Schaub, F., & Weber, M. (2011). diretto: A toolkit for distributed reporting and collaboration. In M. Eibl (Ed.), *Mensch & Computer 2011* (pp. 151–160). Chemnitz: Oldenbourg Wissenschaftsverlag.

Goldstein, B. E. (Ed.). (2011). *Collaborative resilience—Moving through crisis to opportunity* (p. 376). Cambridge, MA: MIT Press.

Gomez, E., & Bartolacci, M. (2011). Crisis management and mobile devices: Extending usage of sensor networks within an integrated system framework. *Proceedings of the ISCRAM*, Lisbon.

Guerrero, L., Ochoa, S. F., Pino, J., & Collazos, C. (2006). Selecting computing devices to support mobile collaboration. *Group Decision and Negotiation, 15*(3), 243–271. doi:10.1007/s10726-006-9020-3.

Heath, C., & Luff, P. (1992). Collaboration and control: Crisis management and multimedia technology in London Underground Line Control Rooms. *Journal of Computer Supported Cooperative Work, 1*(1), 24–48.

Ho, J., & Tang, R. (2001). Towards an optimal resolution to information overload: An infomediary approach. *Proceedings of the GROUP* (pp. 91–96). New York: ACM.

Kyng, M., Nielsen, E. T., & Kristensen, M. (2006). Challenges in designing interactive systems for emergency response. *Proceedings of the DIS* (pp. 301–310). New York: ACM Press.

Ley, B., Pipek, V., Reuter, C., & Wiedenhoefer, T. (2012). Supporting improvisation work in inter-organizational crisis management. *Proceedings of the conference on human factors in Computing Systems (CHI)*. Austin: ACM-Press.

Lundberg, J., & Asplund, M. (2011). Communication problems in crisis response. *Proceedings of the ISCRAM*, Lisbon, Portugal

Mendonca, D. (2007). Decision support for improvisation in response to extreme events: Learning from the response to the 2001 World Trade Center attack. *Decision Support Systems, 43*(3), 952–967.

Mulder, I., De Poot, H, Verwij, C., Janssen, R., & Bijlsma, M. (2006). An information overload study: Using design methods for understanding. *Proc of the OZCHI* (pp. 245–252). New York: ACM Press.

Naumann, F., & Rolker, C. (2000). Assessment methods for information quality criteria. *Proceedings of International Conference on Information Quality* (pp. 158–162).

Nielsen, J. (1993). *Usability engineering*. San Francisco: Morgan Kaufmann.

Nilsson, E. G., & Stølen, K. (2010). Ad Hoc networks and mobile devices in emergency response—a perfect match? (Invited Paper). *Lecture Notes of the Institute for Computer Sciences, Social Informatics and Telecommunications Engineering, 49*, 17–33.

Normark, M., & Randall, D. (2005). Local expertise at an emergency call centre. In H. Gellersen, K. Schmidt, M. Beaudouin-Lafon, & W. Mackay (Eds.), *Proceedings of the ECSCW* (pp. 347–366). Paris: Springer.

O'Reilly, C. A. (1980). Individuals and information overload in organizations: Is more necessarily better? *Academy of Management Journal, 23*(4), 684–696. doi:10.2307/255556.

Okolloh, O. (2009). Ushahidi, or "testimony": Web 2.0 tools for crowdsourcing crisis information. *Participatory Learning and Action*, *59*(1), 65–70.

Paton, D. (2003). Stress in disaster response: A risk management approach. *Disaster Prevention and Management, 12*(3), 203–209.

Paul, S. A., & Reddy, M. C. (2010). Understanding together: Sensemaking in collaborative information seeking. *Proceedings of the CSCW* (pp. 321–330). New York: ACM Press.

Peng, C. Y., Kao, W. S., Liang, Y. Z., & Chiou, W. K. (2007). The practices of scenario observation approach in defining medical tablet PC applications. *Proceedings of the MobileHCI* (Vol. 4553, pp. 518–524). Beijing: Springer.

Prasanna, R., Yang, L., & King, M. (2011). Evaluation of a software prototype for supporting fire emergency response. *Proceedings of the ISCRAM,* Lissabon, Portugal.

Reuter, C., Marx, A., & Pipek, V. (2012). Crisis management 2.0: Towards a systematization of social software use in crisis situations. *IJISCRAM*, *4*(1), 1–16.

Reuter, C., Pipek, V., Wiedenhoefer, T., & Ley, B. (2012). Dealing with terminologies in collaborative systems for crisis management. *Proceedings of the ISCRAM,* Vancouver, Canada.

Schmidt, K., & Bannon, L. (1992). Taking CSCW seriously: Supporting articulation work. *Computer Supported Cooperative Work, 1*(1), 7–40. doi:10.1007/BF00752449.

Schöning, J., Rohs, M., Krüger, A., & Stasch, C. (2009). Improving the communication of spatial information in crisis response by combining paper maps and mobile devices. In J. Löffler & M. Klann (Eds.), *Mobile response: Second international workshop on mobile information technology for emergency response* (pp. 57–65). Berlin: Springer.

Singh, G., & Ableiter, D. (2009). TwiddleNet: Smartphones as personal content servers for first responders. In J. Löffler & M. Klann (Eds.), *Mobile response: Second international workshop on mobile information technology for emergency response* (Vol. 5424, pp. 130–137). Bonn: Springer.

Stein, E. W. (2011). Supporting real time decision-making. In F. Burstein, P. Brézillon, & A. Zaslavsky (Eds.), *Supporting real time decision-making* (Vol. 13, pp. 13–33). Boston, MA: Springer.

Tamaru, E., Hasuike, K., & Tozaki, M. (2005). Cellular phone as a collaboration tool that empowers and changes the way of mobile work: Focus on three fields of work. *Proceedings of the ECSCW* (pp. 247–266). Paris: Springer.

Toffler, A. (1970). *Future shock. Administrative science quarterly* (Vol. 17, p. 423). Random House. doi:10.2307/2392161.

Vieweg, S., Hughes, A. L., Starbird, K., & Palen, L. (2010). Microblogging during two natural hazards events: What twitter may contribute to situational awareness. *Proceedings of the CHI* (pp. 1079–1088). New York: ACM Press.

Weick, K. E. (1993). The collapse of sensemaking in organizations: The Mann Gulch disaster. *Administrative Science Quarterly, 38*(4), 628–652.

Winterboer, A., Martens, M. A., Pavlin, G., Groen, F. C. A., & Evers, V. (2011). DIADEM: A system for collaborative environmental monitoring. *Proceedings of the CSCW*, New York, NY, USA, pp. 589–590.

Wu, A., Yan, X., & Zhang, X. L. (2011). Geo-tagged mobile photo sharing in collaborative emergency management. *Proceedings of the VINCI* (pp. 7:1–7:8). Hong Kong: ACM Press.

The Social Life of Tunes: Representing the Aesthetics of Reception

Norman Makoto Su

Abstract I report on two years of participant observation of traditional musicians in Dublin, Ireland. In Irish traditional music, players from all walks of life gather at pub sessions to play tunes together. Due to the ethos of traditional music, the *representation* of tunes is a constant aesthetic concern. Drawing on the aesthetics of reception, I show how arriving at the proper "text" of a tune poses unique challenges. Rather than simply reading notes on sheet music, traditional musicians must imaginatively read the creative text on a "virtual space" to create art. Making music involves a nuanced process of learning, knowing, and retaining a tune. The tune is not a static entity but one dynamically shaped by its social context and provenance. The social life of tunes suggests that technologies ought to support the practice of practicing seamlessly across the performance-oriented session and the solitary pursuit of skill, while allowing novices a way to conceptualize the historical flexibility of the tune. I will outline a new agenda of *surveilling tradition* to represent the aesthetics of reception. With the burgeoning interest in the collaborative work of tradition, this work provides new perspectives into the creative processes involved in representation.

Introduction

The problem of *representation* has been well documented in the computer-supported cooperative work literature. The ways in which systems capture the world through models and present "new" realities to be read is problematic when designers ignore the everyday interpretive practices of different communities of users (Robinson and Bannon 1991). The problem of how to represent the world

N. M. Su (✉)
School of Information and Library Studies, Dublin, Ireland
e-mail: normsu@ucd.ie

O. W. Bertelsen et al. (eds.), *ECSCW 2013: Proceedings of the 13th European Conference on Computer Supported Cooperative Work, 21–25 September 2013, Paphos, Cyprus*, DOI: 10.1007/978-1-4471-5346-7_11, © Springer-Verlag London 2013

stems from the reality that human behavior is contradictory and improvisatory (Whalen et al. 2002). Complicating the situation even more, representation is always set in the context of external political (Brown 2001) and cultural forces (Grudin 1988). As a result, representations based on models often do not reflect real-world practice by being too deterministic and inflexible (Shipman and Marshall 1999). Indeed, one might argue that the hallmark of CSCW research is that it has shown how users find creative workarounds to close the gap between what "we must support socially and what we can support technically" (Ackerman 2000).

Robinson and Bannon (1991) bring up the issue of *ontological drift* whereby representations change as they are interpreted by different semantic communities. Like the childhood game of telephone, "the *object of an interpretation* and the *interpretation itself* changes places" between different groups. Their work details how each actor (users, feasibility studies, programmers, etc.) involved in software development subsequently transforms representations of reality, ending up with a final product that is radically different from what users originally wanted.

This paper will expand on the concept of representation. I will present a unique case of a community that has, as its explicit moral and aesthetic concern, the ontological drift of representations, or the sheer heterogeneity of representations. In the community of Irish traditional (trad) musicians, the tune is the object of interpretation. Traditional music implies an orally passed skill, one unencumbered by "modern" artifacts. In contrast to the highly regimented training of classical musicians, traditional music seems to have an almost informal, cavalier attitude towards itself. The following YouTube comment on a famous Donegal fiddler playing outside a pub reflects this ethos:

> [Danny Meehan] was playing fiddle in a pub and a mesmerised classical player asked him about the pizzicato style he was using and Danny looked at him bemused and said "Ah now don't be putting fancy names to just picking at the strings."

While fidelity to a composer's wishes on sheet music is valued in classical music, trad musicians routinely disparage texts that rigidly prescribe music making. Tunes often have numerous variations, and most trad musicians cannot read sheet music.

Drawing from two years of participant observation and interviews of trad musicians in Dublin, Ireland, I will show how the ethos of "tradition" poses challenges for system developers. The trad ethos encourages musicians of all skills to gather in pubs, festivals, and homes to play tunes but paradoxically constrains such musicians by prescribing what are the proper representations of tunes. A trad session is not simply composed of expert players but of players in different stages of skill acquisition (Dreyfus and Dreyfus 2005). This melting pot of musicians is precisely the intersection of semantic communities. Significantly, what counts for the right representation depends on a changing reality of what a tune is. Past research has pointed to the significant work involved to achieve (sometimes inflexible or inadequate) representations of a single reality—for example, the work to ensure accurate timesheets (Brown 2001). However, little research has focused on the fact that representations might need to represent *multiple* realities (Robinson and Bannon 1991).

This paper is not just a story of how ontological drift from reality happens, but, rather, how ontological drift itself is an object of active interpretation. While ontological drift is usually perceived as creeping in an insidious manner, Irish trad musicians are cognizantly aware of and think about drift in the representation of tunes. Drift is not necessarily a bad thing. In fact, the ethos of tradition embraces a meaning of tunes that is transient.

To understand the mercurial nature of tunes, I draw from the aesthetics of reception (Iser 1972; Jauss and Benzinger 1970). This theory of literary criticism helps elucidate how tunes in Irish traditional music only gain meaning when there is text to be "read" (i.e., interpreted and played) by an actor. Tunes are read in both private (solo practice) and public spheres (the session), and their representations have different meanings and readings for those in different skill levels. I will argue that to become part of the tradition requires not only an adeptness in the "virtual work" of reading a text—learning, knowing, and retaining tunes—but an understanding of the aesthetics of reception itself. In other words, the Irish trad musician must be aware that there is no ground truth in a representation and what it represents.

After discussing prior work, I describe the theoretical framework from which I draw my analysis, the aesthetics of reception. My analysis will then detail the process of learning (and creating good art), knowing, and retaining tunes. In each activity, how to read the text and what a text "is" is constantly questioned by me and my fellow musicians. Finally, in the discussion and conclusion, I lay out an agenda for the *surveillance of tradition* to support and represent the aesthetics of reception, thereby bridging novice and professional trad musicians.

Prior Work

Most of the HCI and CSCW research on music has been on Western classical music. Graefe et al. (1996) designed a digital music stand to support the practice and formal performance needs of symphony musicians. Their proposed stand consolidated a tuner and metronome while facilitating personal notations and customized music arrangements. They also cite the need to support communication between orchestral musicians in the pit during rehearsals. Letondal and Mackay (2007) studied classical composers, noting that they rely on paper for creative sketching of pieces but found it hard to integrate computer tools with their paper drafts.

Closest to my research is insightful work by Benford et al. (2012) on the "moral order" of Irish sessions, or "informal gatherings of local musicians in pubs…to play music whose dominant style and repertoire is drawn from the Irish tradition." They provide an account of how musicians maintain and create tradition in the context of sessions. For example, they note how sessions often have an implied hierarchy (a session leader who starts many of the tune sets), frown upon overt use of paper artifacts, and have a shared repertoire. They propose designing for "situated discretion," creating technologies that assist musicians in a session while being discrete enough to not disrupt the moral order. As a case in point, mobile apps for trad musicians might be designed to mundanely integrate with the usual activities in pubs (e.g., chatting and drinking). I wish to differentiate my study in several ways. First, my primary field site is in Dublin as opposed to Nottingham, UK. Unlike the sessions observed by Benford et al., occurrences of other genres of music and the use of paper artifacts (other than at learner sessions) in Dublin sessions were extremely rare. My study also has data from crucial places of learning for trad musicians: festivals and workshops. Second, my focus was less on the dynamics of the session and more on the practices of learning and disseminating tunes. While Benford et al. do call for bridging preparation and performance, I will argue that the boundary between the two is much more hazy. Finally, my work examines in detail the actual usage of technology in the social life of tunes.

There is a body of work on the sociology of the Irish trad community. Such research sometimes describe the availability of technological artifacts, but their particular relevance to the everyday practices of musicians is unknown. For example, O'Shea's (2008) study mentions recordings only in passing and focuses on how one gradually becomes accepted as a "regular" in a session. Work by Fleming (2004) examines the controversy over the institution of government-supported competitions in Irish trad music. Titon (2001) gives a personal account of fiddle jams and their spontaneity but without detail of how musicians bridge solo and session playing. While Waldron and Veblen (2008) show how sheet music is a "skeleton for learning [Celtic Trad Music]" and provide a useful categorization of learners on a visual/audio spectrum, my work details how musicians reconcile disparate representations to arrive at a skeleton (here, even sheet music is an inadequate base version of the tune). Forsyth (2011) focuses on the pedagogical practices at a fiddle camp for adult learners. She gives a good overview of debates in using sheet music versus audio transcripts but not on how students actually use such artifacts. Veblen (1996) provides a "snapshot" of stability and change with respect to the oral transmission of Irish trad music. While a good intro to trad culture, it omits mention of sessions.

The above works focus on fieldwork in pedagogical settings, not on solo and session settings and discuss little about the social aspects of tunes. Veblen (2008) provides an ontology of online sources for trad musicians but does not discuss how such sources in practice are used. Morton (2005) looks at sessions and non-verbal communication but mostly to advance "performance ethnography."

The Aesthetics of Reception

In this paper, I draw from the reception theory/history or the aesthetics of reception school of thought from the Konstanz School, namely Wolfgang Iser (1972) and Jauss and Benzinger (1970). These theories are differentiated from other schools of literary criticism that seek to evaluate or interpret literature on the basis of the author's intent or the text as a self-contained script.

The aesthetics of reception (Iser 1972) posits that a literary work is neither the text nor the realization of the text accomplished by the reader. Rather, the literary work is only brought into existence in a *virtual space* (p. 279) where the reader's horizon (horizon being the context or background in Heideggerian terms) and the horizon within which the text appears merge. Iser uses the phrase virtual not in the modern technological medium sense but to convey that this "convergence can never be precisely pinpointed" (p. 279). There is significant work involved in instantiating a literary text that goes beyond both the reader and the blanket text.

Furthermore, each reading, even from the same person, results in a different literary work. Iser (p. 283) says that:

> [E]ach reading can never reassume its original shape, for this would mean that memory and perception were identical, which is manifestly not so....Thus, the reader, in establishing these interrelations between past, present, and future actually causes the text to reveal its potential multiplicity of connections. These connections are the product of the reader's mind working on the raw material of the text, though they are not the text itself—for this consists just of sentences, statements, information, etc.

There is a temporal aspect in reading. Text is made meaningful in moments of time through rereading (Jauss and Benzinger 1970, p. 10). Readers view the "text through a perspective that is continually on the move" (Iser 1972, p. 285), establishing a new virtual dimension of the text. Literary texts reconfigure reading into an ongoing *creative* process.

Part of literary criticism's raison d'être is to establish the canon. According to the aesthetics of reception, literature with *value* must "be conceived in such a way that it will engage the reader's imagination in the task of working things out for himself, for reading is only a pleasure when it is active and creative....The 'unwritten' part of a text stimulates" (Iser 1972, p. 280). This pleasure stems from the work done in the virtual space which in turn is helped by a creative text and an imaginative reader.

A good text defies readers' expectations, allowing multiple variations of interpretations. The tension in "simultaneously having expectations and [the] feeling that...probably they will be violated" (Fry 2009) gives us aesthetic pleasure. Good fiction must balance between presenting an "illusion" (Iser 1972, p. 289) where we comfortably imagine ourselves in a purely unrealistic world (e.g., trashy romance novels) and merely restating the reality we already know.

Iser suggests that wider, external factors have a relation to the virtual dimension. Upon encountering a text, readers can immediately grasp "a repertoire of familiar literary patterns...together with allusions to familiar social and historical contexts" (p. 293). This *repertoire* is "continually backgrounded or foregrounded with a resultant strategic overmagnification, trivialization, or even annihilation of the allusion" (p. 293).

Jauss and Benzinger (1970) expand on Iser, creating a broader picture of reader-reception theory. They outline a historical perspective of the aesthetics of reception in three ways (p. 23, paraphrased): diachronically in the relationship of literary works based upon reception, synchronically with reference to current literature, and with relation to the immanent literary development to the general process of history. A historical perspective brings into focus that there is a variable distance between the immediate and potential meaning of a literary work. Jauss and Benzinger (1970) define the "aesthetic difference" as the distance between the given horizon of expectations and the appearance of a new work. When the aesthetic distance between new work and expectations is too large, a long process of reception or other later, new work may need to appear to widen the horizon of expectations and thus close the distance (p. 26). This distance can be measured *historically* in the "spectrum of the reaction of the audience and the judgment of criticism (spontaneous success, rejection or shock, scattered approval, gradual or later understanding)" (p. 14). Hence, the history of reception, the history of changing horizons of expectations, is important. That is, in the context of the past and present, reception theory posits that to ask how a text is to be understood is to ask what texts the author could expect his or her readers to know in the future.

Reader-reception theory offers a useful lens to critically examine representation as a creative process. In my analysis, I will illustrate how the process of music making in Irish traditional music can be conceptualized as the work done in the virtual dimension where the text and reader's horizon meet.

Methodology and Field Site

I have been previously trained as a classical musician in piano and have a minor in music in which I was educated in (Western) music theory and musicianship. With no prior experience in traditional music, I took active steps to gain enough proficiency in an instrument to sit and participate in sessions. Field work in Dublin, Ireland consisted of enrolling in a tin whistle class for approximately one year at the Dublin People's College, taking informal Irish flute lessons for approximately one year, participating in sessions, and competing in the Dublin Fleadh (festival). Pub sessions in Dublin and learner sessions at the Comhaltas Headquarters (a government-sponsored, non-profit group formed in 1951 to preserve and promote Irish trad music) were regularly attended (at least once a week). Learner sessions are primarily for adult beginners and allow the use of sheet music or other learning aides. In the course of fieldwork, informants also invited me to attend several house sessions: sessions held at someone's house. I also joined a group of musicians, learned a set of performance tunes, and competed in the Grúpa Cheoil; this allowed me to gain a perspective into the pedagogical practices of Comhaltas.

I attended two events outside Dublin, the Leitrim Country Fleadh and the Cruinniú na bhFliúit (The Flute Meeting), a gathering of Irish flute musicians (equivalent gatherings are done for pipers, concertina players, and other trad instrumentalists) in Ballyvourney, an Irish speaking region in Cork. Detailed field notes were taken, and, when allowed/appropriate, photos and audio were also captured.

While the data collected above gives a sense of the amateur's practices in the trad music scene, it excludes the practice of seasoned musicians. For this, I conducted 20 semi-structured interviews with Irish traditional musicians in Dublin. I snowball sampled from an initial pool of informants provided by contacts at the Irish Traditional Music Archive (http://www.itma.ie) and O'Donoghue's pub. Interviews ranged from 45–90 min. Informants are identified as P1–20. All non-anonymized proper names in this paper are of well-known professional trad musicians. My methods in part draw inspiration from Fine's (1998) immersive ethnography of amateur mushroom hunters and academic mycologists. In that work, Fine became an active member of the mushroom-hunter community, participating in many of their activities while interviewing professional mycologists.

Tunes Through the Aesthetics of Reception

To set the stage, I will present a brief introduction to music making in Dublin sessions. A session is a gathering of musicians, often in the snug of a pub, to play music together. Musicians play *sets* of *tunes* in a session. A set is two or three tunes played in succession without a pause. Tunes in a set usually have the same meter/rhythm (e.g., jig, hornpipe, or reel). Each tune in a set is typically repeated three times in a row. In turn, most tunes have an A and B part, both of which are repeated twice. The musician who starts a tune is usually expected to lead (i.e., choose) what tunes follow after (thus forming a set).

I now describe how it is that Irish traditional musicians conceptualize tunes. I argue that the concept of the tune can be described in terms of three central processes: learning, knowing, and retaining. All three processes involve both the interaction between text and reader in an uneasy convergence and judgment on what constitutes a good text/representation and reader. These practices bring the tune into existence and are a subject of ongoing discourse in the Irish traditional community. Inherent in this discourse is whether the ways of representing reflect the traditional ethos.

Learning a Tune

Once a trad musician gains some proficiency to play notes on their instrument, lessons nearly always follow the same format no matter what the venue: they begin with a tune. The bare skeleton of the tune is first presented aurally. For example, in my flute lessons, my teacher, Brandon, would first ask me to start my digital recorder, play the tune once slowly, and then a second time closer to session speed (the speed you would play in public). As I got more comfortable with translating phrases heard into the fingerings of the flute, the lesson would take a more dynamic approach. Brandon would play the tune phrase by phrase, asking me to repeat each phrase on the flute back to him. Slowly, each individual phrase would be added together to form the entire tune. This pedagogical method would give him an opportunity to correct my mistakes and suggest technical exercises or embellishments on the tune.

In more structured settings like the classroom, the teacher might also provide students with what are colloquially called the "ABCs" (a simplified notation system for monophonic music often used for folk music). Figure 1a illustrates Conal O'Grada teaching a jig at the Cruinniú na bhFliúit. I mostly encountered what I will call the shorthand form of ABC notation: notes on the second octave are notched with an apostrophe, rhythm is only roughly expressed with spaces, and notes held longer than a single beat are followed by a dash. The left hand side of Fig. 1a shows Conal's proprietary key for his flute specific notation of ornaments (e.g., scrapes, glottal stops, and tickles).

That the tune can be represented in ABC notation suggests the existence of the "base version" or "skeleton" (Waldron and Veblen 2008) of a tune. It is from this base version trad musicians can develop their "literary work." The tune here represents merely a text from which the reader must engage with at the virtual dimension to create a literary work. Where does one get the base version of a tune? In lessons, getting the base version is easy—the teacher provides the text and then proceeds to explain how one might "read" and thus create an aesthetically informed work from it. In one of my earlier lessons, Brandon gave me a set of tunes from Kevin Henry's album, *One's Own Place*. He explained that this older style of playing, with a slow rhythmic breathing style, would be useful for a beginner. By explicating the origin of the set with a record source, he is legitimizing both the set (that the tunes are interesting, and that the tunes belong together in a set) and his version of the tunes. P15 mentioned that he was trying to

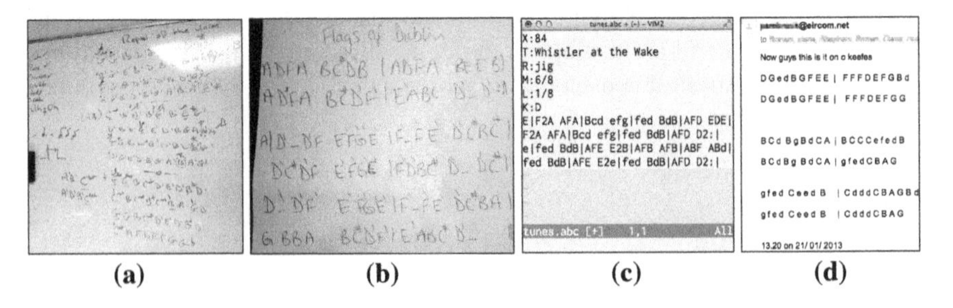

(a) (b) (c) (d)

Fig. 1 *Left* to *right*: Tune taught at The Flute Meeting, digital photo of tune written in shorthand ABC at a learner session, computer ABC notation of a tune, and shorthand ABC of a tune sent in an email

learn a waltz from Eddie O'Gara but had trouble remembering a certain end phrase: "I mean just this…<plays one phrase>, I just couldn't remember which one to do…<plays another, similar phrase>…I must actually sit down and find out what <laughs>, what exactly the notes that Eddie's doing there are." Here, P15 has a great admiration and respect for Eddie and believes his version to be the right one; i.e., it is the right representation from which to read.

In other cases, a representation may be politically sanctioned. The learner sessions I went to in the Comhaltas Headquarters sell the *Foinn Seisiún* collection. Sometimes jokingly called the "Bible" in Dublin, this volume of three books has a set of three tunes on each page "based on a consensus achieved at our regular Wednesday night sessions held at the Cultúrlann in Monkstown over a two year period." The sets in Foinn Seisiún have become a sort of book of standards around Dublin, and it is not unusual to hear sets from that book (which themselves are sometimes based on sets from famous recordings).

However, aside from official and professional sources, for many of my informants, whatever the source that instigated the liking of a tune becomes the base version. Musicians will sometimes record a "lovely" tune they heard in a session to learn it, but "if I was listening to somebody who was doing an awful lot of variations…I wouldn't always know which was the tune and which was the variation" (P4). Instrument peculiarities can exacerbate the difficulty in learning the base version. For example, because of the limited breath available to flautists, notes are often left out. At The Flute Meeting, an integral part of lessons was to also query the class about which notes could be tastefully left out. What is one to do when he or she records a tune played on the flute? Are the notes left out because of the player's preference or does the "true" skeleton of the tune have a rest (moment of silence) at that moment? The reader here is left questioning the "real" representation of the tune before him or her because of the possibility that it is a model that veers far off from the original reality.

Many trad musicians go further than the initial hearing and look up multiple texts of the tune to triangulate representations. Online tune repositories are commonly used by beginning trad musicians, especially those with a classical background. The Session (http://thesession.org) is by far the most popular site for tunes, but over time trad musicians come to understand that the quality of representations posted can be questionable. A common problem I encountered were transcriptions that were too accurate or literal (picking up on all the ornamentations and variations of a recording). Going to the tune's discussion section is imperative: "a lot of people in the sessions[.org] will go in and say, 'Here, this is a load of bollix; here's the settin' I have.' So you generally go down…and…get a better setting of the tune" (P13). When looking up McGibney's Fancy (hornpipe), P12 browsed through the comments and found a link to a YouTube clip of "a flute player…June McCormack…It was a very nice arrangement so I decided to learn it [her version]." At times, discussion sections point to better tune repositories (Henrik Norbeck's Abc Tunes are well regarded).

Again, we see here that the legitimacy (by whatever metric one's own trad ethos has) of a base representation is important. Yet, learning from professional or historic recordings can have the same problems as tunes gleaned from sessions. For example, to learn tunes composed by Josie McDermott, I went to the Comhaltas Archive (http://www.comhaltasarchive.ie) and found clips of Josie playing his own tunes, but even his playing of the same tune differed across clips. Which is the correct one?

Discerning the quality of a tune representation from which to begin the task of "reading" to create a personal version is a learned skill. Expert trad musicians intelligently amalgamate a "heterogeneity of content" (Chalmers and Galani 2004) to arrive at the text. Trad musicians think hard about the context in which the tune will be played. P2 called this finding the "session version" of the tune: "a common accepted version…that's played in your average session." P18 learned a tune from a Brian Hughes CD and once she tried playing it in sessions she found that "with that high part in it…I'd hear other musicians say that's not the [standard] way….So I'd kind of change then till I'm…more similar with those."

One might imagine that if you learned the tune from its composer, that would add credence to your version. Yet, even a transcription written down by the composer has no guarantee of its usability. Michael Clarkson records tunes for people to learn on his blog (http://irishflute.podbean.com). Ed Reavy's Maudabawn Chapel (reel) has the following post: "I tried looking at Reavy's book 'Where the Shannon Rises'…but this just reinforced my view that none of his tunes are normally played the way he wrote them….Here's an attempt at an average of the myriad settings of this tune."

Creating Value Art

Learning a tune means finding the tune's base text. I described the multitude of ways to reach this text. Once a suitable text is found, however, the work begins to create art in the virtual space—where text and the reader's horizon must reconcile. Professionals build upon the base text to create value art, art that is aesthetically valuable. Yet, this reading is not done in isolation; there is a balancing act in reconciling one's own personal vision of a tune with that of the session standard. The session is where history comes into play and aesthetic differences can be measured.

Indeed, the trad ethos is against a mechanistic reading of the text. Ornaments (embellishments such as cuts and rolls on existing notes) and variations (adding or deleting notes) are always introduced to the base version of the tune. Echoing the trad musician's spirit in The Flute Meeting, Conal O'Grada called the word "ornament" a misnomer; without ornaments, trad music loses its essence (e.g., rhythm lift, melodic excitement). P8, a teacher of trad music to primary school children, emphasized the need to not become "over-taught," becoming a clone of Mary Bergin [a famous tin whistler] and playing "every tune exactly as the person who taught you."

Trad musicians learn to discern when a variation is tasteful for a session. While lacking formal training in music theory, they have an instinctual feel for what variations will *harmonize* with the players' versions (or the standard session version). If the variation you have veers too far, "they can actually clash and make it uncomfortable for one…or both players" (P2). One flute player I met at The Flute Meeting told me she tried to learn The Copperplate reel from a recording by Seamus Tansey, but his version varied so far from what was played in Dublin that she had to "relearn" it. Harmonizing is not just about pitch but utilizing complementary timbres; P17 notes "the fiddle compensated for the flute player having to take breaks…[by playing] a long note." Of course, the session, with its critics, does not override the player's own aesthetic. P4 "would have a mixture of other people's variations and my own variations and whatever you're playing at the time." Likewise, P18 ended up forming a personal version of a tune where she would "play the second part differently and then the next time round I might…half [play it] the right way and then maybe change it around." The "right way" refers to the (local) session version of the tune.

Musicians not only create value art by reading a base text, but by determining whether a tune has the potential for value when read. P17 related how she was preparing for a gig in Belgium, and the leader of the band wanted her to learn The Mystery reel. She recorded him playing the tune on her mobile phone. Yet, when she played back her recording she "thought there is a lot more to that tune than that":

> Sometimes for me the music is a bit empty or something like that, there isn't enough in it to really show the tune for *what it is*…and I sort of thought, I think that Mystery reel is a nice tune but I'm not really hearing it there so I [had to] look it up somewhere else. [emphasis added]

P17 searched on YouTube and found Frankie Gavin playing The Mystery reel 20 years ago in *Come West Along the Road* (an Irish documentary show of trad musicians) and "thought, wow, this is a great tune!" Here is an example where the base version alone does not reveal the multiple variations of interpretation possible with it. One needs to hear how others have read the tune. To draw the analogy, other players serve as artistic critics. By showing how the text is full of possibilities, one can see the value of the text itself—how it is full of unexpected readings. P17 deemed The Mystery reel as a value text, one to add to her repertoire to share with others.

I have described the "testing" of an art piece in the public; in other words, the testing of the personal vision of a tune in a session. Trad musicians become deft at recognizing good transcriptions, performances, and recordings before synthesizing these versions with his or her style. A performed tune represents consideration of its social properties.

Knowing a Tune

What does it mean to *know* a tune? You can learn a tune, but to know a tune is a different thing altogether. P6 muses that “comfort is relative....There’s...gigs, playing solo on a stage, playing in a band on the stage, there’s different layers....I could just practice it [tunes] today and have them ready....I would call that still knowing the tunes, you know?...They’d never be 100%. I’m resigned to that at this stage.” Informants conceptually separated their solo repertoire from their other tunes. The solo repertoire is meant for gigs and “party pieces” (virtuoso tunes).

While the session is a place to demonstrate one’s aptitude in folk art, it can also serve as a support mechanism for *incomplete knowledge*. P8 says that the practice for a session tune might be different: “there are certain tunes you might just play once or twice at home just so you have it for a session but it mightn’t be one that you’d call up on to perfect it for other reasons.” P20 noted that she has “hundreds of tunes that you can play to a 50% standard in a group situation, but once you put a microphone in front of you, you really have to...play tunes that I know very well, and they are definitely the tunes that I’ve sat down and played for an hour or two at home.” One can see the session as a place where people take risks. Players sometimes look for sessions with enough people so you can “hide” amongst them. P11 related an attempt at trying out a new tune in a session: “I tried to play it in the session. I didn’t play it that < laughs >, but the other people didn’t know it you see.” P19 abhors this notion of knowing many tunes incompletely: “I think it’s much more important to have a bunch of tunes that at least you can play well.” Trad musicians generally admonish solo playing in sessions because (1) it seems to violate the moral code of collaborative music (Benford et al. 2012), and (2) it puts the technical prowess of the player in the spotlight. The risk of unintentional solo playing occurs when one misjudges the repertoire of the session or is unable to play at least the beginning of the tune recognizably so. P7 noted that “you want to avoid them hearing you by yourself...for even a few seconds, you’d rather not that they hear you.” Thus, musicians, when starting sets, often draw from their solo repertoire; at The Flute Meeting, I observed professional musicians often playing tunes from their CD albums. For trad musicians, the “correct” representation may be bits and pieces of text that can be filled in by others in situ in a session.

Indeed, all informants except for one dismissed any sort of routine practice regimen; instead, they relied on the session to practice tunes *iteratively*. On the rare occasions when particular tunes remained imperfect for lengths of time despite repeated session visits, informants would then actively practice. P13 remarked that he kept hearing the same tune in a session but never could get a certain part down: “I actually sat down to learn it properly...cause I half had it [a Paddy O’Brien tune], I played it thinking I was right, but I wasn’t sure.” P11 says, “if it’s a session tune, you kind of half know it, [if] there’s little bits that are quite tricky, it’s quite useful to see it written down. To get the details, you know?” Here, conversely, incomplete knowledge gained through a session can be ameliorated through formal representations of tunes. Thus, solitary practice is only part of the picture. As P1 put it, "I regard...playing in sessions as a form of practice." P20 emphasized that "if you're not meeting people, to keep up the motivation to practice is very difficult." The session and private place are mutually constitutive spaces for practice.

To say that the musician's repertoire is what tunes he or she knows is an oversimplification. All trad musicians rely on a hazy form of representation that only comes into shape within a session. This collaborative aspect of readers with text brings tunes into existence. Of course, those tunes that the musician are comfortable with have a form of representation not as dependent on their peers in the session. For seasoned musicians, the act of finding tunes is never about seeking solid representations of tunes (i.e., books or collections): "I haven't felt the need to go and look for tunes in books because I...often hear new tunes at sessions and at parties and things" (P4). These musicians absorb the tunes through intuition (Dreyfus and Dreyfus 2005), describing it as osmosis through iterative exposure to the representations of music making. It is less about *finding* tunes but, rather, *stumbling* upon them. In fact, many musicians almost describe it as inevitable, no matter how long, that the tune will become part of them. One musician (P15), without any hint of shame, remarked that the "process took about two years" to know a particular tune.

Retaining a Tune

A perennial problem for trad musicians is retaining a tune. Seasoned musicians know thousands of tunes. While they can play them, they don't know their names. Sometimes, the tune's name can serve as a recall device for the melody. Tunepal (Duggan and O'Shea 2011), a mobile app that records a tune, transcribes it, and queries a database to find its name, was by far the most popular app for trad music encountered in my observations. In this section, I will focus on other contextual cues used to retain a tune.

Tunes are associated with people, places, and events. Family, friends, hometowns, holidays, etc. all serve to dust off old sets of tunes. P4 called them "associations": "you might remember who you heard playing it and what it sounded like and where you heard it." P20 noted that she has "a friend in Antrim and we would always play [the] Paddy O'Brien jig <sings melody>. We would always play that together but it was because we learned it together." P17 related, "a guy...from Westmeath, he plays accordion, there's always tunes that I play with him and I always call them the 'Wexford tunes.'" Whenever I attend a session, seeing people's faces immediately summons up possibilities of playing: their favorites and styles. For example, I know Mary Begley, the concertina player, likes to play steady barn dances and hornpipes.

P17 stated that if you knew of the tune's *provenance*, "information about the composer or why it was composed or what the name means or...the style, or where you learned it or the style of that player," you would retain the tune because, as P1 explained, "it's a hook into your memory." This sentiment was echoed by all the informants. It could be said that all trad musicians have a bit of the ethnomusicologist (academic) in them (Fine 1998). Calling back to Iser, texts are imbued with a sociohistorical context that influence our expectations when we read. Ergo, the meaning of the tune goes beyond its notes. Provenance allows us to place the tune in a situated repertoire of tunes in the past, present, and future to create new art (legitimizing it). A common question amongst trad musicians in a session is not just, "What is the name of that tune?" (Benford et al. 2012) but, "Where did you hear that tune from?" A story about the tune, perforce, follows in answer to the latter question.

Other than Tunepal, the most common artifact encountered was a paper notepad (or mobile app equivalent) where musicians would notate in their own shorthand tunes they heard. Other than audio recordings, tune names, or actual notes of the tunes, informants also added contextual clues. P20 knew that she would not get back to her recordings the next day, so she would always "leave myself clues in the [file]names [of the recordings]." For example, one recording was labeled, "Roaring Barmaid Nathalie 3 versions," indicating three versions of the tune played by Nathalie.

Novices: Representation and Conflict

The above findings primarily show the practices of seasoned traditional musicians. For novices, though, there is a clearer distinction between home and session practice; for example, when P11 first started playing she would keep a list of "all the tunes they played in Hughes [pub] in 1990…on the computer." Similarly, I kept a list of tunes to learn (notated with how comfortable I was with each tune) that codified the repertoire of the pub.

The repertoire of the pub is ever changing. Tunes go in and out of fashion. During a learner session, the leader of the group explained that we would be learning a new tune every few weeks. She expressed a desire to teach us common tunes heard "now." She explained that while the Foinn Seisiún books has common tunes, many of them are not played as much anymore in Dublin. Depending on the musician and session, there can sometimes be a stigma against common tunes. P2 explained his observations that "I have seen certain musicians…put down their instruments [to not play a tune]—certain really advanced musicians when you play one of…those baseline tunes." The Foinn Seisiún volumes can, depending on the skill of the player, represent an especially inflexible representation because it prescribes what are the proper sets—what tunes belong in a set. Players can feel bored when they expect and know what the next tune is. There is no, as Iser puts it, "illusion"; instead, there is simply a restatement of the reality informed by the Comhaltas agency and no opportunity for possibilities. Good texts have a balance of the familiar and unfamiliar; if our expectations are always fulfilled, there is no chance for pleasure in reading. In a house session I attended, the guitarist complained that because each page had room for three tunes, sometimes you get two tunes that belong together with one "straggler" that seems forced in the set. One professional related to me that he attended a session in the Comhaltas Headquarters in Monkstown, Dublin; when he played a set of tunes that did not follow the order prescribed by the Foinn Seisiún, he was told that next time he needed to play them in the "correct" order. My informant was less than pleased by this. Creating sets is creating art.

The formal representation of ABC notation can impede novices. As Fig. 1 shows, there is the computer and shorthand version of ABCs. For example, the computer ABCs, which can be compiled into a MIDI or sheet music image, represents notes on the second octave with a lower case note letter. Note durations are specified by multiplying the note by a number (e.g., "a2" means to hold the note "a" on the 2nd octave for two beats). All online repositories of folk tunes store tunes in the computer ABC format. Beginners, who cannot read sheet music, often end up printing the computer ABCs and have difficulty interpreting them as they differ from the shorthand ABCs used by teachers. The difficulty of ABCs is further exacerbated when attempting to reconcile sheet music with shorthand ABCs. Figure 2 shows the handouts passed by Comhaltas when preparing for the Grúpa Cheoil competition: an ensemble performance of tunes. Here, instruments are asked to come in and leave at certain points of the music. The teacher has specified line numbers of the music with respect to the shorthand ABCs. These lines do not match up with the lines of the sheet music; as a result, I had to notate my sheet music with the respective lines. This caused constant confusion during rehearsals between those who used a sheet music representation and the ABC representation. Finally, because of its ubiquity, shorthand notation is often sent electronically (Fig. 1b); Fig. 1d shows an email sent to me regarding a tune called O'Keefe's heard on the radio. My colleagues had trouble deciphering his ABCs because there is no indication of the rhythm (e.g., slip jig versus jig versus slide); each space separated notes rather than rhythmic phrases.

Novices trained in classical music may face difficulty reconciling their formal training with the apparent flexibility of trad music. In classical music the distinction between wrong and right notes is clear. Parents of some informants had their children initially enroll in classical music to learn the proper posture for holding a fiddle but "were really conscious…of taking me out" (P1). Classical music can interfere with trad practices. P13 says it "demands a clarity in the note being made that…doesn't sound proper in a traditional idiom." The flute for example is capable of producing a note between C-sharp and C-natural. Below is an excerpt from my fieldnotes where I had to force myself to relax the strictness of my classical training (no easy task):

> My teacher asked me to listen to Kevin Henry's CD. I used the Amazing Slow Downer application to hear each note, but on one tune, *Paddy Jim Frank*, I could not tell what the note in a particular phrase was despite repeated listening. I couldn't even tell what octave it was on. To make matters worse, the recording quality was poor. Thinking it was my own inability to discern the pitch, for my next lesson, I sat down with my teacher (Brandon),

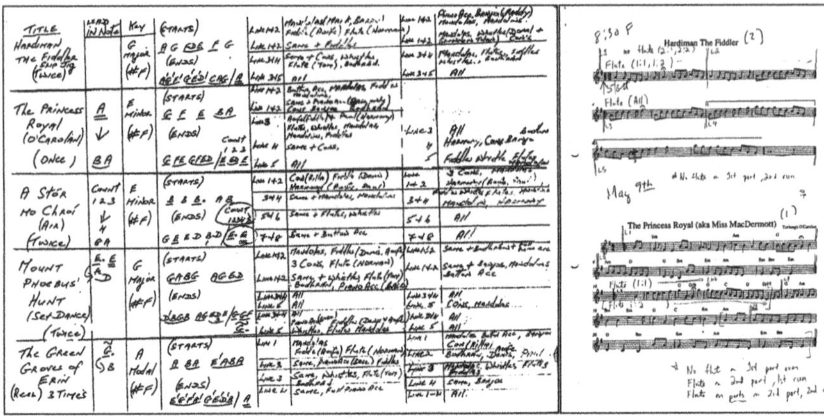

Fig. 2 Arrangement of tunes for the Grúpa Cheoil competition. *Left*: shorthand ABC notation for the arrangement; *Right*: sheet music equivalent for the arrangement

> played the recording, and stepped through the tune to the problematic phrase and asked "What note is this?" Brandon simply grinned and shrugged. For him it wasn't a big deal, as if I could decide what note it was!

Indeed, certain tunes take advantage of this ambiguity (on each tune repeat one might make the pitch ambiguous, switch between two different pitches, etc.). P8 rebuked adult learners who "follow what's written so exactly that…it just doesn't have a traditional feel to it." Thus, transcriptions, as opposed to aural learning, "aren't great if you're just coming from outside…[it's] just the skeletal framework." (P8) Sheet music has codified notation for ornaments (e.g., grace notes); this can cause novices to interpret notated ornaments as set-in-stone (as part of the skeletal tune). The rhythm of a transcription can be misleading; Tunepal allows MIDI playback of ABC transcriptions. P2 related that "it doesn't sound like Irish music at all…no swing." Only with mastery of trad music can you sensibly use a transcription.

Underneath all these issues of representation is an explicit ethos that learning by ear is the only way to know and retain a tune. Musicians constantly told me that tunes learned from sheet music do not stay in the head long. The sheet music is artificially separated from the *context* (e.g., provenance) of the tune. Consider also that learning from recordings or sessions allows one to hear the tune repeated several times by the same player(s). These different readings enable us to imagine the possibilities of the text. We listen to the critic. Next, I will consider how we might be able to support and hence represent the aesthetics of reception intrinsic in trad music.

Representing the Aesthetics of Reception

Every tune is an opportunity…to make it interesting.–P2 “Drift” in ontological drift brings to mind representations whose meanings progressively meander away from the truth. However, in the case of traditional musicians, there is no single truth to a representation. Each time a tune is played, masters of Irish traditional music literally make art anew in the virtual space where the musician’s horizon and the horizon within which the tune’s representation resides intersect. Finding the right representation of a tune is not easy. Sometimes, the text proves too literal or restrictive, reducing the possibilities of interpretation. Other times, the text proves too abstract and vague, masking its value and making it unattractive for musicians to read. These texts reflect the observation of Lee (2007) that “unstandardized artifacts that are partial, incomplete, or are intermediary representations are ubiquitous in collaborative work.” When Star and Griesemer (1989) and Lee (2007) talk of boundary (negotiating) objects, they speak of material artifacts. However, instead of trying to decipher when a tune becomes “materialized” (e.g., when it is played), I believe it more constructive to emphasize the creative process involved in representation via the lens of reader-reception theory.

By highlighting how representation of a tune is a central, ongoing concern for trad musicians, we can move towards a more nuanced notion of what it means to become proficient in the tradition. Benford et al. (2012) suggest several requirements for the “sequencing of tunes” that certainly would follow my own findings about tunes—for example, knowing who is present (and what tunes they know) and what tunes are popular in a session. However, I am interested in how novices can go beyond being what informants disparagingly called “tune fiends” or “tapeworms.” How might a novice move past simplified representations of tunes to attain the intuitive (Dreyfus and Dreyfus 2005) grasp of tunes that experts of trad music have?

I have shown how experts of trad music have learned how to attain a balance of their own aesthetic vision of tunes with the ethos and history of sessions by adroitly synthesizing heterogeneous actors. The tune, personal and social at the same time, is a careful amalgamation of the session, teachers, associations, audio/video clips, ABCs, aesthetic values, etc. Artifacts to support budding musicians must recognize this aesthetic sensibility of the Irish tradition. That is, how would the novice know that the transcription they have is a good one to base their creative pursuits on? “Good” might be based on the author of the transcription or who played the tune. How does the novice know that their variation harmonizes with others’ variations (and at what point does the variation become distasteful)? Musicians must also take a risk (e.g., introducing new tunes) to prevent a session from going stagnant. How might one know that a tune will be absorbed into the session repertoire? This also raises the question of how a musician would recognize that the tune offers creative reading. Systems supporting musicians may need to automatically or via crowd-sourcing methods rate the quality of a transcription (on different levels such as its suitability for particular instruments). In other words, we need to support the *criticism* of tunes.

The flexible and social nature of tunes in its various processes poses non-obvious constraints for tools to model/organize tunes. Current software for folk musicians (e.g., ABC tune organizers, media library apps) still rigidly represent tunes. Tunepal adjusts algorithmically for variation in tunes, but its tune manager simply is a list of static ABC tunes by their name. Tune transcriptions and audio recordings that are posted on online repositories are often divorced from their context. How might systems assist musicians in retaining tunes not only by their titles but by their provenance?

My results suggest it useful to conceptualize the session not merely as the performance apex, but rather a place of active practice. Incomplete knowledge of tunes, even amongst experts (who are adept at cheating—filling in harmonious patterns—to figure out a tune on the fly), is the sine qua non of being a traditional musician. Indeed, an ideal for many novices to reach is an ability to pick up and learn tunes in the session itself. In the past, the old guard players like Patsy Hanly had to rely on their memory, picking up phrases here and there each time they went to a teacher or session. Learning was an iterative, aural, and social process. How might this ability to practice in, rather than for, sessions be facilitated? Moreover, how does a musician choose *how to know* tunes (whether to rely on incomplete knowledge or not)?

Finally, the tension between classical and Irish traditional music pedagogy can pose a challenge for novices. I observed some musicians never being able to take that extra step to go beyond merely playing tunes as written or heard; every reading of the text satisfied expectations, leading to the creation of a soulless literary work. Are there ways to represent the interpretive flexibility of tunes for novices who lack the aural skills of masters? Can artifacts show the stylistic possibilities for a base tune? For example, websites featuring a single tune played by many masters (e.g., http://rjhetc.blogspot.ie) are a useful resource when practicing alone to understand that there are many tunes inscribed in a single tune.

What I am suggesting here is that we support and represent the aesthetics of reception. As a literary theory, the aesthetics of reception asserts that all literary works only take shape when text and reader cross a virtual space. However, I believe that reader-reception theory is especially appropriate for Irish trad music because its moral and aesthetic imperative is the active creation of value tunes through persistent participation in sessions. Refocusing our gaze from the reader, from the text, and instead to the virtual dimension in which the two converge, allows us to see that music making in the tradition is about creative texts and imaginative readers constituted in their sociohistorical contexts to create tunes. How can we represent this in a way that will help both novices and professionals? In the next section, I suggest one approach that might help bring novices to adopt the aesthetics of reception.

Surveilling the Aesthetics of Reception

Below, Jauss and Benzinger (1970, p. 295) define literary criticism's utility:

> Perhaps this is the prime usefulness of literary criticism—it helps to make conscious those aspects of the text which would otherwise remain concealed in the subconscious; it satisfies (or helps to satisfy) our desire to talk about what we have read.

I have shown that being a trad musician involves an expanded notion of what it means to learn, know, and retain a tune. Becoming a folk musician involves cultivating a musical taste that balances between one's own aesthetic goals and that of session players. The tune, the text, itself is not a static entity, but rather shaped by its sociohistorical context. Neither is the reader a static entity. The implication here is that technology should support a musician's practice in a seamless boundary between the ostensibly performance-oriented session and solitary pursuit of skill. Furthermore, technology ought to allow one to discuss the aesthetics of reception in the trad community. How might this discussion be realized?

The aesthetics of reception involves virtual work in the tune's representation when learning, knowing, and retaining a tune. If we were able to observe, collect, and report data on solo and session practice—what variations are played, what sources the tune's text comes from, who played the tunes—we could create a history of reading, or a history of the aesthetics of reception. A historical archive of reception would alleviate the rigidity of computational representations of tunes. Such an archive would illuminate what texts are valued right now in its sociohistorical context (i.e., synchronically and diachronically). By making the music-making practices of people and sessions overtly public, we make reading practices public, thereby supporting the practice of practicing both privately and in the session. Just as the "quantifiable self movement" makes everyday activities visible, might musicians as well present their own quantified data about their tune practices? This suggests a future agenda to designing tech for folk arts: *how can we best surveil tradition*?

Establishing an agenda of the surveillance of tradition brings with it the following lines of inquiry:

- How can we visually support active reading during a session, where practice often happens? Can we visually present the tune or set being played in a session and its variations? How can session participants add their own information/comments into such a system (e.g., adding provenance data or critiques to the tune they just played to the system)? These representations should be accessible to both classically and traditionally trained musicians while being flexible, demonstrating the possibilities of the tune.
- How can we intelligently combine solo and public practices together visually and aurally to support the history of reading? How can we present what tunes are currently popular (synchronic), have been popular in the past (diachronic), are often combined with other tunes in a set, and are often associated with a

particular musician? What tunes seem to never take off? Can we *characterize* a session's aesthetic (e.g., fast-paced or influenced by the East Clare style)?
- What are the implications for creative practices in a session when trends of tunes are presented visually and immediately? For example, will musicians suddenly be conscious that they often play the same tunes? Will they worry about becoming stale and change their habits, defying expectations?
- What are the implications in making the history of the aesthetics of reception available to those outside the session? We might not only present the history of reception locally, but also on the Internet (e.g., on Twitter or a continuously updated website). Will this encourage novices or non-regulars to attend pub sessions? Will Dublin practices of reading exert a powerful influence over other locales' reading practices?
- What are the ethical implications of so closely surveilling tradition (i.e., unblackboxing the mystique of tradition transmitted orally)? My use of the word "surveil" is to deliberately bring such controversies to the forefront. Technologies that enable the surveillance of tradition may be rejected by the community (Mainwaring et al. 2004) as being the very antithesis of tradition.

With the developer of Tunepal (Duggan and O'Shea 2011), I am currently designing and developing TuneTracker, a system to surveil tradition in a Dublin pub. This system will be permanently and continuously running inside a pub. Tunes and their variations that are recognized in the pub's sessions will be publicly displayed in the pub and also online on a website. Part of the challenge will be in designing an interface that allows users to engage with and comprehend an archive of music-making practices. While continuing my participation in the session, this "social experiment" will allow me to see how the history of tradition (reception) might help or hinder both novices and professionals in the social life of tunes.

Chalmers and Galani (2004) suggest that interactive systems be designed to provide a "heterogeneity of content…when users have different past experiences to draw from, when they have different tools available and yet wish a shared experience, and when the designer's and the users' interest is in the ambiguous or contradictory." Irish traditional musicians are exactly these users; I have shown that deft trad musicians draw from multiple and sometimes ambiguous or contradictory representations to realize a tune in the session experience. The history of tradition via surveillance can achieve a heterogeneity of content and "make past activity across media a resource for ongoing or synchronous activity in each medium" (Chalmers and Galani 2004).

Following Jauss and Benzinger (1970), I believe that exhibiting the "process of the history of reception" can allow novice musicians to assimilate the aesthetics of reception so central to Irish traditional musicians. Surveilling tradition, when designed properly, might give some structure to novice players without losing the inherent ambiguity and flexibility of tune representation that allows tradition to be aesthetically enjoyable. I have described the difficulties that Irish trad musicians have in both finding an adequate representation of a tune and in simply defining what is the true reality of a tune. According to the skill expertise of musicians, conflicts of representation pose barriers for musicians to move towards achieving value tunes. By making explicit not only the now but the past, we can understand the process by which tunes are creatively made part of the canon of the future.

Acknowledgment I am grateful for Danny Diamond, Bryan Duggan, Brendan Knowlton, and Padraic Lavin's invaluable assistance in data collection. Leslie S. Liu and Lisa Shields provided helpful feedback on my drafts.

References

Ackerman, M. (2000). The intellectual challenge of CSCW: The gap between social requirements and technical feasibility. *Human-Computer Interaction, 15*(2/3), 181–203.

Benford S., Tolmie P., Ahmed, A.Y., Crabtree, A. (2012). Supporting traditional music-making: Designing for situated discretion. In *Proceedings of CSCW'12* (pp. 127–136). New York: ACM.

Brown, B. A. T. (2001). Unpacking a timesheet: Formalisation and representation. *Computer Supported Cooperative Work, 10*(3–4), 293–315.

Chalmers, M., & Galani, A. (2004) Seamful interweaving: Heterogeneity in the theory and design of interactive systems. In *Proceedings of DIS'04* (pp. 243–252). New York: ACM.

Dreyfus, H. L., & Dreyfus, S. E. (2005). Peripheral vision expertise in real world contexts. *Organization Studies, 26*(5), 779–792.

Duggan, B., & O'Shea, B. (2011). Tunepal: searching a digital library of traditional music scores. *OCLC Systems and Services, 27*(4), 284–297.

Fine, G. A. (1998). *Morel tales*. Cambridge: Harvard University Press.

Fleming, R. C. (2004). Resisting cultural standardization: Comhaltas Ceoltóir Éireann and the revitalization of traditional music in Ireland. *Journal of Folklore Research, 41*(2), 227–257.

Forsyth, M. C. (2011). Teaching "Trad": A fiddling ethnomusicologist's reflections on fiddle camp. *Canadian Folk Music/Musique folklorique canadienne, 45*(2).

Fry, P. H. (2009, January 30). Configurative reading [http://oyc.yale.edu/transcript/454/engl-300]. ENGL 300: *Introduction to theory of literature*. Lecture conducted from New Haven, CT: Yale University.

Graefe, C., Wahila, D., Maguire, J., & Dasna, O. (1996). Muse: A digital music stand for symphony musicians. *Interactions, 3*(3), 26–35.

Grudin, J. (1988). Why groupware applications fail: Problems in the design of organizational interfaces (pp. 85–93). In *Proceedings of CSCW'88*. New York: ACM.

Iser, W. (1972). The reading process: A phenomenological approach. *New Literary History, 3*(2), 279–299.

Jauss, H. R., & Benzinger, E. (1970). Literary history as a challenge to literary theory. *New Literary History, 2*(1), 7–37.

Lee, C. P. (2007). Boundary negotiating artifacts: Unbinding the routine of boundary objects and embracing chaos in collaborative work. *Computer Supported Cooperative Work, 16*(3), 307–339.

Letondal, C., & Mackay W. E. (2007). The paperoles project: An analysis of paper use by music composers. In *Proceedings of the 2nd International Workshop on Collaborating over Paper and Digital, Documents (CoPADD'07).*

Mainwaring, S. D., Chang, M. F., & Anderson, K. (2004). Infrastructures and their discontents: Implications for ubicomp. In *Proceedings of Ubicomp'04* (pp. 418–432). Berlin: Springer.

Morton, F. (2005). Performing ethnography: Irish traditional music sessions and new methodological spaces. *Social and Cultural Geography, 6*(5), 661–676.

O'Shea, H. (2008). *The making of Irish traditional music*. Cork: Cork University Press.

Robinson, M., & Bannon, L. (1991). Questioning representations. In *Proceedings of ECSCW'91* (pp. 219–233). Norwell, MA: Kluwer Academic Publishers.

Shipman, F. M., & Marshall, C. C. (1999). Formality considered harmful: Experiences, emerging themes, and directions on the use of formal representations in interactive systems. *Computer Supported Cooperative Work, 8*(4), 333–352.

Star, S. L., & Griesemer, J. R. (1989). Institutional ecology, 'translations' and boundary objects: Amateurs and professionals in Berkeley's museum of vertebrate zoology. *Social Studies of Science, 19*(3), 387–420.

Titon, J. T. (2001). *Old time Kentucky fiddle tunes*. Lexington: University Press of Kentucky.

Veblen, K. K. (1996). Truth, perceptions, and cultural constructs in ethnographic research: Music teaching and learning in Ireland. *Bulletin of the Council for Research in Music Education, 129*, 37–52.

Veblen, K. K. (2008). The many ways of community music. *International Journal of Community Music, 1*(1), 5–21.

Waldron, J. L., & Veblen, K. K. (2008). The medium is the message: cyberspace, community, and music learning in the Irish traditional music virtual community. *Journal of Music, Technology and Education, 1*(2/3), 99–111.

Whalen, J., Whalen, M., & Henderson, K. (2002). Improvisational choreography in teleservice work. *The British Journal of Sociology, 53*(2), 239–258.

Achieving Continuity of Care: A Study of the Challenges in a Danish and a US Hospital Department

Naja L. Holten Møller

Abstract Continuity of care is a central topic for healthcare practice and is closely related to issues of collaboration. Thus, studying continuity of care from a CSCW perspective can help us understand what makes continuity of care in practice. In this paper, we show how collaborative technologies are appropriated differently in two cases, one in Denmark and the other in the US. We illustrate how this appropriation is dependent on challenges particular to the organizational context of work. Studying the practices in two different hospital departments we found that in practice achieving continuity of care depends on two main characteristics in the organization of work, namely (1) the constitution of roles and (2) the responsibility for care linked to the appropriation of collaborative technologies. These characteristics of the organization of work create different solutions to the challenges of discontinuity when physicians appropriate mundane collaborative technologies: patient records and pagers. To understand how continuity of care is achieved in practice we have to study the appropriation of technologies, the paper argues, and by comparing across cases we may begin to discern challenges that cut across context—and their different origins.

Introduction

This paper focuses on continuity as a central aspect of clinicians' work and a topic for CSCW research (Ellingsen and Monteiro 2006; Fitzpatrick and Ellingsen 2012). Continuity of care is regarded as a principle that applies in different clinical settings despite the various contexts through which collaborative technologies for support of continuity of care are appropriated (Denmark's Board of Technology 2006; US Office of the National Coordinator for Health Information Technology 2010).

N. L. Holten Møller (✉)
Technologies in Practice, IT University of Copenhagen, Copenhagen, Denmark
e-mail: nhmo@itu.dk

O. W. Bertelsen et al. (eds.), *ECSCW 2013: Proceedings of the 13th European Conference on Computer Supported Cooperative Work, 21–25 September 2013, Paphos, Cyprus*, DOI: 10.1007/978-1-4471-5346-7_12, © Springer-Verlag London 2013

When continuity of care has to be enacted in practice, the challenges of context-dependent discontinuity become apparent in how technologies are appropriated. To support continuity of care we thus need to understand what characterize these challenges to continuity in different contexts.

Consequently, previous research has pointed out how, for example, the particular characteristics of private healthcare in the US challenge continuity of care when patients move between various providers (Cebul et al. 2008). Or, how in a Danish context of public healthcare continuity becomes a challenge when the provider forms one tremendously variegated organization that physicians have to maneuver within (Mønsted et al. 2011). The challenges experienced in relation to computer support of continuity of care still imply technical issues; however, the context-related issues in terms of the sociological, cultural, and financial challenges are equally important (Fitzpatrick and Ellingsen 2012).

Context is traditionally rendered important in CSCW-studies: Continuity of care is considered in relation to the appropriating of technologies and artefacts in the particular context of work where they are used (Bardram and Hansen 2004). Context, this research shows, is highly relevant for how clinicians' appropriate technologies. For example, a comparative study across two oncology clinics in Austria shows how practices diverge due to the differences of the organizational context determined by the organization of work spatially and by the information systems (Schmidt et al. 2007). To handle the challenge of differences in a design context, the study suggests a focus on higher-order commonalities in the coordinative practices:

> Here the focus is not on the rationale of specific practices in order to determine what is 'essential' and what is 'accidental', but to identify, if possible, the elements and rules of combination out of which coordinative artefacts and protocols are or could be combined and recombined (Schmidt et al. 2007: 9).

Meanwhile, commonalities have been explored mainly from the perspective of technologies and artefacts focusing on, for example, clinical documents and how they are generally used for several purposes (Schmidt et al. 2007) or how repositories of clinical information are made relevant in the particular context (Winthereik and Vikkelsø 2005). Few (Schmidt et al. 2007; Balka et al. 2008) have paid attention to what commonalities characterize the organization of hospital work in terms of the higher-order challenges that are embedded in these artefacts and technologies.

The importance of understanding the organization of work is illustrated in a comparative study of clinical work in Canada and Austria suggesting that (1) the political—and policy-making—context, (2) the institutional/organizational context, and (3) the system and workplace design context are all relevant for understanding how technologies are appropriated (Balka et al. 2008). Within each of these levels of context, a range of interdependent and interlinked factors inform the understanding of the use of technology, including, for example, staffing and how relationships with external services are managed throughout the clinical work (ibid):

> Here the wider organizational issues that directly frame the space for systems design and that in turn are responses to policy and administrative measures taken by municipal and state agencies are negotiated and implemented (Balka et al. 2008: 518).

Addressing continuity of care from this perspective we need to investigate the *linking practices* by which technologies are appropriated in local contexts to handle challenges of discontinuity. By studying continuity of care in terms of linking practices across empirical settings in two different contexts we are thus able to conceptualize the broader commonalities. This paper in this way extends and contributes to the line of previous CSCW-research (Schmidt et al. 2007; Balka et al. 2008; Boulus and Bjørn 2010) that brings about broader aspects of healthcare (e.g., in terms of commonalities) by studying context-dependent issues (e.g., staffing and relationships with external services) of in-depth empirical cases.

This paper brings empirical observations from a Danish and a US hospital medical department, both of which deploy electronic patient records (EPRs) and pager technology to support continuity of care. However, the appropriation of these technologies, we show, is quite diverse and different across the settings. The research question explored in this paper is: How is continuity of care achieved in everyday practice, and what are the commonalities that characterize the challenges of discontinuity across the two settings? In this way, the contribution of the paper is two-fold: To provide empirical observations of how continuity of care is achieved in two different contexts as well as to conceptualize the basic characteristics of technology use in continuity of care as the way responsibility of care and constitution of roles are performed in healthcare practices.

The rest of the paper is organized as follows: We begin with related research addressing the interrelationships that characterize clinical work in studies of collaborative technologies, focusing in particular on EPRs, phoning, and pagers ("Related Research"). The research method follows, including the Danish case and the US case ("Research Method"), before turning to the analysis ("Analysis: Two Stories of How Continuity of Care is Achieved as Part of Everyday Practice") that forms two narrative stories of how continuity of care is achieved on a particular day as part of everyday use of EPRs and pagers in the Danish and the US cases. Next, we discuss the challenges to continuity of care ("Discussion: Challenges in Continuity of Care"), but from a comparative perspective so that issues that cut across the two cases on (a) responsibility of care and (b) constitution of roles become visible. Finally, the paper is concluded ("Conclusion"). Here, we end with suggestions for a conceptualization of broader conditions and challenges for continuity of care that drive the technology use as well as the required technology support of practice.

Related Research

To support continuity of care is a matter of ensuring coordination and effective communication so that tasks are not disintegrated in the complex organization of clinical work (Strauss et al. 1985). Therefore, collaborative technologies are also central for support of continuity of care (Meum et al. 2011). By linking the clinical specialties through collaborative technologies such as the EPR, it becomes possible for clinicians to handle complex issues (Berg 1998). Continuity of care is a social practice of appropriating technologies and the various interrelated artefacts within the situation where they are used (Bardram and Hansen 2004). To achieve continuity of care is particularly important where several specialties get involved in the care of a patient (US Institute of Medicine 2001). This means that when specialties collaborate around a certain organization, as, for example, teams, this shapes the hospital clinical work and how coordination and effective communication is achieved in practice (Strauss et al. 1985).

The effort to support continuity of care in hospitals is documented by studies of EPRs (Hartswood et al. 2003; Heath and Luff 1996; Berg and Winthereik 2003). These studies show that it is difficult to support electronic sharing of subtle nuances of clinical work between the various clinicians involved in the care of patients (Cabitza et al. 2009). In fact, clinicians (still) rely on informal documentation to handle tasks such as "abstracting" to get the big picture of the status of their patients and planning within their particular context (Heath and Luff 1996; Hartswood et al. 2003; Park et al. 2013). Previous CSCW-research also found that physicians translate rather than transfer clinical information sent electronically between providers for it to be useful in the specific context of work (Winthereik and Vikkelsø 2005; Meum and Monteiro 2011, Mønsted et al. 2011). When new care providers have to make sense of other physicians' entries, the correct interpretation of a patient's record can be hard to decipher (Mønsted et al. 2011).

Consequently, phoning and consults supported by pager technology play a crucial role for how clinicians link their individual and yet interrelated activities (Brown and Randell 2004; Bardram and Hansen 2004; Scholl et al. 2007, Lee et al. 2012). The pager technology enacts the assignment of roles, and previous research of a hospital emergency department (ED) points out how pagers are effective for interrupting or getting a hold of a particular specialist or type of staff (Lee et al. 2012). Clinicians typically perceive this type of interruption as a problem causing errors in hospital clinical work (Brown and Randell 2004; Bardram and Bossen 2005). To make a positive difference to the care of patients within the larger organization of work, including letting clinicians prioritize between tasks and patients, it is crucial that interruptions are qualified, for example, by providing text messaging as an integrated part of the pager design (Lee et al. 2012). This allows the clinicians to make judgments about the urgency of the call relative to the particular task or patient being treated while taking into consideration the larger organization of work.

What is not clear from this previous research is how context-dependent challenges in terms of the wider organizational issues matter for how technology is appropriated. Previous CSCW-research illustrates how clinicians' interlinked activities are carried out across specialties, and why studies of collaborative technologies often address the interrelationship of clinical specialties as a basic condition in how clinical work is organized and carried out. Yet how clinicians make relevant the collaborative technologies in everyday practice to handle challenges to continuity of care that are specific to their particular context remains unclear. This paper will explore how mundane collaborative technologies: EPRs and pagers are appropriated to achieve continuity of care in two different contexts, and by comparing across cases we may begin to discern the broader commonalities of challenges—and their different origins.

Research Method

To explore how continuity of care is acted out across different contexts, two workplace studies were conducted in hospital medical departments between August 2009 and December 2011—one in Denmark and one in the US. By studying this subject across settings, and by also relating it to previous studies (Strauss and Corbin 1998; Schmidt et al. 2007), the paper contributes to a better understanding of challenges to how continuity of care is achieved in practice.

The US medical department is located in a large teaching hospital (university hospital). The hospital employs more than 3,500 personnel serving more than 300,000 outpatient visits to the hospital and nearly 17,000 inpatient visits per year. The medical department, which this study focused on, is organized into six teams. Each team consists of an attending physician (specialist), a senior resident, two residents, and two medical students. During weekends an attending physician and a resident cover for a team. Each team admits up to 20 patients, and the teams are usually on-call 2 days a week. While the team is located on a particular floor of the hospital, patients are spread out on different floors. Teams of physicians, however, are not sub-specialized within the field of internal medicine—only wards are organized by sub-specialization. At each of the wards located on the different floors a "nurses' station" is placed on the ward close to the patients. The medical department staff includes nursing assistants, nurses, tele-monitoring technicians, physicians specializing in internal medicine, and residents who are not yet specialized.

The Danish medical department is located in a teaching hospital that is in the process of becoming a university hospital. The hospital employs more than 1,300 people serving more than 110,000 outpatient visits to the hospital and more than 39,000 inpatient visits per year. The medical department under study is organized into five wards. The wards are sub-specialized in, for example, initiating diagnosis and treatment of medical patients with general symptoms of disease (AVA), or specialized diagnosis and treatment of gastroenterological patients, endocrinological patients, etc. Each ward counts 1–2 attending physicians (specialists) at all hours, 1 senior resident, 1 resident, and numerous medical students. Patients are admitted seven days a week and at all hours. On weekends, 1–2 attending physicians cover patients that are admitted. The medical department staff includes secretaries (nursing assistants), nurses, physicians specialized in internal medicine, residents not yet specialized, and medical students. All staff of the ward are located in one conference room.

In total, the author spent 51 h in the Danish hospital medical department and 40 h in the US hospital medical department observing practices and conducting in situ and semi-structured interviews. The data collection and analysis followed an iterative approach emphasizing the ad hoc collection and challenging of data for rigor analysis (Klein and Myers 1999; Ellingsen and Monteiro 2006). The data from these two studies were analyzed through several rounds of analytical writing to identify themes across the cases (Emerson et al. 1995). This iterative process resulted in a comparison of the US workplace study and the Danish workplace study focusing on how continuity of care is achieved to handle challenges specific to each context. The process of writing continued until the point where there was only marginal change in the analysis (Eisenhardt 1989).

Analysis: Two Stories of How Continuity of Care is Achieved as Part of Everyday Practice

The following two narrative stories, although based on observations across several clinicians and on several days, are told from the perspective of a single day, focusing on the subtleties of how technologies are appropriated as part of everyday practice.

Danish Case

The first story begins in the medical sub-section AVA. This section initiates diagnosis before sorting patients to other subs-sections of the medical department that consists of 5 outpatient clinics and 5 sub-sections (wards)—including AVA. The medical department uses a monthly rotation plan resulting in different physicians present at the AVA every day, with the exception of a permanent attending physician. This arrangement means that the larger group of physicians gets time to see patients in the outpatient clinics the days they are not on-duty. The outpatient clinics are of particular interest to the physicians because they allow them to follow patients and treat them for a longer period of time.

Linking Clinical Information

On this particular morning the permanent attending physician, Dr. V, together with the attending physician, Dr. M, and a senior resident, runs AVA. A resident physician helps out admitting patients. The day begins at 8:05 am with a morning conference together with the rest of the medical department's physicians. An hour later the overall coordination across sub-sections is accomplished and the physicians head back to the ward. AVA operations have a straightforward goal (initiating diagnosis), and all jobs are tied together by the monthly work plan of the medical department prescribing the specific jobs of physicians on every day of the month as a central tool for how work is carried out.

As the physicians return from the morning conference to AVA a little before 9 am, the rest of the staff (nurses and secretaries) have already prepared status reports for patients that are ready to be seen by a physician. AVA's conference room is located on the ward and works as both a nurses' station and physician and secretary workspace. Patients are distributed between the two attending physicians and the senior resident, all of whom are preparing to do rounds at patients' bedsides. AVA admits patients on all days, and whenever a patient is transferred to

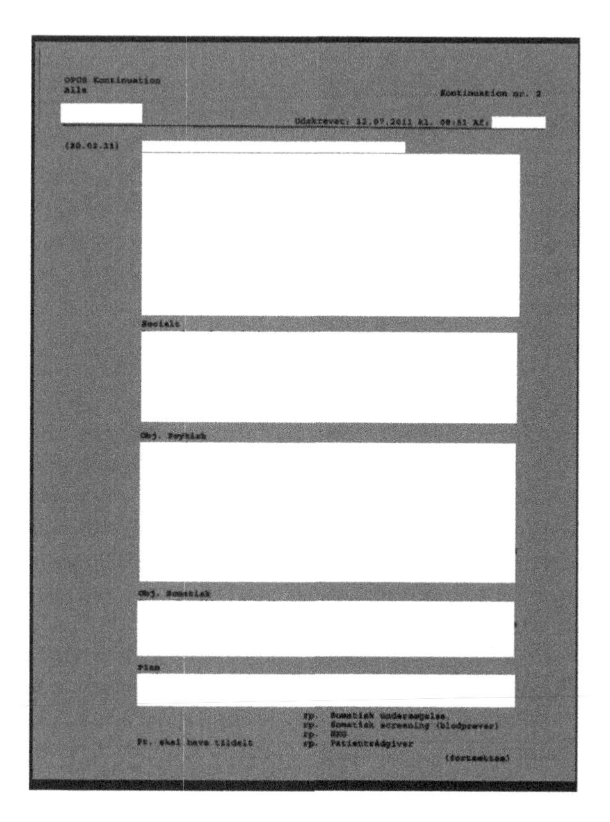
OPUS Kontinuation
Kontinuation nr. 2
Udskrevet: 12.07.2011 kl. 09:51 Af:
(20.02.11)
Socialt
Obj. Psykisk
Obj. Somatisk
Plan
rp. Somatisk undersøgelse.
rp. Somatisk screening (blodprøver)
rp. EKG
Pt. skal have tildelt rp. Patientrådgiver
(fortsættes)

Fig. 1 Ex. of continuation form in the Danish case

one of the other sub-sections new patients are admitted. This means that there is typically a constant flow of patients in AVA.

The hospital requires that an electronic form, the "continuation" (Fig. 1), be filled out as part of everyday practice to prevent the slip in responsibility that could occur from the organization of work around clinicians' specialties. This organization of work is further complicated by the fact that hospitals in the local health region divide responsibility between them on different levels of specialization and specialties. The distribution of responsibility between public hospitals is regulated by the national government and managed by the regional government to ensure that standards of care are high. The principle of organization is that practice makes perfect; the rare conditions are therefore only handled by a few hospitals.

The continuation form can be accessed from all regional hospitals. As part of the EPR, the continuation provides information on the patient's admissions described chronologically, one after the other, and information on the patient's anamnesis, dispositions, and allergies. The continuation also includes what clinical activities have been initiated during a particular admission. In principle the provider is the public, but in practice the patient moves between various providers of healthcare that will depend on what the chief complaint of the patient is, how critical it is, and which hospital treats this condition. Therefore, AVA may also receive patients from other hospitals and/or transfer patients. Although the referring physician is expected to decide what hospital the patient is sent to, in practice this is a negotiation with the receiving hospital department.

Dr. M's first patient of his morning rounds is an 83-year-old woman, and the continuation indicated she most likely has a lung infection. The patient was previously admitted to a different hospital in the local health region, Dr. M notes, at which time she was also quite ill. He turns to the list of medications. As he prepares to the patient's bedside he consults the nurse responsible for this patient. The nurse record (kardex) with the patient's vitals (e.g., the pulse and the patient's general condition) is on the desk in front of them as they discuss the patient. The patient keeps having water in the lungs.

The monthly schedule often results in patients potentially seen by the same physician only once: with the exception of the permanent attending physician, the physicians typically rotate to other jobs the next day. For example, the monthly rotation plan assigns the job of "front-line" physician to residents and the job of "backup" to attending physicians. Because the attending physician is seeing this patient for the first (and maybe last) time, reviewing the patient's records (electronically and on paper) takes time. The free-text in the continuation is made up of sections up to 35 lines in length separated by headings; the text is a uniform typeface and size that makes it challenging to get the overall picture of the relationship between previous admissions.

Both of the attending physicians are rather busy as 21 of AVA's 24 beds are occupied, and they work through their patients without interfering with each other. Dr. M notes down a few details from the patient record on a piece of paper before finally going to the patient's bedside. He keeps the paper with the extract of clinical information in his pocket all day. During the day Dr. M takes out the paper several times, crossing out and adding things, for example, as the change of a patient's vitals requires that his first calculation of medication is adjusted. While the continuation assembles clinical information about patients from a long-term perspective, the piece of paper that he keeps in his pocket visualizes to Dr. M his interpretation of what is done presently.

Back in the conference room Dr. M calls the hospital's general acute care section that admitted the 83-year-old woman to discuss with them her previous admissions because he believes there is a problem of co-morbidity (multiple diagnoses). The patient's condition does not get better because she cannot tolerate diuretics. Dr. M. realizes this when carefully going through the continuation where it was stated that the patient was previously admitted to the nephrology department for kidney problems. The acute care section agrees on his analysis and they decide to change the patient's treatment.

Linking Clinical Specialties

A third attending physician, Dr. J, shows up in the AVA conference room. He is the attending physician responsible for consults that day. Physicians in the medical department carry a pager that is assigned to them in the monthly rotation plan of the medical department along with a specific responsibility (e.g., backup). Since there is a new team each day, the pagers specifically facilitate these shifts so that getting a hold of a particular type of specialist is straightforward. A small display shows the phone number of the ward that paged the physician.

As the attending physician, Dr. J, begins his round, he carries with him a pager corresponding to the role of "backup". He leaves AVA to carry out a consult for a patient in one of the wards of the surgical department. Consults may be requested electronically or by calling the pager number, or by contacting a specialist personally in cases where this person is known to have a certain experience. The office of the attending physician, Dr. J, is located a little away from the ward; he does not spend much time there but just checks that no one has left any messages for him.

Whether a physician carries a pager or not depends on his or her assignment. It is crucial that there are no "stray" pagers if the system is assigning roles by pagers and the monthly rotation plan is to work securely. When Dr. J arrives at the surgical department he walks straight to the conference room, which is also the nurses' station. The senior resident there is worried about a patient, a 17-year-old boy that had surgery in the colon recently, who now has dark stool, which may suggest bleeding from the colon. The patient was referred for surgery by the medical department.

Dr. J is the backup but he is also regularly seeing patients in the outpatient clinic specializing in gastroenterology, and Dr. J in this case remembers the patient from a previous admittance. To confirm to himself that it is in fact the same patient that he saw previously, Dr. J recalls details about the patient from memory and has the resident confirm them from what is stated in the patient's record. Together they flip through the paper record. The attending physician confirms the medication of the patient and they agree to have the patient's colon checked again. Dr. J then returns to AVA to see what the next consult is.

The pager technology reduces the interruption of the larger group of physicians. However, for Dr. J carrying the pager work becomes slightly more cumbersome, it appears, when the pager goes off several times in a row and he is not able to trace the call—or return it while the line remains busy. The simplicity of the pager design, which does not support texting, means that there is never any doubt whether a call was followed-up when the pager shifts hands. However, to the physician carrying the pager (Dr. J), it is cumbersome to make judgments about the particular call.

Dr. J is paged several times within a short time, which makes him worried when he cannot tell from the information displayed by the pager who might be calling him. To mitigate this he walks to the information desk located centrally in the hospital. The information desk is able to trace all in-house numbers, including this one. When Dr. J arrives at the ward paging him, he learns that a resident there simply got confused about the system of paging and the procedures for requesting a consult. And while Dr. J in this case is not interrupted in his work, he feels that he has to investigate the matter straight away.

What the Danish case shows is how physicians achieve continuity of care by appropriating patient records and pagers as they go about their everyday work: The patient record requires some appropriation to be useful in the context where inquiries are listed continuously. The relation between the inquiries is not clear for the physician that has to visualize this on a piece of paper that he keeps in his pocket and edits throughout the day; it takes some linking across cases before he actually sees the reason why the patient continues to have water in her lungs (her previous admittance to the nephrology department reveals to him that she has kidney problems). The challenges to continuity of care are thus interdependent with the context and how EPRs are shared between different clinical specialties sometimes located at different regional hospitals depending also on their level of specialization.

The complex organization of work where a different team of physicians runs AVA every day (and the other wards as well) also makes the linking of care across specialties rather complex. To keep responsibility clear within this complex organization of work, the pagers only provide simple forms of communication. However, where possible the particular physician still tries to link previous acquaintance with the patient in the consults as he goes about his work and also to use his personal acquaintance with the patient when deciding what the next step should be.

We will now turn to the story of how physicians achieve continuity of care as part of daily practice in the US medical department by appropriating patient records and pagers so that challenges in the particular context are met.

US Case

The story in the US case begins with Team B in the medical department. Six teams run the medical department that admits patients in a rotation; two days a week each of the teams is responsible for admitting patients. Team B is one of these teams. The teams run for a month each before another team of physicians takes over while the old team rotates to other activities and departments. Team B resides in one of the six conference rooms off the ward, separate from the nurses' stations. During the two days of their rotation the team admits patients within all areas of internal medicine. The days where Team B is not admitting patients it focuses on following up on patients' conditions and on discharging patients that are ready either to return home or to a nursing facility.

Linking Clinical Information

Team B consists of the attending physician, Dr. A, whose specialty is internal medicine; the senior resident, Dr. G, training to become a specialist in internal medicine; 2 resident physicians, Dr. J and Dr. M, and 2 medical students. These

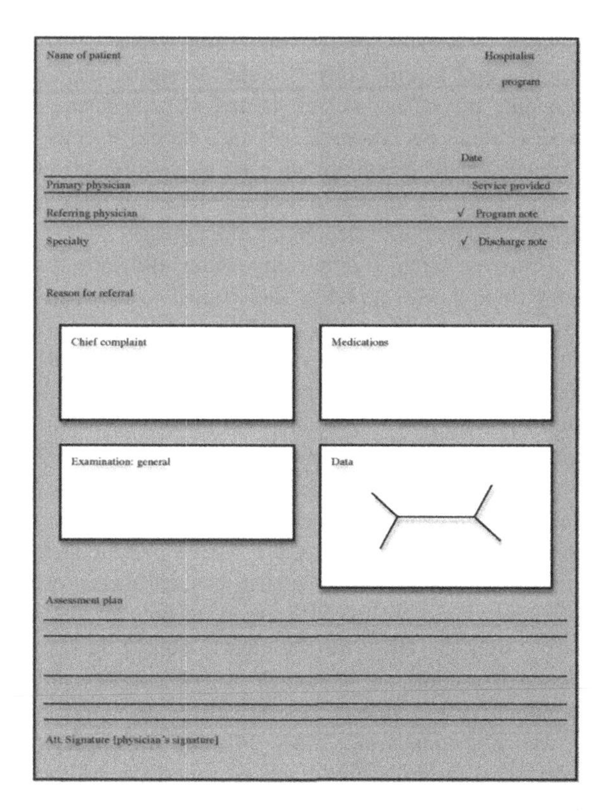
Name of patient
Hospitalist program
Date
Primary physician
Service provided
Referring physician
✓ Program note
Specialty
✓ Discharge note
Reason for referral
Chief complaint
Medications
Examination: general
Data
Assessment plan
Att. Signature [physician's signature]

Fig. 2 Ex. of follow-up note in the US case

physicians form Team B for a month. When the attending physician arrives in Team B's conference room at 8 am, the rest of the team has already been at the hospital for a while checking on their patients. Either one or the other of the two residents is responsible for each patient. Yet should an acute situation emerge, the attending physician has to be available at all hours.

The conference room is, in general, central for Team B's work practices. The team meets here for the morning rounds. As part of the morning rounds the residents, Dr. J and Dr. M, prepare "follow-up notes" (Fig. 2) for all patients, assembling the medical values (e.g., blood pressure), medications, and the plan for the patient. The hospital requires that a follow-up note is filled out each day of the admission for each patient and signed by the attending physician by the end of the day. The note forms a kind of patient résumé similar to that found in the EPR of the hospital, but focusing on the patient's condition on that particular day.

The follow-up note has an important relationship to the patient's health insurance because it is the hospital's documentation to bill procedures and to potential patient lawsuits because it sums up the patient's condition and the steps taken. How patients are covered depends on their health plan (Medicaid, Medicare, or by health insurance as part of their employment). The interpretation of the patient's insurance conditions is an integrated part of the work of Team B's physicians throughout a patient's admission.

The 3-layered carbon paper of the follow-up note ensures that it is completed in 3 copies: a bluish copy (for the billing department), a yellow copy (for the paper record), and a pink copy (for the attending physician's personal records). The attending physician later explained that the handwritten notes make the clinical process stand out more clearly and, should it come to a lawsuit, the adding and crossing out of text helps give an expression of the process nature of the work done. Over time, through a process of various tests and observations, in most cases it will be possible to decide on a diagnosis.

However, Team B's morning rounds illustrate that the follow-up note is, at the same time, a central part of the clinical work when physicians closely follow the development of a patient's condition on every day of the admission. At the center of the follow-up note the newest medical information is visualized. The current state of the patient is crucial to making decisions about the next step. And, while the follow-up note is formally completed for administrative purposes, it is also a convenient daily visualization of the direction of the patient's condition.

The patient's possible change of provider between admittances means that the residents cannot be sure that the electronic record is complete except for the current admittance. The patient's employment is typically what determines the type of health plan the patient has and therefore at what hospital the patient is admitted. The hospital EPR is one source of the information registered in the follow-up note. However, by closely analyzing the patients' conditions, the physicians overcome the challenge of discontinuity in the EPR when information is explored by the same person day-after-day.

Morning rounds take place either in the conference room or at patients' bedsides. This morning physicians sit down around the conference table where they admitted several patients the day before, and this makes it convenient to discuss the details of patients' conditions. The attending physician flips through the follow-up notes laid out on the table in front of him until he finds the patient that Dr. J is presenting to the team. He looks at the follow-up note and starts to ask the team questions about the possible reasons for the increase in this patient's ammonia level. They will not begin any treatment until they have all of the lab results, the attending physician concludes, and he makes a few notes on the follow-up note.

Linking Clinical Specialties

As the morning rounds end, the attending physician leaves to carry out consults that were ordered by other departments. Meanwhile, the residents make sure the next diagnostic steps for Team B's patients are carried out. Two types of consults may be requested: (1) the formal "request for a specialist consult", and (2) the informal "curbside consult", where specialists discuss the diagnosis at the patient's bedside. A third option is family meetings, which is a formal meeting set up with several specialists and the family of the patient.

Consults are requested through the hospital's intranet, which is connected to the system of pagers, or by using the pager number of a certain physician directly. Much of the physicians' work takes place as they are traversing the hospital corridors; pagers make them available for communication while they are seeing patients. The pager also allows the physician to receive a text message and take a quick look at it to decide if the request is urgent enough to disrupt whatever he or she is doing. If the physician is in the middle of a physical examination of a patient, for example, the text message allows the physician to respond later, if the request is not acute.

The pagers are personal and follow Team B's physicians throughout their rotation. In this way the pager allows the physicians to build relationships through both formal and informal consults. The pager provides the physician with the possibility of texting similar to SMS. On her way to see a patient, the resident, Dr. M, stops by the nurses' station to text the senior resident in the nephrology department "Hi, this is M, I have a consult for you regarding patient no _ _ _ _". The resident physician, Dr. M, had already discussed her patient with the senior resident from nephrology several times that week. When the senior resident in the other department responds to her request for a consult that was communicated by paging, they both already know the details of the patient. The senior resident returns the call shortly after and they discuss the details of the patient that concern whether it is Team B or the urology department that should perform a certain procedure. They quickly come to the conclusion that this must be the responsibility of Team B, and Dr. M writes down a few notes that she later types into the EPR. This formal communication is kept as part of the EPR, in contrast to pager communication.

The pager thus supports the possibility that pager messages can be used as more than just an advanced "alarm" that goes off when someone needs to get in touch with the physician. The option of paging also provides the physicians with a less formalized way of communicating with other specialties about what the next clinical step should be. The pagers, in this way, provide a space for the physicians' informal communication that in the end may seem like detours but are actually important in the process of excluding other possibilities in the patient's condition.

What the US case shows is how physicians achieve continuity of care by appropriating patient records and pagers as they go about their everyday work. The EPR in this case requires some appropriation to be useful in the context where it mainly supports an overview of radiology, lab results, and the record of the current admission. However, it does not support an overview across the patient's admissions other than in the particular hospital. The organization of work by month-long teams helps the physician to overcome challenges of discontinuity because it is the same physician that collects and interprets the clinical information throughout the patient's admittance.

Physicians in the US case operate within a context where the course of events can mean a lawsuit. The process nature of the follow-up note and pagers provide them with a way of communicating effectively about a patient's condition. Support for this process cannot be taken for granted within this particular context. Yet the appropriation of patient records and pagers in this way is only possible because of the limited reach of the organization to other specialties within the same hospital.

Teams constituted for a month at a time (also in other clinical specialties) means that physicians' linking of the clinical work may rely on a certain degree of recognition in relation to the specific patient. This is clear from how the pagers allow physicians in Team B to link their work across their formal job title (e.g., senior resident), but also by their experience with the patient in question, when the same senior resident has given advice concerning a particular patient over a period of time.

Discussion: Challenges in Continuity of Care

Continuity of care is a central aspect of clinical work suggesting that it is collaborative by nature when several specialties get involved to handle patients' various conditions. By linking across the organization of work in terms of the clinical information and the clinical specialties it becomes possible to handle complex issues—which has also been a main driver for support of clinical work by collaborative technologies, for example, EPRs (Berg 1998). Thus, from this perspective continuity of care defines a practice of linking so that tasks are not disintegrated in the complex organization of clinical work (Strauss et al. 1985).

Continuity of care is achieved in the Danish and the US hospital medical departments through addressing similar concerns for providing the best possible care under the particular circumstances. Both departments accept patients with a wide spectrum of symptoms that are handled routinely in morning rounds where the patients are discussed in relation to the change in their condition to decide on the next step.

The technologies that the two medical departments deploy are also similar. EPRs offer an overview of radiology and lab-results, inquiries of the patient, and the plan for what ought to be done next. The pagers in both cases work by the roles of physicians depending on their level of specialization (e.g., senior resident) and clinical specialty (e.g., nephrology). Pagers support the linking of specialties by providing a way that consults may be requested.

However, there are significant differences between the two cases. The staffing (continuous vs. shifting physicians), spaces (off the ward vs. on the ward), and interrelationships with services outside the hospital (defined vs. distributed organization) make the US case and the Danish case different in essential ways. The challenges of achieving continuity of care are thus different in the two cases, despite their common medical aim. Nonetheless, they both illustrate how continuity of care is accomplished.

The major difference lies in how roles are constituted around the responsibility for care. In the US case the roles of the physicians are continuous over a period of a month, which makes the extra effort of handling roles in clinical work less cumbersome. The same people seeing the same patients make hand-over less of an issue. This is quite different in the Danish case, where the change in responsibilities places more focus on the work of handling roles, which is illustrated by the physicians' use of pagers as mainly connecting "functions" rather than facilitating interpersonal communication.

Continuity of care is challenging in the US case in the way that the patients might have quite discontinuous admittances depending on their healthcare coverage. This means that the entries on the patient's admissions are often incomplete and there might be aspects that are overlooked in the clinical work. In contrast, in the Danish case the entries across the patient's admissions are continuously added within the region's hospitals, increasing the length of the continuation document. Because of the shifting physicians in the Danish case the written documentation becomes critical in the hand-over between physicians from day-to-day, but also when patients move between hospitals.

In this way, continuity of care is handled by the appropriation of the EPR in the Danish case and by pager communication in the US case to overcome the challenges specific to the different contexts of work. Only by comparing the appropriation of technologies in the two cases from the perspective of context, the broader commonalities across the Danish and the US case becomes visible. Here we see how physicians' appropriation of EPRs and pager technology is different across cases. The comparative analysis of the workplace studies makes visible how in the Danish case and the US case the challenges that make physicians appropriate technologies are context-dependent.

In the US case the responsibility of physicians is evident in the hospital's documentation practices, but links back to the general individual responsibility of physicians in the US in case of lawsuits. This is illustrated by how the hospital and the individual physician both keeps a copy of the follow-up note, because, according to the attending physician, the adding and crossing out of text helps give an expression of the process nature of the work done. The follow-up note is thus crucial both formally and in practice when physicians decide on the direction of a patient's condition.

In the Danish case only the hospital keeps a copy of the patient's record. The collective responsibility of a patient's care is evident in how the hospital organizes the clinical work, as illustrated by the listing of one admission after the other in the continuation, which makes the physician extract information to understand the nature of the patient's current problem. The responsibility of the patient's care is thus linked through the entries in the continuation, and is made relevant by the attending physician on a day-to-day basis.

Previous CSCW-research on how Danish physicians decipher the entries of other physicians (Winthereik and Vikkelsø 2005; Mønsted et al. 2011) supports this finding on challenges of clinical entries into EPRs in the Danish case, which are, however, context dependent. The challenges to physicians' work making entries in the EPR relevant to their particular context are not simply a matter of the nature of that clinical work (Heath and Luff 1996), this paper and previous CSCW-research illustrate, but are also a matter of politics and the organization of work in which the EPR is used.

To elaborate, whereas the key challenge in the Danish case is the hand-over via long-term entries into the EPR and that patients very seldom see the same physician, the key challenge in the US case is the lack of long-term entries into the EPR. These challenges are also accommodated differently in the two cases. In the Danish case the long-term entries into the EPR seek to handle challenges specific to the complex organization, whereas in the US case the instance of creating a short-term linking between physicians and patients means the challenges of incomplete long-term entries lessen.

The pager technology in both the Danish case and the US case relies on different roles for the physicians to link clinical work across specialties when consults are requested from other departments. Physicians in the US case collaborate as a team constituted for a month at a time, whereas in the Danish case most physicians rotate between tasks of the medical department from day-to-day—but in a steady routine over months. The linking of specialties by consults in the Danish case is thus one of many jobs that physicians are assigned by the monthly work plan to run the medical department.

The linking of specialties in the Danish case takes place as physicians coordinate—and negotiate—what is the right combination of specialty and level of specialization. Different hospitals specialize in different types of patients. In the US case the range of this type of negotiation is restricted to a single hospital. The comparative analysis of the US case and the Danish case suggests that physicians' linking of clinical specialties is dependent on both the organization of work (e.g., the monthly work plan), but also the distribution of responsibility beyond the particular hospital.

The appropriation of the pager technology in the US case thus shows how physicians appropriate the pager technology to support the organization of work limited to the particular hospital. Other hospitals are mainly relevant if patients are transferred there, but then it is more so a matter of the conditions in the patient's health plan. The challenges particular to the context in the US case concern issues of how physicians may also create a space for their informal communication on the process of care, which is not saved in the same way as information entered into the EPR.

The commonalities from both cases that bring forward how continuity of care is achieved in practice are that continuity of care is acted out based upon politics and how work is organized in terms of the responsibility for care and the constitution of roles. Both responsibility and roles are organized differently and provide certain conditions and challenges for continuity of care, which then also drive the technology use as well as the required technology support of practice.

The essential contribution of this paper is the identification of (a) responsibility for care and (b) the constitution of roles as important elements and rules of combination in relation to how technology is appropriated within the particular context where it is used; the empirical cases illustrate how continuity of care is acted out in practice. These two interdependent and interlinked factors—responsibility of care and constitution of roles—can thus help us understand in broader terms the challenges across context of technologies to support continuity of care.

The challenges to continuity are characterized in essential ways by the patients' circulation between providers, which makes practices of linking across the organization of work part and parcel of physicians' everyday work. This aspect of clinical work is often promoted as a way to politically raise awareness about the provision of healthcare across time, setting, and specialty (Ellingsen and Monteiro 2006: 443). This paper points to the importance of understanding what continuity of care comes to mean in practice as it is interrelated and interdependent with politics and the organization of work.

Conclusion

This paper explored how continuity of care is achieved through the appropriation of technology as part of everyday practice in a Danish and a US hospital medical department. Comparing these two cases at the level of the broader commonalities (Schimdt et al. 2007), it becomes clear how the linking of clinical work is challenged in both cases across lines of responsibility of care and the constitution of roles, although the origin of the challenges is context-dependent.

Our data illustrate how the challenges of continuity of care in the US case concern the lack of long-term documentation of the patient's condition in the EPR, whereas in the Danish case the lack of continuity lies squarely in the parade of changing physicians for each patient. While the challenges are different in the two cases, they both mirror the broader political and organizational structure of healthcare provision in a Danish and a US context and the challenges that are addressed by different appropriations of technologies.

To accommodate challenges of lack of documented care for a patient over time due to conditions of private healthcare where patients move between providers depending on how they are covered by their health plan, the relative continuity between the patient and the physician becomes central in the US case to support the clinical work. Differently, to accommodate the challenges of public healthcare where there is one provider but the patient still moves between hospitals depending on their condition, physicians rely on the long-term documentation of the care of a patient in the Danish case.

It is not up to this paper to promote either of these approaches. Rather, the paper attempts to shed light on how continuity of care is achieved as part of everyday practice—and what role context plays. In both in the US case and the Danish case valuable lessons can be learned from the ways technologies are appropriated to accomplish continuity of care in practice if the goal is new, improved practices. These lessons concern how exactly responsibility and roles are organized differently in the US case and the Danish case and provide certain conditions and challenges for continuity of care, which then also drive the technology use as well as the required technology support of practice.

Acknowledgments A great thank you to all of the medical department staff at the US hospital and the Danish hospital for always being open and welcoming. Also, a special thank you to Yunan Chen for arranging for me to conduct the US case study. The US study was carried out under the IRB number UCI HS# 2009-6754. I am grateful to Pernille Bjørn, Nina Boulus-Rødje, Yunan Chen, Christopher Gad, Gunnar Ellingsen and Irina Shklovski for their constructive discussion and comments in the process of writing this paper.

References

Balka, E., Bjørn, P., & Wagner, I. (2008). Steps toward a typology for health informatics, *Proceedings of the 2008 ACM conference on Computer Supported Cooperative Work* (pp. 515–524).

Bardram, J.E., & Hansen, T.R. (2004). The AWARE architecture: supporting context-mediated social awareness in mobile cooperation, *Proceedings of the 2004 ACM conference on Computer Supported Cooperative Work* (pp. 192–201).

Bardram, J. E., & Bossen, C. (2005). Mobility work: The spatial dimension of collaboration at a hospital. *Computer Supported Cooperative Work, 14*, 131–160.

Berg, M. (1998). *Order(s) and disorder(s): Of protocols and medical practices, in Differences in Medicine. Unraveling Practices Techniques and Bodies* (pp. 226–246). Durham and London: Duke University Press.

Berg, M, & Winthereik, B.R. (2003): Waiting for Godot. Episodes from the history of patient records, *in Health Information Management: Integrating Information and Communication Technology in Healthcare Work* (pp. 10–42). London, UK: Routledge.

Boulus, N., & Bjørn, P. (2010). A cross-case analysis of technology-in-use practices: EPR-adaption in Canada and Norway. *International Journal of Medical Informatics, 76*(6), 97–108.

Brown, B., & Randell, R. (2004). Building a context-sensitive telephone: some hopes and pitfalls for context sensitive computing. *Computer Supported Cooperative Work, 13*, 329–345.

Cabitza, F., Simone, C. Zorzato, G. (2009): ProDoc: An electronic patient record to foster process-oriented practices, *Proceedings of the 11th European Conference on Computer Supported Cooperative Work* (pp. 85–104).

Cebul, R. D., Rebitzer, J. B., Taylor, L. J., & Votruba, M. (2008). Organizational fragmentation and care quality in the U.S. health care system. *Journal of Economic Perspectives, 22*(4), 93–113.

Denmarks Board of Technology (2006). *Sundhedsydelser med IT. Pervasive Healthcare I den Danske Sundhedssektor* [Healthcare Services by IT. Pervasive Healthcare in the Danish Healthcare Service]. Teknologirådets rapporter 2006/11.

Eisenhardt, K. M. (1989). Building theories from case study research. *Academy of Management Review, 14*(4), 532–550.

Ellingsen, G., & Monteiro, E. (2006). Seamless integration: Standardisation across multiple local settings. *Computer Supported Cooperative Work, 15*(5–6), 443–466.

Emerson, R.M.; Fretz, R.I., & Shaw, L.L. (1995). Writing ethnographic fieldnotes. Chicago and London: The University of Chicago Press.

Fitzpatrick, G., & Ellingsen, G. (2012). A Review of 25 years of CSCW research in healthcare: Contributions, challenges and future agendas, *Computer Supported Cooperative Work, 12*, 1–57 (published online 21 June 2012).

Hartswood, M., Procter, R., Rouncefield, M., & Slack, R. (2003). Making a case in medical work: Implications for the electronic medical record. *Computer Supported Cooperative Work, 12*(3), 241–266.

Heath, C., Luff, P. (1996). Documents and Professional Practice: 'bad'organisational reasons for good clinical records, *Proceedings of the 1996 ACM Conference on Computer Supported Cooperative Work* (pp. 354–363).

Klein, H., & Myers, M. (1999). A set of principles for conducting and evaluating interpretive field studies in information systems. *MIS Quarterly, 23*(1), 67–94.

Lee, S., Tang, C., Park, S.Y., & Chen, Y. (2012). Loosely formed patient care teams: communication challenges and technology design, *Proceedings of the 2012 ACM Conference on Computer Supported Cooperative Work* (pp. 867–876).

Meum, T., Monteiro, E., & Ellingsen, G. (2011). The pendulum of standardization, *Proceedings of the 12th European Conference on Computer Supported Cooperative Work* (pp. 101–120).

Mønsted, T., Reddy, M.C., & Bansler, J.P. (2011): The use of narratives in medical work: A field study of physician-patient consultation, *Proceedings of the 12th European Conference on Computer Supported Cooperative Work* (pp. 81–100).

Park, S.Y., Pine, K.H., & Chen, Y. (2013). Local-universality: Designing EMR to support localized informal documentation practices, *Proceedings of the 2013 ACM Conference on Computer Supported Cooperative Work.*

Schmidt, K., Wagner, I., & Tolar, M. (2007) Permutations of cooperative work practices: A study of two oncology clinics, *Proceedings of the International ACM conference on supporting group work* (pp. 1–10).

Scholl, J., Hasvold, P., Henriksen, E., & Ellingsen, G. (2007). *Managing communication availability and interruptions: a study of mobile communications in an oncology department, in Pervasive Computing Innovations in Intelligent Multimedia and Applications* (pp. 234–250). Berlin, Heidelberg: Springer.

Strauss, A; Corbin, J. (1998). *Basics of Qualitative Research. Techniques and Procedures for Developing Grounded Theory.* Thousand Oaks, CA, Sage Publications.

Strauss, A. L., Fagerhaugh, S., Suczek, B., & Wiener, C. (1985). *Social Organization of Medical Work.* New Brunswick (USA) and London (UK): Transaction Publishers.

US Institute of Medicine (2001). *Crossing the Quality Chasm: A New Health System for the 21st Century.* Washington, DC: The National Academies Press.

US Office of the National Coordinator for Health Information Technology (2010): *Health Information Technology: Initial Set of Standards, Implementation, specifications, and Certification Criteria for Electronic Health Record Technology; Final rule.* Department of Health and Human Services, July 28 2010.

Winthereik, B. R., & Vikkelsø, S. (2005). ICT and integrated care: Some dilemmas of standardizing inter-organisational communication. *Computer Supported Cooperative Work, 14*(1), 43–67.

Fostering Collaborative Redesign of Work Practice: Challenges for Tools Supporting Reflection at Work

Michael Prilla, Viktoria Pammer and Birgit Krogstie

Abstract Reflection is a well-known mechanism to learn from experience. Often, it has been investigated from an educational viewpoint or as a formalised procedure such as in project debriefing. Based on an analysis of three case studies, we show that collaborative reflection is much more embedded in daily work and that it supports collaborative, bottom-up redesign of work. We found that processes of work redesign alternate between individual and collaborative reflection and identified reasons for collaborative reflection as well as criteria for selecting reflection partners. We also identified perspective exchange, attribution and (re-)appraisal of past situations to be decisive for collaborative reflection and how it supports finding adequate levels of work redesign and partners needed to implement change. From this, we describe five themes for the design of support for collaborative reflection as a means for work redesign.

Introduction

Reflection on work is a typical mechanism of (implicit) learning in the workplace (Boud et al. 1985; Eraut 2004; Kolb and Fry 1975; Schön 1983): People think about whether they acted appropriately in a certain situation or whether their cooperation with others runs smoothly and how things can be improved. Reflection can be understood as re-evaluation of experience(s) for the purpose of guiding

M. Prilla (✉)
Ruhr-University of Bochum, Bochum, Germany
e-mail: michael.prilla@rub.de

V. Pammer
TU Graz and Know Center, Graz, Austria
e-mail: vpammer@know-center.at

B. Krogstie
Norwegian University of Science and Technology, Trondheim, Norway
e-mail: birgitkr@idi.ntnu.no

O. W. Bertelsen et al. (eds.), *ECSCW 2013: Proceedings of the 13th European Conference on Computer Supported Cooperative Work, 21–25 September 2013, Paphos, Cyprus*, DOI: 10.1007/978-1-4471-5346-7_13,

future behaviour (Boud et al. 1985). It helps people make sense of an experience, handle difficult emotions, or find a way of solving a concrete problem, by transforming experience into knowledge applicable for daily work as part of a learning cycle (Kimmerle et al. 2010; Stahl 2000). Reflection thus combines "codified knowledge" and "cultural knowledge" (Eraut 2004), giving people the chance to learn from past work and to *redesign future work*—the latter outcome transcends approaches of enabling people to actively shape their work as currently known in CSCW and will be the focus of this paper.

Reflection has a strong social dimension (Boud et al. 2006; Hoyrup 2004) and is often accomplished collaboratively by a team or working unit. *Collaborative reflection* means that people reflect together by exchanging (similar) experiences, discussing them and deriving insights together. Accordingly, we can understand collaborative reflection as external, communicative process, in contrast to individual reflection which is an internal, cognitive process. Collaborative reflection then transcends individual reflection, as it enables participants to learn from each other and to craft new knowledge from shared experiences (Daudelin 1996; Hoyrup 2004). A lot of work on collaborative reflection investigates singular events such as project (Kerth 2001), but little is known about other processes of collaborative reflection and how technology can be designed to support reflection through which people can influence their work environment.

We investigated processes of collaborative reflection in three different cases (hospital, IT consulting, social care). We found that collaborative reflection may lead to a *redesign of work* that is *triggered and implemented by workers* rather than experts, managers or other superordinate roles. This means that workers identify discrepancies or difficult situations during work, derive a proper understanding of the experience and on that basis implement changes in the work practice on their own. Such democratization of work design may speed up change processes in organizations and raise the satisfaction of employees. Within this paper, we take a deeper look on the question of how to support processes of collaborative reflection that finally lead to redesigning work. This work is especially relevant for the CSCW community as it shows how by collaborative reflection people can bypass hierarchical barriers and redesign group work on their own. As collaborative reflection is a frequent, yet hardly investigated mechanism, there is a need to understand it better to tap on this potential.

In what follows, we describe the three case studies on which this work is based, including examples of collaborative reflection from the cases. We then describe characteristics of collaborative reflection by relating foundational work on reflection to our examples. Analyzing the cases, we show how collaborative reflection leads to work redesign and that it is based on an interplay of individual and collaborative reflection sessions. This leads to questions of what triggers collaborative reflection, what mechanisms happen inside collaborative reflection, and how results are created collaboratively. We answer these questions by analyzing the cases more deeply, identifying support needs for collaborative reflection. On this basis we derive *five themes for the design of tool support* for collaborative reflection as a means for work redesign.

Related Work

Collaborative reflection is close to other concepts in CSCW. We will briefly discuss sensemaking, collective mind, collaborative problem solving and decision support according to their slight, yet decisive differences to reflection.

Sensemaking (Weick 1995) has a clear relation to reflection in that it is a process of understanding previous events better. Weick (1995) describes it as a process of creating clearer picture of what has happened concerning a particular event in order to "rationalize what people are doing". While it may also contain asking about what new insights may mean in terms of future actions, reflection has a much clearer focus on the future than sensemaking, by stressing "outcomes". *Collective mind theory* (Weick and Roberts 1993) goes beyond sensemaking and describes a conscious process of conversation, which is close to communication during reflection, and recapitulation, which contains replaying and reanalyzing important events (Crowston and Kammerer 1998). The latter, however, is a process of building a shared identity rather than deriving change for the future and makes it a routinized group building process rather than a practice of *work redesign*, as which we understand collaborative reflection at work here.

Reflection in groups typically involves considering alternatives and agreeing on outcomes, i.e. it incorporates decision processes. (Group) *Decision Support Systems (DSS)*, which can be understood as "interactive computer-based systems that help people use computer communications (…) to solve problems and make decisions" (Power and Sharda 2009), are about decision making in teams. Their focus, even for distributed DSS (Gray et al. 2011), is on the decision making task and not on other aspects of collaboration (Dennis et al. 1988) or on reflection.

Collaborative problem solving (Roschelle and Teasley 1995) describes a process of constructing and maintaining a joint problem space and, by acting and communicating, learning together how to solve a problem. In such processes there is, however, a tendency to focus on information that is shared among all its members from the start, which is called the "shared information bias" (Baker 2010). Collaborative reflection, in which group members share different experiences, may overcome this, as shared information is on the type of experience rather than on particular events.

Collaborative reflection differs from these concepts in its clear focus on the re-assessment of experiences and creating outcomes that affect future work. While both might be relevant for processes such as problem solving, sensemaking, creating collective mind or supporting decisions, the emphasis on going back to experiences, re-evaluating them and drawing conclusions for the future makes collaborative reflection a unique phenomenon that is deeply embedded into daily work. Therefore, it may benefit from solutions for any of the concepts mentioned above, but a thorough analysis and understanding of its occurrence and needs in practice is needed first.

Reflection in Practice: Three Cases

The findings in this paper are based on investigations of three cases, including a hospital, a consulting company and care homes for elderly people.

The Cases

Case 1: Reflection in a hospital

In Case 1, we investigated a ward in a German hospital in which acute stroke patients are treated. Due to the demands of this work, the staff is highly trained. Their primary motivation is a desire to help people by providing good care to improve the quality of patients' lives. Work is organized in shifts: physicians work in two shifts covering days and nights, nurses work in shifts in the morning, the afternoon and the night. Between shifts, handovers are done within and between these two professional groups. Regular meetings are held bi-weekly to discuss issues on the ward. Work in the ward is constrained by time pressure and emotional stress. Often, due to time pressure, mandatory documentation is done after shifts to guarantee that it does not interfere with caring properly for patients. Emotional stress results from work with patients who are unable to articulate what they need or who are getting gradually worse. In addition, physicians need to make decisions affecting patients' lives, and they need to talk to relatives of the patients, which often includes bringing bad news. Supervision and mutual help are accordingly considered important among staff.

We observed a physician and a nurse for two days each and conducted four interviews with nurses and physicians. We conducted focus group workshops with four nurses and three physicians to identify support needs and options.

Case 2: Reflection in IT Consulting

The consulting case study was carried out at a German IT company selling and personalizing customer relationship management software to help analysing and optimising the marketing, sales and service processes of their customers. The company has about 60 employees, most of them based in the headquarters. Many meetings with customers are held at the customers' sites, which requires internal preparation and post-processing. Daily work is heavily focused on customers' needs. Therefore, consultants need a high degree of flexibility in their work. We found that consulting and sales thus involves a high degree of reflection on interaction with the customer. As a consequence, knowledge management and sharing is considered to be a major challenge in this organization. Consultants mainly work in small teams of two to three people and often talk to each other about their work. We conducted interviews with five consultants and observed two consultants for 2 days each.

Case 3: Reflection in social care

The care home case study was carried out in two nursing homes in the UK (referred to as homes A and B). A growing challenge for both homes is the higher proportion of elderly residents suffering from dementia. These people often show what is called 'challenging behaviour', during which they react aggressively to unfamiliar surroundings or events. This requires a lot of reflection on the side of the caregivers, as there is no one-size-fits-all solution when dealing with people suffering from dementia. To deal with them one needs to understand the individual and their complex life history. Most of the care staff, except for the registered nurses, who are responsible for medical issues, are not educated to a degree level, and have only been trained for at most a few weeks. In home A, we observed meetings during two days and interviewed four caregivers. In home B, we interviewed three caregivers and observed one and a half day of work practice.

Methodology

The analysis of the three case studies uses material gathered during field visits, including work observations and interviews. For each case, two researchers followed two staff members for two days each, observing their daily practice with a special emphasis on reflection, taking notes on their observations. For case 3 (social care), in home B different members of staff and their tasks were observed during one and a half day. In addition, semi-structured interviews were conducted with staff in all cases, asking about reflection in practice and related aspects such as learning, knowledge transfer and communication in their work environment. The interviews were audiotaped and transcribed. In Case 1, also focus groups were created and interviewed on their needs and current habits of reflection.

The resulting material was analysed in an approach aligned to Grounded Theory (Strauss and Corbin 1998). Additionally, we used indicators for reflection as described by van Woerkom and Croon (2008) during analysis to identify reflection in the material and to differentiate it from other occurrences of thinking about past events. The combination of interviews and work observations provided a holistic overview of reflection in the cases, as interviews provided more general information on needs and habits than what could be seen from the observation. Conversely, the observations provided better insights into the specific work environment and reflection practice than could be inferred from the interviews.

Reflection in the Cases by Example

To illustrate our understanding of occurrences of reflection, we provide examples of successful reflection from the three cases below. The examples serve as proxies for many others and will be used in the paper to illustrate our findings from an analysis of the three cases and the need for support in less optimal cases.

Example 1: Starting the alarm procedure in a hospital ward

During our observation, a patient with an acute stroke and in very bad condition was admitted to the emergency room of the ward. The responsible physician realized that this was a very critical case. The standard procedure is to start an internal alarm, which causes the head physician and an emergency team to immediately come to the ward. The present nurse tried to start the alarm with her internal telephone, as there was no alarm button in the room. However, the alarm did not go off and the helpers did not arrive in the next minutes. The nurse then called the head physician and the emergency team directly, and they came to the emergency room and took care of the patient.

After this situation, the nurse reflected on the problem by repeatedly going through the procedure he had applied in the emergency room. He did not find a reason for the problem and therefore asked the head nurse to reflect on the issue together. She had had a similar experience, and together they realized that using the telephone for the emergency procedure as it was described in the hospital's quality manual was too complicated in emergency situations. After this, the head nurse recalled other similar situations she had been in and thought about the resolutions she had come up with then. To clarify the issue, she finally added it to the agenda for the upcoming ward meeting and asked the nurse who had experienced the problem to explain it to the others, including the reason they had come up with. Some of the other nurses present reported similar problems. As a result of sharing the experiences, the nurses agreed to practice essential procedures more often and to change the telephone emergency procedure. As the latter could not be implemented by the nurses, but is subject to hospital-wide standards, the head nurse agreed to talk to the responsible quality manager to change the procedure.

Example 2: Losing sales pitches in an IT Consulting Company

After a time of success, some sales consultants in the company realized that they were losing more pitches than they used to. Each consultant had thought about this, but nobody had an idea of how to change the situation. In the monthly meeting of sales consultants, in which they usually iterate through current activities, one consultant mentioned this problem. The other consultants reported similar impressions. They focused the meeting on pitches that had been lost recently and started to reflect on what had happened there to find reasons for the losses. Going through the experiences, they found that in most cases the critical issue had been the customer asking for an interactive demo system. The company usually did not provide customers with demo systems, but invited them to the site of a reference customer to show them an operational system. The consultants reported that customers had often been dissatisfied with the lacking demo system, as competitors had provided demo systems, and that they had struggled with this dissatisfaction during the remainder of the pitch. They decided that from now on they would have a demo system for customers. The head consultant agreed to talk to the IT department in order to set up such a demo system. He also reported this to the management, who agreed to change the company standards to include demo systems in the sales process.

Example 3: Challenging behaviour in a care home

In home A, caregivers often discuss challenging behaviour of residents, possible reasons for such behaviour and how to deal with it. This is done in what is called "reflective meetings", in which a senior caregiver meets with other staff and asks them if there is something bothering them or worth discussing for other reasons. In one of these meetings a young caregiver, who had started work only weeks before, reported a problem: A resident of the care home had approached him multiple times, asking when she would be allowed to leave the care for her own home. The young man was very sad for her and because he did not know what to tell her. Some of the other, more experienced caregivers reported similar experiences, and told him that this also affected them much when they were younger and proposed what could have caused the lady's behaviour. They also described how they had dealt with these situations and the emotions caused by them. This gave the junior caregiver alternative ways to deal with the situation and showed him that the problem was relevant not only to him. In addition, the group decided that the best way to react in such situations was to be honest and tell the residents that they are in a care home and that this was their permanent home. They agreed that this should be the standard procedure for the future.

(Collaborative) Reflection in the Cases

Below, we relate the examples from the cases to insights and terminology from prior work on reflection that influences our research.

The Reflection Process

Our understanding of reflection is closely aligned to that of Boud et al. (1985), who identify three main steps in the reflective learning process.

(1) **Going back to experiences** that happened in the past,
(2) **re-evaluating and understanding these experiences** in the light of current knowledge or experiences and
(3) **deriving insights for future behaviour** from this assessment.

The steps are explained in Table 1 by referring to the examples given above.

Boud et al. (1985) emphasise the *non-linear structure* of reflection in practice. In contrast to other models of learning from experience (e.g., Kolb and Fry 1975),

Table 1 Reflection steps in the model of Boud et al. (1985) with examples from the cases

Case/step	Going back to experiences	Re-evaluating and understanding exp.	Deriving insights for future work
Case 1: Hospital	*Individual*: Thinking about the problem *Collaborative*: Exchanging experiences on the emergency procedure	Realizing that the stressful situation afforded too much attention to care and that the alarm procedure was too complicated	Agreeing to practice standard procedures more often and to modify the emergency procedure
Case 2: Consulting	*Individual:* Thinking about lost pitches *Collaborative*: Exchanging reports on pitches	Realizing that many similar experiences had in common that the client asked for a demo system	Agreeing to add demo systems to the standard procedure for customer visits
Case 3: Social care	*Individual*: Thinking about dealing with the resident *Collaborative*: Talking about similar situations	Discussing previous solutions of and understanding that the truth was the best option	Changing the way to talk to the old lady and agreeing on a standard procedure for this

they include explicit loopbacks between the steps. They also focus on the *process* of reflection rather than reflection as a mind-set (e.g., Reynolds 1999) or professional attitude (e.g., Schön 1983). This helps to identify reflection in practice, differentiate it from other ways to think about past (work) events (see related work) and to support reflection appropriately. The model by Boud et al. should be considered a *blueprint* and not as a normative process, as formalizing the reflection process too much may inhibit reflection as it evolves in practice, and may also lead to resistance among reflection participants (Boud et al. 2006).

Reflection Sessions

Reflection takes place in *sessions*, "a time-limited activity of reflecting" (Krogstie et al. 2012) distinguished by a specific time span, a place, a particular set of participants and whether it is spontaneous or planned. It may take place "in action", being inextricably linked to work activity, or "on action", in which case the reflection session can be arbitrarily separated in its characteristics from work activities (Schön 1983). Reflection on the same topic may span several sessions such as in the example from the hospital, in which at first the two nurses had a reflection session before the head nurse started another session in the meeting.

Collaborative Reflection as a Means to Redesign Work Practice

In the cases, successful collaborative reflection at work was often a means to redesign work processes. This highlights new opportunities for work redesign: While this is often left to experts and superiors, *reflection offers the opportunity to enable workers to redesign their work and implement this change*.

Redesigning Work

Redesigning work means questioning and changing norms, procedures and their underlying rationales and can thus be understood as double-loop learning as explained by Argyris and Schön (1978). Understanding collaborative reflection as a means to redesign work, we can also see workers reflecting collaboratively as a design community in the (broad) sense of "being concerned with 'how things ought to be'" (Fischer and Ostwald 2003).

In the case studies, we found many situations in which reflection helped a group to analyse the structure and rationales of (collaborative) work and identify potential improvements as well as people needed to implement them. The group of nurses in example 1 realized that in addition to changes in the procedure for the alarm (implementation that would need approval by management), they needed to intensify their training on the ward (implementation feasible within the team). In the case of the care home (example 3), the group did not only help the junior caregiver to deal with his emotions, but also decided that being honest to residents should be a leading paradigm in similar situations from now on, thus transforming what had started as peer help to a collaboratively achieved redesign of work for the whole group. The consultants in example 2 agreed to use a demo system in future pitches, adding this to the best practice procedure of their company.

Overall, our observations indicate that collaborative reflection can create a dynamic in which a *group of workers becomes enabled to redesign work, thereby creating a change within the organization*. This is in line with Engeström et al. (1996), who also show how data on past experiences can support the change of work practices. However, extending this and other approaches, it also shows that such work redesign is not bound to scheduled sessions, but happens continuously and ubiquitously through reflection. In addition, it shows that in some cases, the group is itself able to implement changes, while in other cases the group needs to enlist additional actors in order to implement the solution.

Back and Forth Between Individual and Collaborative Reflection

The road to collaborative redesign of work can be regarded as a continuous interplay of individual and collaborative reflection sessions (see also Engeström et al. (1996)). Each of our examples contains sessions in which individuals reflect alone and sessions in which they reflect together with others. These sessions build on each other, as the social care case (example 3) shows: The caregiver had reflected on his own before he told his colleagues about it (individual). Hearing his account, the colleagues recalled similar experiences and reflected on them (collaborative reflection). The consultants in example 2 had reflected on lost pitches (individual) before addressing the issue in the meeting and discussing similar experiences (collaborative reflection). Collaborative reflection in this case was amplified by the earlier reflection as participants could bring their insights into the discussion. The process of an individual seeking the assistance of others is typical for dealing with negative experiences. It may also get more complex: In example 1, the nurse had approached the head nurse for collaborative reflection. After this, the head nurse started to reflect on her experiences with the problem (individual) and decided to bring this topic up for collaborative reflection of all nurses in their next meeting. These observations show how processes of reflection may take multiple iterations between individual and collaborative reflection and how these loops amplify the created outcomes (see also Fig. 1).

Towards Designing Technology that Supports the Reflective Process of Work Redesign: Research Questions

Our analysis shows that collaborative reflection can contribute to work redesign and that this redesign relies on loops of collaborative and individual reflection. The redesign process is often started by an individual approaching others with the

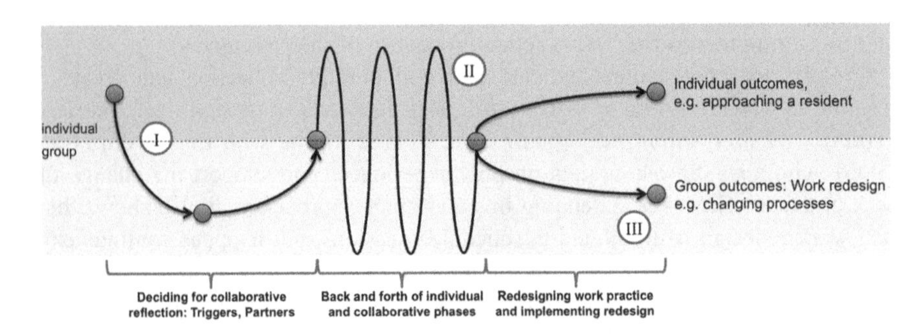

Fig. 1 The process of collaborative reflection for redesigning work

purpose of reflecting together, by sharing experiences (e.g., on lost pitches) or asking for experiences with similar issues (e.g., problems with the alarm procedures). It results in outcomes for the individual or the group (Fig. 1).

In the multitude of situations we observed to run less smoothly than the examples used in this paper, tools could support people to reflect together by providing data on work and the perspectives of others on this data as a basis for reflection (Knipfer et al. 2011). The challenge for tools is then to enable transitions between individual and collaborative reflection, to help people identify needs for redesign and to support the implementation of insights gained through reflection. Given the usual course of reflection as described above, designing such support needs answers to the following research questions:

(1) **Initializing collaborative reflection**: Why and how do people engage in collaborative reflection? What motivates them to share their observations and solutions? (no. I in Fig. 1)
(2) **Reflecting collaboratively**: What are the particular characteristics of collaborative reflection and what is necessary to create solutions for redesigning work? (no. II in Fig. 1)
(3) **Outcomes of collaborative reflection**: How do the reflection actors move from collaborative reflection to redesigning work? What kind of work can be redesigned? (no. III in Fig. 1)

Understanding Collaborative Reflection

Below, we analyze our cases driven by the three research questions.

Initializing Collaborative Reflection: Triggers and Partners

In practice, collaborative reflection is often initialized by an individual approaching others and articulating her experiences. But what actually causes the individual to approach colleagues, that is, what triggers collaborative reflection? Among the scarce literature on such triggers, van Woerkom and Croon (2008) only list typical situations in which collaborative reflection is initiated such as asking for feedback or questioning norms, but do not investigate the underlying reasons why people ask for feedback or question norms. Our cases provide more insights: In the case of the failed emergency alarm (example 1), the nurse wanted *clarification* on the reasons for the problem and approached the head nurse. The head nurse went from individual reflection to a group session of reflection because she wanted the whole group to become *aware* of the problem and *solve it together*—she knew that the chances of finding a solution and implementing it would be higher if the group was involved. The consultant from example 2 speaking up in the meeting initially wanted to *get feedback* on this problem. In the care home example, the junior caregiver was *seeking help and advice* in a situation that he felt bad about. Finally, although we were not able to observe this, in examples 1 and 2 people who were *needed for implementing the identified solutions* (the change in the procedure and the demo system) were contacted. This can be regarded as another trigger for collaborative reflection.

Once individuals realise that they want to reflect with others, there is a question of whom to approach. Just like reasons for choosing communication partners are diverse (Sykes 1983), choosing reflection partners is not straightforward, but depends on the problem to be reflected on and the purpose of reflection. Individuals may approach people with *more competence or experience* to get advice from them (as in example 1). This may not necessarily lead to collaborative reflection if the answer is known by the more experienced partner, but this is often not the case and collaborative reflection is initialised (as in example 1). In other cases, individuals approach people who can *give emotional support* in addition to advice (trusted peers or experts, as in example 3). We also observed the choice of *people with less experience or awareness of a problem* as reflection partners. Here, the rationale was to make others learn: For example, senior caregivers told us in interviews that they often approach a younger colleague to tell them to carry out tasks differently. After that, they would give a story about a similar situation in which the approach in question did not work and reflect on both situations with the younger caregiver. Moreover, people may be addressed because they are supposed to support the creation or implementation of a solution—in example 1, reflection was started among nurses to include them in the decision process, and management was involved to implement the change in the procedure. Finally, we also observed partner choice as chance encountering, when the choice of partners resulted from doing certain tasks together or doing similar tasks. In such situations, reassurance on work done was the main purpose of reflection.

Merging our insights on triggers and reflection partners, we find three categories of triggers and related choice of reflection partners:

- **Seeking clarification or resolution**: The category we observed most frequently was an individual seeking input and support by others. This includes triggers such as clarification and seeking help as well as choosing partners based on their experiences or emotional sensitivity.
- **Seeking support for solution implementation**: Reflection partners are often chosen to support the creation or implementation of solutions.
- **Creating awareness**: A subtle category consists of making reflection partners aware of a certain problem or supporting them in learning about it. This was the case with the senior careers reflecting with younger colleagues in care homes, and the head nurse involving the all nurses in reflection.

Reflecting Collaboratively: Looking Inside Collaborative Reflection

Articulation and Perspective Exchange

Collaborative reflection consists of a continuous process of *perspective taking and perspective making* (Boland and Tenkasi 1995): To understand experiences better, the participants exchange their perspectives on the topic reflected, assess their perspectives mutually by looking at the problem from the angle of the respective other and intertwine their views to create a solution. This can be seen in example 1, where nurses exchange their views on how to deal with the emergency alarm, and in example 3 where caregivers discussed different perspectives on how to approach residents who have tough questions. This process, as Boland and Tenkasi (1995) explain, requires from its participants the "ability to take the perspective of another into account". In the examples, workers did this by evaluating whether the solutions stemming from the perspectives of others could have helped them. In the meeting of caregivers, for example, perspectives had included lying to the resident, avoiding a clear answer by changing the topic, or being honest. In this process of exchanging perspectives, articulation (Suchman 1996) plays a decisive role (Prilla et al. 2012a): Making the rationales behind perspectives and proposed solutions explicit enables reflection participants to take the perspectives of others into account and arrive at a common solution. In example 3, the agreement to be honest to residents was made because one caregiver argued that this would also help the caregivers protect themselves against emotional stress stemming from lying to the residents.

Problem Understanding: Attribution

The shaping of attribution in the sense of "the perception of causality, or the judgement of why a particular incident occurred" (Weiner 1972) plays a decisive role in redesigning work as a result of collaborative reflection. Often, individuals stick to well-known attributions in problematic situations, such as ascribing a problem with using a computer to technical failure. Being able to create attributions based on a better problem understanding enables people create better, more sustainable solutions and thus redesign work. Collaborative reflection, as we observed, helps a group to critically discuss attributions stated by individuals and to shape the attribution of the group to be more elaborate.

In example 1, standard attributions such as blaming a problem to own inabilities or to technical issues did not work for the nurse, and he approached the head nurse. In example 2, the consultants losing pitches had attributed the losses to bad luck or difficult customers—only through a collaborative effort he learned that the real reason was different: when the group collaboratively reflected that they came up with attributions that really made a difference. We observed this shift more clearly in another example from Case 1: A group of physicians sat together to reflect on recent conversations with relatives, using notes from these talks to explain them to the others. While they explained the problematic situation in these conversations, their colleagues repeatedly stated that they should have stayed calm to avoid the problems—we were told later that this is a standard phrase that clinical educators teach young physicians. In one discussion about a talk in which a relative had become angry with a physician, the group decided not to stick with this simple attribution and found that conflicting statements given to the relatives by different physicians had actually caused the problem.

These examples show how collaborative reflection shapes the understanding of work and how successful reflection can alter work practice by making reflection participants aware of a way to go beyond standard attributions for problems and think more deeply about them.

Perceiving Work: Appraisal of Emotions

Besides understanding rationales behind work, people also need to understand and manage their own emotions and those of others (Hochschild 1979). This is particularly clear in sectors such as healthcare, in which displaying friendliness or empathy is essential in interacting with patients. However, emotions also need to be managed in the interaction with colleagues in collaborative work, as collaborators affect each other emotionally. This happens partially via emotional contagion and partially via *appraisal* of others' emotions (Parkinson and Simons 2009). Appraisal theory (Lazarus and Folkman 1984) states that emotion is about how people perceive situations, and that this perception influences subsequent emotion, and thus further action and interaction. Appraisal thus addresses the cognitive aspect of emotion. Reflection can help learners appraise emotions differently in a similar work situation in the future. As reflection on emotional experience entails re-living the emotions of the experience, reappraisal can also be a part of the reflective process. In example 3, the caregiver had been emotionally affected by the lady, who repeatedly asked whether she would be allowed to go home. During the reflection session, others directly addressed his emotional reaction with their reports and proposal. These perspectives helped the young caregiver to understand why he was affected so much and to change his perception of such situations.

Outcomes of Collaborative Reflection

Levels of Outcomes

Outcomes of reflection can be changes in attitude or perspective, or can be work redesign as we often observed in our case studies. Even if we consider only the outcome of "work redesign", this may happen at differing levels: Redesign may affect the work of individuals, teams or entire organizations, and the redesign may concern very precise, fine-granular tasks or very large, only roughly-designed procedures or guidelines for action (such as best practices, or practices originating in organisational culture). In the care home (example 3), the work of the young caregiver was redesigned in that he would approach differently the resident asking him about going home (individual and single task affected) but also the general approach of interacting with residents was changed (group and broad process affected). In the IT company, each consultant learned from the meeting how to better work with clients (individual, task) and, by agreeing to use a demo system, the consultants also changed organisational practice. The nurses agreed to change their training procedure (group, task level) and to ask for changes in the emergency procedure (organisation, process level). This shows how collaborative reflection also affects the *decision for the level of outcomes*: it not only helps the group agree on suitable solutions, but also prevents individuals from focusing solely on individual change and helps them to find an appropriate level of outcomes to sustainably change work practice.

Implementing Solutions

Collaborative reflection also includes dynamics concerning the participants of reflection: Often, solutions on a chosen level cannot be implemented by the participants of a group reflecting and, in order to implement solutions, people have to be included, who have the power, expertise or any other means to put a solution into practice. In our examples the nurses could not change the hospital emergency procedure themselves, which caused them to include management into the process, and the consultants needed to ask other colleagues to create the demo system for them. This is consistent with the finding that one reason for initialising collaborative reflection can be that a person or a group of people is required in order to find a solution at all. On the other hand, to keep up the motivation to critically reflect on own work (Kerth 2001), it is important within collaborative reflection to *also find solutions that the group can implement itself*, as it was the case for the nurses, who could change their training procedures themselves.

Representation of Redesigned Work

The outcomes of reflection can have different levels of formalization: Redesigned work may be expressed or reified in tangible artefacts, e.g., a demo system used by sales people. It may also be expressed in formal or informal rules such as the standard emergency procedure in the process manual of the hospital, or the decision to be honest to residents in the care home, which is an unwritten, informal rule. The results of work redesign may also become manifest in outcomes of work, e.g., increased success rates in sales pitches or better handling of emergencies in a hospital. For all of these targets of change, there is a need to keep track of consequences stemming from change, that is, whether new artefacts and rules actually create benefit and whether changes in work practice are feasible and effective in the sense of actually supporting work.

Implications: Needs and Challenges for Supporting Collaborative Reflection as Means to Work Redesign

Looking at our insights on reflection as a means of collaborative redesign from the perspective of tool and process support, we identified five major themes: *Connecting sessions* and *sharing and communicating in context* are general themes of collaborative reflection support, while *creating solution teams*, *articulation that talks back* and *linking and awareness* are focused on redesigning work by means of collaborative reflection. These themes describe socio-technical support needs that *complement existing interaction and communication practices*, which, as our examples underpin, need to be in place to make reflection work.

Connecting Sessions

We found that collaborative reflection is an iterative process including *multiple reflection sessions*. Such sessions can be planned or spontaneous, individual or collaborative, and in different iterations, collaborative reflection sessions will have different participants. The alternations between individual and collaborative reflection go beyond an individual briefly reflecting within a collaborative reflection session, and show how individuals consciously switch to collaborative reflection in order to better understand and redesign work practice. Thus, a process of collaborative reflection may be scattered across multiple sessions and adequate support needs to connect reflection sessions, allowing insights to be sustained across sessions and to be related to each other.

Sharing and Communicating in Context

Looking at the motivations to start collaborative reflection as an individual, we found that two major reasons are seeking clarification or resolution and creating awareness—both reasons are based on the need to re-think certain issues together with others with the intention of getting a better understanding of practice. During collaborative reflection, perspective making and taking as well as articulation play major roles, as participants need to engage in communicative interaction on shared experiences. This fits the reasons to start collaborative reflection as described above. Combining these needs to share and communicate about experiences with the intention to understand them better, tools for supporting collaborative reflection need to create a space for *sharing and communicating* in a context of experiences (see also Boud et al. 2006). There is need to *relate all communication to its context*, that is, the articulations made and experiences documented, allowing people to e.g., comment on documented experiences or criticise attributions of others (Prilla et al. 2012a). One aspect of support can be *finding and addressing reflection* partners, including filters relevant for selecting reflection partners. This need transcends known solutions for finding experts or staff with certain skills in organisations (e.g., Farrell et al. 2007; Reichling et al. 2007): To be an adequate reflection partner may take experience with situations, emotional sensitivity, expertise, power or even a lack in awareness or knowledge.

Creating Solution Teams

More specifically bound to work redesign, we found that collaborative reflection can also be triggered by *seeking support for solution implementation*—individuals are aware that the group of reflection participants needs to include people able to implement changes and thus include these people explicitly. This also holds true for the creation of outcomes from collaborative reflection, as during the creation of outcomes, people may understand which expertise, power or other abilities are needed to implement outcomes. This means that in order to be able to redesign work, there is a need to find and address these experts. Beyond this, this may mean to include them immediately into the reflection process, e.g., by sharing the context of reflection or the group communication with them remotely and immediately in order to ensure follow-up implementation of outcomes. Postponing the inclusion of necessary people after the reflection process can create a barrier caused by extra effort or lacking knowledge of whom to contact.

Learning to Understand Better: Articulation that Talks Back

In the cases, we saw repeatedly that if collaborative reflection is to lead to work redesign, the group should not stick with initial assumptions, beliefs and solutions, but has to seek a better (deeper) understanding of the solution. We found this in the improvement of (individual, simple) attribution and appraisal of emotions that resulted from group reflection sessions, when participants criticized standard or simple attributions and went deeper into understanding a problem such as e.g., why the alarm procedure did not work (Case 1). Similarly, we found that collaborative reflection shapes the level of work redesign: in many cases groups opted for a sustainable, but potentially more effort-demanding solution (e.g., changing the organizational alarm procedure instead of local changes).

The processes of reaching a better understanding by criticizing attributions, commenting emotion appraisal and questioning initial solutions play a decisive role in whether collaborative reflection leads to work redesign. The benefit and feasibility of changes derived from reflection depends on the depth of problem understanding and the associated quality of solution approaches. Going into the necessary depth needs support in which articulations of reflection participants "talk back" (Fischer and Ostwald 2003) to their authors, that is, in which attributions and other proposals are not easily accepted, but critically processed. This can be done, for example, by encouraging other participants to criticize proposals or by reminding people to create a higher level of understanding.

Linking and Awareness

Representations of redesigned work can differ a lot—from digital artefacts (e.g., demo system or process specifications) to being very informal (different attitude "agreed upon" in team). Technology support for redesigning work therefore needs to relate outcomes and their implementation to existing artefacts or rules of an organisation. When work redesign relates to implicit norms (e.g., not lying to residents, example 3), support needs to make people aware of outcomes agreed upon and remind them to take them into account in practice. Both relating to existing artefacts and making people aware might be best done if reflection support is coupled to other systems providing knowledge and supporting learning or communication in an organisation.

Conclusion and Outlook

In this paper, we investigated collaborative reflection, its potential to support iterative processes of bottom-up work redesign, and five themes for technological support for such outcome-oriented collaborative reflection. These findings affect a broad variety of workplaces, as collaborative reflection is an integral work activity at many modern workplaces and as the cases we have analyzed represent a broad bandwidth of different domains and qualification levels among workers.

The importance of collaborative reflection for organizations clearly lies in its power to enable workers to design and implement work changes bottom-up. Such redesign often performed by higher levels in organisations or by external actors such as consultants. Redesign by reflection enables people to gain an understanding of their work practice and create solutions for future work. Their group then makes sure that the solutions have an adequate quality and that they can be implemented. This, however, also creates a shift in power and responsibility that has to be embedded into existing structures and cultures, and in the end needs to be formally permitted and appreciated within the hierarchy of the organization.

Further work will address these issues as well as the implementation and evaluation of the support challenges described in this paper.

Acknowledgments MIRROR is funded under the FP7 of the European Commission (project number 257617). We would like to thank our colleagues for their contributions and valuable input during discussions. Special thanks go to Andrea, Anne, Dominik, Ian, Kevin, Manuel, Malcolm, Samia and Volker for allowing us to gain deep insights into reflection in their respective organisation.

References

Argyris, C., & Schön, D. A. (1978). *Organizational learning: A theory of action perspective*. Addison-Wesley.

Baker, D. F. (2010). Enhancing group decision making: An exercise to reduce shared information bias. *Journal of Management Education, 34*(2), 249–279.

Boland, R. J., & Tenkasi, R. V. (1995). Perspective making and perspective taking in communities of knowing. *Organization Science, 6*(4), 350–372.

Boud, D., Cressey, P., & Docherty, P. (2006). *Productive reflection at work: Learning for changing organizations*. Routledge.

Boud, D., Keogh, R., & Walker, D. (1985). Promoting reflection in learning: A model. In D. Boud., R. Keogh, & D. Walker (Eds.) *Reflection: Turning experience into learning* (pp. 18–40). London: Kogan Page.

Crowston, K., & Kammerer, E. E. (1998). Coordination and collective mind in software requirements development. *IBM Systems Journal, 37*(2), 227–245.

Daudelin, M. W. (1996). Learning from experience through reflection. *Organizational Dynamics, 24*(3), 36–48.

Dennis, A. R., George, J. F., Jessup, L. M., Nunamaker Jr, J. F., & Vogel, D. R. (1988). Information technology to support electronic meetings. *MIS Quarterly, 12*(4), 591–624.

Engeström, Y., Virkkunen, J., Helle, M., Pihlaja, J., & Poikela, R. (1996). The change laboratory as a tool for transforming work. *Life Long Learning in Europe, 2*(2), 10–17.

Eraut, M. (2004). Informal learning in the workplace. *Studies in Continuing Education, 26*(2), 247–273.

Farrell, S., Lau, T., Wilcox E., Nusser, S., & Muller, M. (2007). Socially augmenting employee profiles with people-tagging. In: *Proceedings of UIST* (pp. 91–100). New York: ACM.

Fischer, G., & Ostwald, J. (2003): Knowledge communication in design communities. In: R. Bromme, F. Hesse, & H. Spada (eds.) *Barriers and biases in computer-mediated knowledge communication* (pp 213–242). Dordrecht: Kluwer Academic Publishers.

Gray, P., Johansen, B., Nunamaker, J., Rodman, J., & Wagner, G.R. (2011). GDSS past, present, and future. In D. Schuff (Ed.) *Decision support* (pp. 1–24) Dordrecht, Heidelberg, London New York: Springer.

Hochschild, A. R. (1979). Emotion work, feeling rules, and social structure. *American Journal of Sociology, 85*(3), 551–575.

Hoyrup, S. (2004). Reflection as a core process in organisational learning. *Journal of Workplace Learning, 16*(8), 442–454.

Kerth, N.L. (2001). *Project retrospectives*. Dorset House.

Kimmerle, J., Cress, U., & Held, C. (2010). The interplay between individual and collective knowledge: Technologies for organisational learning and knowledge building. *Knowledge Management Research & Practice, 8*(1), 33–44.

Knipfer, K., Prilla, M., Cress, U., & Herrmann, T. (2011). Computer support for collaborative reflection on captured teamwork data. In: *Proceedings of the 9th International Conference on Computer Supported Collaborative Learning* (pp. 938–939).

Kolb, D.A., & Fry, R. (1975). Towards an applied theory of experiential learning. In C. Cooper (Ed.) *Theories of group processes* (pp. 33–58). London: Wiley.

Krogstie, B., Prilla, M., Wessel, D., Knipfer, K. & Divitini, M. (2012). Computer support for reflective learning in the workplace: A model. In: *Proceedings of the 2012 IEEE International Conference on Advanced Learning Technologies (ICALT 2012).*

Lazarus, R.S., & Folkman, S. (1984): *Stress, appraisal, and coping.* Springer.

Parkinson, B., & Simons, G. (2009). Affecting others: Social appraisal and emotion contagion in everyday decision making. *Personality and Social Psychology Bulletin, 35*(8), 1071–1084.

Power, D.J., & Sharda, R. (2009). Decision support systems. In *Springer handbook of automation* (pp. 1539–1548). Springer.

Prilla, M., Degeling, M., & Herrmann, T. (2012a). Collaborative reflection at work: supporting informal learning at a healthcare workplace. In: T. Finholt, H. Tellioglu, K. Inkpen, & T. Gross (Eds.) *Proceedings of the ACM International Conference on Supporting Group Work (GROUP 2012)* (pp. 55–64).

Prilla, M., Pammer, V., & Balzert, S. (2012b). The push and pull of reflection in workplace learning: Designing to support transitions between individual, collaborative and organisational learning. In A. Ravenscroft, S.N. Lindstaedt, C.D. Kloos, & D.H. Leo (Eds.) *Proceedings of the 7th European Conference on Technology Enhanced Learning* (pp. 278–291).

Reichling, T., Veith, M., & Wulf, V. (2007). Expert recommender: Designing for a network organization. *Computer Supported Cooperative Work, 16*(4), 431–465.

Reynolds, M. (1999). Critical reflection and management education: rehabilitating less hierarchical approaches. *Journal of Management Education, 23*(5), 537–553.

Roschelle, J., & Teasley, S. (1995). The construction of shared knowledge in collaborative problem solving. In: *Computer supported collaborative learning* (pp. 69–97). Heidelberg: Springer.

Schön, D. A. (1983). *The reflective practitioner.* New York: Basic Books.

Stahl, G. (2000). A model of collaborative knowledge-building. In: *Proceedings of ICLS 2000* (pp. 70–77). Ann Arbor: Lawrence Erlbaum.

Strauss, A.L., & Corbin, J.M. (1998). *Basics of qualitative research: Techniques and procedures for developing grounded theory.* Sage Publications.

Suchman, L. (1996). Supporting articulation work. In R. Kling (Ed.) *Computerization and controversy: Value conflicts and social choices* (pp. 407–423).

Sykes, R. E. (1983). Initial interaction between strangers and acquaintances— A multivariate analysis of factors affecting choice of communication partners. *Human Communication Research, 10*(1), 27–53.

Van Woerkom, M., & Croon, M. (2008). Operationalising critically reflective work behaviour. *Personnel Review, 37*(3), 317–331.

Weick, K.E. (1995). *Sensemaking in organizations.* Sage Publications.

Weick, K.E., & Roberts, K.H. (1993). Collective mind in organizations: Heedful interrelating on flight decks. *Administrative science quarterly*, 357–381.

Weiner, B. (1972). Attribution theory, achievement motivation, and the educational process. *Review of Educational Research, 42*(2), 203–215.

The Challenges of Microfinance Innovation: Understanding 'Private Services'

Muhammad Adeel, Bernhard Nett, Turkan Gurbanova, Volker Wulf and David Randall

Abstract The organization, technology and operation of microfinance have undergone much change and differentiation. Muhammad Yunus, a Nobel-prize winner first demonstrated the possible empowerment of poor people by means of microfinance. Even so, certain cases have indicated that this empowerment does not necessarily occur and that microfinance can even be damaging. In this paper, we describe a case study which describes some of the value clients do receive from an initiative of this kind but notes that this value sometimes lies in unofficial, 'private', advice and help. To this end, we conducted an ethnographic study in a microfinance institution (MFI) in Azerbaijan. We found a special pattern of interaction between MFI-staff members and customers, which both regarded as beneficial. Since, from the point of the organization, it was not recognizably part of their work, we call it a "private service". We think that the identification of similar private initiatives may help to identify new possible synergies between the operation, organization and technology in the microfinance sector. All of them are decisive for the identification of promising human–computer interaction patterns and the design of supportive computer applications.

M. Adeel (✉) · B. Nett · T. Gurbanova · V. Wulf · D. Randall
University of Siegen, Siegen, Germany
e-mail: adeel.muhammad@uni-siegen.de

B. Nett
e-mail: bernhard.nett@uni-siegen.de

T. Gurbanova
e-mail: tuerkan.qurbanova@student.uni-siegen.de

V. Wulf
e-mail: volker.wulf@uni-siegen.de

D. Randall
e-mail: d.randall@mmu.ac.uk

O. W. Bertelsen et al. (eds.), *ECSCW 2013: Proceedings of the 13th European Conference on Computer Supported Cooperative Work, 21–25 September 2013, Paphos, Cyprus*, DOI: 10.1007/978-1-4471-5346-7_14,

Introduction

During the course of the 20th century there have been many attempts to provide a credit infrastructure for the 3rd world. These programs were often very large scale but failed to reach one important target group—poor rural households—most of the time (Lipton 1977; Robinson 2001). Subsequently, the notion of microfinance became popularized as a potentially superior alternative for development and as a means to support basic needs (see e.g. Ledgerwood 1999). Muhammad Yunus, a prime mover in this shift, received the Nobel Prize for his work in the establishment of the Grameen Bank, Bangladesh, which combined the provision of financial services to the poor with mobilization, education and community building.

Today microfinance has become one of four major instruments of the United Nations in fighting extreme poverty. About one billion people live in households with a per capita income of one dollar per day (Murdoch 1999) and exclusion from credit facilities still prevails. Microfinance aims to rectify this through the provision of loans and basic financial services to the poor. At the same time, institutional factors are seen to intervene in the effectiveness of microfinance provision and it is sometimes argued that microfinance institutions (MFIs) have proved to be better equipped for this purpose than banks (Parikh et al. 2006). One basic aim is that of increasing productivity, which in turn ought to enable the repayment of debt.

From the point of view of recipients, microfinance can be used to overcome liquidity constraints (not only for investment) for instance, in lean periods of the year (Adugna 2000; Heidhues 1995; Navajas et al. 2000; Diagne and Zeller 2001). Demand for funds is often a response to crises such as diseases, accidents, legal problems, or similar unexpected events (Friedman 1992). However, these objectives are not automatically met. Market limitations and volatility may endanger success. It has been suggested that such "unproductive" credit use may even increase individual dependency and marginalization leading, in extreme cases, to despair and suicide (Biswas 2010).

Exclusion from modern infrastructure and services is at its worst in peripheral, rural areas. People do not have large financial resources at their disposal, and moreover have little experience with savings mechanisms or of interaction with modern financial organizations. For MFIs, this involves a double problem: even if the overhead costs for repayment management were more or less fixed, profit would decrease when credit declined. Further, repayment management becomes more problematic when credit-takers are inexperienced re-payers, and live in peripheral areas. As a consequence, costs are higher and such financing is unattractive for banks. It is also a reason why microfinance is either characterized by comparably high interest rates or ongoing needs for subsidies.

Thus, efforts have tended to concentrate on mere cost reduction. Rhyne and Otero (1992), for instance, argue that MFIs with a high outreach are more sustainable and, therefore, better suited for poverty alleviation. Focusing on extensive growth and economies of scale is often accompanied by a reductive policy of equating microfinance with credit management, and technology development with automation. As a result, microfinance initiatives have been subject to some critique. Hence: *"not all microfinance produces favorable results, especially for poor people working in low-return activities in saturated markets that are poorly developed and where environmental and economic shocks are common"* (Hulme 2000).

According to Buckley (1997) the commonly used success indicators of microfinance reveal nothing about their impact on poverty. The impact of microfinance upon poverty reduction, it is argued, can only be identified by studying socio-cultural and economic factors in specific cases over a longer period of time (De Angela et al. 2004). Such evaluative measures, however, have not often been taken since they entail significant effort, not to mention cost, and require expertise. One result is that we have very few studies which tell us how clients use their loans.

The lack of such knowledge makes it very difficult to envision appropriate services and products, for instance, in terms of financial education of clients, management-support, value-chain enhancement and other 'social' services. Microfinance, that is, cannot in and of itself be a guaranteed solution for all development problems, nor even for poverty reduction. Such issues are seldom addressed in discussions on the role of technology for microfinance, which is thus hitherto characterized by little interest in enabling opportunities in terms of product, techniques and/or technology (Buckley 1997).

If, as we have suggested, microfinance initiatives are mediated by institutional and cultural factors then it is worth examining how these operate. It would seem, given the obstacles to growth on the part of MFIs and the paucity of knowledge about the behavior of borrowers and the possible affordances of new technology (Tamgaki 2006) that empirical investigation might prove valuable.

It is known that MFIs attempt to control the process by limiting loans in various ways and by providing 'coaching' for credit-takers, or by otherwise supporting them. The Grameen Bank, for instance, gives its mostly female credit-takers significant educational and community-building support. This work shapes customer relations, which are seen as central to the lending process (Churchill and Halpern 2001). In this way, microfinance can in principle produce known "side-effects" such as education, community building and mobilization.

Much of the "side-activities" which have made Yunus' Grameen Bank sustainable in its efforts to reduce poverty might be supported or even enabled by means of computer technology. Our point, however, is that this will not happen without a systematic understanding of the particularities of microfinance. Cultural factors, infrastructural fallibility (or indeed its absence when talking specifically about internet capacity), educational background and low levels of literacy, as well as the nature of institutional practice may all be relevant. How the interplay between economy, technology and culture might be understood and mobilized, then, is the topic of our enquiries.

Method

We are still far from an understanding of the interplay between operation, organization and technology in the microfinance sector. Nugroho and Millies (2009) differentiate between "innovation for microfinance" and "microfinance for innovation": the automation of credit-data management being an example for the first, and the introduction of an information service about current fish prices offered to fisher clients by an MFI of the second. Nugroho and Millies point out that, in spite of the crucial importance of the latter for poverty-reducing impacts of microfinance, it is receiving much too little attention.

One reason is, as Datar et al. (2008) argue, that most MFIs are still institution-centered, focusing only on high customer numbers. Effective microfinance clearly requires that support for clients be maintained and, if possible, improved via the use of new technology and/or new organizational procedures. How this can be done is evidently a question that goes beyond mere automation.

Further, quite distinct problems occur when one is researching the behavior of microfinance clients- problems which include ethics and privacy issues as well as the practical difficulties associated with researching for special and disadvantaged user groups, for example, disabled people (Pullin and Newell 2007) or illiterate users (see e.g. Mehdi et al. 2009). Below, we argue that researching MFIs entails some development of the ethnographic enterprise.

The work we describe can be thought of as belonging to the 'turn to the social' which moved design concerns away from the merely technical towards serious consideration of the relationship between the computer artifact and the use to which it is put. Much of the debate about this has been focused on the problem of 'requirements' or, in its later version, 'implications for design'. Classically, of course, requirements were thought of in functional (task completion) terms, or non-functional (satisfying a need). The critique of this policy largely had to do with both the naïve conception of task and of 'need' implied in this vision.

Requirements engineering, hitherto conceived of in mainly technical terms (IEEE 830 1993) slowly moved towards a view which hinged on the notion of 'work'- what it is that people actually do when they go about their business. Key to this was the recognition that technical functionality does not necessarily prescribe the use to which the technology will be put (or indeed, whether it will be used at all). Of course, this also entailed various methodological moves, and ethnographic stances became popularized. This, in turn, required ethnographic traditions to undergo some transformation.

The classic view of ethnography as the 'stranger' arriving at distant shores and becoming enculturated over a period of (usually) years has turned into something very different, and often contested. Ethnography, as practiced in CSCW and HCI is not (and cannot be—see Clifford and Marcus 1984) an exercise in complete understanding of a culture but approximates instead to a systematic attempt to understand what features of cultural practice are relevant to the putative introduction of new technology and how we should deal with its consequences (see e.g. Randall et al. 2007). Exactly how this is to be done is an unresolved question.

This is made increasingly complex when we consider a further aspect. If we consider research of the kind we describe to be, broadly, part of HCI for development, something distinctive may be implicated in relation to 'customer facing' work. Many CSCW studies have historically focused mainly on institutional arrangements (see e.g. Harper et al. 2000), in development-related work our understanding of the cultural features entailed in 'being a customer' are equally, if not more, important.

It is anything but illegitimate to claim that ethnographic and other documentary practice in CSCW and HCI should have some relationship to design. However, the question is what kind of relationship it should be. There has to be some relationship between qualitative studies of the kind exemplified by 'ethnography' and - in the end—a product specification. That is, the design business is and must be predicated on both technical and 'social' aspects.

Meta-design (Fischer 1999), we suggest, provides a means to reflect upon the designer-client relation as well as the design of a product which supports both user practices and innovation possibilities. Meta-design is intended to overcome the problems of the 'present' as against the 'future' embedded in the work study-design relationship by combining participation and support for design experience in processes of seeding, evolutionary growth and reseeding (Fischer 1998): thus it does not simply delegate the responsibility for problems to the clients, but tries to use the design experience of the experts to enable and facilitate participation and ultimately organizational change (Wulf et al. 1999).

We draw here on Schütz and Luckmann (1973), who attempted to explain why the construction of technology is complicated and error-prone through their conception of the "natural attitude". The assumption is one of simplicity—we assume others' motives for behavior are much like our own, born of routine experience. As such, the world has a 'taken for granted' character which is not ideal for the reflective consideration of change possibilities. Conscious reflection on critical exceptions and new possibilities necessitates an orientation to the world of the 'other'. This requires something more akin to the 'scientific' attitude, in Schütz and Luckmann's terms.

In CSCW, a conceptual locus for discussions of this kind has been that of the 'boundary object' (Star and Griesemer 1989) and 'articulation work' (Schmidt and Bannon1992), both terms appropriated in origin from Strauss (1988). Articulation work is something that (often) takes place over and above immediate task- based behavior and can have an "invisible" character (see Star and Strauss 1999). For Schmidt and Bannon (1992) the identification of articulation work is a prerequisite for the design of technological support for cooperative work, the mutual dependencies of which might otherwise become disregarded and possibly disabled. Cabitza et al. (2009) show how different influences on work within one organization (i.e. a hospital) may be modeled as an inter-articulation of different work systems which strive for maintenance. However, microfinance for innovation does not only have to deal with work systems beyond the MFI, it also has to address the fact that these systems may not exist at the time of investigation.

As a result, ethnographic approaches to the design of microfinance technology have concentrated upon innovation in microfinance. Ratan et al. "digital slate" allows automatically validated data input in areas without electrical- and internet connection, while allowing data transfer at a later moment, when the slate may be read out and data sent when field officers return to well-connected places. Their "digital slate" thus addresses the problematic "last mile" of development. Nevertheless, it concentrates on the automation of credit management as its primary objective.

To understand the relationship between technology, organization and operation in microfinance, rather than accept an 'automation' agenda uncritically, we conducted ethnographic research in an MFI in Azerbaijan, which we will call "ABC". This institution was also an application partner. We should point out here that research of this kind, which relies on the participation of new institutions, may be politically and ethically sensitive. It may involve research subjects with a limited point of view and can be fraught with difficulty (see Wulf et al. 2011).

This became painfully clear to us when our first application partner, a Pakistan MFI, unexpectedly stopped its collaboration with the first author of this paper, a native Pakistani, without clear explanation after a first ethnography (Adeel et al. 2010) had been conducted. As a result, we had to look for some other organization open for cooperation with us. We subsequently contacted a number of organizations by means of email or phone. A promising reply came from an umbrella organization for MFIs in Azerbaijan. This led to a workshop where we presented our research-and-development interests. This workshop was attended by staff members from diverse Azeri MFIs. Although CEOs were not present, the workshop opened doors, and meetings with the CEOs of two MFIs were arranged. One of these MFIs (as already mentioned we shall call it "ABC") became our application partner.

Our first research visit in Azerbaijan focused on branches in Baku, and in Sumgait and Sabirabad. Sumgait is close to Baku, while Sabirabad is located in a remote area more than 200 km from Baku (the MFI provided us with transportation facilities). Approximately 25 semi-structured interviews were conducted. A native speaker (co-authoring this paper) assisted by translating, interpreting and transcribing. The CEO of ABC announced our study to the bank staff and asked for support. Subsequent interviews with staff lasted from 2 to 2.5 h and were largely unproblematic. Interviews with clients were not so straightforward. At first, the clients to be interviewed were selected by the management of the MFI. We felt that a second round with a more—as far as possible—independently arrived at sample and some more in-depth questioning should be found and used. Even so, such interviews tended to be much shorter (an average of 10 min).

At our second research visit, we selected the regions of Imishli, Sabirabad and Saatli, as we wanted to re-use some of our initial contacts as well as new ones. New contacts were furnished through cascading. Initial contacts, after some trust building work, often proved willing to introduce us to other clients. We used a semi- structured interview protocol and focused on the kinds of problem that credit- seekers faced. Some loan officers allowed us to accompany them to the field area, where we could directly observe each detail of the process from application till disbursement.

After our return, the more than 40 digitally recorded interviews were transcribed and translated into English. Strauss and Corbin's (1998) Grounded Theory was used to analyze the data by help of MAXQDA. Both field notes and interview data were coded and the categories further analyzed under an articulation-work perspective which differentiated between formal work organization and actual work practices.

Poverty in Azerbaijan

In spite of the fact that the agriculture produces only 6 % of GDP, it constitutes the workplace of, and subsistence for, almost 40 % of the Azerbaijan labor force. In the long run, the availability of land and natural resources has made agriculture an attractive income source (World Bank Report 2011) but the very small average size of farms and the poor infrastructure are poverty risks.

Poverty became a greater problem in Azerbaijan in the years 1988-1992 due to separation from the Soviet Union and the Karabagh war following it. Prior to this, farmers had been working in large, bureaucratic kolkhozes. Income was secure if not substantial, productivity was limited, and there were only a few incentives to increase it. According to the Survey of Living Conditions (Encyclopedia of the United Nations (w/o year) 2010) the percentage of the population below the poverty line rose to 61 % in the post-war period. The former *kolkhoz* land was largely appropriated by a group of influential people who started to rent it to the former farm workers. Due to this insecure situation, the latter widely accepted land reform, in which 95 % of the plowed land was given to the farmers (the rest of 5 % is owned by the government) (Habibov 2011).

Responsibility for the provision of rural infrastructure and rural services such as water and gas was allocated to the so-called "*belediye*" (a communal institution) after the abolition of the *Kolkhozes* and this transition has caused some difficulties. Although school education remains mandatory in every region in Azerbaijan, higher education remains problematic on the countryside, mainly because rural young need to support household effort (Habibov 2011).

In urban areas, documented poverty has declined from 46.7 % (2003) to 29.3 % (2005) as governmental programs and the oil boom have helped ameliorate the urban situation, in particular in the capital, Baku (State Program on Poverty Reduction and Sustainable Development 2008). Thus, the differences between the rural and metropolitan areas are large. For instance, while in urban areas many women tend to have jobs, female work in the countryside is mostly household-based and thus without an individual work contract. In turn, while agricultural performance has remained more or less stable when compared to other non-oil activities, rural areas remain those with the lowest income levels (State Program on Poverty Reduction and Sustainable Development 2008).

Findings

The Microfinance Institution "ABC"

ABC is an MFI which was established in 1996 to fight poverty in Azerbaijan after the Karabagh war. ABC is part of an international microfinance fund. In 2003, ABC became a limited-liability company and started working as an MFI. The goal of ABC is to provide loans to individuals who are too poor to get a loan at commercial banks. Sometimes ABC cooperates with local non-government- and capacity-building organizations.

ABC's operation is divided into geographical units such as regions and branches. However, ABC operates mainly in urban areas, one focus being the capital Baku. Currently, 350 staff members are serving 48,515 active clients. There is a 'top down' approach to organizational change, as one might expect in a highly centralized and somewhat bureaucratic institution.

ABC is actually trying to further formalize the process of loan-management and installment-collection. In this context, loan officers are expected to be mere policy executors instead and local initiative in respect of policy innovation is not encouraged. It is interesting to note that, according to the CEO of ABC, our talks provided inspiration for the MFI to reflect on its customer relationships and the potential for restructuring. That is, insights from 'outsiders' seemed to be valued more highly than those offered by local experts.

Among the criteria required to become a client is the necessity to reside in the branch cover area, to not be in default of loans from another bank and to own a running business. ABC offers an agricultural and an urban micro-loan and an agriculture small loan as well (all of them an individual and group-based version). Moreover, there are family loans and household loans. Loan products range from 15 to 20,000$ with 2.7 to 3.5 % interest rate (interest is calculated only on the principle amount). The ratio of female clients is low. ABC is taking initiatives to increase the number of female clients and looks favorably on initiates for social development.

The Loan Process

The loan process starts with the application. The client needs to come to the bank by him-/herself to be informed about the conditions of any loan. This is done on a face-to-face basis (Fig. 1). We should remind ourselves that this can mean clients travelling 50 km or even more. The client has to provide some basic information which later on is used for the "full" application. The next document to be filled out is the poverty scoring card containing a table of items such as cars, computers, the number of family members and children. (Missing) crosses indicate that these (do not) exist in the household of the client. Additionally, the client must provide the

Fig. 1 Field officer (second from *right*) in a discussion about a group loan

loan officer of ABC with his personal ID and a marriage certificate, if such document exists.

Subsequently, and in a monitoring process, the household or business of the potential client is visited and evaluated. On this occasion, the loan officer informs the client about a possible maximum loan amount available for him. In case of acceptance the loan officer forwards the documents to the *loan committee,* which consists of a branch accountant, a branch manager, and the Senior Loan Officer.

When the client is informed about the committee decisions, he/she is asked again about willingness to take the loan and the consequences of the decision. When the response is positive, the loan officer makes the client sign the documents and forwards these documents to the accountant. The accountant elaborates all the necessary documents (i.e. payment record, time table of installment payback, pledge record if necessary), a process of 3–5 days. In the rather widespread case of a gold pledge (gold is a standard measure of wealth in rural areas), a gold smith comes to the branch and values the gold in presence of the account officer, the senior officer and the client, before the senior loan officer packs and seals it in front of all present people. The gold will be returned on maturity of the loan.

At the end, the client may take the money from the cashier. Some years ago, ABC only used third-party commercial banks for this purpose (and to collect payments, as well). Due to increasing competition, ABC has started its own money service.

The Media Infrastructure

The international fund of which ABC is part has tried to establish one identical software solution for all their MFIs worldwide by establishing the software used in its US organizations, but for various reasons beyond the scope of this paper, has failed. In a next step, a MIS was bought from a Swiss company to be implemented in all MFIs, an effort which failed again. As a result, ABC has invested into in-house-developed IS, but there are still problems around it. Currently the international fund's MFIs in Caucasus region are trying to develop a new common standard MIS for the region.

ABC has invested a large amount of money into ICT. As a result, all branches are equipped with a basic ICT infrastructure including computer, fax, telephone, internet. On the branch level, however, it remains the case that the number of computers is much lower than the number of staff members. LOs do not have access to the MIS and thus cannot reach the MIS data in their own portfolio, in particular, the records of "their" clients. This is a significant problem for them, as they quite often have to deal with problems of clients.

In respect of technological innovation, the IT department plays an important role. But there is a big gap between this department and the rest of the company. In a repetition of classic scenarios historically found in more developed organizations, we find little communication between the IT department and other departments, partly because users are not regarded as competent in the use of ICT. The IT department had never used any empirical or participatory method when dealing with future users such as cashiers, accountants or loan officers. At present, ICT is playing no significant role in interactions between clients and LOs.[1]

The Poverty Scoring Card

As evaluation of the impacts of microfinance is not easy (Brau and Woller 2004), poverty scoring cards were proposed by Mark Schreiner, Microfinance Risk Management LLC. The international fund directed ABC to make use of this instrument. As a result, ABC hired international consultants for the design of a poverty scorecard. Only the second version was accepted and implemented with the participation of the marketing department of ABC.

This poverty scoring card is effectively a 'spotlight' on the socio-economic situation of a client applying for a loan. Generated before the loan and without diachronic sensitivity, it provides no means to observe effects of microfinance on

[1] There was one exception: ABC tried to automatically send SMS to clients in order to remind them of upcoming installment deadlines. However, the clients obviously interpreted this service as disruptive and an imputation of unreliableness, which they resented. In turn, ABC stopped the service.

clients over time. So the poverty scoring card appears to be mainly a device for analyzing the status of people who apply for loans, not for assessing whether the loans have any positive effect.

In fact, LOs have little sense of what the poverty score card might or might not be used for beyond their immediate context. For them, it acts primarily as an informal 'risk assessment' tool: if the sum of weighted criteria was below a certain threshold, the applicant is not considered attractive.

Articulation Work

The poverty scoring card actually becomes a primary resource for record keeping among LOs, but not in its original form. Loan officers, in fact, habitually input the data it contains into other, locally managed, records. Some loan officers with their own computers store the local records on them, others use handwritten notebooks. This means that while data is stored in a central MFI, there is no mechanism at the field level to digitalize valuable additional data and make them accessible to other loan officers.

Among the informal data collected and maintained in this manner is the loan period, the appearance of the client, his/her ownership of certain goods, the number of children, the kind of home, monthly spending on meat, sweets, education etc., all of which are documented in a variety of ways. Further information is collected about mobile phone numbers, address, type of business, additional persons of importance, structure of family, qualifications and competences, etc. The data collected differs from one loan officer to another one. Loan officers verify the data during their visit to the client.

Loan officers also, in much the same way, develop client histories (thus developing precisely an informal version of the information that the poverty scoring card does not provide). Often they use their local records as kind of workaround, bypassing problems of lack of access to the MIS: instead of asking a cashier or an accountant, loan officers effectively use their own local data-bases. This has much in common with historical problems associated with the use of MIS systems documented by Harper et al. (2000) in their discussion of the 'bibles' that building society operatives preferred to MIS data. Managing local records in this way is a kind of 'articulation work' because it is a significant resource in the management of lending officer- client relations and for making local comparisons with other lending officers and with cashiers.

It turns out that loan officers are more involved in their clients' lives than appeared at first sight. They often, for instance, used informal sources of information to clarify the poverty level of the clients (for instance, well-informed local individuals). In case of payment delay they sometimes used the close ties with the village location of a client by, for instance, informing the father or uncle of the defaulter. Loans, in other words, have a normative dimension.

This is also true in relation to advice. Loan officers reported the need to be extremely careful about responding to questions and to requests for help by the clients. In this context, many interviewees (not only loan officers) report that they have experienced difficulties as a result of advice given. This becomes particularly difficult in cases where advice about possible collaboration is given: one case was reported to us, for instance, in which one party claimed compensation for a collaboration which failed, but which had been initiated on advice from the bank. Helping clients turns out, in other words, to be as risky in normative terms as it is in economic terms. It also, of course, implicates a work overhead. Nevertheless, the loan officers sometimes provide assistance. Partly this was to maintain their portfolio, the critical indicator for their success in the bank: they were, put simply, dependent upon satisfied clients if they want to find new ones.

Further Practices

The help of the loan officers generally rested on personal relationships rather than institutional policy. Usually their help lay in providing information, as they were often the only access the poor had to expert knowledge or market information. For instance, information about market prices of vegetables was frequently given to vegetable-growing clients.

Transportation, for instance, was a major issue in the rural areas especially for rural working poor. Clients such as dairy farmers or cattle/sheep owners often reported themselves to be in need of transportation. Currently their opportunities appear to be very limited, and if they cannot find a transport provider, they suffer losses. For poor people who do not posses many goods it is extremely important to be able to share transportation facilities, or to share orders for the use of a tractor or truck, since to do so alone would be much too expensive. Transportation of such small units of goods seems to be critical for rural poor in Azerbaijan. Such information was also shared with clients.

One loan officer reported using his local records on individual clients to help other clients. He provided a client eager to buy a satellite receiver with the phone number of a client who ran a shop selling this kind of product. This meant that the service provided was more akin to that of a 'community broker' or 'human yellow pages' and was beyond that expected by the MFI. The point here is that landlines are scarce and mobile phones often not internet-enabled. Finding relevant information, then, is difficult.

Discussion

Supporting Articulation Work

Like most MFIs, ABC is looking for high numbers of loans and payments with equal attention being paid to the possibilities for profit and the minimization of potential loss. But for ABC such high numbers are a challenge, among others, as technological "help" from outside (i.e. the MIS systems) has not really been helpful in enabling them to assess these risks. When even basic data management is not running at an optimum, further information demands (for instance, for a poverty scoring card) can easily appear as nothing more than another external irritation for the organization.

Partly as a result, ABC is focusing on clients with an income just below that of clients of the commercial banks, not on the poorest groups in society: as the cost of managing payments is more or less independent of the value of the payments, higher loans are better for the financial sustainability of an MFI than small ones. This was one underlying reason for ABC to act like a mini-bank. A senior MFI staff member spoke about strategies to "grow with the clients", giving ever larger credits to clients in order become more like a regular bank over time. In contrast, their image as an MFI, especially among lower level staff, was sometimes a source of pride when contrasted with the machinations of regular banks.

Besides the development of the MIS, the IT department is currently only invoked in cases of media breakdowns or purchasing necessities. When designing the new MIS, the IT department neither communicated with local actors nor made any attempt to understand the practical information difficulties or needs of local officers. Articulation work of the kind we describe has not been rendered visible in ICT development. Integrating it into the definition of technological visions should make technology decisions much better informed.

In technological terms there is no obstacle to an integration of the local records into the MIS, as loan officers could share the available computers on the basis of differentiated user access rights and be integrated by means of existing internet connections. However, as already indicated in approaches such as Integrated Organization and Technology Development (OTD) (Wulf et al. 1999), organizational measures may be a necessary precondition of technological ones.

In this regard, one can envisage a process where loan officers establish a common scheme for locally managed client data. This would allow a more constructive poverty scoring card to be developed as well as conferring other potential benefits such as the sharing of data. The establishment of common metadata does not prevent the loan officers from storing individual data of their own, as well. In order to do so, organizational policy concerning the private versus the public nature of data would have to be developed. As we have pointed out, some of this data has normative consequences.

Private Services

However, and as we have tried to stress, the routine practices of loan officers went well beyond procedural matters entailed in the management of local records. The personal help related to the information about a satellite shop was only possible by using the resources (data) of the organization, but in an improvised, private manner. From the point of the organization it was not recognizably part of their work, but a private initiative. Furthermore, there was no obvious inter-dependency: the organization did neither win nor lose in any direct sense- at least in the short term. To put this into a more 'managerial' form, the organization had no formal customer relationship model (CRM), and was unaware of the potential benefits of customer support to the long term future of the organization.

Schumpeter (1934), when analyzing the role of theory (i.e. technological inventions) on social change, argued that to transform inventions into innovations is to embed ideas into social conditions. The social and normative arrangements we outlined above do not constitute a product or service in any strict economic sense and remain a largely private and personal kind of support. In this sense they are beyond the articulation of work in the MFI. Nevertheless they constitute 'social capital' of the organization. This concept, originating with Coleman (1988), is being increasingly used in the context of organizational development and knowledge management (see e.g. Nahapiet and Ghoshal 1998; Burt 2005). These non-material resources are regarded as increasingly important in the development of expertise both on an institutional and on a personal level.

Burt's notion of 'brokerage' and 'closure' is of relevance here. Brokerage refers to the activities of people who live at the intersecting of social worlds, who can see and develop good ideas. This accurately describes the role of loan officers in the MFI. Closure is the tightening of coordination on a closed network of people. The long-term development of client and loan officer competence arguably necessitates, whether through technology or other means, strategies for sharing and developing social capital for the appropriate network of people, and what that 'appropriate' network will look like is a matter of organizational learning.

We have given only a few examples of the kinds of knowledge and expertise that local officers are able to deploy in support of client relationships but all such knowledge, at least of the kind we have described can, in principle, be embedded in systems of one kind or another—systems which might be used at the organizational level we have been working with but which, again in principle, might also be deployed directly to clients in the future. Transportation information and transport sharing networks are one simple example of this.

Thus, local records may thus become important seeds (Fischer 1998) for user-centered services. The necessary data already exist, but in private and local forms. Translating this information into standard formats is non- trivial. Moreover, some forms of knowledge-kinship and other arrangements, for instance-imply some very serious ethical issues. Even so, and our argument here is very much to do with the need for organizations like MFIs to embed themselves in a more real way in the lives and experiences of local populations, this is a vehicle for developing trustful client—officer relations.

Such development is, of course, not without risks. Even among the providers of the private services, there was widespread scepticism against systematic help for the clients, motivated by examples in which help had proven problematic. Our view is that such occasions are in large part a function of their 'private and personal' status and of the unequal relationship between officers and clients.

Again, and in the long term, developing a customer relationship through the building of social capital might render this relationship less unequal, and might reduce risk both for the organization and for the client.

This is a speculation, and we should not exaggerate the possibilities. We need to consider what would be needed to transform the individual, unsystematic help for clients into organizationally supported products for clients. Such a development requires a relationship with our application partner which involves not only the development of a technological apparatus to be used in ways not previously envisaged- as an information resource for local loan officers and ultimately for clients- but also reflection on the part of the organization about the role of its IT department and on its vision of necessary skill levels as against procedural forms on the part of loan officers. Such transformations are not easily arrived at.

Conclusion

Our work forms part of the burgeoning interest in HCI for development (HCI4D-see Ho et al. 2009 for a useful summary of issues). As Ho et al. say: *"We contend that appropriate, human centered designing and contextually sensitive designs of digital ICTs are necessary, although clearly, these have not been sufficient conditions to enable effective use of ICT to support development outcomes. Kleine and Unwin (2009) have recently raised concerns that the discourse in ICT4D… is paying too little attention to the role of previous generations of information and communication technologies, such as writing, printing, telephony, radio, and TV. Because of its concern with properly understanding contexts before designing ICT interventions, HCI4D research (when done well) pays careful attention to existing information and communication technologies and practices."*

To which we can only add that insufficient attention is often paid to the way in which local cultures (and attendant levels of knowledge and expertise) and institutional arrangements (with their attendant levels of knowledge and expertise) intersect. To change this necessitates an amalgam of skills rooted in, but not encompassed by, those of the traditional ethnographer. The ethnographer, in such a context, needs all of the cultural sensitivities as well as the methodological competencies that are conventionally reported.

The demand for client-centered innovation in microfinance (Datar et al. 2008) is one specific case. Technological innovation in microfinance does not seem to be satisfying for exactly the reasons that Ho et al. outline. Indeed, visible in the demand for standardized international formats, it even sometimes appears to be driving in the opposite direction (Adeel et al. 2010).

Considering microfinance for innovation Waterfield and Ramsing's (1998) description of the MIS in microfinance as little understood may be reformulated: the cultural context of microfinance has not yet been studied enough. At the same time, the ethnographer needs the capacity to judge what technological possibilities there might be in the context of local material and infrastructural conditions and how those technologies might be embedded in an organization with an existing technology infrastructure. In the context of HCI4D—and in a number of related contexts (see e.g. Wulf et al. 2013 forthcoming)—the nature of the sensitivities and skills that are required is not yet fully understood.

We have shown how—in the context of microfinance—there is only a very limited body of work, which tries to reflect these conditions. Most research on microfinance and technology focuses on innovation in microfinance, not on microfinance for innovation. Ethnographic approaches such as Ratan et al. (2010) are no exception in this respect. This may have to do with economic interests, but may partly also be a result of the lack of competences which engage with both the technical and the social elements that are implied with meta-design (Fischer 1999): the task of finding promising applications that support microfinance for innovation involves identifying the disempowerment which is to be overcome, the human–computer-interaction patterns that might help—and methods to identify both.

We found that for the latter purpose, private services could be of heuristic value. Using organizational resources to satisfy existing demands on an unofficial level means private services are operated in a grey (sometimes even illegal) zone. Even so, in the case we describe, the private service was beneficial for the organization; nevertheless it was beyond the legal operation of the MFI: by way of example, debtors′ information documented in local records was used on one occasion to help a person to find a shop in which he could buy a certain product.

Any transformation of private services into products or technologies would require a change of the overall strategy of the organization—and implicates a change which could be problematic. Private services are- obviously- private. This means no-one else, including management, has access to this information. Sharing them requires careful consideration of who should be entitled to use this information and when. The identification of private services could, therefore, improve strategic reflexivity. At the same time, as we have demonstrated, it could help to identify existing needs and opportunities of microfinance for innovation.

References

Adeel, M., Nett, B., & Wulf, V. (2010). Innovating the field level of microfinance—A Pakistan case study, In: *Proceedings of the International Conference on Information and Communication Technologies for Development,* ISBN: 978-1-4503-0787-1. New York:ACM.

Adugna, H. S. (2000). The comparative study of rotating credit associations. *Journal of the Royal Anthropological Institute, 94*(1), 201–229.

Biswas, S. (2010). India's micro-finance suicide epidemic. In: *BBC News South Asia* http://www.bbc.co.uk/news/world-south-asia-11997571.

Brau, J. C., & Woller, G. M. (2004). Microfinance—A comprehensive review of the existing literature. *Journal of Entrepreneurial Finance and Business Ventures, 9*(1), 1–26.

Buckley, G. (1997). Microfinance in Africa: Is it either the problem or the solution. *World Development, 25*(7), 1081–1093.

Burt, R. S. (2005). *Brokerage and closure: An introduction to social capital.* Oxford: Oxford University Press.

Cabitza, F., Simone, C., & Sarini, M. (2009). Leveraging coordinative conventions to promote collaboration awareness. *Journal Computer Supported Cooperative Work, 18*(4), 301–330.

Churchill, C. F., & Halpern, S. S. (2001). *Building customer loyalty*. http://centerforfinancialinclusionblog.files.Wordpress.com/2011/10/building-customer-loyalty.pdf.

Clifford, J., & Marcus, G. E. (1984). *Writing culture. The poetics and politics of ethnography*. Berkeley, CA: University of California Press.

Coleman, J. S. (1988). Social capital in the creation of human capital. *American Journal of Sociology, 94*, 95–120.

Datar, S., Epstein, M., & Yuthas, K. (2008). Clients must come first. In: *Microfinance, Stanford Social Innovation Review* vol. 9. Stanford: Leland Stanford Jr. University Publisher.

De Angela, A., Athavankar, U., Joshi, A., Coventry, L. M., & Johnson, G. (2004). Introducing ATMs in India: A contextual inquiry. *Interacting with Computers, 16*(1), 29–44.

Diagne, A., Zeller, M. (2001). *Access to credit and its impact in Malawi*. Washington, D.C: International Food Policy Research Institute (IFPRI) (Research Report No. 116).

Encyclopedia of the United Nations (w/o year). (2000). http://www.nationsencyclopedia.com/economies/Asia-and-the-Pacific/Azerbaijan-POVERTY-AND-WEALTH.html.

Fischer, G. (1998). Seeding, evolutionary growth and reseeding: Constructing, capturing and evolving knowledge in domain-oriented design environments. *Automatic Software Engineering, 5*(4), 447–464.

Fischer, G. (1999). *Symmetry of igorance, social creativity, and meta-design creativity and cognition* (pp. 116–123). Loughsborough, U.K.: ACM.

Friedman, J. (1992). *Empowerment—The politics of alternative development*. Oxford: Blackwell.

Habibov, N. (2011). *Caucasus Analytical Digest No. 34*. December 21st, 2011, Windsor, Canada. http://www.css.ethz.ch/publications/pdfs/CAD-34-13-15.pdf.

Harper, R., Randall, D., & Rouncefield, M. (2000a). *Fieldwork for design theory and practice*. London: Springer.

Harper, R., Randall, D., & Rouncefield, M. (2000b). *Organisational change and retail finance: An ethnographic perspective*. London: Routledge.

Heidhues, F. (1995). Rural finance markets—An important tool to fight poverty. *Quarterly Journal of International Agriculture, 34*(2), 105–108.

Ho, M. R., Smyth, T. N., Kam, M., & Dearden, A. (2009). (2009): *Human-computer interaction for development: The past, present, and future. USC Annenberg School for Communication & Journalism, 5*(4), 1–18. Published under creative commons attribution—Non commercial-share alike, Winter.

Hulme, D. (2000). Is microdebt good for poor people? A note on the dark side of microfinance. *Journal of Small Enterprise Development, 11* (1), 26–28.

IEEE. (1993). *IEEE Standard 830-1993, Recommended Practice for Software Requirements Specifications*.

Ledgerwood, J. (1999). *Microfinance handbook: An institutional and financial perspective*. Washington, DC: World Bank.

Lipton, M. (1977). *Why poor people stay poor. Urban bias in world development*. London: Temple Smith.

Medhi, I., Gautama, S. N. N., & Toyama, K. (2009). A comparison of mobile money-transfer UIs for non-literate and semi-literate users. In: *HCI '09 Proceedings of the 27th International Conference on Human Factors in Computing Systems*, pp. 1741–1750.

Morduch, J. (1999). The microfinance promise. *Journal of Economic Literature 37*(XXXVII), 1569–1614.

Nahapiet, J., & Ghoshal, S. (1998). Social capital, intellectual capital, and the organizational advantage. *Academy of Management Review, 23*(2), 242–266.

Navajas, S., Schreiner, M., Meyer, R. L., Gonzales-Vega, C., & Rodrigues-Meza, J. (2000). Microcredit and the poorest of the poor: Theory and evidence from Bolivia. *World Development, 28*(2), 333–346.

Nugroho, Y., & Milies, I. (2009). *Microfinance & Innovation.* Mini study: Global review of innovation intelligence and policy studies. http://grips-public.mediactive.fr/knowledge_base/dl/786/orig_doc_file/..

Parikh, T., Javid, P., Sasikumar, K., & Ghosh, K. (2006). Mobile phones and paper documents: Evaluating a new approach for capturing microfinance data in rural India. In: Proceedings SIGHCI 2006 (pp. 551–560). New York: ACM.

Pullin, G., Newell, A. F. (2007): 'Focussing on extra-ordinary users. In: *Proceeding HCII 2007*, Beijing, 22–27 July (Lecture Notes in Computer Science). ISBN: 978354073278-5, pp. 253–262.

Randall, D., Harper, R., & Rouncefield, M. 2007. *Fieldwork for design.* London: Springer.

Ratan, A. L., Chakraborty, S., Chitnis, P. V., Toyama, K., Ooi, K. S., Phiong, M., & et al. (2010). Managing micro-finance with paper, pen and digital slate, In: *Proceedings of the International Conference on Information and Communication Technologies for Development, ISBN: 978-1-4503-0787-1.* New York: ACM.

Rhyne, E., & Otero, M. (1992). Financial services for microenterprises: Principles and institutions. *World Development, 20*(11), 1561–1571.

Robinson, M. (2001). *The microfinance revolution sustainable finance for the poor.* Washington, DC: World Bank.

Schmidt, K., & Bannon, L. (1992). Taking CSCW seriously: Supporting articulation work, In: *Computer Supported Cooperative Work (CSCW) 1*(1), 7–40 (An international journal).

Schumpeter, J. A. (1934). *The Theory of Economic Development: An inquiry into profits, capital, credit, interest and the business cycle.* Cambridge, Mass: Harvard University Press.

Schütz, A., & Luckmann, Th. (1973). *The structures of the life-world.* Evanston, Illinois: Northwestern University Press.

Star, S. L., & Griesemer, J. R. (1989). Institutional ecology, "Translations" and boundary objects: Amateurs and professionals in Berkeley's museum of vertebrate zoology. *Social Studies of Science, 19*(1989), 387–420.

Star, S. L., & Strauss, A. L. (1999). Layers of silence, arenas of voice: The ecology of visible and invisible work. *Computer-Supported Cooperative Work (CSCW): The Journal of Collaborative Computing, 8*, 9–30.

State Program on Poverty Reduction and Sustainable Development. (2008). In: The Republic of Azerbaijan for 2008–2015 (w/o year). http://www.cled.az/pdf/others/Azerbaijan%20Poverty%20Program%20for%202008-2015.pdf.

Strauss, A. L. (1988). The articulation of project work: An organizational process. *The Sociological Quarterly, 29*, 163–178.

Strauss, A. & Corbin, J. (1998).*Basics of Qualitative Research Techniques and Procedures for Developing Grounded Theory.* London: Sage.

Tamagaki, K. (2006). *Effectiveness of ICTs on the dual objectives of microfinance.* www.waseda.jp/assoc-cioacademy/pdf/tamagaki.pdf.

Waterfield, C., & Ramsing, R. (1998). *Management Information Systems for Microfinance Institutions. A Handbook.* New York: Pact Publications. ISBN 1-888753-11-0.

World Bank Report. (2011). http://documents.worldbank.org/curated/en/home.

Wulf, V., Krings, M., Stiemerling, O., Iacucci, G., Maidhof, M., Peters, R. Fuchs-Frohnhofen, P., Nett, B., Hinrichs, J. (1999). Improving inter-organizational processes with integrated organization and technology development. *Journal of Universal Computer Science V*(6), 339–365.

Wulf, V., Rohde, M., Pipek, V., & Stevens, G. (2011). Engaging with practices: design case studies as a research framework in CSCW. In: *2011 International Conference on Computer Supported Cooperative Work.* pp. 505–512, New York: ACM Press.

Wulf, V., Aal, K., Abu Ktesh, I., Atam, M., Schubert, K., Yerousis, G. P., Randall, D., & Rohde, M. (2013). Fighting against the wall: Social media use by political activists in a Palestinian village. In: *Proceedings of the 31st International Conference on Human Factors in Computing Systems* (CHI '13). Paris, France: ACM-Press (in press).

Motivation-Targeted Personalized UI Design: A Novel Approach to Enhancing Citizen Science Participation

Oded Nov, Ofer Arazy, Kelly Lotts and Thomas Naberhaus

Abstract We report a preliminary exploration of the effectiveness of motivation-targeted UI design—a novel personalized approach to enhance online participation. The empirical setting was Butterflies and Moths of North America (BAMONA), a large-scale citizen science project. Using a combination of design intervention and classification of users based on their collective identification motivation, we show that stating the community's mission on its website increases the likelihood of contribution among those who strongly identify with the project, but decreases likelihood of contribution among those with weak identification with the project. The findings contribute to theory and practice of social systems design by demonstrating how motivation-targeted design that can enhance online participation.

Introduction and Background

In this paper we report a preliminary exploration of a novel approach to enhancing web-based citizen science participation: building on insights from social psychology, we explore the effectiveness of personalized UI design targeting users' motivations.

O. Nov (✉)
Polytechnic Institute of New York University, Brooklyn, New York, USA
e-mail: on272@nyu.edu

O. Arazy
University of Alberta School of Business, Edmonton, Alberta, Canada
e-mail: oarazy@ualberta.ca

K. Lotts · T. Naberhaus
Butterflies and Moths of North America, Bozeman, Montana, USA
e-mail: lotts@exchange.montana.edu

T. Naberhaus
e-mail: tnaberhaus@exchange.montana.edu

O. W. Bertelsen et al. (eds.), *ECSCW 2013: Proceedings of the 13th European Conference on Computer Supported Cooperative Work, 21–25 September 2013, Paphos, Cyprus*, DOI: 10.1007/978-1-4471-5346-7_15,

Extant HCI and CSCW research use insights from social psychology to inform the design and development of social participation technologies (Dabbish et al. 2012; Farzan et al. 2011; Kraut and Resnick 2011). In such design-based studies, controlled experiments are often used to test the effect of UI design features on user behavior (Dabbish and Kraut 2008; Ling et al. 2005). In particular, such studies often focus on identifying effective ways to encourage volunteered contribution of public goods in online settings (Burke et al. 2009; Choi et al. 2010). This approach enables researchers to draw conclusions about design effectiveness. However, to a large extent, studies based on this approach do not account for differences in users' personal attributes, such as their personalities or motivation.

A highly complementary stream of research involves individual differences and online engagement. Studies in this field showed how participants' personal attributes are correlated with online contribution. In particular, the role of motivational factors in has been explored and demonstrated in studies of a wide range of settings (Chen 2007; Fugelstad et al. 2012; Peddibhotla and Subramani 2007; Zhang 2008), such as Wikipedia (Bryant et al. 2005; Nov 2007), open source software projects (Hertel et al. 2003; Lakhani and Wolf 2005), and citizen science projects (Nov et al. 2011b; Raddick et al. 2010; Wiggins and Crowston 2011). This stream of research is different from the design-centered stream in term of the methodologies used, drawing primarily on survey-based data rather than experimental studies.

Building on these two streams of research, in the present study we examine the effectiveness of design features targeting users' motivations, as a method to increase participation. In other words, we explore the effects of the interaction between user motivation and a UI design feature on user online behavior. To follow a medical metaphor, this approach is analogous to a medical treatment that is applied to an individual based on her specific genetic profile, and may therefore be more effective than treatment applied to the entire population.

Relevant to our research is the literature on personalization (e.g. (Chu and Park 2009; Felfernig et al. 2010; Liu et al. 2010)). Work in that area often involves user models based on users' task-specific interactions. Our motivation-targeted UI design approach, on the other hand, involves classifying users based on preexisting categories informed by psychology research (motivations, in this case). In other words, while personalization often involves defining user personas based on task-specific prior activities, we define user profiles based on more fundamental user attributes such as their motivations.

In the related field of adaptive UI, there has been prior experimental work on the interaction between personality traits and UI design features (Goren-Bar et al. 2006; McGrenere et al. 2002). The primary objective of these studies has been to reduce users' cognitive load and make their interaction with the computer more efficient. The differences in goals between such studies and ours (reduce cognitive load vs. influence online participation), make them different in terms of the applicable design manipulations.

Two recent papers we explored the effectiveness of personality-targeted design (Nov and Arazy 2013; Nov et al. 2013). For example, they showed how users' extroversion levels determine their response to a particular design intervention (manipulating an indicator presenting the number of past visitor in a social recommender system). In the present study we build on and extend this line of research by moving beyond targeting personality traits to targeting users' motivations. Motivation was shown to be an important driver of participation in volunteer-based collaborative efforts online, and therefore in the present study we explore the feasibility of catering to users' motivations through UI design features.

Interaction Between Motivations and UI Design Intervention

In the present study we address the following general research question: can differences in users' motivation explain the effects of design interventions on users' contribution to an online volunteer-based collaborative effort?

A motivational factor which is highly relevant to understanding users' response in collaborative efforts is identification with the online community (Hertel et al. 2003; Nov et al. 2011b; Rotman et al. 2012). As a person develops an appreciation of the social groups he belongs to and attributes significance to this group membership, he develops a social identity (Tajfel 1978). And when an individual is identified with an organizations or a group he will tend to define herself in terms of the defining features of that group (Hogg and Abrams 1988) and exhibit a more autonomous motivation, resulting in both higher quality of engagement and a more positive experiences (such as enjoyment, sense of purpose, and well-being) (Ryan and Deci 2001).

In the context of computer-mediated communication, it has been argued that technology mediation causes de-individuation, which in turn gives rise to a strong social identification (Postmes et al. 1998; Spears et al. 2002). In online communities, identification was linked to a social influence exerted from the collective, such that the individual defines himself in terms of the membership in the group (Bagozzi and Dholakia 2002). Since online communities are usually sustained by voluntarily user-created content, identification has also been used to explain participation and knowledge contribution (Dholakia et al. 2004; Schroer and Hertel 2009). It is interesting to note that some prior empirical studies did not find a significant correlation between identification and participation in online communities (Hertel et al. 2003), including recent works in the particular context of our study—voluntary participation is citizen science projects (Nov et al. 2011b).

We speculate that such inconsistencies in terms of the effects of identification may result from the interaction between identification and other contextual factors. Our focus in on the interaction between identification and messages displayed on the community's web site, in particular messages stating the community's mission.

The effects of such a UI design feature could be explained through the theory of Attraction-Selection-Attrition (ASA), which describes how individuals become assimilated in organizations (with a focus on work settings) (Schneider 1987). According to ASA, people often self-select into situations consistent with their personality, and leave situations inconsistent with their personality. While part of a group (or community), individuals still maintain stable self-views, which provide them an essential source of coherence and a means of defining their existence (Swann et al. 2003). In the selection process, individuals make implicit judgments of the congruence or fit between their own aspiration, motivation and ideology, and the group's goals. Those individuals who fit with the organization are more motivated and committed, and their overall performance is high (Schneider 1987). In the context of online communities, ASA has been applied to explain the formation of online groups (Templeton et al. 2012) and participation levels (Kuk 2004).

Viewed through ASA, displaying on the community's website a message that states the community's identity acts to make fit (or misfit) more salient, by prompting members to contrast this collective identity with their own values (Postmes et al. 2005). Individuals unconsciously self-categorize on the basis of available cues related to the social identity; the more an identity information dominates a person's working memory, the more salient self-categorization processes are (Hogg and Terry 2000). In computer-mediated communication, members tend to be more sensitive to any salient social identity cues, because they seek to reduce the uncertainty in social interaction (Lea et al. 2001).

Identity salience is most often elicited by external factors (Forehand et al. 2002). Prior research has investigated various contextual factors, such as: visual images and words (Aquino and Reed 2002), group symbols and priming (Devine 1989). In the context of online communities, these contextual factors are mainly integrated into the design of the community's website. For example (Shen and Khalifa 2010) showed that messages on a community's website can influence members identification.

In the present study we investigate a particular UI design feature: presenting a message stating the community's mission on the website. Such a message establishes the community identity as stable, significant and a salient target for identification. When features of social context serve to make a given social identity salient, individuals are triggered to contrast that identity with their own, producing pressure to comply with the group norms and values (Tajfel 1978; Turner 1982). We hypothesize that when the fit between person and the community is revalidated, the likelihood of participation becomes higher; on the other hand, when misfit becomes apparent, dissonance increases, resulting in lower participation.

Methodology

The setting of the present study is citizen science. Citizen science projects enable members of the public to take part in scientific research (Cohn 2008; Wiggins and Crowston 2011), often through web-based contribution (Hand 2010). As such, citizen science offers a participatory approach for conducting scientific research, and requires good understanding of user motivation (Hand 2010; Nov et al. 2011b; Rotman et al. 2012; Wiggins and Crowston 2009; Wiggins and Crowston 2011).

As citizen science is based both on computer systems to manage large amounts of distributed resources on the one hand, and on attracting and retaining volunteers who contribute their time and effort to a scientific cause, recent research explored the motivations of citizen scientists (Nov et al. 2011b; Raddick et al. 2010; Rotman et al. 2012; Wiggins and Crowston 2010). In the present study, we build on these studies to apply the knowledge gained on the factors that drive citizen science participation to offer motivation-targeted UI design insight.

In this experimental study, we focused on Butterflies and Moths of North America (BAMONA)—a large-scale citizen science project that collects and makes available expert-verified butterfly and moth distribution in North America (Opler et al. 2009). The BAMONA website contains data contributed by more than 3,000 volunteers on more than 5,000 species, including species profiles, photographs, and dynamic distribution maps showing verified species occurrences (see Fig. 1 for an example). More than fifty collaborating lepidopterists volunteer as regional coordinators tasked with quality control. They utilize an online system to review each individual submission and determine the species identification. The BAMONA database contains nearly 300,000 individual records.

During the experiment period, the BAMONA landing page invited participants to answer a short questionnaire which included motivation items. Self-report surveys are commonly used in social science research to identify personal attributes, and have been used extensively in HCI and CSCW studies (McElroy et al. 2007; Seay and Kraut 2007). The questionnaire items used a 7-point Likert scale and were adapted from social psychology research of voluntary participation in social movements (Klandermans 1997; Simon et al. 1998). The same questionnaire items were used in studies of participation in open source software development (Hertel et al. 2003), Wikipedia editing (Schroer and Hertel 2009), and citizen science (Nov et al. 2011a, b). We classified high and low-identification volunteers by performing a median split: respondents whose identification score was above the sample median were classified as high- identification and those below the median as low- identification respondents. The experimental manipulation included a presentation of the project's mission at the top of the website's landing page.

During the 45 days in which the experiment ran, we recorded the participation levels of participants in the four experimental conditions (above vs. below identification median X presentation of the community's mission vs. no presentation).

In order to examine the effects of motivation, UI design, and the interaction between them, we used a factorial logistic regression in the statistical analysis. The independent variables in the analysis included identification (high = 1, low = 0), community mission UI design feature intervention applied (intervention = 1, control (no intervention) = 0), and the interaction between them.

We used system log data to identify users who made at least one contribution in the 45 days prior to the experiment. Many citizen scientists contribute very little and we therefore wanted to focus on regular contributors—those who together

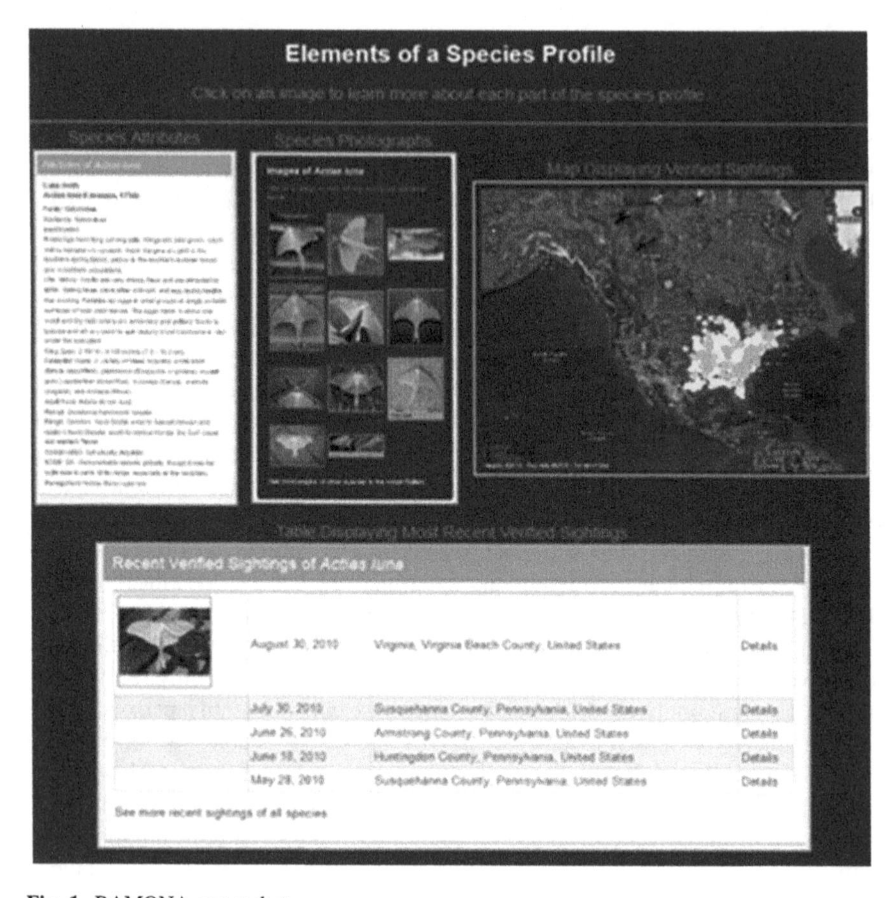

Fig. 1 BAMONA screenshot

make up the bulk of contributions. As an illustration, the top 10 % of the sample's volunteers contributed more than 88 % of its content.

Since we were interested in understanding how the independent variables affect the likelihood that a user will keep contributing content, the outcome variable was contribution, defined as providing at least one contribution during the 45 days of the experiment, when the design feature intervention was active (contributed = 1, not contributed = 0).

Results

Of the 462 volunteers who took part in the study, 73 made at least one contribution in the 45 days prior to the experiment and were included in the data analysis. Of these, 53 % were in the UI intervention condition and 47 % were in the no-intervention condition. As is common in many large scale volunteer-based projects, contribution made by volunteers was characterized by a power-law distribution, in this case with an average contribution of 8.44 photos (S.D. = 17.9).

There were no statistically significant effects of either the design intervention or the level of identification on the likelihood of contribution. That is, identification levels across the entire population were not correlated with participation; similarly, when considering the entire population, the UI design feature was not correlated with participation. The results of the logistic regression showed that the main effects of the independent variables were statistically insignificant ($B = -1.46$, $Wald = 3.62$, $p > 0.05$ for identification and $B = -0.96$, $Wald = 2.25$, $p > 0.05$ for the UI intervention).

However, as hypothesized, when examining the interaction between the independent variables a more intricate relationship was revealed (see Fig. 2): the interaction between identification and the UI intervention and its effect on contribution, was found to be significant ($B = 1.97$, $Wald = 3.89$, $p < 0.05$).

The results of the logistic regression showed that the main effects of the independent variables were statistically insignificant ($B = -1.46$, $Wald = 3.62$, $p > 0.05$ for identification and $B = -0.96$, $Wald = 2.25$, $p > 0.05$ for the UI intervention). The interaction between identification and the UI intervention—the focus of our analysis—was found to be a significant predictor of contribution ($B = 1.97$, $Wald = 3.89$, $p < 0.05$).

Discussion and Conclusions

The findings support the hypothesis that the effectiveness of a UI design intervention whereby the project's objective is made visible depends on users' level of collective identification. In other words, in line with our hypothesis, making the

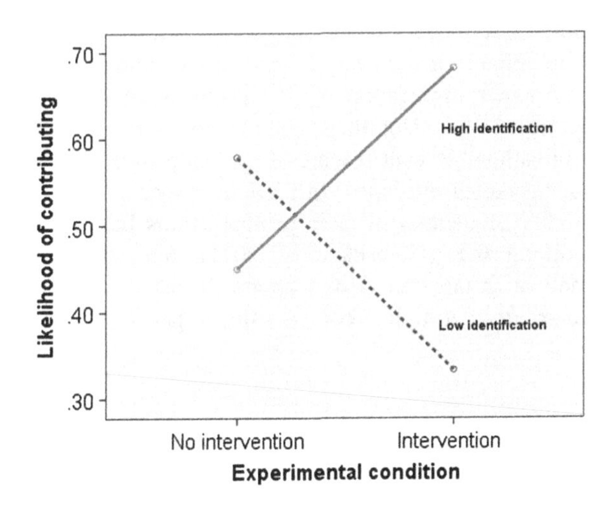

Fig. 2 The interaction of UI intervention and the identification motivation: the combined effect on the likelihood of contribution

community's mission visible to contributors leads to increased likelihood of contribution among those who strongly identify with the project, but to decreased likelihood of contribution among those with weak identification with the project (see Fig. 2).

The findings inform the research on collective identification in computer-mediated communication (Postmes et al. 1998, 2005; Spears et al. 2002) and in online communities (Dholakia et al. 2004; Hertel et al. 2003; Schroer and Hertel 2009; Shen and Khalifa 2010). Our primary contribution to this literature is in demonstrating that external factors—a UI design feature that presents a message stating the community's mission—can moderate the relationship between identification levels and online participation, such that the UI design feature would strengthen the positive effects of identification in some users, but reverse its effect in others.

In terms of CSCW research, the results highlight the potential effectiveness of a more nuanced, targeted approach to UI design in general, and the practice of making a community's mission visible in particular: providing cues that highlight the mission in a large collaborative project may be an effective way to increase participation among those identify with the project, but should be avoided when users do not identify with it.

More broadly, our proposed approach to targeted design highlights the need to tailor design features to idiosyncratic personal characteristics, such as their motivations, and as such, it complements the literature on use of personal attributes in design, such as the work on motivational affordances (Zhang 2008) personality-targeted design (Nov and Arazy 2013; Nov et al. 2013). In recent years, a number of studies have investigated the effects of users' personal traits on UI design. For example, studies of persuasion have shown how personality determines people's reaction to persuasive messages (Kaptein and Eckles 2012) and suggested that this approach is applicable to the design of system interfaces (McElroy and Dowd 2007). Studies on adaptive UI have demonstrated that personality-based design can reduce users' cognitive load (Furnham et al. 2012; Goren-Bar et al. 2006). Our study builds on such prior work, showing that motivation-targeted design can enhance contribution.

Another implication of the results is the need to develop systems that can automatically adapt their features to users' personal attributes—such as their motivations. Recent research explores possibilities for unobtrusive adaptation to user personal attributes. In particular, recent research has demonstrated the feasibility of identifying user personal traits based on their activity in social networking sites (Golbeck et al. 2011). A combination of such methods and the motivation-targeted design approach has the potential to dramatically increase contribution to online communities in general, and citizen science in particular.

References

Aquino, K., & Reed, A. (2002). The self-importance of moral identity. *Journal of Personality and Social Psychology, 83*(6), 1423–1440.

Bagozzi, R. P., & Dholakia, U. M. (2002). Intentional social action in virtual communities. *Journal of Interactive Marketing, 16*(2), 2–21.

Bryant, S., Forte, A., & Bruckman, A. (2005). Becoming wikipedian: Transformation of participation in a collaborative online encyclopedia. In *International ACM SIGGROUP Conference on Supporting Group Work* (pp. 1–10). Sanibel Island, FL: ACM.

Burke, M., Marlow, C., & Lento, T. (2009). Feed me: Motivating newcomer contribution in social network sites. In *27th International Conference on Human Factors in Computing Systems CHI 2009*. Boston, MA.

Chen, I. (2007). The factors influencing members' continuance intentions in professional virtual communities—a longitudinal study. *Journal of Information Science, 33*(4), 451–467.

Choi, B., Alexander, K., Kraut, R. E., & Levine, J. M. (2010). Socialization tactics in wikipedia and their effects. *Proceedings of the 2010 ACM conference on Computer Supported Cooperative Work (CSCW).*

Chu, W., & Park, S. -T. (2009). Personalized recommendation on dynamic content using predictive bilinear models. *Proceedings of the 18th International Conference on World Wide Web* (pp. 691–700). Madrid, Spain: ACM.

Cohn, J. (2008). Citizen science: Can volunteers do real research? *BioScience, 58*(3), 192–197.

Dabbish, L., & Kraut, R. (2008). Awareness displays and social motivation for coordinating communication. *Information Systems Research, 19*(2), 221–238.

Dabbish, L., Farzan, R., Kraut, R., & Postmes, T. (2012). Fresh faces in the crowd: Turnover, identity, and commitment in online groups. *Proceedings of the ACM 2012 conference on Computer Supported Cooperative Work* (pp. 245–248). Seattle, Washington: ACM.

Devine, P. G. (1989). Stereotypes and prejudice: Their automatic and controlled components. *Journal of Personality and Social Psychology, 56*(1), 5–18.

Dholakia, U. M., Bagozzi, R. P., & Pearo, L. K. (2004). A social influence model of consumer participation in network-and small-group-based virtual communities. *International Journal of Research in Marketing, 21*(3), 241–263.

Farzan, R., Dabbish, L., Kraut, R., & Postmes, T. (2011). Increasing commitment to online communities by designing for social presence. *ACM 2011 Conference on Computer Supported Cooperative Work (CSCW).* Hangzhou, China.

Felfernig, A., Mandl, M., Tiihonen, J., Schubert, M., & Leitner, G. (2010). Personalized user interfaces for product configuration. *Proceedings of the 15th International Conference on Intelligent User Interfaces.* Hong Kong, China.

Forehand, M. R., Deshpandé, R., & Reed II, A. (2002). Identity salience and the influence of differential activation of the social self-schema on advertising response. *Journal of Applied Psychology; Journal of Applied Psychology, 87*(6), 1086–1099.

Fugelstad, P., Dwyer, P., Moses, F. J., Kim, J., Mannino, C. A., Terveen, L., & Snyder, M. (2012). What makes users rate (share, tag, edit…)?: Predicting patterns of participation in online communities. *Proceedings of the ACM 2012 conference on Computer Supported Cooperative Work.*

Furnham, A., Boo, H. C., & McClelland, A. (2012). Individual differences and the susceptibility to the influence of anchoring cues. *Journal of Individual Differences, 33*(2), 89.

Golbeck, J., Robles, C., Edmondson, M., & Turner, K. 2011. Predicting personality from twitter. *IEEE International Conference on Privacy, security, risk and trust (PASSAT).*

Goren-Bar, D., Graziola, I., Pianesi, F., & Zancanaro, M. (2006). The influence of personality factors on visitor attitudes towards adaptivity dimensions for mobile museum guides. *User Modeling and User-Adapted Interaction, 16*(1), 31–62.

Hand, E. (2010). Citizen science: People power. *Nature, 466*(7307), 685–687.

Hertel, G., Niedner, S., & Herrmann, S. (2003). Motivation of software developers in open source projects: An Internet-based survey of contributors to the Linux kernel. *Research Policy, 32*(7), 1159–1177.

Hogg, M. A., & Abrams, D. (1988). *Social identifications: A social psychology of intergroup relations and group processes*. London: Routledge.

Hogg, M. A., & Terry, D. J. (2000). Social identity and self-categorization processes in organizational contexts. *Academy of Management Review, 25*(1), 121–140.

Kaptein, M., & Eckles, D. (2012). Heterogeneity in the effects of online persuasion. *Journal of Interactive Marketing, 26*, 176–188.

Klandermans, B. (1997). *The social psychology of protest.* Oxford: Blackwell.

Kraut, R. E., & Resnick, P. (2011). *Evidence-based social design: Mining the social sciences to build online communities*. Cambridge: MIT Press.

Kuk, G. (2004). Selection, cliques and knowledge sharing in open source software development communities. *Proceedings of the IADIS International Conference on Web-Based Communities*. Lisbon, Portugal

Lakhani, K., & Wolf, R. (2005). Why hackers do what they do: Understanding motivation effort in free. In B. F. J. Feller, S. Hissam, & K. Lakhani (Eds.), *Perspectives in Free and Open-Source Software*. Cambridge: MIT Press.

Lea, M., Spears, R., & de Groot, D. (2001). Knowing me, knowing you: Anonymity effects on social identity processes within groups. *Personality and Social Psychology Bulletin, 27*(5), 526–537.

Ling, K., Beenen, G., Ludford, P., Wang, X., Chang, K., Li, X., Cosley, D., Frankowski, D., Terveen, L., & Rashid, A. (2005). Using social psychology to motivate contributions to online communities. *Journal of Computer-Mediated Communication, 10*(4)

Liu, J., Dolan, P., & Pedersen, E. (2010). Personalized news recommendation based on click behavior. *Proceedings of the 15th International Conference on Intelligent User Interfaces*. Hong Kong, China.

McElroy, T., & Dowd, K. (2007). Susceptibility to anchoring effects: How openness-to-experience influences responses to anchoring cues. *Judgment and Decision Making, 2*(1), 48–53.

McElroy, J. C., Hendrickson, A. R., Townsend, A. M., & DeMarie, S. M. (2007). Dispositional factors in internet use: Personality versus cognitive style. *MIS Quarterly, 31*(4), 809–820.

McGrenere, J., Baecker, R., & Booth, K. (2002). An evaluation of a multiple interface design solution for bloated software. *Proceedings of the SIGCHI conference on Human factors in computing systems*.

Nov, O. (2007). What motivates wikipedians? *Communications of the ACM, 50*(11), 60–64.

Nov, O., & Arazy, O. (2013). Personality-Targeted Design: theory, experimental procedure, and preliminary results. *Proceedings of the ACM Conference on Computer Supported Cooperative Work (CSCW 2013)*. San Antonio.

Nov, O., Arazy, O., & Anderson, D. (2011a). Dusting for science: motivation and participation of digital citizen science volunteers. *iConference*. Seattle.

Nov, O., Arazy, O., & Anderson, D. (2011b). Technology-mediated citizen science participation: A motivational model. *Proceedings of the AAAI International Conference on Weblogs and Social Media (ICWSM 2011)*. Barcelona, Spain.

Nov, O., Arazy, O., Lopez, C., & Brusilovsky, P. (2013). Exploring personality-targeted UI design in online social participation systems. *Proceedings of the ACM SIGCHI Conference on Human Factors in Computing Systems, CHI 2013*. Paris, France.

Opler, P., Lotts, K., & Naberhaus, T. (2009). BAMONA: Butterflies and Moths of North America.

Peddibhotla, N., & Subramani, M. (2007). Contributing to public document repositories: A critical mass theory perspective. *Organization Studies, 28*(3), 327–346.

Postmes, T., Spears, R., & Lea, M. (1998). Breaching or building social boundaries? SIDE-effects of computer-mediated communication. *Communication Research, 25*(6), 689–715.

Postmes, T., Spears, R., Lee, A. T., & Novak, R. J. (2005). Individuality and social influence in groups: inductive and deductive routes to group identity. *Journal of Personality and Social Psychology, 89*(5), 747–763.

Raddick, M. J., Bracey, G., Gay, P. L., Lintott, C. J., Murray, P., Schawinski, K., et al. (2010). Galaxy zoo: Exploring the motivations of citizen science volunteers. *Astronomy Education Review, 9*, 010103.

Rotman, D., Preece, J., Hammock, J., Procita, K., Hansen, D., Parr, C., Lewis, D., & Jacobs, D. (2012). Dynamic changes in motivation in collaborative citizen-science projects. *Proceedings of the ACM 2012 conference on Computer Supported Cooperative Work.*

Ryan, R., & Deci, E. (2001). To be happy or to be self-fulfilled: A review of research on hedonic and eudemonic wellbeing. *Annual Review of Psychology, 52*, 141–166.

Schneider, B. (1987). The people make the place. *Personnel Psychology, 40*(3), 437–453.

Schroer, J., & Hertel, G. (2009). Voluntary engagement in an open web-based encyclopedia: Wikipedians and why they do it. *Media Psychology, 12*(1), 96–120.

Seay, A., & Kraut, R. (2007). Project massive: Self-regulation and problematic use of online gaming. *ACM Conference on Human Factors in Computing Systems, CHI 2007.*

Shen, K. N., & Khalifa, M. (2010). Explaining virtual community participation: Accounting for the IT artifacts through identification and identity confirmation. *European Conference on Information Systems (ECIS).* Pretoria, South Africa.

Simon, B., Loewy, M., Stürmer, S., Weber, U., Freytag, P., Habig, C., et al. (1998). Collective Identification and social movement participation. *Journal of Personality and Social Psychology, 74*(3), 646–658.

Spears, R., Lea, M., Corneliussen, R. A., Postmes, T., & Ter Haar, W. (2002). Computer-mediated communication as a channel for social resistance the strategic side of SIDE. *Small Group Research, 33*(5), 555–574.

Swann, W. B. J., Rentfrow, P. J., & Guinn, J. S. (2003). Self-verification: The search for coherence. In M. R. Leary & J. P. Tangney (Eds.), *Handbook of self and identity* (pp. 367–383). New York: Guilford Press.

Tajfel, H. E. (1978). *Differentiation between social groups: Studies in the social psychology of intergroup relations.* Oxford: Academic Press.

Templeton, G., Luo, X. R., Giberson, T. R., & Campbell, N. (2012). Leader personal influences on membership decisions in moderated online social networking groups. *Decision Support Systems, 54*, 655–664.

Turner, J. C. (1982). Towards a cognitive redefinition of the social group. In H. E. Tajfel (Ed.), *Social identity and intergroup relations* (pp. 15–40). Cambridge: Cambridge University Press.

Wiggins, A., & Crowston, K. (2009). *Designing Virtual Organizations for Citizen Science.* OASIS 2009.

Wiggins, A., & Crowston, K. (2010). Developing a conceptual model of virtual organisations for citizen science. *International Journal of Organisational Design and Engineering, 1*(1), 148–162.

Wiggins, A., & Crowston, K. (2011). *From conservation to crowdsourcing: A typology of citizen science*

Zhang, P. (2008). Motivational affordances: Reasons for ICT design and use. *Communications of the ACM, 51*(11), 145–147.

Author Index

O. W. Bertelsen et al. (eds.), *ECSCW 2013: Proceedings of the 13th European Conference on Computer Supported Cooperative Work, 21–25 September 2013, Paphos, Cyprus*, DOI: 10.1007/978-1-4471-5346-7, © Springer-Verlag London 2013

Printed in the United States
By Bookmasters